# Review Manual
# for
# SPEECH, LANGUAGE,
# and
# HEARING

by

NORMAN J. LASS, Ph.D.

LEIJA V. McREYNOLDS, Ph.D.

JERRY L. NORTHERN, Ph.D.

DAVID E. YODER, Ph.D.


by

**JERRY L. NORTHERN, Ph.D.**

Head, Audiology Division
University Hospital
Professor, Department of Otolaryngology
University of Colorado Health Sciences Center
Denver, Colorado

W. B. SAUNDERS COMPANY

Philadelphia   London   Toronto   Mexico City   Rio de Janeiro   Sydney   Tokyo

W.B. Saunders Company:    West Washington Square
Philadelphia, PA    19105

1 St. Anne's Road
Eastbourne, East Sussex BN21 3UN, England

1 Goldthorne Avenue
Toronto, Ontario M8Z 5T9, Canada

Apartado 26370—Cedro 512
Mexico 4, D.F., Mexico

Rua Coronel Cabrita, 8
Sao Cristovao Caixa Postal 21176
Rio de Janeiro, Brazil

9 Waltham Street
Artarmon, N.S.W. 2064, Australia

Ichibancho, Central Bldg., 22-1 Ichibancho
Chiyoda-Ku, Tokyo 102, Japan

Review Manual for Speech, Language, and Hearing        ISBN 0-7216-6874-7

Last digit is the print number:    9   8   7   6   5   4   3   2

# This review has been adapted from material contributed by the following individuals:

JAMES H. ABBS, Ph.D.

Professor, Department of Communicative Disorders, University of Wisconsin. Staff, Speech Motor Control Laboratories, Waisman Center on Mental Retardation and Human Development, University of Wisconsin, Madison, Wisconsin.

*Basic Neurophysiological Mechanisms Underlying Oral Communication; Neurophysiological Processes of Speech Movement Control*

DOROTHY M. ARAM, Ph.D.

Assistant Professor, Department of Pediatrics, Case Western Reserve University School of Medicine. Speech Pathologist and Director of Communication Disorders, Rainbow Babies and Childrens Hospital, Cleveland, Ohio.

*The Diagnostic Process*

NICHOLAS W. BANKSON, Ph.D.

Professor and Chairman, Department of Communication Disorders, Sargent College of Allied Health Professions, Boston University, Boston, Massachusetts.

*Articulation Assessment*

JOHN E. BERNTHAL, Ph.D.

Associate Professor and Head, Department of Communicative Disorders, University of Northern Iowa, Cedar Falls, Iowa.

*Articulation Assessment*

FRED H. BESS, Ph.D.

Professor and Director, Division of Hearing and Speech Sciences, Vanderbilt University School of Medicine. Director, Bill Wilkerson Hearing and Speech Center, Nashville, Tennessee.

*Basic Hearing Measurement*

JANE W. BLALOCK, Ph.D.

Assistant Professor, Department of Communicative Disorders, Northwestern University, Evanston, Illinois.

*Problems of Mathematics in Children with Language Disorders*

HUGH W. BUCKINGHAM, Jr., Ph.D.

Director, Interdepartmental Program in Linguistics; Associate Professor of Linguistics, Department of Speech, Louisiana State University, Baton Rouge, Louisiana.

*Neuropsychological Models of Language*

DONALD R. CALVERT, Ph.D.

Professor and Chairman, Department of Speech and Hearing, Washington University. Director, Central Institute for the Deaf, St. Louis, Missouri.

*Articulation and Hearing Impairment*

WILLIAM E. CASTLE, Ph.D.

Vice President, Rochester Institute of Technology. Director, National Technical Institute for the Deaf, Rochester, New York.

*The Deaf*

ROBIN S. CHAPMAN, Ph.D.

Professor, Department of Communicative Disorders, University of Wisconsin, Madison, Wisconsin.

*Issues in Child Language Acquisition*

CAROL G. COHEN, M.S.

Instructor, Division of Special Education and Rehabilitation, Syracuse University. Director, Schneier Communication Unit, Cerebral Palsy Center, Syracuse, New York.

*An Overview of Augmentative Communication*

THOMAS A. CROWE, Ph.D.

Assistant Professor, Department of Communicative Disorders, University of Mississippi, University, Mississippi.

*Language Delay*

JAMES R. CURRAN, M.S.

Director, Auditory Research, MAICO Hearing Instruments, Minneapolis, Minnesota.

*Aspects of Contemporary Hearing Aids*

NATALIE HEDBERG DAVES, Ph.D.

Associate Professor, Department of Communication Disorders and Speech Science, University of Colorado, Denver, Colorado.

*Models of Auditory Linguistic Processing*

WILLIAM M. DIEDRICH, Ph.D.

Professor in Speech Pathology, Department of Hearing and Speech, The University of Kansas College of Health Sciences and Hospital, Kansas City, Kansas.

*Toward an Understanding of Communicative Disorders*

MARION P. DOWNS, M.A.

Professor, Department of Otolaryngology, Division of Audiology, University of Colorado Health Sciences Center, Denver, Colorado.

*Early Identification of Hearing Loss*

JUDITH FELSON DUCHAN, Ph.D.

Associate Professor, Department of Communicative Disorders and Sciences, State University of New York at Buffalo, Buffalo, New York.

*Problems in Assessing Children's Language*

MARY F. ELBERT, Ph.D.

Assistant Professor, Department of Speech and Hearing Sciences, Indiana University, Bloomington, Indiana.

*Articulation Disorders of Unknown Etiology and Their Remediation*

GERALD M. ENGLISH, M.D.

Clinical Professor, Department of Otolar-
yngology, University of Colorado Health Sciences Center. Chief, Division of Otolaryngology, combined staff of Porter and Swedish Hospitals, Denver. Attending Physician, St. Luke's Hospital, Denver Children's Hospital, St. Anthony's Hospital, Presbyterian Medical Center, Denver, and Lutheran Medical Center, Wheat Ridge; Consultant, Fitzsimons Army Medical Center, and Veterans Administration Hospital, Denver, Colorado.

*Medical and Surgical Treatment of Hearing Loss*

DONALD G. FERGUSON, Ed.D.

Associate Dean, College of Education, New Mexico State University, Las Cruces, New Mexico.

*Education of Hearing Impaired Learners*

JOHN W. FOLKINS, Ph.D.

Assistant Professor, Department of Speech Pathology and Audiology, University of Iowa, Iowa City, Iowa.

*Speech Production*

FRANCES JACKSON FREEMAN, Ph.D.

Assistant Professor, Callier Center for Communciation Disorders, University of Texas, Dallas.

*Prosody in Perception, Production, and Pathologies; Stuttering*

ROBERT GOLDSTEIN, Ph.D.

Professor, Department of Communicative Disorders, College of Letters and Science, University of Wisconsin, Madison, Wisconsin.

*Neurophysiology of Hearing*

JAMES W. HALL, III, Ph.D.

Assistant Professor and Chairman of Audiology, Department of Otorhinolaryngology and Human Communication, University of Pennsylvania School of Medicine, Philadelphia. Director of the Speech and Hearing Center, Hospital of the University of Pennsylvania, Philadelphia, Pennsylvania.

*Impedance Audiometry*

**DOIN E. HICKS, Ed.D.**

Vice President of Research and Professor of Administration, Gallaudet College, Washington, D.C.

*Education of Hearing Impaired Learners*

**RAYMOND H. HULL, Ph.D.**

Professor and Chairperson, Department of Communication Disorders, and Director of Audiology, University of Northern Colorado, Greeley, Colorado.

*Aural Rehabilitation in Adults*

**JAMES F. JERGER, Ph.D.**

Professor of Audiology, Department of Otorhinolaryngology and Communicative Sciences, Baylor College of Medicine. Consultant, The Methodist Hospital, Texas Childrens Hospital, and Veterans Administration Hospital, Houston, Texas.

*Impedance Audiometry*

**DORIS J. JOHNSON, Ph.D.**

Professor, Department of Communicative Disorders, Program of Learning Disabilities, Northwestern University, Evanston, Illinois.

*Problems of Mathematics in Children with Language Disorders*

**JUDITH R. JOHNSTON, Ph.D.**

Assistant Professor, Department of Speech and Hearing Sciences, Indiana University, Bloomington, Indiana.

*The Language Disordered Child*

**JOEL C. KAHANE, Ph.D.**

Associate Professor, Department of Audiology and Speech Pathology, Memphis State University, Memphis, Tennessee.

*Anatomy and Physiology of the Organs of the Peripheral Speech Mechanism*

**ROBERT W. KEITH, Ph.D.**

Professor, Department of Otolaryngology, University of Cincinnati College of Medicine. Director, Division of Audiology and Speech Pathology, University of Cincinnati Medical Center, Cincinnati, Ohio.

*Central Auditory Tests*

**JESSE G. KENNEDY, III, Ph.D.**

Assistant Professor, Department of Communicative Disorders, University of Wisconsin. Staff, Speech Motor Control Laboratories, Waisman Center on Mental Retardation and Human Development, University of Wisconsin, Madison, Wisconsin.

*Basic Neurophysiological Mechanisms Underlying Oral Communication; Neurophysiological Processes of Speech Movement Control*

**DAVID P. KUEHN, Ph.D.**

Assistant Professor, Department of Speech Pathology and Audiology, University of Denver, Denver, Colorado.

*Acoustics of Speech; Speech Production; Assessment of Resonance Disorders*

**PATRICIA K. KUHL, Ph.D.**

Associate Professor, Department of Speech and Hearing Sciences, University of Washington. Affiliate, Child Development and Mental Retardation Center, University of Washington, Seattle, Washington.

*Speech Perception: An Overview of Current Issues*

**CHARLES R. LARSON, Ph.D.**

Research Assistant Professor, Department of Speech and Hearing Sciences, University of Washington, Seattle, Washington.

*Neuroanatomic Bases of Hearing and Speech*

**NORMAN J. LASS, Ph.D.**

Professor and Chairman, Department of Speech Pathology and Audiology, West Virginia University; Joint Appointment, Department of Otolaryngology, School of Medicine, West Virginia University, Morgantown, West Virginia. Consultant, Audiology and Speech Pathology Service, Veterans Administration Medical Center, Martinsburg, West Virginia.

*Acoustics of Speech*

**MARGARET L. LEMME, Ph.D.**

Assistant Professor, Department of Speech Pathology and Audiology, University of

Denver. Assistant Clinical Professor, Physical Medicine and Rehabilitation, University of Colorado Health Sciences Center, Denver, Colorado.

*Models of Auditory Linguistic Processing*

DAVID M. LIPSCOMB, Ph.D.

Professor, Department of Audiology and Speech Pathology, University of Tennessee, Knoxville, Tennessee.

*Anatomy and Physiology of the Hearing Mechanism*

MALCOLM R. McNEIL, Ph.D.

Assistant Professor, Department of Communicative Disorders, University of Wisconsin. Staff, Speech Motor Control Laboratories, Waisman Center on Mental Retardation and Human Development, University of Wisconsin, Madison. Consultant, Veterans Administration Medical Center, Madison, Wisconsin.

*The Nature of Aphasia in Adults*

LEIJA V. McREYNOLDS, Ph.D.

Professor, Department of Hearing and Speech, University of Kansas College of Health Sciences and Hospital School of Medicine, Kansas City, Kansas.

*Articulation Disorders of Unknown Etiology and Their Remediation*

THOMAS MURRY, Ph.D.

Veterans Administration Medical Center, and Department of Surgery, University of California, San Diego, California.

*Phonation: Assessment and Remediation*

JAMES E. NATION, Ph.D.

Professor and Chairman, Department of Communication Sciences, Case Western Reserve University. Speech-Language Pathologist, Craniofacial Defects Clinic, Rainbow Babies and Childrens Hospital, Cleveland, Ohio.

*The Diagnostic Process; Management of Speech and Language Disorders*

J. DOUGLAS NOLL, Ph.D.

Professor, Department of Audiology and Speech Sciences, Purdue University, West Lafayette, Indiana.

*Remediation of Impaired Resonance Among Patients with Neuropathologies of Speech*

CASSANDRA A. PETERS, M.Ed., M.A.

Graduate Research Assistant and Ph.D. Candidate in Linguistics, Department of Communication Arts and Sciences, Howard University, Washington, D.C.

*Sociolinguistics and Communication Disorders*

SALLY J. PETERSON-FALZONE, Ph.D.

Associate Professor, Center for Craniofacial Anomalies and Department of Otolaryngology, Abraham Lincoln School of Medicine, University of Illinois Medical Center, Chicago, Illinois.

*Resonance Disorders in Structural Defects; Articulation Disorders in Orofacial Anomalies*

GLENN S. PFAU, Ph.D.

Director, Office of Sponsored Research, and Professor, Department of Foundations and Research, Gallaudet College, Washington, D.C.

*Education of Hearing Impaired Learners*

BRYAN E. PFINGST, Ph.D.

Research Assistant Professor, Department of Otolaryngology, University of Washington School of Medicine. Research Affiliate, Regional Primate Research Center, University of Washington, Seattle, Washington.

*Neuroanatomic Bases of Hearing and Speech*

JOANNE S. ROSENBERG, M.A.

Private Practice, Audiology.

*Hearing Screening*

PHILIP E. ROSENBERG, Ph.D. (Deceased)

Professor of Audiology, Director of Audiology Section, Temple University Health Sciences Center. Professor, Audiology-Otorhinology Section, Temple University Medical School, Philadelphia, Pennsylvania.

*Hearing Screening*

JAY W. SANDERS, Ph.D.

Professor of Audiology, Division of Hearing and Speech Sciences, Vanderbilt University School of Medicine. Staff, Bill Wilkerson Hearing and Speech Center, Nashville, Tennessee.

*Diagnostic Audiology*

RUTH S. SARGENT, M.A.

Clinical Audiologist, Colorado Otolaryngology, P.A. Englewood, Colorado.

*Medical and Surgical Treatment of Hearing Loss*

HOWARD C. SHANE, Ph.D.

Associate Professor, Department of Pediatrics, Harvard Medical School. Speech-Language Pathologist, Hearing and Speech Division and Developmental Evaluation Clinic, The Children's Hospital Medical Center, Boston, Massachusetts.

*An Overview of Augmentative Communication*

JUNE E. SHOUP, Ph.D.

Associate Professor and Chairperson, Department of Communication Arts and Sciences, University of Southern California. Director, Speech Communications Research Laboratory, Inc., Los Angeles, California.

*Acoustics of Speech*

ORLANDO L. TAYLOR, Ph.D.

Graduate Professor, Department of Communication Arts and Sciences, Howard University, Washington, D.C.

*Sociolinguistics and Communication Disorders*

LAWRENCE J. TURTON, Ph.D.

Associate Professor, Division of Speech Pa-

thology and Audiology, Indiana University of Pennsylvania, Indiana, Pennsylvania.

*Communication and Language Instruction for Severely Handicapped Children and Youth*

GERALDINE P. WALLACH, Ph.D.

Associate Professor, Department of Communication Disorders, Emerson College, Boston, Massachusetts.

*Language Processing and Reading Deficiencies: Assessment and Remediation of Children with Special Learning Problems*

DONALD W. WARREN, D.D.S., Ph.D.

Kenan Professor and Chairman, Department of Dental Ecology, School of Dentistry, University of North Carolina; Kenan Professor, Department of Surgery, University of North Carolina School of Medicine; Administrative Director, Oral, Facial and Communicative Disorders Program, University of North Carolina, Chapel Hill. Attending Physican, Hospital Dental Service, North Carolina Memorial Hospital, Chapel Hill, North Carolina.

*Aerodynamics of Speech*

CAROL LYNN WARYAS, Ph.D.

Executive Director, Arondale House (for Autistic Children), Houston, Texas.

*Language Delay*

JANET M. ZARNOCH, M.A.

Instructor, Department of Otolaryngology, University of Colorado Health Sciences Center. Clinical Audiologist, University Hospital, University of Colorado Health Sciences Center, Denver, Colorado.

*Hearing Disorders: Audiologic Manifestations*

# PREFACE

There are as many different methods by which to study as there
are students involved in learning.  Each student has a unique way by
which he or she learns most effectively.  However, there is no easy
way to learn!  Learning is a time-consuming process.  This Review
Manual is intended to help you study, learn and review the material
presented in the campanion textbook, SPEECH, LANGUAGE and HEARING
published by W.B. Saunders.  The materials within this study guide
are in no way intended as a substitute for thorough reading of the
textbook, but they should enable you to detect areas of weakness in
your knowledge.

SPEECH, LANGUAGE and HEARING is the most complete textbook
of its kind, and assimilation of the mass of information presented
within the three volumes is difficult.  Each chapter from the textbook
is represented in this Review Manual by an outline and several study
questions.  You should read the appropriate textbook chapter prior
to using the Review Manual.  Make notes in the margin of the Review
Manual to clarify the outline or emphasize information that is especially
important to you.  Studies have verified when material is reviewed or
rehearsed immediately after reading it is retained much better than
material which has not been so reviewed.

Then answer the review questions based on your reading of the
chapter in the textbook.  Active learning is more beneficial than simple
passive reading.  Check your answers in the back of the Review
Manual.  Items on which you made mistakes should be noted so you can
go back and re-read the appropriate passages in the textbook.

It is important to set study goals for each study session and
a good plan is to follow a standard study procedure with one chapter
at a time.  Some students find it valuable to read the text and
compare it with the outline in the Review Manual at the same time.
Or the outline may be utilized to emphasize major ideas and concepts
to be sure full comprehension of the textual material is achieved.

This Review Manual should be especially useful as a study guide
to those persons preparing for the NTE National Examinations in Speech
Pathology and Audiology.  Since the NTE Examinations are usually taken
after graduation from academic coursework, during or following the
Clinical Fellowship Year, this Review Manual can be used for independent
study.

Remember...you will receive as much benefit from this Review
Manual as you put effort and time into using it.  Good Luck!

Jerry L. Northern, Ph.D.
University of Colorado Health Sciences Center

I would like to extend my sincere appreciation to Baxter Venable of W.B. Saunders for his help and encouragement in all aspects of this project. Appreciation is also extended to many of the authors from SPEECH, LANGUAGE and HEARING for their part in helping prepare materials for this Review Manual. I am especially grateful to Theresa Perry, M.S., for her work on numerous outlines, and to Patsy Tormey-Meredith for her tolerance, diligence and care in typing the manuscript.

# CONTENTS

NORMAL PROCESSES

# Chapter 1

# NEUROANATOMIC BASES OF HEARING AND SPEECH

*Charles R. Larson and Bryan E. Pfingst*

I. Overview

    A. Structure of the Nervous System:

        1. The nervous system is divided into two components:

            a. central nervous system (CNS) which includes the brain and spinal cord;

            b. peripheral nervous system (PNS) which includes sensory receptors and nerves outside the CNS.

        2. The brain is divided anatomically into:

            a. medulla (myelencephalon);

            b. midbrain (mesencephalon);

            c. hypothalamus and thalamus (diencephalon);

            d. brain stem (includes the medulla, pons, mesencephalon and diencephalon);

            e. cerebellum and pons (metencephalon);

            f. cerebral cortex and basal ganglia (telencephalon).

    B. Structure of the Nerve Cell:

        1. Soma – cell body.

        2. Dendrites – small fibers that carry nerve impulses towards soma.

        3. Axon – fiber carrying nerve impulses away from soma.

4.  Myelin sheath – insulating sheath wrapped around some axons.

5.  Nodes of Ranvier – small gaps in the myelin sheath.

C.  Synapse – a space over which one neuron communicates with another.

D.  Cluster of cell bodies in CNS is called a <u>nucleus</u> ; in the PNS the cluster is called a <u>ganglion</u>.

E.  Nerve fibers are divided into 2 categories:

1.  Afferent – carries information toward a reference point (usually CNS).

2.  Efferent – carries information away from a reference point (usually CNS).

II.  The Auditory Pathway:  Eighth Nerve to Inferior Colliculus

A.  <u>Acoustic Nerve</u>:

1.  Auditory portion of VIIIth nerve consists of 31,000 nerve fibers.

2.  95% of afferent fibers innervate inner hair cells – <u>inner radial fibers</u>.

3.  Remaining 5% of afferent fibers innervate outer hair cells – <u>outer spiral fibers</u>.

4.  The VIIIth nerve is tonotopically organized.

5.  The VIIIth nerve enters the brain stem and immediately terminates in the <u>cochlear nucleus complex</u>.

B.  <u>Cochlear Nucleus</u> (CN):

1.  Divided into three areas (each tonotopically organized):

a. anteroventral cochlear nucleus (AVCN);

b. posteroventral cochlear nucleus (PVCN);

c. dorsal cochlear nucleus (DCN).

2.  Various cell types within each division of the CN differ in their innervation patterns.

3.  All VIIIth nerve fibers synapse on cells in the cochlear nucleus (obligatory synapse).

C.  Acoustic Striae:

1.  Projections from the cochlear nucleus form three
    distinct striae:

    a.  stria of Monakow (dorsal);

    b.  stria of Held (intermediate);

    c.  trapezoid body (ventral; largest of the three).

D.  Superior Olivary Complex (SOC):

1.  Collection of six nuclei located in the caudal-to-mid pons.

2.  Largest nuclei are the lateral superior olive and the
    medial superior olive (accessory nucleus).  Both nuclei
    contain an orderly tonotopic frequency map.

3.  The SOC is the first point along the auditory pathway
    at which interaction from both ears is possible.  The
    medial superior olive is particularly important in this
    regard.

E.  Olivocochlear Bundle:

1.  Best documented efferent pathway with cell bodies located
    in the superior olivary complex.

2.  Ultimately parallels the VIIIth nerve to terminate on inner
    and outer hair cells.

F.  Stapedius Reflex Pathway:

1.  Stapedius muscle in middle ear is innervated by a branch
    of VIIth nerve.

2.  Pathway for stapedius reflex involves the acoustic nerve,
    the AVCN, the MSO, and the VIIth nerve.

G.  Nuclei of the Lateral Lemniscus:

1.  Contains two nuclear groups:

    a.  dorsal (LLD);

    b.  ventral (LLV).

2.  Both nuclei contain an orderly tonotopic frequency map.

H.  Inferior Colliculus (IC):

1.  Generally considered to be the second obligatory synapse in the auditory pathway.

2.  Comprised of a large, tonotopically organized central nucleus and small overlying nuclei.

3.  Primary afferent projection of the IC is to the ipsilateral medial geniculate nucleus in the thalamus.

III.  The Thalamus

A.  Thalamus is the major relay nucleus to the cerebral cortex for all sensory systems – except olfaction.

B.  Medial Geniculate Body (MGB):

1.  Ventral division of MGB is the major relay to the primary auditory cortex.

2.  Ventral division probably contains two tonotopic maps.

3.  Medial and dorsal divisions of MGB are less directly involved in the primary auditory pathway.  The medial division projects to secondary auditory cortical fields (see IV, B, 3).

C.  Thalamic Areas Related to Speech:

1.  The pulvinar, ventral lateral, and ventral anterior nuclei of the thalamus are probably involved in speech control.

2.  Sensory information from the orofacial region projects to the ventral posterior medialis nucleus (VPM) of the thalamus – such sensory information may be used in speech control mechanisms.

IV.  Cerebral Cortex

A.  Overview:

1.  The structure of the cerebral cortex is marked by numerous convolutions.

2.  Sulci are the fissures between the convolutions.

3.  Gyri are rounded portions of convolutions.

4.  Cortex comprises layers of cell bodies and fibers (gray matter) overlying massive fiber tracts (white matter).

5. Cerebral cortex is divided into two hemispheres (left and right); the two halves are connected by a band of fibers called the corpus callosum.

6. Each hemisphere contains five lobes:

   a. frontal;

   b. occipital (containing cortex);

   c. temporal (containing cortex);

   d. parietal;

   e. insular.

B. Auditory Cortex:

   1. Located on the superior, medial and lateral surfaces of the superior temporal gyrus and thus buried for the most part within the Sylvian fissure.

   2. Primary auditory cortex (area AI.or auditory koniocortex) has a complete frequency tonotopic representation.

   3. Area AI is surrounded by several distinct secondary auditory cortical areas (belt areas).

   4. The primary auditory cortex sends projections to the surrounding belt areas, to the contralateral area AI, and to subcortical nuclei; the auditory belt areas send projections to each other and to a number of nonauditory cortical areas.

C. Cortical Speech Areas:

   1. Two primary areas involved in speech control named after the men who first described them:

      a. Paul Broca;

      b. Carl Wernicke.

   2. Speech and language are controlled primarily in the left hemisphere (except for a few left-handed individuals who may have a dominant right hemisphere for speech).

   3. The motor aspects of speech production are controlled in the left hemisphere in Wernicke's and Broca's areas, in most individuals.

D.  Sensorimotor Cortex:

1.  Important for speech and other types of voluntary movement control.

2.  This cortical area lies along the central sulcus, the boundary between the frontal and parietal lobes.

3.  Three important aspects of sensorimotor cortex:

    a. the medial areas regulate the lower limbs and the lateral areas regulate upper limbs, head and face;

    b. cortical areas regulating muscular systems requiring precise motor control, such as the areas involved in speech production, tend to be longer than areas regulating less precisely controlled systems;

    c. right half of body is controlled by the left sensorimotor cortex and vice versa – although bilateral control seems to exist for most speech structures.

V.  Cortical Motor Output

A.  Pyramidal System:

1.  Originates in motor cortex and travels without interruption to the motor nuclei of the brain stem and spinal cord.

2.  Pyramidal system is extremely important for speech as a lesion may result in paralysis of the muscles of speech.

B.  Extrapyramidal Mechanisms:

1.  Extremely complicated motor system that projects from the cerebral cortex to several subcortical nuclei, primarily the basal ganglia.

2.  Outputs from this system may go to the brainstem regions containing motor nuclei or back to the cerebral cortex.

3.  Abnormalities may result in speech disorders such as observed in Parkinsonian patients.

C.  Cerebellum:

1.  Large area of brain important for motor control.

2.  Damage to cerebellum results in speech disorder known as ataxic dysarthria.

3. Possible that integration of auditory information and other forms of sensory feedback by the cerebellum could be important for speech control.

D. Brain Stem:

1. Brain stem nuclear groups provide the final common pathway for nerve signals being sent from the CNS to the muscles regulated by cranial nerves.

2. Trigeminal System:

   a. largest of brain stem nuclear groups;

   b. contains four major nuclei:

      (1) the motor nucleus;

      (2) chief sensory nucleus;

      (3) spinal nucleus;

      (4) mesencephalic nucleus of the trigeminal (Vth) nerve.

3. Facial Nucleus:

   a. facial complex supplies sensory innervation for taste, part of the external ear canal and the auricle;

   b. also supplies motor fibers for the face and lips.

4. Nucleus Ambiguus:

   a. supplies motor fibers to the IXth (glossopharyngeal), Xth (vagus) and XIth (accessory) cranial nerves;

   b. the input to the nucleus ambiguus is varied but involves pathways involved in the voluntary control of the larynx and pharynx for speech as well as involuntary reflex mechanisms.

5. Nucleus of Solitary Fasciculus: afferent fibers from the facial, glossopharyngeal, and vagus nerves, upon entering brain stem form a bundle of fibers which gives off fibers to the nucleus of the solitary tract. The vagus afferents carry sensory information from the larynx.

6. Central Mechanism of Respiration: in addition to involuntary respiratory mechanisms located in reticular formation of medulla, there are cortically mediated voluntary mechanisms important for speech.

7. Hypoglossal Nucleus: supplies the motor innervation for muscles of the tongue.

VI. Peripheral Motor Pathways

A. Trigeminal Nerve:

1. Largest cranial nerve.

2. Three branches with both motor and sensory function:

a. ophthalmic;

b. maxillary;

c. mandibular.

3. The maxillary nerve provides sensory innervation to the midfacial region:

a. branches of the maxillary innervate the soft palate, uvula, and tonsils, nasal portion of the pharynx, teeth, gums, cheeks;

b. branches of the mandibular innervate the tensor veli palatini, tensor tympani, masseter, temporal, lateral pterygoid, and medial pterygoid muscles;

c. lingual branch supplies sensory fibers to mucous membrane of anterior 2/3 of the tongue.

B. Facial Nerve:

1. VIIth cranial nerve with motor and sensory functions has numerous branches. The buccal and mandibular branches are important for their innervation of facial muscles used in speech production.

C. Glossopharyngeal Nerve:

1. Both sensory and motor.

2. Motor innervates the stylopharyngeus muscle.

3. Sensory fibers to portions of the middle ear and mucous membrane of the pharynx.

D. Vagus Nerve:

1. Many functions related to cardiovascular and visceral activities.

2. Also supplies sensory fibers to pharynx, larynx, soft palate, tympanic plexus, trachea.

3. Motor fibers to larynx and pharynx.

4. Many functions of the vagus nerve to larynx are duplicative with the accessory nerve.

5. The recurrent laryngeal nerve is the main motor nerve of the larynx and sensory nerve for the trachea and lower laryngeal region.

6. The superior laryngeal nerve is the main sensory nerve for the larynx but also contains motor fibers to the cricothyroid muscle.

E. Accessory Nerve:

1. It is possible that most of the laryngeal motor fibers may actually be part of the accessory nerve.

F. Hypoglossal Nerve:

1. Main motor nerve for the tongue, but probably also has proprioceptive sensory fibers.

G. Respiratory Nerves:

1. The phrenic nerve contains motor and sensory fibers for the diaphragm.

2. The motor and sensory nerves that innervate other muscles of respiration arise from cervical, thoracic and lumbar regions of the spinal cord.

VII. Summary

A. Auditory system:

1. Has direct pathways for rapid, precise conveyance; minimum of 3 synapses between VIIIth nerve and cortex.

2. Also more complex pathways to permit very intricate analysis of information.

3. Variety of crossed and uncrossed pathways connecting auditory nuclei.

4. Each station in auditory pathway has afferent and efferent input creating complex patterns of information processing and feedback control.

B.  Speech system:

1.  Involves a broad area of the cerebral cortex and a number of simple and complex parallel motor pathways.

2.  Complex network of neural impulses, sensory and motor, insure that the neural signals sent to the "speech muscles" are coordinated in such a way as to produce intelligible speech.

C.  Redundancies in auditory and speech systems:

1.  These redundancies make the pathway fairly resistant to disruption by small lesions or other disturbances.

2.  Disadvantage is that small malignant defects are difficult to detect until they have grown to dangerous proportion.

3.  Speech, language and hearing are perhaps man's most sophisticated sets of behavior – and thus depend on extensive neural systems and structures.

**REVIEW QUESTIONS**

1.  All of the following are parts of a neuron EXCEPT:

    A.  Axon
    B.  Soma
    C.  Ganglion
    D.  Dendrite
    E.  Membrane

2.  The auditory portion of the eighth cranial nerve in a young adult human consists of how many fibers?

    A.  800
    B.  3,000
    C.  31,000
    D.  52,000
    E.  4-5 million

3. What is the minimum number of synapses crossed in the transmission of information from the auditory nerve to the auditory cortex, including one synapse at the cortex?

A. 2
B. 4
C. 6
D. 7
E. 10

4. What major nucleus in the auditory pathway is located between the superior olivary complex and the medial geniculate nucleus?

A. The central nucleus of the inferior colliculus.
B. The cochlear nucleus.
C. The medial inferior olivary nucleus.
D. The spiral ganglion.
E. The olfactory proboscis.

5. Which of the following neural elements is essential for normal function of the acoustic stapedius reflex?

A. The olfactory nerve.
B. The lateral geniculate nucleus.
C. The medial geniculate nucleus.
D. The third cranial nerve.
E. The seventh cranial nerve.

6. The first opportunity in the auditory pathway for information from the two ears to interact is the:

A. Eighth nerve.
B. Cochlear nucleus.
C. Superior olive.
D. Inferior colliculus.
E. Brachium of the inferior colliculus.

7. Which of the following has the clearest tonotopic organization?

A. The dorsal division of the medial geniculate body.
B. Broca's area.
C. The mesencephalic nucleus of the trigeminal nerve.
D. The medial superior olive.
E. Area CM of the auditory cortex.

8. Primary auditory cortex (auditory koniocortex) receives direct, essential projections from:

A. The ventral division of the medial geniculate body.
B. The anteroventral cochlear nucleus.
C. The lateral preolivary nucleus.
D. The stria of Monakow.
E. The ventral nucleus of the lateral lemniscus.

9. All of the following thalamic nuclei are probably involved in speech and hearing control EXCEPT:

A.  Medial geniculate nucleus.
B.  Pulvinar.
C.  Ventral lateral nucleus.
D.  Lateral geniculate nucleus.
E.  Ventral posterior medialis nucleus.

10. Ataxic dysarthria would most likely result from damage to which area of the brain?

A.  Lobes VI and VII of the cerebellum.
B.  Red nucleus.
C.  Globus pallidus.
D.  Lateral hemispheres of the cerebellum.
E.  Vermis.

11. The pyramidal and extrapyramidal systems differ in which of the following respects?

A.  Neuronal cell bodies of the pyramidal system are triangular in shape while those of the extrapyramidal system are round.
B.  Fibers of the extrapyramidal system pass through the "Extrapyramidal Tract".
C.  Pyramidal tract fibers pass through the external capsule while the extrapyramidal fibers pass through the internal capsule.
D.  Pyramidal tract fibers originate from Broca's and Wernicke's areas exclusively.
E.  Pyramidal tract fibers make their first synapse at or near a motor neuron while extrapyramidal fibers project to one of several subcortical nuclei many synapses removed from motor neurons.

12. The mandibular branch of the trigeminal nerve:

A.  Provides motor fibers to the muscles of mastication and sensory fibers to the soft palate.
B.  Provides motor fibers to muscles of mastication and facial expression.
C.  Provides motor fibers to masseter, temporalis, medial pterygoid, lateral pterygoid, tensor veli palatini and tensor tympani muscles.
D.  Provides sensory innervation to the hard palate mucous membrane, gums, soft palate, uvula and tonsils.
E.  Provides sensory innervation to the upper 2/3 of the face.

13. Which part of the cerebral cortex would probably be least involved in speech control?

A.  Frontal lobe.
B.  Broca's area.
C.  Wernicke's area.
D.  Planum temporale.
E.  Sensorimotor cortex.

14. A lesion of the brainstem that involved the nucleus ambiguus would result in:

   A. Loss of sensation of the face.
   B. Paralysis of laryngeal muscles.
   C. Paralysis of respiratory muscles.
   D. Loss of pure-tone auditory discrimination.
   E. Paralysis of tongue muscles.

15. In which of the following ways do the lingual and hypoglossal nerves differ?

   A. The lingual nerve supplies motor fibers to muscles of the tongue while the hypoglossal supplies sensory fibers.
   B. The lingual nerve carries taste and proprioceptive afferent fibers while the hypoglossal carries only motor fibers.
   C. The lingual nerve innervates the anterior part of the tongue while the hypoglossal innervates the posterior, or lower part of the tongue.
   D. The lingual is the only nerve innervating the tongue; the hypoglossal innervates pharyngeal tissues below the base of the tongue.
   E. The lingual nerve supplies sensory innervation for the mucous membrane of the anterior part of the tongue while the hypoglossal carries motor and proprioceptive sensory fibers.

16. Label the following figures:

   1-1

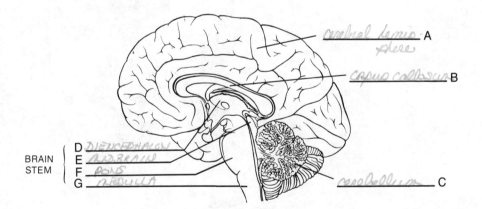

cerebral lamina here — A

capus callosum — B

BRAIN STEM
   D DIENCEPHALON
   E MIDBRAIN
   F PONS
   G MEDULLA

cerebellum — C

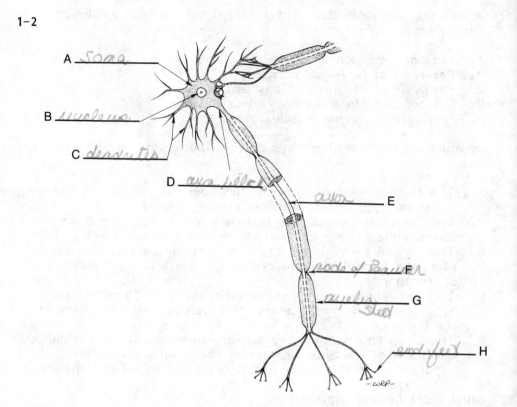

A _soma_

B _nucleus_

C _dendrites_

D _axon hillock_

E _axon_

F _node of Ranvier_

G _myelin sheath_

H _end feet_

—WRP—

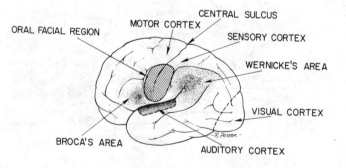

ORAL FACIAL REGION

MOTOR CORTEX

CENTRAL SULCUS

SENSORY CORTEX

WERNICKE'S AREA

VISUAL CORTEX

AUDITORY CORTEX

BROCA'S AREA

—R. Poston—

# Chapter 2

# BASIC NEUROPHYSIOLOGICAL MECHANISMS UNDERLYING ORAL COMMUNICATION

*Jesse G. Kennedy, III, and James H. Abbs*

I.  Identification of the Basic Unit of the Nervous System

    A.  Two schools of thought:

        1.  Hans Held and Camillo Golgi:  Syncytium or continuity theory.

        2.  Ramon y Cajal and contemporaries such as Sherrington, Forel, and His:  contact theory.

    B.  Waldeyer (1891) summarized and provided the basis for delineation of the neuron doctrine.

        1.  Each neuron is an independent outgrowth from a single primitive neuron cell (a neuroblast).

        2.  Neurons have a certain polarity.

        3.  Neurons are the basic units of the nervous system.

        4.  Neurons demonstrate physiological and functional specificity.

II.  The Basic Unit of the Nervous System

    A.  The Neuron.

        1.  The CNS is estimated to be composed of more than 10 to the 11th power neurons, each according to the neuron doctrine, acting as independent functional entities.

    B.  Basic Neuronal Morphology.

        1.  Dendritic Zone:  specialized for reception of impulses.

            a. dendrites – cytoplasmic extensions;

            b. soma – neuronal cell body;

            c. axon – transmits neural information impulses away from soma.

(1) axon hillock – point where axon attaches to soma;

(2) axon terminal and plates – end buttons or end feet.

   d. plasma membrane – encloses the neuron (differentially) permeable).

2. Intracellular – inside the cell membrane.

3. Extracellular – outside the cell membrane.

4. Ion Channels – pores that interrupt the membrane continuity and selectively allow inorganic ions to penetrate. These pores operate through selectivity and gating.

C. The Resting Neuron.

1. Membrane potential – potential electrical difference between the extra- and intracellular environment.

2. Resting potential – membrane potential in the resting cell.

3. Electrical potential:

   a. cations – positively charged ions on surface of the membran

   b. anions – negatively charged ions on the opposite surface.

4. Active transport – chemical system in the cell membrane which moves substances through the cell membrane.

5. Passive transport – transport of ions by diffusion through the cell membrane.

6. Effectiveness of transport depends on:

   a. differences in concentration of ions across the membrane (the concentration gradient);

   b. differences in the electrical charge on the membrane (the electrical gradient).

D. The Active Neuron.

1. Action potential is due to a rapid change in membrane potential due to changes in membrane permeability and depolarization;

   a. conductance – dilation of the membrane channels for sodium;

b. polarization – ions flow into the cell, creating a positive charge;

c. depolarization – positive potassium ions flow out of the cell making its electrical charge less negative;

d. reversal potential – reverses polarity of the cell membrane;

e. all-or-none – starting and continuation of the events of the action potential.

E. Propagation of the Action Potential.

1. Conduction Velocity is the speed at which the wave of depolarization traverses the neural membrane and is dependent on:

a. fiber diameter;

b. nerve temperature;

c. the presence or absence of insulating myelin.

2. Mode of propagation of neural impulse.

a. local circuit propagation (membranes without myelin);

b. saltatory propagation (myelinated neurons);

c. eddy circuit depolarizes the adjacent segment spreading the impulse to the termination of the membrane.

F. Efficiency of Action Potential Excitation is due to several factors including:

1. Accommodation.

2. Excitability curve.

3. Refractory Period – immediately following the reversal potential there is a period of time during which the membrane remains depolarized.

a. absolute refractory period – initial refractory stage which completely blocks production of action potential;

b. partial refractory period – follows absolute refractory period during which an action potential can be elicited only with difficulty.

III. Fundamental Neuronal Integration

    A. The Synapse - interface between two neurons or between a neuron and a muscle.

        1. Synapse is an integrator which regulates transmission of neural information.

            a. the most complex of neuronal system behavior.

    B. Central Nervous System Synapses: Neuron to Neuron - two basic types of synaptic transmission:

        1. Electrical Synapses.

        2. Chemical Synapses - rely on chemicals called neurotransmitters

        3. Basic Structures of a Central Synapse:

            a. presynaptic terminal - terminal knob or bouton terminaux;

            b. mitochondria - provide chemicals necessary for synthesis of neurotransmitters;

            c. synaptic vesicles - contain specific amounts of neurotransmitters;

            d. postsynaptic membrane - the membrane to which the neural impulse is being transmitted.

        4. EPSP - Excitatory postsynaptic potentials - local, subthreshold depolarization in the postsynaptic membrane.

        5. IPSP - Inhibitory postsynaptic potentials - local, hyper-polarizing potential change in the postsynaptic membrane.

        6. Two ways to facilitate the creation of an action potential:

            a. temporal facilitation;

            b. spatial facilitation.

    C. Peripheral Nervous System Synapses: Nerve to Muscle.

        1. Neuromuscular Junction (myoneural junction) - the synapse between a nerve and a muscle.

            a. presynaptic structure includes:

                (1) motor end-plate - invaginates the muscle fiber:

                    (a) synaptic gutter - the depression in the muscle in which the end plate resides;

(2) EPP - end-plate potential - potential generated (is local and may be graded in amplitude).

2.  Neurotransmitters of Synaptic Action:

    a.  acetylcholine (ACh) - may function as an excitatory or inhibitory agent;

    b.  dopamine;

    c.  norepinephrine;  } excitatory agents

    d.  serotonin;

    e.  gamma aminobutyric acid (brain); } apparent inhibitory
    
    f.  glycine (spinal cord).           } neurotransmitters

IV.  Principles of Grouped Neuron Interactions

A.  Basic Organizational Principles.

    1.  Convergence - a single neuron is controlled by multiple, converging inputs.

    2.  Divergence - may function to amplify effects with a single neuron innervating varying numbers of muscle fibers.

B.  The Input to the System:  Sensory Mechanisms.

    1.  Sensory receptors - body requires constantly updated environmental information.

    2.  Afferent neurons - transmit information from sensory end organs to neuronal processing centers.

C.  Basic Characteristics of Sensor Mechanism:

    1.  Mechanoreceptors - provide the nervous system with information regarding touch, movement, mechanical deformation of deep tissue, and hearing.

        a.  encapsulated;

        b.  unencapsulated.

    2.  Two general principles apply to all receptors:

        a.  differential sensitivity - different afferent nerves elicit different sensations;

        b.  adaptation - describes the response of the nerve to continued stimulation.

D.  Four Stages of Sensory Function:

1.  Application of an appropriate stimulus to a sensory end organ.

2.  Membrane permeability leads to a generator current within the receptor.

3.  Generator current induces a local membrane depolarization called generator potential (receptor potential).

4.  Generator potential electronically spreads as a nonpropagating impulse.

E.  The Output of the System:  Motor Apparatus.

1.  Three types of muscle:

    a. striated muscle (somatic);

    b. unstriated muscle (smooth, visceral);

    c. cardiac.

2.  Characteristics of muscle fiber contraction:

    a. isometric - length of muscle is held constant;

    b. isotonic - length of muscle changes as it contracts against a constant load.

3.  Regulation of muscle contraction:

    a. motor unit - the basic element of control of muscle contraction:

        (1) single motoneuron;

        (2) muscle fibers (innervation).

    b. regulators of muscle may be achieved by:

        (1) varying the frequency at which motor units fire;

        (2) modulating the number of motor units that are simultaneously fired.

    c. multiple unit summation (recruitment).

F.  Functional Classification of Muscles:

1.  Phasic - show short contraction time, high levels of force and rapid fatigue.

2.  Tonic - long contraction times, less force, and high resistance to fatigue.

V.  Interactions Between Input and Output:   Reflexes

A.  Reflexes.

1.  Based on "hardwired" neuron circuits that are present before birth, do not require learning.

2.  Predictable from the nature and magnitude of the stimulus.

3.  Triggered by, and time-locked to external stimuli.

4.  Stereotypic.

5.  Utilized to regulate or protect the organism.

6.  Involuntary, unconscious and automatic responses.

7.  Observed with shorter time delays between the stimulus and consequent motor reactions than are observed with "voluntary" reactions.

B.  Reflexes Observed in the Spinal Cord:

1.  Afferent pathway - centripetally conducts sensory information from the peripheral sensory end organs.

2.  Integrating interconnection - located within the central grey matter of the spinal cord.

3.  Efferent pathway - centrifugally conducts motor commands to the peripheral musculature.

C.  Intrasegmental Spinal Reflexes - utilize a single level of the spinal cord.

1.  Monosynaptic reflex arc:

a. stretch reflex (muscle spindle or myotatic reflex);

b. intrinsic reflex.

2.  Polysynaptic reflexes:

a. tendon reflex (inverse myotic reflex).

3.  Propriospinal neurons - afferent axons that also synapse on central grey neurons in the spinal cord that ascend and descend in propriospinal tracts to terminate on different segments of the spinal cord.

D.   Basic Characteristics of Reflexes:

1.   Reflex fatigue – decrement in the amplitude of a reflex response during maintained application of the stimulus.

2.   Reflex rebound – changes in reflex threshold which occur following removal of the stimulus.

3.   After-discharge – the persistence of reflex activity following removal of the stimulus.

4.   Reflex time – the time between stimulation and reflex response.

5.   Reflex response – corresponds to the intensity of the stimulus.

E.   Brain Stem Reflexes – show similarities and differences to spinal cord reflexes.

F.   Utility of Reflexes – clinical examination of <u>reflex</u> <u>profiles</u> provides information about the nature, extent and location of neural lesions.

**REVIEW QUESTIONS**

1.   Match the following statements identified with the <u>syncytium</u> or <u>continuity</u> theory (1) or with the <u>neuronal</u> or <u>contact</u> (2) theory.

_1_ A. Neurons share a common cytoplasm.
_2_ B. Each neuron is an independent outgrowth from a single primitive <u>neuroblast</u>.
_2_ C. Neurons demonstrate physiological and functional specificity.
_2_ D. Neurons have a certain polarity, with information entering through dendrites and soma and exiting through the axon.
_1_ E. The axon membrane of one neuron directly contacts and pierces the membrane of another.

2.   Fill in the blanks:

The neuron consists of a (A) _dendritic_ _zone_, which is a specialized area for reception of impulses and includes numerous cytoplasmic extensions called (B) _dendrites_ that profusely branch and taper to be covered with gemmules on their distal terminations; a (C) _soma_ (neuronal cell body); an (D) _axon_, which arises from the (E) _hillock_ of the soma.

3. The speed at which the wave of depolarization traverses the neural membrane is called _conduction_ _velocity_ and depends on at least three factors:

   A. _fiber diameter_
   B. _nerve temperature_
   C. _presence /absence of myelin)_

4. Immediately following the reversal potential there occurs a period of time during which the membrane remains depolarized and a second stimulus cannot elicit a new action potential. This general period of time is called the (A) _refractory_ _period_; the initial stage of this period is characterized by total inactivation and is labeled the (B) _absolute_ _refractory period_; following this initial stage there is a period during which a second action potential may be elicited with difficulty – this stage is called the (C) _relative_ _refractory_ _period_.

5. The two basic types of synaptic transmission are labeled by virtue of the synaptic stimulus as either (A) _electrical_ or (B) _chemical_.

6. Name the two basic organizational principles which influence the transfer of information in the nervous system:

   A. _convergence)_
   B. _divergence)_

   Define each term:

   A. _a single neuron is controlled by_
      _multiple, converging input)_
   B. _one neuron may innervate varying_
      _numbers of muscle fibers or multiple_
      _neuron tracts)_

7. Put the following 4 statements in proper order to describe the process by which nerve endings fulfill their functions as transducers:

   _3_ A. The generator current induces a local membrane depolarization.
   _4_ B. The generator potential spreads as a nonpropagating impulse.
   _2_ C. The change in membrane permeability leads to a generator current.
   _1_ D. An appropriate stimulus is applied to the sensory end organ.

8. Histologically there are three types of muscle. Name them.

A. _____striated_____
B. _____unstriated_____
C. _____somatic_____

9. Functionally muscles may be classified as phasic or tonic. Identify each general statement below as a description of a (1) phasic or (2) tonic muscle:

_1_ A. fatigues rapidly
_2_ B. long contraction time
_2_ C. highly resistant to fatigue
_1_ D. fast discontinuous movements
_1_ E. short contraction time
_1_ F. high level of force generated
_2_ G. red
_1_ H. white

10. What is the concept of <u>differential sensitivity</u>?

theory that a nerve fiber will transmit only one modality of sensation regardless of how the nerve is stimulated

24

# Chapter 3

# NEUROPHYSIOLOGICAL PROCESSES OF SPEECH MOVEMENT CONTROL

*James H. Abbs and Jesse G. Kennedy, III*

I.  Introduction

    A.  Research Methods

        1.  Prior to 1965 two main research methods on spinal motor system:

            a. electrophysiological or mechanical stimulation while recording evoked potentials;

            b. observation of behaviors following introduction of lesions.

        2.  Current Research Methods:

            a. result from converging ideas and approaches from several different scientific fields, such as experimental psychology and neurophysiology;

            b. correlation of single nerve activity within a portion of the brain with specific voluntary movement or muscle contraction;

            c. use of reversible lesions;

            d. analysis of modeling techniques of engineering and cybernetics.

        3.  Speech motor neurophysiology written prior to 1970 or 1975 has been reduced to historical value by newer developments.

II.  Current Concepts of the Neuromotor Control of Voluntary Movement

    A.  How does the nervous system program, coordinate, and regulate voluntary movement?

1. According to Delong (1971):

    a. the appropriate muscles must be selected;

    b. each participating muscle must be activated or
       inactivated in proper temporal relation to the others;

    c. the appropriate amount of excitation or inhibition
       must be exerted on each muscle.

2. With preprogrammed playback, descending patterns must
   be modified and refined at one or more levels of motor
   execution by ascending afferent information.

3. While certain aspects of motor behavior are prelearned,
   these patterns are modulated and manipulated to fit
   the changing environment.

4. The most critical question in motor control is "How and
   to what extent, is motor output controlled by sensory input?"

III. An Overall Framework for Neuromotor Control

   A. Normal motor control appears to be the result of delicate
      interactions among a hierarchy of cascaded neural pathways.

      1. Motor equivalence: implies a set pattern of coordinated
         muscle contractions and/or set of movements involved may
         vary from one repetition of a defined motor task to
         another -- implying a sort of automatic flexibility in
         both the programming and execution of the act.

   B. Current views of normal motor control concerns the moment-
      to-moment contribution of afferent information to multiple
      control pathways.

   C. To evaluate these multiple pathways involved in the control
      of movement is the introduction of precisely controlled
      perturbations (steps of force or displacement) to limbs or
      digits during the performance of a learned motor task.

      1. The responses often reflect simultaneous operation of:

         a. short-latency, automatic pathways;

         b. long-latency, voluntary pathways;

         c. one or more additional pathways operating between
            these extremes.

26

D. Some evidence exists to show interactions between perturbation parameters (i.e., velocity, displacement, rate of force, etc.) and the type of movement in determining specific pathway involvement.

E. Experience, degree of motor skill and/or the intentions of the subject may have influence on the particular pathways involved.

F. Thus, it appears that the particular neuromotor mechanisms involved in programming and execution of a motor gesture may be determined by a complex interaction of many variables.

   1. The dynamics of the movement.

   2. The novelty of the motor task.

   3. The subject's intentions.

   4. Possible movement-to-movement and system-to-system differences in the nature of the controlled movement output.

IV. Possible Mechanisms of Motor Coordination

A. Eye-head coordinative interactions are an excellent example of a feedforward open-loop control mechanism.

B. A closed-loop feedback system is one in which the efferent consequence of afferent discharge acts to reduce or eliminate the "error" at the site where that error was "sensed".

C. It has been suggested that feedforward, open-loop regulation may be more common in the nervous system than the more classic feedback, closed-loop processes.

V. Possible Mechanisms of Motor Learning

A. The general hypothesis under study is that the afferent channels normally activated during movement have special capabilities in providing short-latency voluntary control of that movement.

   1. With extended learning, kinesthetic stimuli yield much shorter reaction time latencies than comparable auditory or visual stimuli.

B. It appears that the nervous system has an ability to transfer a particular afferent-to-efferent response from conscious mediation to a less conscious level with a substantial reduction in response latency.

C. Expectation of errors may be an important factor in motor control.

    1. It seems likely that as a part of motor learning one becomes aware of those particular subcomponents in which errors are most likely to occur.

D. There obviously are circumstances in which afferent control is neither feedback nor closed-loop.

E. Some intended responses have latencies and a degree of automaticity previously associated only with reflexes.

F. Some reflexes have been shown to be modifiable by instruction, experience, etc., and hence may be under voluntary control.

VI. Neurophysiology of Speech Movement Control

A. The role of afferent mechanisms is of major importance in appreciating nervous system execution of speech movements.

    1. However, methodological problems have restricted inferences that could be made concerning important moment-to-moment neurophysiological control processes.

    2. Experiments often have been contaminated by multiple sources of nervous system adaptation.

B. Multiple hierarchical Pathways appear to be operative in speech production.

    1. The orofacial system serves many functions in addition to speech so a nervous system capability for on-line adaptive adjustment is necessary.

C. Motor equivalence adjustments to descending speech motor commands implies a repetition-to-repetition flexibility.

    1. Speech motor commands may be adjusted to assume that individual articulators reach a semi-invariant target position, despite a substantial degree of variability in their starting positions.

    2. Individual muscles appear to "trade-off" in their combined contribution to an individual articulatory movement -- as do the articulators.

D. The hierarchical, multipathway process underlying the programming and execution of speech movements does not require that we view speech production as a closed-loop process.

E.  Many experiments show the flexibility of the speech motor control system's <u>motor equivalence</u> adjustment capabilities, and the remote yet differentiated nature of ascending afferent actions.

F.  Another experimental approach involves temporary structural alterations of the peripheral speech apparatus such as <u>bite blocks</u> between the teeth, and observing the readjustment of tongue and lip movements to permit the production of <u>normal</u> speech.

G.  There are many reasons to hypothesize that <u>the motor subsystems of the speech production mechanisms are not controlled in a uniform manner</u>.

VII.  Speculations Concerning Speech Motor Learning

A.  Little is known concerning the nature and characteristics of speech motor <u>learning</u>.

B.  The learning process of speech motor development involves sensorimotor exploration and integration.

C.  There may be different control mechanisms operating within the normal population.

VIII.  General Implications for Disorders of Speech Production

A.  Caution should be exercised in drawing conclusions concerning speech motor aberrations based on neurological assessments.

B.  Need to refine measures used to describe and study populations of speech motor disorders.

C.  The apparent dependency between coordination of normal speech movements and sensory information may suggest directions for rehabilitation contributions.

D.  The movement/control requirements between the different subsystems of the speech production mechanisms that generally follow upper motor neuron damage may yield substantial variation in motor impairment.

E.  General views of the speech mechanism as a single neuromotor system must be changed if more effective treatment is to result.

<u>In summary</u>, we need to temper our thinking with the knowledge that the neurophysiological mechanisms of speech control cannot be separated functionally from the less-well-understood neural processes involving (a) motivation; (b) attention; (c) conceptualization; and (d) sensory awareness.

**REVIEW QUESTIONS**

1.  Identify the two major classic methods of neurophysiological study on the spinal motor system.

    A. _electrophysiological stim. of various parts of NS & record evoked potentials_
    B. _observation of motor behaviors following intro of lesion_

2.  Delong (1970) listed 3 basic requirements that must be fulfilled by the central nervous system for motor movements to be generated.

    A. _the approp. muscle must be selected_
    B. _each muscle must be activated in proper temporal relation_
    C. _the approp. amt of excitation/inhibition must be exerted on each muscle_

3.  What is the apparent hierarchy phenomenon called when a particular pattern of coordinated muscle contractions and/or set of movements involved may vary from one repetition of a defined motor task to another, implying a sort of automatic, yet controlled, flexibility in the final motor details of both programming and execution?

    _motor equivalence_

4.  One of the most powerful and popular methodologies for the study of nervous system pathways in the control of movement involves precisely controlled _perturbations_ to the limbs or digits during the performance of a learned motor task.

5.  Identify three subject attributes that have been shown to influence the particular pathways involved in a motor gesture.

    A. _experience_
    B. _degree of motor skill_
    C. _intentions of the subject_

6.  A (closed-loop) (open-loop) feedback system is one in which the efferent consequence of afferent discharge acts to reduce or eliminate the "error" at the site where that error was "sensed".

7. "Bite block" experimentation has essentially documented the ability of the speech production system to be capable of a wide variety of adaptations. Identify the following statements, based on "bite block" studies, as true or false.

_T_ A. Specific actions of the speech production system can be documented only by observation of multiple variables and careful specification of the motor task.
_T_ B. Particular compensatory actions may vary from one replication of the task to another.
_T_ C. Absolute vowel formant frequencies can vary substantially without loss of perceptual "acceptability".

8. Can you suggest one reason that an individual with a repaired cleft palate retains many speech errors even after the apparent source of the speech problem has been corrected?

Due to the concept of learned motor compensatory movements.

# Chapter 4

# ANATOMY AND PHYSIOLOGY OF THE ORGANS OF THE PERIPHERAL SPEECH MECHANISM

*Joel C. Kahane*

I. Introduction

    A. Negus (1929) maintained that <u>speech</u> is <u>overlaid</u> upon other more negative functions.

II. The Respiratory System

    A. Postnatal Developmental Changes.

        1. Although the respiratory system is capable of supporting life at birth, it is still structurally immature.

        2. The tracheobronchial tree:

            a. trachea in newborn is 1/3 of adult size;

            b. bronchi in newborn is 1/2 of adult size;

            c. bronchioles are only 1/4 of adult size.

        3. Although the bronchioles and alveoli reach adult size and number by age 8, the lung continues to grow into adulthood.

        4. The shape and morphology of the thorax changes from birth to adulthood as a result of upright posture and changes in respiratory needs.

        5. Frequency of breathing decreases with age.

        6. In infants the abdomen moves greatly during respiration; after age 7, thoracic wall movements predominate.

B. Anatomy and Physiology of the Respiratory System.

1. The <u>upper respiratory tract</u> is composed of the nasal cavities, oral cavity, pharynx and larynx.

   a. these organs serve several functions including respiration, mastication, deglutition, resonation and phonation.

2. The nasal cavities serve 3 functions:

   a. humidification;

   b. warming of inspired air;

   c. protection of the upper airways.

3. The pharynx is relatively passive in respiration.

4. The larynx muscles control the size of the <u>rima glottidis</u> – the inlet through which inspired air enters the lower respiratory tract.

   a. the larynx moves with cyclical, rhythmic oscillations during respiration;

   b. the central role of the larynx in respiration is to maintain a patent glottal airway;

   c. the glottis becomes larger when the volume of inspired air increases and when the rate of air flow increases;

   d. a wide variety of opinions exist regarding the roles of specific laryngeal muscles during respiration.

5. The lower respiratory tract consists of all the airways below the larynx – referred to collectively as the <u>tracheobronchial tree</u>.

6. The <u>trachea</u> is composed of 16-20 C-shaped hyaline cartilage rings, and lined with typical respiratory epithelium.

   a. the cartilaginous rings and smooth muscles provide rigidity to the walls of the airway, insuring its patency.

7. The <u>bronchial tree</u> consists of all the passageways below the tracheal bifurcation.

   a. although the diameter of the bronchi passages decreases with each subsequent subdivision, the total surface area of the bronchial tree increases geometrically – resulting in an enormous increase in sites for gaseous exchange in alveoli.

33

8. The lungs:

   a. the right lung is shorter and broader than the left lung and has 3 lobes;

   b. the left lung has only 2 lobes;

   c. the basic functional unit of the lung is the <u>primary lobule</u> or <u>lung unit</u> which consists of the respiratory bronchiole, alveolar ducts, alveolar sacs, and alveoli plus their blood and lymph vessels and nerves;

   d. as the lungs expand, the fibers uncoil and become stretched, while the respiratory bronchioles and alveolar ducts expand, allowing the inspired air to reach the alveoli;

   e. during expiration, the recoil forces stored in the stretched fibers restore them to their unstretched state – which results in pushing air out of the air space into the main conducting tubes.

9. Pleural linkage:

   a. the lungs and thoracic cavity are lined by a serous membrane called the <u>pleura</u>;

   b. two layers of pleurae separated by a narrow fluid-filled pleural space – the fluid reduces surface tension and friction – this arrangement is called <u>pleural linkage</u>;

   c. pleural linkage allows forces from the chest wall to be directly transmitted to the lungs, enabling the lungs to expand in accordance with changes in the chest wall.

C. The Thoracic Skeleton.

   1. The bony thoracic skeleton consists of 12 thoracic vertebrae, 12 ribs and the sternum.

   2. Ribs are named for their relationship to the sternum and numbered 1 through 12:

      a. vertebrosternum – 7 pairs of ribs;

      b. vertebrochondral – 3 pairs or ribs;

      c. vertical (floating) – 2 pairs of ribs.

D. The Respiratory Muscles.

    1. The muscles of inspiration are:

        a. diaphragm;

        b. external intercostal muscles;

        c. internal intercostal muscles (interchondral portion);

        d. sternocleidomastoid and scalene;

        e. pectoralis major and pectoralis minor.

    2. The expiratory muscles include:

        a. the abdominal muscles;

        b. internal intercostals.

III. The Larynx

A. An infant's larynx differs from its adult counterpart in size, consistency of tissues, position in the neck, and shape.

    1. The position of the larynx descends from infancy through childhood and puberty, assuming its adult position at the cricoid cartilage.

    2. The male larynx undergoes significantly more growth than the female larynx – the male vocal folds undergo more than twice the growth of the female vocal folds.

    3. The thyroid cartilage and cricoid cartilage are joined bilaterally at the cricothyroid joints (CTJ).

        a. contraction of the cricothyroid muscles approximates the cricoid and thyroid cartilages to lengthen the vocal folds.

    4. The cricoarytenoid joints (CAJ) are central to laryngeal function and maintenance of an adequate airway during respiration.

        a. the CAJ is formed by the articular facets of the cricoid and arytenoid cartilages;

        b. the two principal movements of the CAJ are sliding and rocking, and brings the vocal folds together for sound production;

c. movements of the arytenoid cartilages are complex and result  in simultaneous displacement of parts of the cartilages in horizontal, vertical and depth planes.

5. Muscular forces in the larynx:

   a. the intrinsic muscles are small, delicate and among the fastest contracting muscles in the body and richly innervated;

   b. as a group the intrinsics work synergistically:

      (1) change relationships of the laryngeal cartilages to each other;

      (2) alter the size and shape of the rima glottidis;

      (3) modify the physical properties of the vocal folds;

      (4) influence glottal resistance.

   c. the intrinsic laryngeal muscles and their functions:

      (1) cricothyroid – lengthens and tenses vocal folds;

      (2) lateral cricothryroid – adducts vocal folds; narrows the rima glottidis;

      (3) posterior cricoarytenoid – abducts vocal folds; widens rima glottidis;

      (4) interarytenoids – adducts vocal folds, particularly the posterior region;

      (5) thyroarytenoid:  thyrovocalis portion – shortens vocal folds and increases tension; thyromuscularis portion – adducts vocal folds and reduces tension.

   d. the extrinsic laryngeal muscles are divided into suprahyoid and infrahyoid groups:

      (1) sternohyoid – lowers thyroid cartilage and lowers larynx;

      (2) thyrohyoid – raises thyroid cartilage; raises larynx; lowers hyoid bone.

B.  The Human Vocal Folds.

   1.  The vocal folds are composed of three layers that are
       differentiated on the basis of structure and mechanical
       properties:

       a. cover – superficial layer;

       b. transitional – comprise the intermediate and deep layers.

IV.  The Pharynx

   A.  The pharynx plays essential roles in respiration, deglutition
       and resonance.

   1.  Postnatal developmental changes are significant and
       related to growth of the tongue and larynx and to
       establish the unique spatial relationships for the
       development of the vocal tract.

   2.  Growth of the pharynx is continuous through age 16
       in both sexes.

   3.  There is interest in the growth pattern of the
       nasopharynx and adenoids because of their potential
       effects on velopharyngeal competence during speech.

       a. the adenoids are noticeable by six months to
          1 year of age; by 2 years they are well developed
          and occupy nearly 1/2 of the nasopharyngeal area;
          peak growth of adenoids is reached between 9–15
          years of age; after age 15, the adenoids begin to
          atrophy and reach complete atrophy by age 25 years.

   B.  The muscles of the pharynx are arranged in 2 layers:

   1.  Inner layer of muscles:

       a. stylopharyngeus;

       b. palatopharyngeus;

       c. salpingopharyngeus.

   2.  Outer layer of muscles:

       a. superior constrictor;

       b. middle constrictor;

       c. inferior constrictor.

3.  The wall of the pharynx is composed of four functionally specialized layers:

    a. mucous membrane;

    b. muscular wall;

    c. pharyngeal raphe and buccopharyngeal fascia;

    d. loose areolar tissue.

4.  The pharynx is conventionally subdivided into 3 regions on the basis of openings in its anterior wall:

    a. the epi- or nasopharynx;

    b. the meso- or oropharynx;

    c. the hypo- or laryngopharynx.

5.  The nasopharynx is almost exclusively involved in respiration – although it also facilitates aeration and drainage of the middle ears via the eustachian tube and drainage of the nasal cavities and sinuses – and serves as a resonator during speech.

6.  The oropharynx and hypopharynx serve both respiratory and digestive functions:

    a. peristalsis – the primary motor function of the pharynx creating a positive muscular force which drives the food bolus caudally.

V.  The Soft Palate and Velopharyngeal Mechanism

    A.  The soft palate is highly mobile because of its muscular structure and strong because of its connective tissue elements.

    B.  The soft palate (or velum) consists of five pairs of muscles:

        1.  Tensor veli palatini.

        2.  Levator veli palatini.

        3.  Uvulae.

        4.  Palatoglossus.

        5.  Palatopharyngeus.

C. The velum and lateral pharyngeal walls contribute to obturation of the velopharyngeal portal.

D. The velum elevates posterosuperiorly and makes contact with the posterior pharyngeal wall.

E. Passavant (1869) was the first to describe a forward displacement of the posterior pharyngeal wall during velopharyngeal closure during speech.

   1. Several subsequent investigators have shown that anterior displacement of the posterior pharyngeal wall rarely accompanies velopharyngeal closure.

   2. The frequent appearance of Passavant's pad in cleft palate patients and those with velopharyngeal insufficiency suggests that it is a compensatory mechanism to improve valving for speech.

F. Lateral pharyngeal wall movement.

   1. The predominant direction of movement is medial.

   2. The movement is extensive.

   3. The primary site of motion or displacement is at the level of the hard palate.

G. Bloomer (1953) proposed a dichotomous classification of velopharyngeal valving:

   1. Pneumatic tasks – speech, blowing, whistling.

   2. Nonpneumatic tasks – swallowing, gagging.

VI. The Tongue

A. The tongue is an extraordinarily versatile organ which is important in mastication, deglutition, taste and speech.

   1. The tongue increases in all dimensions from birth to adulthood.

   2. The dorsal surface of the tongue is divided into an anterior two thirds (blade) and a posterior one third (root).

3. The surface is characterized by epithelial uprisings – the <u>lingual</u> <u>papillae</u> – which are specialized for taste:

   a. filiform papillae;

   b. fungiform papillae;

   c. circumvallate papillae.

B. <u>Intrinsic</u> muscles of the tongue:

   1. <u>Superior longitudinal</u> – shortens tongue, turns tongue tip and sides upward.

   2. <u>Inferior longitudinal</u> – shortens tongue, lowers tongue tip and sides.

   3. <u>Transverse</u> – narrows tongue and increases its height.

   4. <u>Vertical</u> – flattens tongue and widens it.

C. <u>Extrinsic</u> muscles of the tongue:

   1. <u>Styloglossus</u> – retracts and elevates tongue.

   2. <u>Genioglossus</u> – retracts and depresses tip.

   3. <u>Hyoglossus</u> – lowers tongue.

   4. <u>Glossopalatinus</u> – elevates back of tongue.

VII. The Temporomandibular Joint (TMJ) and Craniomandibular Musculature

A. The TMJ is highly specialized and differs from other movable joints in numerous ways.

B. The TMJ is really a bilateral articulation in which both joints may be active to an equal extent, undergoing similar movements, or where one condyle may be active while the other is passive.

C. There are five pairs of muscles which move the mandible (muscles of mastication):

   1. Temporalis.

   2. Masseter.

   3. Medial (internal) pterygoid.

   4. Lateral (external) pterygoid.

   5. Anterior digastric.

D. <u>Sliding</u> and <u>rotation</u> are the basic movements of the mandible.

E. Functional movements of the mandible result from a combination of sliding (translational) and rotatory (or hinge) activity.

VIII. The Facial Muscles

A. Facial muscles are important in such diverse activities as speech, facial expression, swallowing and in helping to maintain normal occlusion and proper alignment of the teeth.

B. Unique properties of the facial muscles:

1. Organized into flat sheets that are located superficially in close proximity to the skin.

2. The muscle fibers course through a layer of adipose tissue on their way toward insertion into the facial skin or mucous membrane.

3. Facial muscles lack fascial sheaths and typical tendinous attachments found in most other striated muscle fibers.

4. There is great inter- and intrasubject variability in size and shape of facial muscles.

5. Nerves innervating facial muscles approach them from their deep surface rather than more superficially, as is customarily seen in other striated muscles.

C. The facial muscles can be divided into four distinct groups:

1. Muscles surrounding the eyes:

   a. <u>orbicularis</u> <u>oculi</u>;

   b. <u>corrugator</u> <u>supercilii</u>;

   c. <u>procerus</u>.

2. Muscles related to nasal function:

   a. <u>nasalis</u>;

   b. <u>compressor</u> naris;

   c. <u>dilator</u> naris;

   d. <u>depressor</u> septi.

3. Muscles of the external ear and the scalp:

    a. <u>anterior auricularis</u>;

    b. <u>superior auricularis</u>;

    c. <u>posterior auricularis</u>;

    d. <u>occipitofrontalis</u>.

4. Muscles that insert into the region surrounding the opening into the mouth:

    a. referred to as the <u>oral group</u> or the <u>perioral muscles</u>.

1. In the space provided, enter the letter corresponding to the item in Column II that is most related to the item in Column I.

### Column I

*D* (1) Lungs-thorax (pleural) linkage
*A* (2) Dimensions of thorax increased by action of the diaphragm
*C* (3) Dimensions of thorax increased by action of external intercostals
*G* (4) Non-muscular forces
*H* (5) Role of expiratory muscle forces
*F* (6) Role of inspiratory muscle forces
*E* (7) Ribs whose movements primarily affect the transverse dimensions of the thorax
*B* (8) Ribs whose movements primarily affect anteroposterior and transverse dimensions

### Column II

A. Vertical
B. Ribs 2-7
C. Anteroposterior and transverse
D. Results from anatomical arrangement of pleural membranes which allows forces from chest wall to be directly transmitted to lungs
E. Ribs 8-10
F. Increase size of thoracic cavity and control ingressive flow of air
G. Restore chest wall towards resting state through elastic recoil forces; relaxation pressure
H. Decrease size of thoracic cavity and control egressive flow of air

2. Rocking and rotatory (rotation) motions have been ascribed to the:

A. Cricothyroid joint (CTJ) and Cricoarytenoid joint (CAJ) respectively.
B. CAJ
C. CTJ
D. CAJ and CTJ, respectively
E. Thyroepiglottic joint

3. As a group, the intrinsic laryngeal muscles perform all of the following tasks <u>EXCEPT</u>:

   A. Increase tension of vocal folds.
   B. Abduct and adduct vocal folds.
   C. Change size and shape of the rima glottidis.
   D. Lengthen vocal folds.
   E. Alter vertical position of the larynx in the neck.

4. The complex structure of the vocal folds has become better understood because of Hirano's recent electromicroscopic studies. According to him, the vocal folds:

   A. Are composed of two layers called the cover and body.
   B. Are composed of three layers, the stiffest of which is at the vibrating margin.
   C. Are composed of three layers – cover, transition and body.
   D. Vibrate as a single body.
   E. Vibrate like a string.

5. In addition to voice production, list three other biological functions served by the larynx:

   A. _____

   B. _____

   C. _____

6. The vocal tract consists of the following anatomical constituents:

   A. The pharyngeal cavities.
   B. The pharyngeal cavities and the oral and nasal cavities, which may be differentially coupled.
   C. The pharyngeal cavities and the oral cavity.
   D. The oral and nasal cavities.
   E. The pharyngeal cavities and nasal cavities.

7. Indicate the item that is <u>not</u> true about the pharynx.

   A. Composed mainly of 3 V-shaped muscles arranged cranio-caudally.
   B. Pharyngeal constrictors extend from the base of the skull to the oblique line of the thyroid cartilage and to the cricoid cartilage.
   C. Pharyngeal muscles transport a bolus by peristaltic contractions.
   D. Pharyngeal muscles are partially overlapped and united at midline by a raphe.
   E. The shape of the pharynx is tubular.

8. Velpharyngeal closure is normally accomplished by:

    A.  Superior displacement of the velum.
    B.  Superior displacement of the velum and anterior displacement of the posterior pharyngeal wall.
    C.  Posterosuperior displacement of the velum and medial and posterior displacement of the lateral pharyngeal walls.
    D.  Posterior displacement of the velum.
    E.  Posterosuperior displacement of the velum and superior movement of the lateral pharyngeal walls.

9. Research on velopharyngeal valving by Bloomer (1953) and Shprintzen (1973) has shown that:

    A.  Velopharyngeal valving for speech is a unique form of closure.
    B.  Males and females exhibit identical patterns of velopharyngeal closure.
    C.  Velopharyngeal valving for speech and swallowing are similar.
    D.  Velopharyngeal valving for speech, whistling, and blowing are similar.
    E.  Passavant's pad is a normal component of the velopharyngeal mechanism during speech.

10. Choose the item containing the pair of muscles which best completes this sentence:

    Among the muscles of the soft palate the _____ muscle is the prime elevator of the velum while the _____ muscle dilates the eustachian tube.

    A.  Tensor veli palatini; palatopharyngeus
    B.  Levator veli palatini; tensor veli palatini
    C.  Levator veli palatini; tensor tympani
    D.  Levator veli palatini; uvula
    E.  Levator costarum; dilator tubae

11. The principal muscles that cause movement of the mandible are:

    A.  Muscles of mastication.
    B.  Facial muscles.
    C.  Posterior digastric muscle.
    D.  Buccinator muscle.
    E.  Mylohyoid muscle

12. Opening and closing movements of the mandible result from complex movements of the temporomandibular joint because:

    A.  They involve movements restricted to the upper joint cavity.
    B.  They involve movements restricted to the lower joint cavity.
    C.  They result from a sliding movement followed immediately by a hinge movement.
    D.  They result from hinge movement immediately followed by sliding movement.
    E.  They result from hinge movement.

13. Distinguish the functional difference in the roles of the extrinsic and intrinsic tongue muscles.

14. Facial muscles exhibit all of the following characteristics EXCEPT:

    A.  Organized into flat sheets located close to the skin.
    B.  Insert into skin of the face and mucous membrane.
    C.  Contraction of muscles changes contour and shape of face.
    D.  Richly innervated and thus capable of performing refined or subtle movements.
    E.  Exhibit little morphologic variability.

15. Sphincter function of the circumoral muscles is largely derived from an interlacing of all of the following facial muscles EXCEPT:

    A.  Buccinator
    B.  Depressor anguli oris
    C.  Levator anguli oris
    D.  Mentalis
    E.  Orbicularis oris

# Chapter 5

# ANATOMY AND PHYSIOLOGY OF THE HEARING MECHANISM

*David M. Lipscomb*

I.   The Inner Ear

   A.   Comprised of 3 subdivisions:

      1.   The vestibule.

      2.   The semicircular canals.

      3.   The cochlea.

   B.   The <u>vestibule</u> – serves as middle region and opens into both the semicircular canals and the cochlea.

      1.   Contains <u>utricle</u> and <u>saccule</u>.

      2.   Contains <u>vestibular</u> aqueduct.

      3.   <u>Endolymphatic duct</u> (only contact the inner ear has outside its boundaries).

   C.   The three <u>semicircular canals</u> open posteriorly from the vestibule.

      1.   Contain <u>cristae</u>: the sensory end organs for balance.

      2.   Each canal located in a different body plane.

      3.   The three canals are unequal in length and each has one larger end, the <u>ampulla</u>.

      4.   The superior semicircular canal joins the posterior semicircular canal to form the <u>crus commune</u>.

      5.   The <u>horizontal</u> (or lateral) semicircular canal is the shortest in length.

D.  The cochlea is similar in shape to a snail shell.

1.  Located at anterior end of inner ear.

2.  The cochlear canal winds around a central bony core, the modiolus for 2 and 2/3 turns.

E.  The inner ear is a membranous system within a bony cavity, known respectively as the membranous and osseous labyrinth systems.

1.  Osseous labyrinth contains perilymph fluid.

2.  Membranous labyrinth contains endolymph fluid.

F.  A bony ledge, the osseous spiral lamina, projects into the cochlear canal.

1.  Osseous spiral lamina divides the cochlear canal into two major divisions (scalae).

2.  Bony opening at base of the cochlea, the internal auditory meatus which carries nerve fibers of VIIIth cranial nerve (acoustic) to the brainstem.

G.  Sensory end organ for hearing is the organ of Corti.

1.  Organ of Corti rests on basilar membrane.

2.  Basilar membrane attached at one end to the osseous spiral lamina and at the other end to the spiral ligament.

3.  Reissner's membrane separates the cochlear canal into three distinct sections:

a. scala vestibuli – uppermost chamber filled with perilymph – opens into vestibule;

b. scala tympani – lowermost chamber also filled with perilymph – terminates at the round window;

c. scala media – central chamber that contains endolymph and organ of Corti.

H.  Vestibule contains two membranous sacs:

1.  Utricle – larger sac.

2.  Saccule – shaped like a globe.

3.  Two sacs connected by <u>utriculosaccular</u> duct.

4.  Sensory end organs are the <u>maculae</u>.

5.  Provide information regarding acceleration, deceleration and rotation.

I.  Organ of Corti:

1.  <u>Pillars of Corti</u> (or <u>inner and outer rods</u>) form a triangular tunnel, the <u>tunnel of Corti</u> filled with <u>Cortilymph</u>.

2.  Supporting cells for the organ of Corti:

    a.  <u>phalangeal processes</u> arising from <u>Dieter's cells</u> to form the <u>reticular lamina</u>; next come Hensen cells and Claudius cells.

3.  Two types of sensory hair cells:

    a.  single row of <u>inner hair cells</u> total number is 3500–4000; pear shaped;

    b.  3 to 4 rows of <u>outer hair cells</u> number 12,000; column shaped;

    c.  nearly 95% of all <u>afferent</u> (sensory) CNS nerve fibers serve the fewer inner hair cells;

    d.  remaining 5% of afferent CNS nerve fibers are shared by the more numerous outer hair cells;

    e.  cilia atop inner hair cells are arranged in slight crescent formation, whereas cilia of outer hair cells shaped as "W";

    f.  inner hair cells held in place rigidly by supporting cells; outer hair cells are more free-standing;

    g.  outer hair cells subjected to more mechanical activity – thus may be more sensitive to lower levels of sound stimulation;

    h.  tops of longest cilia of outer hair cells are rooted in the underside of <u>tectorial membrane</u>, but cilia of inner hair cells are not attached at top;

    i.  nerve connections of outer hair cells are restricted to bottom of cell; inner hair cells have nerve connections over 2/3 of the cell;

   j. exactly how inner and outer hair cells respond to fluid pressure waves in the scala media is not yet fully understood.

II. Cochlear Blood Supply

 A. Rich vascular organization in cochlea:

  1. Intricate vascular cycle:

   a. blood enters cochlea through several arterial links beginning with <u>subclavian artery</u>, <u>vertebral artery</u> and <u>basal artery</u>;

   b. basal artery branches off into the <u>inferior anterior cerebral artery</u> which has a smaller branch, the <u>labyrinthine artery</u> – which enters the internal auditory meatus;

   c. smaller arteries include the <u>anterior vestibular artery</u>, the <u>vestibular -cochlear artery</u>, and <u>spiral modiolar artery</u>

   d. radiating arterioles supply blood to the dense capillary network known as <u>stria vascularis</u>.

  2. Venous drainage system from inner ear:

   a. <u>vein of scala tympani</u> collects blood from stria vascularis;

   b. <u>vein of scala vestibuli</u> joins vein of scala tympani by uniting with <u>spiral modiolar vein</u>;

   c. at base of cochlea the veins flow into the <u>vein of the cochlea</u> aqueduct which empties ultimately into the <u>jugular vein</u> and on to the heart.

III. Cochlear Mechanics

 A. Exactly how cochlea works is still unknown.

  1. Anatomic parts are microscopic.

  2. Anatomy is largely inaccessible due to the protection afforded by dense temporal bone.

 B. Key concept: cochlear fluids are incompressible, and pressure applied at any one point is instantly transferred to other points in the system.

 C. <u>Traveling wave</u> on basilar membrane reaches an instantaneous crest according to frequency of the stimulus. Human frequency response is 20 Hz to 20,000 Hz.

D.  Cochlea uses some form of analogue frequency displacement transformation for frequency analysis.

E.  High frequencies represented at <u>basal</u> end of basilar membrane; low frequencies located toward <u>apical</u> end.

F.  Amplitude of sound, perceived as "loudness", is represented in cochlea by greater amplitude of displaced basilar membrane, thus involving a larger number of sensory end organs.

G.  Cochlea is capable of discriminating 280 intensity changes in a stimulus from softest to most intense; also, 1400 pitch changes can be perceived when swept through the audible frequency range.

. Hearing Theory

A.  <u>Resonance</u> <u>Theory</u>:

1.  Associated with Helmholtz during middle 1800's.

2.  Frequency resolution achieved by "tuned" fibers, signaling to the sensory cells, and ultimately the nerve fibers.

3.  However, fibers in basilar membrane are not free to vibrate in "resonance".

B.  <u>Frequency</u> <u>Theory</u>:

1.  Rutherford in 1880 thought that sound stimulating the inner ear was simply changed into neural impulses of the same frequency and transmitted to the brain for perception.

2.  <u>Absolute</u> <u>refractory</u> <u>period</u> of nerve fibers limits the number of times a nerve can fire within a given time period.

3.  Theory may hold for stimulating frequencies below 1000 Hz, but not for higher pitches.

C.  <u>Place</u> <u>Theory</u>:

1.  Bekesy in mid-1900's described the traveling wave of the basilar membrane and the way it encodes frequency and amplitude information by the organ of Corti.

2.  Awarded Nobel Prize in Medicine for his work.

D. <u>Volley</u> <u>Theory</u>:

    1. Wever in the 1950's proposed that groups of nerves could fire in <u>volleys</u>, setting up neural impulses analogous to the frequency of the stimulus.

    2. Volley theory recognizes frequency theory for sounds below 800 Hz; volley principle could explain frequency transmission up to 5000 Hz; place principle employed for frequency information higher than 5000 Hz.

V. The Middle Ear

  A. The middle ear mechanism serves to match impedance of air to that of the inner ear fluids.

    1. Middle ear development was closely associated with changes in lower jaw structure.

    2. Middle ear cavity <u>(tympanic</u> <u>cavity)</u> is an irregular air-filled compartment of about 2 cc in volume capacity.

    3. Middle ear cavity is bounded by the <u>tympanic</u> <u>membrane</u>, <u>eustachian</u> <u>tube</u> <u>orifice</u>, lateral wall of inner ear capsule, the <u>mastoid</u> <u>antrum</u>, and the <u>tegmen</u> <u>tympani</u>.

  B. Middle Ear Structures:

    1. Three densest, tiniest bones in body transmit sound across the middle ear cavity: <u>malleus</u>, <u>incus</u> and <u>stapes</u>.

    2. Two smallest muscles in body attach to the ossicular chain: <u>tensor</u> <u>tympani</u> <u>muscle</u> and the <u>stapedius</u> <u>muscle</u>.

    3. Eustachian tube serves to equalize air pressure between middle ear space and the nasopharynx.

    4. <u>Tympanic</u> <u>membrane</u>, or eardrum, is a 3-layer, cone-shaped membrane which collects acoustic pressure waves and transmits the energy to the ossicular chain.

       a. vibrates only about 40 millionths of a cm to threshold sounds, or less than 1/100 the width of a hydrogen molecule!

VI. Functional Correlates of the Middle Ear

  A. Tympanic membrane position and shape is especially important for efficient transmission of vibration.

B.  Ossicular Chain suspended in the middle ear cavity in such a way as to permit high degree of efficiency.

   1.  Malleus and incus weigh about the same, but stapes is only about 1/10 the mass of the other ossicles to facilitate transmission of high frequency sounds.

   2.  Ossicular motion varies as a function of the frequency and intensity of sound.

   3.  Middle ear muscle action increases tension on ossicular chain, thereby reducing the responsivity of the system.

      a.  muscles serve as limited protection against possible damage to cochlear tissues with high intensity stimulation.

C.  Impedance Matching System of the Middle Ear:

   1.  Acoustic impedance is combination of three factors: acoustic resistance, acoustic mass, and acoustic compliance (or stiffness).

   2.  The middle ear transformer:

      a.  areal relationship – area of tympanic membrane is greater than area of stapes footplate by factor of 21:1, accounts for about 23 dB of amplification;

      b.  lever action – manubrium of malleus is 1.3 times longer than the long process of incus, thereby providing 2.5 dB amplification.

   3.  The two factors, areal relationship and lever action, account for a total transfer value in middle ear transformer system of 25 dB.

   4.  For transformer system to work fully air pressure on both sides of tympanic membrane must be equal, and mobility of all moving middle ear parts must be normal.

VII.  A Secondary Pathway

A.  Although most perceived sounds traverse an air conduction pathway, an alternate pathway of bone conduction can also stimulate the cochlea directly.

B.  Three modes of bone conduction:

   1.  Compressional mode – alternating intense pressure waves cause the skull to move in synchrony with the stimulus, thereby creating pressure waves directly in the cochlea.

2. Inertial Mode - when skull vibrates, the middle ear ossicles also vibrate, but somewhat lag in movement because of inertia; stapes footplate creates pressure waves in the cochlea as a consequence of skull vibrations.

3. Osseotympanic mode - skull vibrations may be transferred to the temporomandibular joint of lower jaw to vibrate the temporal bone directly.

4. In most conditions, all three modes of bone conduction vibration interact together.

VIII. The External Ear

A. External ear is in two parts:

1. External auditory meatus (canal).

2. Auricle or pinna.

B. External auditory meatus is "S"-shaped from canal opening to the tympanic membrane.

1. Outer third of canal contains hairs to filter out unwanted substances; and ceruminous and sebaceous glands which secrete earwax (cerumen).

C. The auricle is the "external ear flap".

1. Contains numerous ridges, convulutions and depressions.

2. Used as aid in sound localization.

IX. Overview

A. Development of hearing is economy of creation.

1. Design and structure of the ear are so complete and so intelligent, it would be impossible to manufacture such a system of equal size and complexity.

1. Which of the following structures are not part of the human auditory mechanism?

   A. Pinna
   B. Ossicles
   C. Labyrinth
   D. Lateral line organ
   E. Organ of Corti

2. The ear developed in a progressive series of steps. Which of the following structures appeared earliest:

   A. External ear
   B. Middle ear
   C. Inner ear
   D. Ossicular chain
   E. Lateral line organ

From the following choices, answer questions 3, 4 and 5:

   A. Malleus
   B. Incus
   C. Stapes
   D. Tensor tympani
   E. Stapedius

3. Which of the ossicles is the most lateral? A

4. What tympanic muscle causes the tympanic membrane to move D medialward when the muscle contracts?

5. The tympanic muscle is innervated by which cranial nerve? VIII E

6. Choose the auditory structure that is found only in mammals.

   A. Auricle
   B. Cochlea
   C. Semi-circular canals
   D. External auditory meatus
   E. Saccule

Match the following for Questions 7, 8 and 9:

A. E.G. Wever
B. G.V. Bekesy
C. Volley theory
D. Volley principle
E. Frequency theory

7. This man is the only Nobel laureate in our profession, being recognized in part for his expansion of the place theory. B

8. A theory that incorporates the strong features of three theoretical concepts or principles. C

9. A theory that was eliminated by the knowledge that nerve fibers can not fire at a rate much above 1000 per second. E

10. The normal middle ear is a(n):

A. Fluid-filled space.
B. Air-filled space.
C. Fluid-filled sac.
D. Fluid-filled cavity.
E. Sealed chamber.

11. One of the following structures is not contained in the inner ear:

A. Tectorial membrane.
B. Vestibule.
C. Promontory.
D. Outer hair cells.
E. Basilar membrane.

12. The inner ear consists of two interrelated fluid-filled compartments, the osseus and membranous labyrinths; the fluid in the osseus labyrinth is:

A. Cortilymph
B. Spinal fluid
C. Perilymph
D. Endolymph
E. Serum

13. When a positive pressure wave causes the tympanic membrane to move medialward, the stapedius muscle is:

A. Unaffected
B. Stretched
C. Contracted
D. Severed
E. Dislocated

14. The middle ear is important to land-dwelling creatures because:

    A.  It keeps fluid levels correct.
    B.  It matches the impedance of air to inner ear fluid.
    C.  It increases the sound striking the tympanic membrane.
    D.  It analyzes sound reducing the demands on the brain.
    E.  It holds the tympanic membrane in place.

15. The mechanical characteristic in the inner ear that provides for great sensitivity of the auditory mechanism is:

    A.  The shearing motion of the organ of Corti.
    B.  The tension on the basilar membrane.
    C.  The springiness of the tectorial membrane.
    D.  The compressibility of the inner ear fluids.
    E.  The tension of the round window membrane.

16. Name the two major contributing features of sensitivity of the ear.

    A.  _middle ear transformer_
    B.  _shearing motion of the inner ear_

17. Name the three components in mechanical impedance and the frequency area (if any) in which each component has the greatest influence:

    A.  _resistance - not freq. dependant_
    B.  _mass       - high freq depend_
    C.  _compliance  - low freq_

18. List three major subdivisions of the ear in the (a) order of embryonic development; (b) in the order air-borne sound passes through the structures.

    (a) A. _inner_      (b) A. _outer_
        B. _middle_         B. _middle_
        C. _outer_          C. _ear_

19. Describe how the tympanic membrane is moved when the stapedius muscle is contracted.

20. Name the five major components in the vestibular sensory system:

    A.  _utricle_
    B.  _saccule_
    C.  _superior   SCC_
    D.  _posterior  SCC_
    E.  _horizontal SCC_

21. Circle the one structure in the following pairs that is the most medially situated:

   A. malleus – incus
   B. auricle – tympanic membrane
   C. tensor tympani muscle – stapedius muscle
   D. external auditory meatus – internal auditory meatus
   E. In the tympanic membrane:  radial fiber layer – mucus layer

22. Describe the interaction between oval window motion and round window motion.

# Chapter 6

# NEUROPHYSIOLOGY OF HEARING

*Robert Goldstein*

I. Behavioral Phenomena

   A. No model of the central auditory nervous system (CANS) can account unequivocally for all auditory phenomena.

      1. We hear with our brain – not our ear.

      2. CANS must preserve some of the information supplied by the peripheral hearing mechanism:

         a. threshold of auditory sensitivity;

         b. sounds heard when attention is diverted;

         c. frequency sensitivity;

         d. awareness of pitch changes.

      3. Threshold sensitivity varies with duration of signal (temporal integration); probably peripheral plus CANS action.

      4. Phenomenon of "backward masking" must involve CANS.

      5. Other auditory activities exist that cannot be explained on basis of the peripheral system alone – most involve CANS interactions.

      6. Auditory localization is usually attributed to CANS processing.

I. Overview of Central Auditory Function

   A. The CANS is so complex that only rudimentary descriptions of its function exist.

1. Most such basic descriptions focus on the <u>primary</u> <u>auditory</u> <u>projection</u> <u>system</u>.

2. Most models agree that the primary auditory projection system transmits and processes auditory signals.

3. Collateral connections exist to the <u>reticular</u> <u>formation</u> and <u>cerebellum</u> presumably initiating reflex responses to sound.

4. Above classic or traditional view of CANS raises two questions:

   a. how can the "slow" reticular formation alert the cortex to react appropriately to signals already received through the faster primary projection system?

   b. if the primary projection system is responsible for auditory sensation, why does not bilateral destruction of both temporal bones produce complete, irreversible deafness?

III. Personal CANS Model

A. The CNS consists of a series of integrating centers; developed phylogenetically.

   1. New pathways, which include the primary projection system, developed to provide rapid reciprocal communication between the integrating centers.

   2. All basic functions are carried out by the integrating centers at each level, but with increasing sophistication at succesively higher levels.

   3. Sensation, including hearing, is not a function of the newer, rapidly conducting systems but of less specific neural systems shared by all modalities.

   4. The core of each integrating center appears to be a neural network that receives and integrates messages delivered from all sensory modalities.

   5. As level ascends from spinal cord up, the central general computer network of the brain increases in size and complexity and in flexibility. Most of the cerebral cortex is part of the reticular system that constitutes the essence of the brain.

B. Control or regulation of lower brains would be impossible if the lower brain completes its action before the necessary message can reach the upper brains, be processed, and a controlling message sent to the lower brain.

1. Upper level control is only possible because fast pathways have evolved, connecting successive brains or integrating centers.

2. The faster myelinated pathways constitute only a small percentage of CNS neurons even though they make up much of the physical bulk of the brain.

3. The remaining neurons, generally appearing less organized, unmyelinated, and multisynaptic are known as reticular formation.

4. Despite its reticular nature, the central computer network is not haphazard in structural organization, but the very essence of the brain.

C. The above generalities apply to all sensory systems – and probably to motor systems as well.

IV. Neuroanatomy and Neurophysiology of the CANS

A. At each brain level a nucleus at which the auditory nerve or primary auditory projection system terminates and synapses.

1. A portion of each nucleus is simple, another portion seems to be more complex.

2. The nuclear way stations at higher brain levels each appear to have portions whose discrete cell arrangements and axonal inter-connections appear to be part of the rapid-transmission system.

3. Each nucleus also has immediate adjacent portions which appear to be local processors.

B. It is likely that the extralemniscal pathways represent older interconnections, while lemniscal pathways are phylogenetically newer pathways.

1. Connections between halves of the brain occur at all levels – the most prominent is the corpus

2. Not every portion of the CANS of each half of the brain connects with its homologue on the other side.

3. Cerebral dominance for any function is difficult to derive from this model.

C. The tonotopic arrangement of the primary projection system is an illustration of the preservation of original signal information as it is transmitted along the lemniscal system.

V.  Macroelectrophysiology

    A.  Difficult to generalize from single-neuron studies about actions of diffuse systems such as the reticular structures of the central, general processor.

        1.  Most audiology-related macroelectrophysiologic studies have been conducted with the "averaged electroencephalic response or AER".

        2.  Considerable confusion exists over the source and significance of AER peaks.

        3.  General description of the auditory AER as a series of 15 waves (Galambos, 1975) seems to have reached general acceptance but may not be valid.

        4.  The earliest activity (initial 10 msec) in response to abrupt-onset stimuli almost certainly reflects activity of the primary auditory projection system up through at least the inferior colliculus.

    B.  General conclusions can be offered about the AER:

        1.  Early brainstem components (2-8 msec) and middle components (8-80 msec) to brief, rapidly-repeated signals arise from the pathways of the auditory rapid-transmission system.

        2.  Late components (50-250 msec) arise from the dedicated processor(s) near Heschl's gyrus.

        3.  Still later activity, beyond 250 msec, arises from large portions of the cortical mantle.

        4.  In terms of function:

            a. early and middle components are related primarily to the physical parameters of stimulus;

            b. late components are also related more to stimulus parameters than to message content;

            c. still later activity appears to be influenced more by the conditions of stimulation, message significance, etc.

. The central auditory nervous system (CANS) does not include the:

A. Superior olivary complex.
B. Inferior colliculus.
C. Medial geniculate body.
D. Spiral ganglion.
E. Dorsal cochlear nucleus.

. The primary auditory projection system is characterized by its:

A. Thinly myelinated nerve fibers.
B. Intimate connections with the primary visual projection system.
C. Indistinct and diffusely organized interconnecting nuclei.
D. Intimate connections with the extrapyramidal system.
E. Heavily myelinated nerve fibers.

. Most models of CANS function traditionally stress the importance of the primary auditory projection system in:

A. Conscious sensing or awareness of auditory signals.
B. Primitive reflex functions.
C. Modulation of vestibular function.
D. Sophisticated speech-motor acts.
E. Suppressing sensation initiated in other modalities.

. The nature of the primary auditory projection system is incompatible with the:

A. Place theory of pitch perception.
B. Role of the reticular formation as an alerting system.
C. Left hemispheric dominance for speech.
D. Role of the superior olive in the acoustic reflex.
E. Volley theory of pitch perception.

. In Goldstein's model of the CANS, a principal purpose of the primary auditory projection system is to provide:

A. A pathway for messages generated within the reticular formation.
B. The substrate for conscious perception.
C. Rapid reciprocal communication between the various levels of the brain.
D. Regulation of responses during sleep.
E. A pathway for messages generated by the autonomic nervous system.

6. The central reticular core of the brain stem:

   A. Is characterized by total flexibility and plasticity in its operation.
   B. Is similar to the bulk of the cerebral cortex in its role.
   C. Differs greatly in its role from the H-segments seen in cross-sections of the spinal cord.
   D. Is similar to the lemniscal systems in all modalities in its major role.
   E. Is independent of descending influences from higher centers.

7. The central or reticular core of the brain appears to:

   A. Receive exactly the same neural signals that are transmitted along the lemniscal pathways.
   B. Process motor and sensory signals independently.
   C. Function without change despite sleep or other changes in a person's state.
   D. Process ascending and descending signals independently.
   E. Receive neural signals that are transformed in some way after being received from the lemniscal pathways.

8. Tuning curves for single neurons in the CANS:

   A. Become distinctly sharper at each successive ascending level of the CANS.
   B. Can be obtained only from the brain stem level portions of the CANS.
   C. Do not change significantly as a function of CANS level.
   D. Can be obtained only from the inferior colliculus or higher CANS levels.
   E. Broaden significantly at each successive ascending level of the CANS.

9. The initial waves (3-10 msec) of the averaged electroencephalic response (AER) to rapidly-repeated clicks probably arise from the:

   A. Brain stem portions of the primary auditory projection system.
   B. Post-auricular muscles.
   C. Brain stem reticular formation.
   D. Stapedius and tensor tympani muscles.
   E. Auditory association areas of the temporal lobe.

10. Auditory thresholds measured by audiometry in which the AER is the response index tells only about the integrity of:

    A. Peripheral auditory mechanism.
    B. Primary auditory projection system.
    C. Brain stem reticular formation.
    D. Left temporal lobe.
    E. Auditory association areas.

11. In general, the later a peak or component of the AER:

A. The lower its frequency spectrum.
B. The less likely it is to be affected by attention.
C. The less likely it is to be affected by drugs.
D. The less likely it is to be affected by sleep.
E. The smaller its amplitude.

12. Single neurons within the CANS:

A. All discharge in a uniform manner.
B. Only respond to stimulus onset.
C. Always respond to both stimulus onset and termination.
D. Only respond to stimulus termination.
E. Vary greatly in their discharge patterns.

13. Neurons in the primary auditory projection system:

A. Are affected only by ipsilateral visual signals.
B. Are affected only by perceived visual signals.
C. Cannot respond to slowly-repeated auditory signals.
D. Are unaffected by visual signals.
E. Are affected only by contralateral visual signals.

14. The descending pathways of the CANS:

A. Originate mainly from the cerebellum.
B. Are an integral part of the rapid transmission pathways.
C. Play a major role in temporal integration.
D. Affect sensitivity for high-frequency signals.
E. Are mandatory for localization.

15. For purposes of threshold audiometry, it is important that:

A. We know the anatomic source of all 15 waves of the AER.
B. The AER waveform bears a predictable relation to stimulus intensity.
C. The AER waveform not be distorted through filtering.
D. The AER be elicited only from awake patients.
E. We know the anatomic source of the first five waves of the AER.

# Chapter 7

# ACOUSTICS OF SPEECH

*June E. Shoup, Norman J. Lass,*
*and David P. Kuehn*

I.   Sound and Vibration (Definition)

    A.  <u>Sound</u> (Hoops) 1969, "a condition of disturbance of the particles of an elastic medium which is propagated in a wave outward in all directions from a vibrating body, and takes the form of displacement of the particles forward and backward from their positions of rest in the direction of the propagation of the wave".

    B.  Elements of Sound:

        1.  Energy source.

        2.  Vibrator.

        3.  Transmitting medium.

        4.  Receiving mechanism (in applying sound to human perception).

    C.  Vibrations:

        1.  All sound waves are created by vibration, a to-and-fro movement of a body about its rest position.

            a. periodic:  vibration repeats itself in a regular pattern, and in equal intervals;

            b. aperiodic:  vibration occurs in an irregular or erratic pattern that does not repeat itself regularly.

    D.  Components of Vibration:

        1.  Mass:  any form of matter capable of vibratory motion.

        2.  Elasticity:  tendency of a medium or object to return to its original condition after some change has been introduced.

3. Inertia: the property which causes a body in motion to remain in motion, and a body at rest to remain at rest.

4. Damping Factor: any force that interferes as a result of energy loss to the system.

E. Sound Waves in Air:

   1. Molecular:

      a. compression (condensation);

      b. rarefaction (expansion);

      c. propagation (movement).

   2. Motion:

      a. simple harmonic motion (sine wave).

F. Properties of Sound Waves:

   1. Displacement.

   2. Amplitude.

   3. Cycle.

      a. period.

   4. Phase.

   5. Frequency – cycles per second.

   6. Period – seconds per cycle.

   7. Velocity (speed).

      a. elasticity;

      b. density;

      c. temperature.

II. Complex Waves

A. Periodic – produced by complex periodic motion.

B. Aperiodic – produced by complex aperiodic waves.

C. Fourier analysis – mathematical analysis of complex waves into their sinusoidal components.

D. Spectrum – graphic representation of the frequencies and amplitudes of the components of a complex wave.

   1. Spectra for complex periodic waves:

      a. discrete spectrum – discrete frequency of each component and its amplitude.

   2. Spectra for complex aperiodic waves:

      a. displays the energy present in complex wave as in a continuous, varying line.

   3. The frequency of each component is a whole-number multiple of the frequency of the lowest component:

      a. fundamental – the lowest component of complex periodic wa

      b. fundamental frequency – the frequency of the lowest component;

      c. harmonics – all components above the fundamental frequenc which are exact multiples of the fundamental frequency.

   4. Sound spectrograph – an instrument that measures and displays the spectra of sound waves.

III. Resonance

   A. Vibrations.

      1. Free – vibrating body, initially set into vibration, is released from the original force which is set into vibration and no outside force continues to move it.

      2. Forced – vibrating body is continuously subjected to an outside force that causes it to vibrate with the frequency imposed upon it by the outside force.

      3. Maintained – outside force keeps a body vibrating without imposing a frequency of its own on the vibrating body.

      4. Resonance – when an object is being driven by an outside force at the same frequency as its own natural frequency the largest vibration occurs.

      5. Resonant frequency – the frequency at which the maximum resonance occurs.

B. Resonance Pertaining to Speech:

    1. Single Helmholtz Resonator:

        a. simple resonator:

            (1) single chamber closed at the glottal end, not open to the nasal cavity, open to the atmosphere through the interlabial channel;

            (2) acoustical properties depend on the volume of the chamber and the dimensions of the channel leading to the atmosphere but not on the exact shape of the chamber.

        b. double Helmholtz resonator:

            (1) the pharyngeal and oral cavities are represented by separate volumes connected to each other by a channel representing the constriction between the tongue and hard palate;

            (2) the oral cavity volume opens to atmosphere through the interlabial channel.

IV. Acoustic Transmission Line

    A. Vocal tract.

        1. A tube closed at one end (glottis) and open at the other end (lip orifice).

        2. Air enclosed will transmit sound waves.

        3. Sound source applied to the closed end sets up a compressional wave which propagates the whole length of the tube.

        4. Reaching open end, a wave of rarefaction is reflected back to the closed end.

        5. Waves are reflected back and forth, which establishes a pattern of standing waves.

    B. Vocal tract transfer function:

        1. The distribution of resonances along the frequency scale.

        2. Forming a ratio between the output signal and input signal for each frequency component.

        3. A given transfer function is completely specified by the center frequency and bandwidth of each resonant mode.

        4. Formant bandwidths are related to vocal tract.

5. Vocal tract transfer functions have many resonant modes, theoretically an infinite number.

6. The vocal tract transfer function may be stimulated electronically using a series of electronic filters (electrical transmission line).

7. Electrical analogue models of the vocal tract have been useful in synthetic speech generation and continue to be used in formulating more accurate models of the acoustic behavior of the vocal tract.

C. Sound Sources.

1. The laryngeal sound source is normally a periodic tone consisting of a fundamental frequency component and a series of higher harmonics.

2. The sound source produced within the vocal tract is an aperiodic noise of relatively long duration.

3. The sound source will be modified by the resonant characteristics of the vocal tract acting as an acoustic filter.

4. All speech sounds, including consonants as well as vowels, are characterized by concentrations of energy along the frequency scale.

D. Vowels.

1. Produced by periodic or quasiperiodic laryngeal sound source.

2. Resonated through the pharyngeal and oral cavities (voiced, oral vowels).

3. In the formation of larger units, such as a syllable, the vowel is the nucleus or central portion.

4. The acoustic identification or discrimination of vowel types is primarily by their first three formants.

5. The size of the vocal tract determines in large measure the range of formant frequencies for the various speech sound formations.

6. The smaller the vocal tract, the higher the formant frequencies.

7. Males have the lower formant frequency ranges, females have somewhat higher formant frequencies, and children have the highest formant frequencies.

8. Bandwidth increases as formant frequency progresses from first to second to third.

9. One of the most common modifications of vowel production is that of nasalization.

E. Nasal Coupling: Acoustic Effect.

1. The complete vocal tract transfer function depends on the resonance properties of the pharyngeal-oral cavity, the nasal cavity, and the interaction between the two cavity systems.

2. (Fant, 1960) If the right and left nasal channels on each side of the nasal septum are perfectly symmetrical, they function acoustically as a single cavity system.

3. Each nasal pathway will contribute its own resonant frequencies.

4. The resonant characteristics of the nasal cavity may also depend on the shunting effect of the maxillary and frontal sinuses which communicate with the nasal cavity and function as additional resonant cavities (Lindquist-Gauffin and Sundberg, 1976).

5. Curtis (1968) pointed out that interaction between the pharyngeal-oral cavity and the nasal cavity is complexly related to the extent of acoustic coupling between them.

6. The distribution of acoustic energy between the nasal cavity and the pharyngeal-oral cavity depend not only on the size of the velopharyngeal opening but also the configuration of the pharyngeal-oral cavity.

7. The addition of a sidebranch resonator such as the nasal cavity will introduce antiresonances in the transfer function of the complete resonator system.

F. Nasal Consonants.

1. The pharynx and coupled nasal cavity represent the primary acoustic resonator for nasal consonants.

2. The oral cavity is the occluded side branch.

3. The nasal consonants are characterized by fairly constant formant frequencies.

4.   The nasal consonants are differentiated according to
     place of articulation by various cues, including vowel
     transitions, second formant frequencies, and the
     frequency positions of the nasal antiresonances.

5.   The longer the side branch, the lower the antiresonant
     frequency; for example:

     a. /m/ approximately 1000 Hz;

     b. /n/ approximately 3500 Hz;

     c. /j/ higher than 5000 Hz.

6.   Discrimination of the nasals is based on varying second
     formant frequencies (Hecker, 1962), with /m/ identified
     when this formant is 1300 Hz, /n/ at 1800 Hz, and /j/
     at 2000 Hz.

7.   Nakatu (1959) found the best judgments of synthesized
     nasals to be with second formants of 1100 Hz for /m/,
     1700 Hz for /n/, and 2300 Hz for /j/.

8.   (Liberman et al., 1954) identified through synthesis
     experiments the vowel transitions as one of the most
     important cues for the discrimination of place of
     articulation of the nasal consonants.

9.   Fujimura (1962) investigated the nasals and reported three
     properties that they had in common:

     a. a low first formant around 300 Hz;

     b. high damping of the formants;

     c. high density of the formants in the frequency domain.

G.   Stop Consonants.

1.   Identified not only by the formant transitions to and from
     adjacent vowels but also by the first of the stop releases
     and by the voice onset time.

2.   The class of consonants includes plosives, implosives,
     clicks, and ejectives, differs from all other consonants
     in their blocking (or stopping) of the air flow, so that
     a burst is possible upon the release of the articulatory
     closure which forms the stop.

3.   Vowels and consonants other than stops are referred to
     as continuants.

4. The acoustic pattern for a stop consonant changes during its production.

5. Voiceless stops /p/, /t/, /h/, no sound produced, no acoustic speech wave present, only silence.

6. Following either the voiceless or the voiced closure, all stop consonants may have an acoustic impulse (burst) at the moment of release of the closure.

7. Halle et al. (1957) early study on the acoustic properties of English plosives.

8. Correlation exists between place of articulation of the stop consonants and second formant transitions of the associated vowels.

9. Blumstein and Stevens (1980) have shown that correct identifications can be made for stop place of articulations from the 10 to 20 ms of speech immediately following the onset of the syllable.

H. Fricatives and Sibilants.

1. Voiced fricatives and sibilants have two simultaneous sound sources:

   a. vibration of the vocal folds for the voicing;

   b. noise produced at the place of articulation.

2. The quasi-random speech waves associated with all fricatives and sibilants are easily identified as distinct from quasi-periodic waves.

3. Acoustic features associated with each of these sounds are resonances, antiresonances, and a broad-band continuous spectrum.

4. Tarnoczy (1954) – summary of literature on the analyses of fricatives and sibilants to determine acoustic properties.

5. Hughes and Halle (1956) developed objective identification criteria by measuring the density spectra of gated segments of fricatives and sibilants.

6. Stevens (1960) – provided a comprehensive study of fricatives and sibilants.

I. Sonorants.

1. Sounds produced with an airflow neither as laminar as that for vowels nor as turbulent as that of fricatives.

2. The speech wave is usually quasi-periodic, occasionally may be quasi-random from the functional property associated with certain sonorant productions.

3. English sounds included in the sonorant groups are semi-vowels such as /w/, /j/, laterals such as /l/, and retroflexed consonants such as /r/.

4. Lehiste (1964) published one of the most thorough studies on the acoustic properties of English sonorants.

5. Lisker (1957b) studied the perception of sonorants in intervocalic position.

6. O'Connor et al. (1957) studied them in the initial position.

## REVIEW QUESTIONS

1. The three elements necessary for sound to be created are:

   A. _a source of energy_

   B. _a vibrator_

   C. _a transmitting medium_

2. All sounds are created by _vibrator_, a to-and-fro movement of a body about its rest position; this motion may be _periodic_ or _aperiodic_.

3. A _MASS_ is any form of matter capable of vibration; _ELASTICITY_ is the tendency of a medium or object to resume its original condition after a change has been introduced; _INERTIA_ is the property of a body in motion to remain in motion and a body at rest to remain at rest. The _damping factor_ is a force that interferes with vibration as a result of energy loss to the system.

74

4. When molecules are nearer each other during the propagation of a wave, a state of _Compression_ exists; when molecules are forced farther apart from each other, a state of _Expansion_.

5. Match the following:

_4_ A. propagation            1. speed
_3_ B. sine wave             2. maximum displacement
_2_ C. amplitude            3. pressure curve
_7_ D. phase               4. movement
_5_ E. wavelength          5. distance between adjacent waves
_6_ F. frequency           6. cycles per second
_1_ G. velocity             7. portion of a cycle

6. The velocity of a sound wave is related to:

A. _Elasticity_

B. _Density_

C. _Temperature_

7. The mathematical analysis of a complex wave into its sinusoidal components is called _Fourier_ _analysis_.

8. Label the common properties of sound waves:

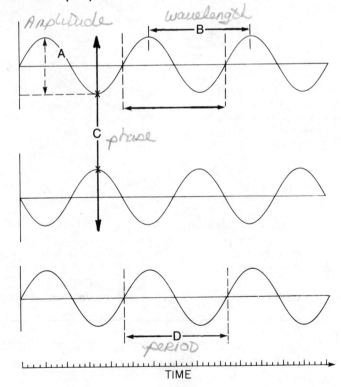

Amplitude     wavelength

A

B

C phase

D
period

TIME

9.  Vibrations can be divided into three categories:

    A.  _Free_

    B.  _Forced_

    C.  _Maintained_

10. In a forced vibration, when an object is being driven by an outside
    force at the same frequency as its own natural frequency, the
    largest vibration occurs, and this response is called _Resonance_

11. When waves continue to be reflected back and forth, so that the
    distribution of minimal and maximal vibrations are exactly the same,
    we have a pattern known as _STANDING_ _waves_ .

12. In reference to vocal tract acoustics, the resonance frequencies are
    called _formants_ ; the lowest is symbolized as $F_0$ ,
    the next highest is symbolized as $F_1$ , and so on.

13. Identify the appropriate average fundamental frequencies for
    English vowels spoken by men, women and children.

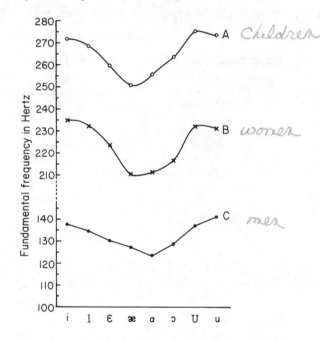

14. The voiced-fricatives and sibilants have two simultaneous sound source
    _vibration of the v.f. for voicing_ a
    _noise produced at place of artic_ .

15. The velocity of sound through air is _1129_ feet per second at room
    temperature.

    _344 m/s_

# Chapter 8

# AERODYNAMICS OF SPEECH

*Donald W. Warren*

I. Introduction

    A. The generation of speech requires precise control of airflow along the respiratory tract.

        1. System is very complex because the specialized aerodynamics of speech is superimposed on the respiratory system.

II. Mechanics of Airflow

    A. Air flows from one region to another because of a difference in air pressure between the two areas.

    B. Airflow is not always smooth because of the branching, irregular shape of the respiratory tract.

    C. Eddying and turbulence occurs at bifurcations, rough surfaces and constricted areas.

III. The Respiratory System for Breathing: The Generation of Pressures

    A. Breathing results from contraction of the respiratory muscles which produce volume changes in the chest cavity.

        1. Whenever chest cavity enlarges, the lungs also enlarge.

        2. At the end of expiration, pressure within the lungs (<u>pulmonary pressure</u>) is atmospheric, and there is no airflow - resting level.

        3. When diaphragm contracts, its dome moves downward, thus enlarging the thoracic cavity.

        4. This enlarges the volume of air within the lungs, pressure falls below atmospheric, and air is drawn into the expanding lungs.

5. Inspiration is an active process; normal expiration is primarily a passive event.

IV. The Work of Breathing

A. The elastic behavior of the respiratory system is usually described in terms of its pressure–volume relationship.

1. The pressure obtained at any lung volume is the result of the elastic forces of the lung and chest wall.

2. Most of the work involved in filling the lung is used to overcome elastic recoil – the energy required is stored during inspiration and utilized during expiration.

3. Compliance of the respiratory system is an important factor in determining the amount of energy required to move air in and out of the lungs.

4. The magnitude of airway resistance is another factor determining the degree of work required for breathing.

5. A third factor related to degree of work in breathing is a special surface film that lines the alveoli of the lungs.

V. Maintenance of Airway Pressure for Speech

A. An almost constant pressure head must be maintained to power the speech mechanism.

1. Since speech occurs during the expiratory phase of breathing, normal expiratory pressure must be modified to some extent.

2. Inspiration and expiratory muscle activity is required to maintain subglottal pressure.

3. The sudden changes in respiratory load that occur when the upper airway closes or opens must be compensated for almost instantaneously if pressure is to be maintained at a near-constant level.

4. Undoubtedly a complicated feedback system regulating pressure and airflow must be involved, probably including higher centers of the brain as well as the medulla.

5. Some system for simultaneous pre-programming of the respiratory system and the articulators is also a possibility.

VI. Lower Airway Dynamics

A. Airflow in the lower airway is influenced by the shape of the alveolar sacs, the bronchi, and the trachea.

   1. The flow of air is also modulated by the glottis and the supraglottal constrictors (i.e., tongue, palate, nose, lips and teeth).

   2. The increase in subglottic pressure that occurs with increased loudness or stress is due to changes in the activity of the respiratory muscles.

      a. larger lung volumes of air are used when loudness is increased;

      b. similarly, respiratory effort is less when the utterance is softer than normal.

B. Laryngeal Activity:

   1. Glottis is the first major constrictor involved in the process of forming speech.

   2. The aerodynamic forces which are exerted on the vocal folds include:

      a. subglottal air pressure;

      b. the Bernoulli force produced by negative pressure created transglottally by high velocity airflow;

      c. supraglottal pressure produced by articulatory constrictions in the upper airway.

   3. The rapid closing and opening of the glottis molds airflow into a modulated stream which provides the basic source of speech.

   4. The vocal folds modify pressure and airflow during speech. The size of the glottal constriction affects the transglottal pressure loss but supraglottal constrictions also play an important role.

   5. To achieve voiced stop consonants, a difference in pressure between the subglottal and supraglottal cavities must occur.

   6. Glottal resistance: the ratio of transglottal pressure to airflow through the glottis.

      a. glottal resistance is lower for voiced fricatives than for vowels, which indicates that the vocal folds do not adduct as much for fricatives as they do for vowels.

7. <u>Whisper</u> – glottal opening is narrow and respiratory effort is considerably increased, noted by increased airflow rates.

   a. increased time and effort are necessary to generate airflow turbulence and produce the sounds of whispered speech.

VII. Upper Airway Dynamics

A. Structures of the upper airway also modulate the air stream into precise patterns.

   1. Air flows more readily through an open oral cavity than it does through the nasal cavity because resistance is approximately half.

   2. Lip, tongue and soft palate movement can modify resistance to airflow and shunt airflow through the nose as in nasal sounds.

B. Aerodynamic patterns vary for each of the speech sounds:

   1. Voiceless plosives.

   2. Voiced plosives.

   3. Voiceless fricatives.

   4. Voiced fricatives.

   5. Vowels.

C. During production of non-nasal sounds, the soft palate and pharyngeal walls form a valve that prevents airflow from entering the nasal cavity.

   1. Nasal resonance is modified if the palatal orifice is not open enough for nasal sounds. Denasal quality results when the opening is small or the nasal airway is blocked.

VIII. Instrumentation for Aerodynamic Studies

A. <u>Spirometer</u> – instrument used to measure pulmonary function; records volume of air flowing in and out of the lungs.

B. <u>Manometer</u> – instrument to measure intraoral pressures during breathing and maximum expiratory efforts.

C. Aerodynamic Devices - flowmeters and pressure transducers.

D. Air Pressure Devices - strain gauge transducers are the most commonly used devices for measuring pressure.

E. Airflow Devices - most accepted instrument for measuring the volume rate of airflow is the heated pneumotachograph, which consists of a flowmeter and a differential pressure transducer.

F. Aerodynamic techniques are used to obtain important information about normal and abnormal speech production - which may involve the application of hydraulic principles and equations.

## REVIEW QUESTIONS

1. The generation of speech requires precise control of airflow along the respiratory tract. This system is complex for at least 3 reasons:

   A. _____

   B. _____

   C. _____

2. What is the first major constrictor involved in the process of forming speech?

   A. Teeth
   B. Oropharynx
   C. Nasopharynx
   D. Glottis
   E. Trachea

3. Air flows from one region to another because of _pressure_ _differences between the two areas_.

4. What 3 factors determine the degree of work required for breathing?

A. _energy required to overcome elastic recoil_
B. _magnitude of airway resistance_
C. _surface tension of the alveoli_

5. During normal conversation the breathing cycle is modified by increasing the depth of inspiration and prolonged expiration.

A. In normal conversation, approximately _25_% of lung capacity is used and _1.2_ to _1.5_ liters of air are involved;

B. During quiet breathing, only _10_% to _15_% of total lung capacity is used and approximately _0.5_ liter of air is moved.

6. When loudness of speech is increased, larger lung volumes are used, perhaps as great as _4_ to _5_ liters.

7. Glottis resistance is:

A. Higher for voiced fricatives than for vowels.
B. Lower for voiced fricatives than for vowels.
C. The same for voiced fricatives and vowels.

8. Respiratory effort is considerably (increased or decreased) during a whisper.

9. Denasal speech results when the _velopharyngeal_ orifice does not open sufficiently and in advance of the _nasal_ _CONSONANT_ sound. This causes diminished _NASAL_ _EMISSION_ of air and the preceding vowel is not nasalized.

10. Match the following instruments and their uses:

_3_ A. Spirometer
_1_ B. Strain gauge transducer
_2_ C. Oral manometer
_4_ D. Pneumotachograph

1. Most common device for measuring pressure
2. measures intraoral pressures
3. used to measure pulmonary function
4. measures the volume rate of airflow

# Chapter 9

# SPEECH PRODUCTION

*John W. Folkins and David P. Kuehn*

I. Methods of Analyzing Speech Production

    A. <u>Aerodynamics</u> – measurement of air pressures and flows at various points along the airway.

    B. <u>Electromyography</u> (EMG) – measurement of small voltages produced by contracting muscle fibers.

        1. EMG cannot be used as an indirect measure of speech articulator movement or muscle force.

    C. <u>Cinematography</u> and <u>Cineradiography</u> – high speed motion picture techniques which involve time-consuming frame-by-frame analysis.

        1. X-ray motion pictures permit study of movements of speech structures normally hidden from view.

    D. <u>Strain Gauge Systems</u> – variable resistor banded to a thin lever; relatively inexpensive, noninvasive and provides an electrical analog of movement; used primarily to measure lip and jaw movements.

    E. <u>Electromagnetic Techniques</u> – involves attachment of small electromagnets to articulatory structures.

    F. <u>Photoelectric Techniques</u> and <u>Fiberoptics</u> – uses variable light transmission to provide an analog of structural movements.

        1. Fiberoptics (bundles of flexible glass fibers) have been used to record movements of velopharyngeal and laryngeal structures.

    G. <u>Ultrasound</u> – uses ultra-high frequency sound produced by a transmitter placed against the skin.

H. Palatography – technique involves measuring points of tongue contact on an artificial palate.

I. No one method of analyzing speech production is best for all purposes.

II. Respiration

   A. The respiratory system builds up air pressures, produces airflow and helps to move structures for sources of speech sounds.

      1. If subglottal air pressure is negative and the larynx is open, air will be drawn into the lungs.

      2. If subglottal air pressure is positive and the larynx is open, air will flow out of the lungs.

   B. Relaxation Pressure – relation between subglottal air pressure and lung volume level produced by recoil.

   C. Electromyography through the Range of Lung Volume Levels.

      1. Ladefoged's work in the 1960's indicated that inspiratory and expiratory muscles each abruptly stopped when the other group was activated.

      2. More recent research suggests that the expiratory muscles do not appear to be turned off when the inspiratory muscles are turned on and vice versa.

   D. Loudness:

      1. Variations in loudness of phonation are related directly to changes in subglottal air pressure.

   E. Body Orientation:

      1. Relaxation pressure of the respiratory system is influenced markedly by the orientation of the body due to forces of gravity.

      2. For phonation sustained throughout vital lung capacity, it is necessary to modify active muscular forces to maintain similar subglottal pressure when body orientation is changed.

   F. During connected speech the change in relaxation pressure is not necessarily accompanied by change in active muscular force.

      1. Desired subglottal pressures are produced at any body orientation by adjusting lung volume levels.

2. Breath group refers to those syllables that occur on the same expiratory movement.

3. In general, speakers control lung volume with both the rib cage and diaphragm-abdominal components.

G. The Search for the Chest Pulse:

1. Stetson and Hudgins (1930) thought that separate, active adjustments of the respiratory system were produced on a syllable-by-syllable basis.

2. During connected speech, phonation is continually started and stopped and therefore the rate of air flow through the glottis is quite irregular.

III. Phonation

A. Vibratory Mechanics:

1. Most widely accepted viewpoint is the aerodynamic-myoelastic theory of sound production.

2. Holds that the generation and control of sound at the larynx involves interaction between aerodynamic forces from respiratory energy and mechanical forces exerted by the larynx.

B. Qualitative Description:

1. Bernoulli effect: low pressure suction between the vocal folds due to relatively high velocity of air particles forced through the glottis.

2. Vocal fold configurations and vibratory patterns differ substantially as a function of pitch, loudness and other factors.

a. as loudness increases, the folds become more tightly adducted;

b. as pitch is increased, the folds elongate and vibrate more rigidly;

c. at very high pitches, vibration appears limited to the anterior and medial aspects of the vocal folds.

C. Models of Vocal Fold Vibration:

1. Hirano (1974, 1977) proposed a three-layer model for vocal fold vibration:

   a. the cover layer;

   b. the transition layer;

   c. the body layer.

2. Flanagan and Landgraf (1968) modeled the vocal folds as a one-mass system possessing a single horizontal degree of freedom.

3. Ishizaka and Matsudaira (1972) proposed a two-mass model of the vocal folds in which the interactions between masses help explain vocal fold vibration.

4. Titze (1973, 1974) formulated a 16-mass, 32 degrees-of-freedom model that incorporates two rows of eight segments each.

D. Pitch:

   1. Pitch Registers - three commonly recognized:

      a. head register - falsetto;

      b. model or chest register - used for normal speech;

      c. vocal fry or pulse register - lowest pitch range.

   2. Vocal pitch is related to the frequency of vocal fold vibration.

   3. Most important factors which influence the frequency of vibration are:

      a. effective vibrating mass;

      b. tension of the vibrating mass;

      c. subglottal pressure.

   4. Vocal folds are lengthened with an increase in pitch up to the falsetto register.

   5. Primary mechanism for increasing pitch is to elongate the folds by contracting the cricothyroid muscle.

   6. Pitch is also increased by contraction of the vocalis muscle as well as the lateral and posterior cricoarytenoid muscles.

7. Loudness change is primarily controlled by respiratory factors.

8. It is not known for sure whether the mechanisms responsible for changes in pitch and loudness are identical for sustained vs. connected speech utterances.

9. Rapid laryngeal adjustments are made for distinctions between voiced and voiceless speech sounds – glottal opening is larger for whispered voiceless consonants.

10. Exact position of the arytenoids (and thus the approximation of the vocal folds in the midline) depends on the speech context.

11. In laryngeal muscle activity for connected speech, the relative contribution of each muscle is dependent upon a number of interacting factors including:

   a. phonetic;

   b. prosodic demands.

IV. Supraglottal Articulation

A. Numerous instances in which little correspondence has been observed between phonetic units and supraglottal movements.

B. The lips are involved in:

   1. Bilabial closure.

   2. Labiodental articulation.

   3. Lip rounding.

   4. Lip movements in relation to phonetics:

      a. upper and lower lips make a consistent contact associated with p, b and m;

      b. labial opening for open vowels is relatively consistent;

      c. lower lip–upper incisor contact is achieved consistently in association with f and v;

      d. relatively slow protrusion gestures often occur for rounded vowels.

5. For most speech tasks, the upper and lower lips are in synchrony.

    a. lower lip is involved in labiodental fricatives whereas upper lip is not;

    b. lower lip movement influenced by jaw movement much more than the upper lip is.

6. A great deal is still unknown about how the forces from different muscles interact to produce labial movements.

C. Range of jaw movements in speech is much less than the total range (envelope) or as used in mastication.

1. Jaw never reaches a completely closed position during speech.

2. Closest speaking space - distance between completely closed jaw position and the most superior jaw elevation during speech.

3. Slight posterior component to jaw movement occurs as jaw is lowered during speech.

4. Jaw is not a primary articulator because there are no speech sounds for which the jaw directly forms part of the closest point of oral constriction.

5. Jaw influences mechanical properties of the labial tissues and muscles.

6. Tongue is also dependent upon jaw position.

7. Not only are other articulators dependent on the jaw but, conversely, jaw movements are dependent on the actions of other articulators.

8. Jaw reaches its most open positions for vowels; degree of jaw opening fits the traditional vowel classification of high, mid, and low.

9. Antagonistic jaw muscles seldom contract simultaneously to a significant extent during speech.

10. Relatively large variations in jaw-muscle EMG activity have been observed within the same experimental session for repeated tokens of the same speech sample.

D. The Tongue:

1. The tongue is the most important supraglottal articulator.

2. Difficult to investigate because its position may vary radically depending on numerous complex, interacting factors.

    a. vowels are traditionally classified by a quadrilateral spacial arrangement of tongue placements;

    b. however, an orderly arrangement of tongue placement is not always observed;

    c. lingual position for a particular vowel depends on adjacent phonemes, the degree of stress and the speaking rate;

    d. location of lingually produced vocal tract constriction for consonants may vary for different speakers;

    e. tongue shapes for English are fairly consistent regardless of the vowel produced;

    f. future studies of the tongue should consider its three-dimensional structure rather than a simple two-dimension configuration as seen in lateral view x-ray studies;

    g. tongue movements during speech are generally studied with high-speech x-ray motion pictures;

        (1) velocity of lingual movement is related to the distance traveled.

E. The Velopharynx

1. Functions as a valve to direct sound energy through the nasal cavities when open and through the oral cavity when closed.

2. If the valving action is not achieved or is inappropriately timed, the result is impaired speech output (i.e., deaf-speech, cleft-palate speech, etc.).

3. Velopharyngeal closure is achieved by elevating and retracting the velum and simultaneously constricting the surrounding nasopharyngeal walls.

4. Velar position varies systematically with the phonetic category of the speech sound produced.

    a. major effect is nasal versus non-nasal.

5. An adequate model of velar timing is not yet available, but must include maturation, language specificity, anatomic variation, etc.

6. Posterior pharyngeal wall movement is often small during speech production.

7. Levator veli palatini – the most important muscle in moving the velum.

   a. other muscles perhaps involved include:

      (1) superior pharyngeal constrictor;

      (2) palatopharyngeus;

      (3) palatoglossus.

## REVIEW QUESTIONS

1. Which of the following techniques used in speech research does not measure articulatory movement?

   A. Electromyography
   B. Cineradiography
   C. Strain-gauge systems
   D. Photoelectric systems
   E. Ultrasound systems

2. An advantage of cineradiographic techniques over strain-gauge transduction systems is in the:

   A. Ease of data reduction.
   B. Lower radiation dosage.
   C. Applicability to the tongue.
   D. Cost of the equipment.
   E. Applicability to different languages.

3.  At which of the following lung volume levels can the largest
    positive subglottal air pressure be produced?

    A.  90% of vital capacity.
    B.  70% of vital capacity.
    C.  36% of vital capacity.
    D.  20% of vital capacity.
    E.  0% of vital capacity.

4.  During a sustained phonation:

    A.  The rib cage will produce expiratory activity only at high
        lung volume levels.
    B.  The diaphragm will produce inspiratory activity only at high
        lung volume levels.
    C.  The rib cage will switch from expiratory activity to
        inspiratory activity when the lung volume level passes through
        the resting level.
    D.  The rib cage will be active only at times when the diaphragm
        is also active.
    E.  The abdominal system will produce expiratory activity even
        when the rib cage is producing expiratory activity.

5.  During connected speech the length of a breath group will depend
    most on the:

    A.  Placement of sentence and phrase boundaries.
    B.  Limitations from the speaker's vital capacity.
    C.  Body orientation relative to gravity.
    D.  Location of the chest pulses.
    E.  Loudness used.

6.  Ishizaka and Matsudaira's two-mass model of the vocal folds:

    A.  Emphasizes that the left and right vocal folds can be
        controlled separately.
    B.  Characterizes the vocal folds as noncompressional tissue
        that is deformed rather than compressed during phonation.
    C.  Attempts to explain how the volume-velocity waveform of
        the laryngeal sound source is related to the glottal area
        function.
    D.  Hypothesizes an aerodynamic coupling between the upper and
        lower portions of the vocal folds.
    E.  Attempts to relate vocal fold mass to vocal registers.

7.  Hixon, Klatt and Mead (1971) found that a 1 cm $H_2O$ increase in subglottal air pressure would have which of the following effects on fundamental frequency?

    A.  20 to 40 Hz increase.
    B.  2 to 4 Hz increase.
    C.  No change.
    D.  2 to 4 Hz decrease.
    E.  20 to 40 Hz decrease.

8.  Increasing activity in the lateral cricoarytenoid muscles during phonation might be expected to:

    A.  Increase subglottal air pressure.
    B.  Increase air flow through the glottis.
    C.  Decrease pitch.
    D.  Decrease loudness.
    E.  Increase laryngeal height.

9.  Which of the following statements about the upper and lower lips is true?

    A.  The upper and lower lips always move at the same time and to a similar extent because movement of both is produced by activity in the orbicularis oris muscle.
    B.  The upper and lower lips tend to move at the same speed during speech.
    C.  The upper lip does not move for production of bilabial closing gestures when immediately preceded or followed by a lip-rounded vowel.
    D.  Bilabial closure for [f] and [v] requires movement by both the upper and lower lips.
    E.  When more movement occurs in one lip for a given opening or closing gesture there is often less movement in the other lip.

10. A major problem with EMG studies in the lip muscles is that:

    A.  It cannot be verified that the activity recorded is from fibers in the intended muscle.
    B.  Lower lip movement is produced by movement of the jaw as well as contraction of the labial muscles.
    C.  EMG activity recorded from the labial muscles is often unreliable.
    D.  Hooked-wire electrodes will not stay in place in the labial muscles.
    E.  Fascial sheaths around the labial muscles cannot be penetrated easily by typical needles used for hooked-wire electrode placements.

11. Ammerman et al. (1970) observed that the magnitude of jaw movements was _____ for sustained vowels than for vowels in connected speech.

A. Always larger.
B. Usually larger.
C. Usually the same.
D. Usually smaller.
E. Always smaller.

12. Which of the following will change most systematically with the vowels of English?

A. The position of the highest point on the tongue.
B. The amount of tongue advancement or retraction.
C. The tongue height combined with tongue advancement.
D. The position and extent of the maximal vocal tract constriction.
E. The shape of the tongue (with the variation due to jaw position removed).

13. The peak velocity of lingual movements during speech is:

A. Directly related to the extent of the movement.
B. Increased when the duration of the movement decreases.
C. Decreased when the duration of the movement decreases.
D. Generally constant even when large undershoot is present.
E. Generally lower than the peak velocity of velar movements during speech.

14. Which of the following statements about velar movement in normal subjects is accurate:

A. A tight velopharyngeal closure will always occur during sustained vowels.
B. The frequency of velopharyngeal patency is greater during low vowels than high vowels.
C. An adjacent nasal consonant will not influence the velar height reached during most vowels.
D. The extreme position reached by the velum during nasal consonants is the same as the resting position of the velum.
E. The extreme position reached by the velum during a nasal consonant will be the same regardless of the vowel context.

15. Which of the following statements reflects the findings from electromyographic studies of the superior pharyngeal constrictor in normal speech production?

A. The superior constrictor and tensor veli palatini are usually active at the same time.
B. The superior constrictor is not active during speech.
C. The superior constrictor is not active at the same time as the palatoglossus.

D. The superior constrictor is not active at the same time as the palatopharyngeus.

E. The studies reporting EMG data from the superior constrictor have produced generally conflicting results.

# Chapter 10

# SPEECH PERCEPTION: AN OVERVIEW OF CURRENT ISSUES

*Patricia K. Kuhl*

I.  Models of the Speech Perception Process

    A.  General Considerations.

        1.  A model or theory aids science in at least 3 ways:

            a. summarizes available data in an economical and coherent framework;

            b. makes predictive statements about outcomes of specific experimental manipulations;

            c. allows establishment of questions and their relevant values.

    B.  Levels of Processing.

        1.  Speech perception greatly influenced by information-processing models which involve hierarchically organized stages of information transformation and storage.

        2.  Level implies successively more abstract forms of representation.

        3.  Decisions at higher "levels" strongly influence processing at lower "levels".

        4.  Levels of processing commonly posited include:

            a. auditory;

            b. phonetic;

            c. phonological;

            d. lexical, syntactic and semantic

C.  An <u>Active</u> Process.

1.  A process in which the listener attempts to recover a string of discrete phonetic units from a continuously varying acoustic waveform

   a. analyzes incoming waveform seeking acoustic cues related to phonetic features;

   b. takes phonetic matrix to generate a hypothesis concerning the exact message form;

   c. checks hypothesis against a stored representation of the incoming waveform;

   d. known as <u>analysis-by-synthesis</u> models.

2.  The model may employ a strategy of "bottom-up" or "top-down".

D.  The Problem of Invariance.

1.  Phonetic units are not defined by invariant acoustic characteristics:

   a. some acoustic event is perceived as a different phonetic unit in different contexts, etc.

2.  The <u>Motor Theory of Speech Perception</u> is that a listener's taut "knowledge" between particular articulatory maneuvers and their acoustic results somehow permits the listener to recover the phonetic unit uttered by the talker.

3.  Speech perception theorists literally dichotomized "auditory" and "phonetic" level(s) of analysis.

   a. auditory processes were conceived to be those of frequency-over-time transformation of the signal – creating a "neural spectrogram";

   b. phonetic processes somehow converted widely diverse acoustic patterns into invariant percepts.

4.  Recent research shows that the classic behaviors thought to dichotomize auditory and phonetic processing no longer do so.

II. Status Report on Contemporary Issues

    A. Categorization of Speech Sounds.

        1. Current emphasis on the perception of <u>boundaries</u> between categories.

        2. Also on the definition of acoustic cues that underlie the perception of similarities (constancy) for any group of exemplars belonging to the same phonetic category.

    B. Auditory Correlates of Acoustic Cues for Phonetic Categories.

        1. Vowel stimuli vowel:

            a. <u>psychophysical</u> <u>approaches</u> for vowel stimuli;

            b. <u>cochlear</u> <u>model</u> <u>approaches</u> utilizing computer-simulated bank of filters;

            c. <u>neurophysiological</u> approaches may include examination <u>of responses from</u> auditory nerve fibers.

        2. Consonant Stimuli:

            a. template matching approaches;

            b. cochlear modeling approaches.

        3. Summary:

            a. previous attempts to look for invariant cues were largely visual displays of speech - such as the sound spectrograph;

            b. advent of cochlear models and neurophysiologic approaches adds important dimension;

            c. recent use of <u>animal</u> <u>models</u> for the study of speech-sound processing.

    C. Categorical Perception.

        1. Occurs when a listener's ability to discriminate two stimuli is predicted by his ability to label them differently.

2. Two tasks must be demonstrated:

   a. subject <u>labels</u> each of the stimuli from an acoustic continuum;

   b. subject attempts to <u>discriminate</u> <u>pairs</u> of stimuli taken from the continuum.

3. Dramatic change in the approach to categorical perceptions has been noted during past five years:

   a. perception of certain <u>non-speech</u> continua produced results that are categorical in nature;

   b. realization of the influence of the psychophysical procedure in producing <u>categorical-like</u> results;

   c. animals demonstrated similar perceptual tendencies when listening to speech sounds.

4. Nonspeech Examples of Categorical Perception:

   a. four clear cases of categorical perception of nonspeech stimuli are available – three auditory and one visual;

   b. criteria for categorical perception:

      (1) the stimuli from each of the continua were perceived as falling into two discrete categories;

      (2) discrimination was significantly better for two stimuli given the same label than for any two stimuli given different labels.

5. Categorical Perception for Speech Depends upon Psychophysical Technique:

   a. two factors frequently mentioned by speech researchers as responsible for the differences produced by psychophysical procedure:

      (1) stimulus uncertainty – refers to the size of the catalogue of alternatives available on each trial;

      (2) memory factors – a longer steady-state vowel is more accessible in auditory memory than a shorter steady-state signal.

6. Animal Data:

   a. recent data suggest that nonhuman listeners also demonstrate the tendency to perceive speech sounds <u>categorically</u>;

b. in chinchillas, discrimination functions agree perfectly with the identification functions in the sense that the peak in performance occurs at the phoneme boundary, while the poorest performance occurs for within-category pairs.

7. Summary:

a. human listeners are capable of discriminating within-category stimuli under certain testing formats;

b. categorical perception exists only under certain testing conditions, while in others the labeling data do not predict the absolute level of discrimination performance;

c. non-speech continua can be perceived categorically;

d. at least some speech-sound continua are perceived categorically by animal listeners.

D. An Alternate Approach: Sensitivity Maxima.

1. Sensitivity maxima - the locations on a continuum where discrimination performance is best.

2. Phonetic boundary effect - places more emphasis on the location of the peak in the discrimination function and less on the absolute level of discrimination performance throughout the function.

3. The degree to which categorical perception results will be obtained directly depends upon the relationship between the step size chosen for discrimination testing and the just-noticeable difference (JND) for the stimuli along the continuum.

4. The alternate approach is to examine the absolute sensitivity at different places along the continuum, defining at each place a difference limen or just-noticeable difference or threshold for the acoustic variable.

E. The Perception of Voicing.

1. A number of reasons exist why researchers have so thoroughly studied the perception of voicing in stop consonants:

a. the voicing distinction is phonemic in most languages of the world;

b. the acoustic cues underlying the voicing distinction in English are varied - includes voice-onset time (VOT), temporal separation between the plosive burst and the onset of voicing, and the presence of low-frequency energy at voicing onset.

2. Perception of voicing is interesting because we have numerous data:

   a. acoustic correlates of the distinction in naturally produced utterances;

   b. on the perceptual relevance of these acoustic cues in isolation and in combination with other cues.

3. Discrimination of stimuli varying in VOT or in tone-onset-time produces non-monotonic functions.

4. Discrimination of unfilled intervals follow Weber's Law - a JND in the duration of a brief-tone interval bounded by tone bursts is proportional to the time interval to be discriminated.

5. The two markers involved in voicing perception (the stop burst and the onset of voicing) are complex sounds which vary in intensity, frequency and duration.

F. The Timing Hypothesis.

1. The primary basis of the discrimination of sounds from a synthetically generated voice-onset time continuum is timing.

2. A natural psychophysical boundary exists which separates events that are perceived as simultaneous and events that are in fact successive presentations of auditory stimuli.

3. Data on voice-onset time, tone-onset time, and noise-buzz signals converge to suggest that perception of timing plays a significant role for adult listeners.

III. Perceptual Adaptation

A. Introduction.

1. Many believe that phonetic recognition involves the detection of features.

2. Complex stimulus events are initially analyzed into parts and then recoded at a higher neural level into wholes.

3. A notion exists that the continuous acoustic waveform representing speech is transformed into a series of discrete features.

4. Selective Adaptation Technique – works on the assumption that whatever neuronal structures were involved in the analysis of the acoustic information in speech, the repeated presentation of a particular acoustic pattern could alter the mechanism in some way, perhaps by fatigue.

   a. in particular the aim was to identify the degree to which the neuronal mechanisms were selectively tuned to particular aspects of a complex stimulus.

5. Recent Studies:  Contingent Adaptation Effects:

   a. recent studies demonstrate that adaptation effects are sensitive to a variety of contextual variations;

   b. adaptation effects are strongest when the adapting stimulus is drawn directly from the test series;

   c. taken as a whole, recent studies tend to refute the notion that the mechanisms affected by adaptation with speech are specifically phonetic in nature:

      (1) marked reduction in the effects of adaptation is noted when the spectral information of the adapting and test stimuli differ;

      (2) adaption effects were predicted by the acoustic information represented in the adapter rather than by the listener's phonetic percept of the adapter;

      (3) reliable shifts in the phonetic boundary were obtained with components of the speech signal, even though these components did not contain critical information about the phonetic unit under test.

   d. thus, the available information suggests that the mechanisms to which we attribute these effects are selectively tuned to a restricted range of values representing a particular phonetic unit;

   e. they are also selectively tuned to a variety of contextual variables.

B.  The Sensory Fatigue Hypothesis.

   1.  We are reaching stronger consensus that the nature of the change brought about by adaptation has something to do with sensory fatigue or desensitization of the detector.

   2.  The adapting stimulus itself will display reduced sensitivity after adaptation.

C.  Adaptation Effects:  One Level or Two?

   1.  Some question exists that in addition to a <u>peripheral</u> level at which mechanisms are fatigued, the data suggest the existence of a more <u>central</u>, integrative level.

D.  Summary:

   1.  In the <u>channels of analysis</u> approach, adaptation studies simply provide another source of evidence that identifies the information in the signal to which the auditory system is paying attention.

   2.  The technique provides an indication of the degree to which the <u>mechanisms</u> that analyze different auditory events utilize <u>common</u> <u>channels</u> for the analysis of these events.

IV.  Conclusion

A.  This chapter reviewed three areas on speech perception:

   1.  Identification of invariant acoustic information for phonetic units.

   2.  Categorical perception.

   3.  Perceptual adaptation.

B.  The most substantial change in research approach is awareness of the importance of understanding the auditory level of analysis.

**REVIEW QUESTIONS**

1. Speech perception models based on information-processing commonly agree on 4 distinct processing levels involved in the transformation from an acoustic signal to a perceived message:

    A. _Auditory_

    B. _Phonetic_

    C. _Phonological_

    D. _Lexical, syntactic, semantic_

2. The study of categorization for speech sounds has focused on two rather different phenomena. Name them:

    A. _Boundaries_

    B. _Constancy_

3. The work on vowel perception has recently involved three approaches including (A) _psychophysical_,
    (B) _cochlear modeling_, and (C) _neurophysiologic_

4. Essentially, <u>categorical perception</u> is said to occur when a listener's ability to discriminate two stimuli is predicted by his ability to label them differently. To demonstrate <u>categorical perception</u> two tasks must be compared:

    A. _____

    B. _____

5. What two factors are frequently identified by speech researchers as responsible for the differences produced by the psychophysical procedures used in categorical perception of speech experiments?

    A. _Stimulus uncertainty_

    B. _Memory factors_

6. Is it (true) or false that experiments have been completed which show that chinchillas produce identification functions (involving synthetically produced stimuli) that are identical to those produced by English-speaking adults?

7. Identify the three categories of voiced and voiceless stops most common across languages:

   A. _voiced stop_

   B. _voiceless - unaspirated_

   C. _voiceless - aspirated_

8. The concept that the primary basis of the discrimination of sounds from a synthetically generated voice-onset time continuum is known as ___the___ ___timing___ ___hypothesis___.

9. Identify the following abbreviations:

   A. VOT ___voice___ ___onset___ ___time___
   B. JND ___just___ ___noticeable___ ___diff___
   C. RT ___reaction___ ___time___
   D. DL ___difference___ ___limen___

# Chapter 11

# NEUROPSYCHOLOGICAL MODELS OF LANGUAGE

*Hugh W. Buckingham, Jr.*

I. The Field of Neuropsychology

    A. <u>Neuropsychology</u> bridges two areas – neurology and psychology.

        1. Most information about normal function in neuropsychology originates from studies of abnormal behavior caused by anomalous growth of, or lesions to, the nervous system.

        2. A large area of neuropsychology is devoted to the study of long-term, intermediate, and short-term memory.

        3. Short-term memory is most important for language processing, both for comprehension and production.

        4. Research in the area covers the development and dissolution of function and how it correlates with the human nervous system.

        5. <u>Neurolinguistics</u> is considered a subdomain of neuropsychology.

II. The Neuropsychological Study of Language

    A. The most problematic aspect is that of locating functions in autonomous regions of the brain.

    B. "<u>Functional vulnerability</u>" holds that various functions or behaviors seem to be vulnerable to disruption secondary to lesions in certain areas of the nervous system.

    C. Neuropsychological models of language:

        1. Initial appearance – Wernicke's monograph of 1874:

            a. correlated sensorimotor association on an anatomical basis at cortical level;

            b. Wernicke is the "father" of cerebral connectionism.

2. **Lichtheim (1885)** first stated that to understand words one needs much more than acoustical information.

   a. he localized lesions that give rise to deficits in one or another function concerning language.

3. **Marie, in collaboration with Foix (1917),** studied patients with traumatic penetrating wounds sustained in World War I.

4. **Penfield and Roberts (1959)** researched cortical electrical stimulation as well as cortical ablation.

   a. felt there must be some subcortical language integrating mechanism – reasoned that it must be the <u>thalamus</u>.

5. **Luria in Moscow (1966–1976)** is a localizer of components which function together in normal case as a complete system.

   a. for Luria, damage to specific cerebral regions results in different syndromes;

   b. characterized sensory aphasia in terms of a phonologic decoding inability which disturbs comprehension.

6. **Geschwind (1965)** revitalized the model of cerebral connectionism in explaining agnosia, apraxia and aphasia.

   a. his explanations of these syndromes are in terms of lesions within functional centers or of lesions which cut one center off from another.

7. **Whitaker (1970)** was one of the first to study aphasia from a linguistic point of view.

8. **Brown (1976)** developed a model for the genesis of language which comprises a bottom to top "unfolding" process from limbic cortex to generalized neocortex to specialized focal neocortex.

   a. Brown's model offers an alternate approach to the classic localization schemes with centers and connections.

III. Conclusions

   A. Practically all neuropsychologists agree that the human brain is <u>not</u> equipotential in the normally functioning adult, but that it is somewhat more in the infant.

B. Almost all concur that early brain damage forces shifts in cortical functional responsibility.

C. Almost all assume that focal damage to one or another region of the language area in the dominant hemisphere will produce predictable symptomatology.

D. Language functions which have been "mapped" onto human cortex are dynamic <u>performance</u> phenomena:

1. Articulate speech.

2. Repeating.

3. Comprehensive acoustic - verbal stimuli.

4. Providing labels for pictured objects.

E. We know much more about performance than about competence - we are a long way from a straightforward mapping between "mind" and "brain".

## REVIEW QUESTIONS

1. The auditory, visual, tactile and motor systems in primates were ultimately shown to have endpoints in the cerebral cortex by:

   A. The middle of the 18th Century.
   B. The end of the 19th Century.
   C. The early 1920's.
   D. The turn of the 19th Century.
   E. The middle of the 17th Century.

2. Collateral blood supply, subsiding edema and amelioration of initial diaschisis all play an important role in:

   A. Callosal agenesis.
   B. Dementia.
   C. Agnosia.
   D. Functional recovery.
   E. Visual field defects.

3. One of the principal goals of the neuropsychology of language is to demonstrate that linguistic functions are:

   A. Separately disruptable.
   B. Mediated equipotentially in the normal human brain.
   C. Non-localizable.
   D. Artifacts of one's analysis.
   E. Specifically located in discretely defined Brodmann areas.

4. Cerebral connection theories are closely linked to:

   A. Freudian psychology.
   B. Abnormal psychology.
   C. Gestalt psychology.
   D. Social psychology.
   E. Association psychology.

5. Who first stipulated that locating the damage that destroys speech and locating speech are two different things?

   A. Karl Wernicke
   B. Paul Broca
   C. John Hughlings Jackson
   D. Henry Head
   E. Kurt Goldstein

6. The phrenological views of Gall and Spurzheim regarding the localization of articulate speech can be traced to Broca through the work of:

   A. Liepmann and Kleist
   B. Bouillaud and Auburtin
   C. Ferrier and Bastian
   D. Freud and Lichtheim
   E. Dax and Wernicke

7. In Wernicke's model as well as in Lichtheim's model, "Leitungsaphasie" was caused by a lesion which disconnected:

   A. The visual cortex from the motor strip.
   B. Broca's area from the supplemental speech region.
   C. The angular gyrus from the splenium.
   D. The motor speech region from the auditory region.
   E. The medial geniculate from Heschl's gyrus.

8. Pierre Marie's "lenticular zone" did not include:

   A. The putamen.
   B. The globus pallidus.
   C. The lateral geniculate.
   D. The internal capsule.
   E. The claustrum

9. In Henry Head's classification of aphasia, which syndrome most closely parallels Broca's aphasia?

    A. Syntactical aphasia.
    B. Global aphasia.
    C. Verbal aphasia.
    D. Semantic aphasia.
    E. Nominal aphasia.

10. Experimental studies involving electrical stimulation of the supplemental motor region for speech have demonstrated that when these areas are excited, the subject:

    A. Becomes mute.
    B. Produces neologistic jargon.
    C. Cannot comprehend verbal stimuli.
    D. Perseverates or vocalizes.
    E. Develops an agnosia for sounds.

11. In Penfield and Roberts' view, what is the common mediating zone for the anterior and posterior cortical language areas?

    A. The thalamus.
    B. The splenium.
    C. The corpus callosum.
    D. The pons.
    E. The cerebellum

12. H.C. Bastian, in 1869, hypothesized that the production of speech was a "glosso-kinaesthetic" function. Which aphasic syndrome in A.R. Luria's scheme uniquely parallels this motor-sensory dichotomy?

    A. Efferent motor aphasia.
    B. Semantic aphasia.
    C. Dynamic aphasia.
    D. Sensory aphasia.
    E. Afferent motor aphasia.

13. In Luria's "paradoxical state," what happens to the Pavlovian "rules of force"?

    A. Nothing.
    B. They are reversed.
    C. Another rule is in force.
    D. They are both strengthened.
    E. Only one is in force.

14. What aspect of Gall and Spurzheim's phrenological theory has recently been investigated by Geschwind, Galaburda and others?

   (A.) The relation between functional difference and cortical asymmetries of size.
   B. The relation between personality traits and cranial prominence.
   C. The location of articulate speech in the anterior region at the frontal orbits.
   D. Their theories on cerebellar function.
   E. Their theories of learning.

15. Match the aphasic syndrome with the prototypical error of that syndrome:

   A. 5 Wernicke's aphasia
   B. 1 Broca's aphasia (apraxic)
   C. 3 Conduction aphasia
   D. 4 Anomic aphasia
   E. 2 Wernicke's aphasia (with jargon)

   1. sub-phonemic error (but correct phonemic selection)
   2. neologism
   3. repetition error
   4. lexical retrieval error
   5. phonemic substitution error (but <u>correct</u> allophonic production for that error)

# Chapter 12

# MODELS OF AUDITORY LINGUISTIC PROCESSING

*Margaret L. Lemme and Natalie Hedberg Daves*

I. Introduction

    A. Theories of <u>auditory</u> <u>processing</u> deal with analysis of the acoustic signal.

    B. <u>Speech</u> <u>perception</u> theories are concerned with the analysis of acoustic patterns and their relationship to the recognition of phonemes.

    C. <u>Information</u> <u>processing</u> theories expand influences to account for how language is understood by the human organism.

    D. Definition of <u>process</u> is "a set of programs that is being executed for a common purpose and for which resources are allocated as a unit."

        1. Structural and control processing:

            a. features appear to reflect levels of storage built into the system in a fixed programmatic sense;

            b. control processes are variable voluntary strategies performed to accomplish a specific task;

            c. similarly the central nervous system is composed of fixed structures whose operations can vary and be selective.

        2. Bottom-up and top-down processing:

            a. bottom-up data are analyzed with increasing finer levels of analysis carried out between input of stimuli at point at which weaning is derived;

            b. top-down processes take into account expectations held by the individual for incoming stimuli.

3.  Passive and active processing:

    a. in passive systems, a perceptual unit is built up by combining previously analyzed fragments;

    b. active systems contain a comparator which matches the input pattern with a pattern that is either stored or generated for purposes of meditation.

4.  Serial and parallel processing:

    a. in serial processing the results of one level of processing are fed into a processor at the next level;

    b. parallel processing allows for multiple levels of analysis to be carried out simultaneously.

II. Neural Basis of Auditory Processing

  A.  Nonspecific Sensory System:

    1.  A diffuse, indirect route through the central core of the brain for auditory information to reach the cortex, including the brain stem reticular formation.

    2.  System is able to decrease or increase excitability of most sensory neurons.

    3.  Arousal is considered a neurophysiological entity resulting from activation of the cortex by the ascending reticular activating system and appears to respond primarily to stimulus change.

  B.  Neural Basis of Attention:

    1.  Attention is defined as focusing of perceptual mechanisms upon input in particular sensory modalities or upon the specific configuration of stimuli which correspond to a unique event.

    2.  Hernandez-Peon et al. (1956) demonstrated suppression of irrelevant auditory input in cats at the level of the cochlear nucleus.

    3.  Brain mechanisms of attention are extremely complex and require contributions from higher level brain structures including the limbic cortex of the temporal lobe and the frontal lobe.

C.  Neural Basis of Memory:

1.  The nature and localization of memory are elusive because memory is probably a complex rather than a single function.

2.  Commonly accepted notion is that the temporal lobes, including the limbic system, play an important role in memory.

3.  Consolidation of memory, or the registration and retention phases, appears dependent upon hippocampal activity.

4.  Long-term memory storage appears to be widely distributed in the cortex.

D.  Cortical Auditory System:

1.  Primary auditory cortex is located within the transverse gyri of Heschl (Brodmann's areas 41 and 42) on the superior aspect of the temporal lobe.

2.  Early cortical mapping identified two auditory areas in the temporal regions having reverse tonotopic frequency projections of each other.

3.  Auditory cortex is essential for sequence of stimulation or amount of stimulation for stimulus patterns.

4.  Unilateral cortical lesions do not influence absolute thresholds for pure tones - but pure tone hearing loss may occur following bilateral cortical lesions.

II. Neural Basis of Language

A.  Cortical Specialization for Language Function:

1.  Cortical specialization for language function in one hemisphere of the human brain, most commonly the left hemisphere, is a well accepted premise.

2.  Right ear preference for speech stimuli, while left ear is more accurate for non-speech stimuli, e.g., melody patterns.

3.  Comprehension of speech may be more diversely or bilaterally represented than speech production.

B.  Localization of Language Function:

1.  Neurolinguistics, a relatively new discipline, seeks to integrate information from other fields to develop language organization models.

2. Much speculation as to how the central language neuronal structures process auditory-linguistic information.

3. Language representation occurs when the activities of the auditory association area and of the angular and supramarginal gyri in the inferior parietal lobe interact.

4. Present literature concerning brain-language theory and function emphasizes the essential role of cortical structures and cortical-cortical connections in subserving man's language system.

IV. Cognitive Correlates of Auditory Processing

A. Structural Theories:

1. First attempt at a complete model of human information processing abilities was made by Broadbent in his book _Perception_ _and_ _Communication_, 1958.

2. Broadbent's model represented the human central nervous system as essentially a single communication channel that has a limited capacity for processing information that operated on a "filter theory".

3. Theories of attention that emphasize structural aspects of information processing were dubbed "bottleneck" theories because they relate the necessity for selecting certain stimuli for further processing.

B. Capacity Theories:

1. Maintain that man has considerable control over the allocation of his attentional resources; certain activities require no attention and others require attention only in later stages of processing; thus concurrent activities may be carried out to the extent of available capacity.

2. Total performance is resource limited.

3. When control is required, the rate of processing by the system is the limiting factor in determining the capacity of the system.

C. Pattern Representation:

1. Ability to recognize patterns is fundamental to all information processing systems.

2. Results of pattern recognition and analysis is represented as an internal representation of the physical pattern.

3. Distinctive features concept introduced by Jakobson et al., 1951.

   a. distinctive features viewed as the ultimate units of language; as such the features represented the differences between phonemes;

   b. discovery of distinctive features and the relations among the features that create a pattern may be thought of as the first stage in recognition of previously learned patterns.

D. Pattern Processing:

1. Passive process: "Pandemonium" pattern perception involves "demons" which search for their likenesses in input stimuli.

2. Active process: decoding is accomplished through an indirect process in which a pattern is recalled or generated to match input stimuli.

E. Memory:

1. Recent studies of memory suggest different coding strategies rather than different storage structures.

F. Acoustic and Semantic Coding:

1. It has been shown that both acoustic and semantic coding are present in both short- and long-term recall tasks.

2. Recall tasks show that short-term memory is affected by acoustic form of words, but not by visual and semantic forms.

3. Long-term memory is primarily affected by the semantic form of the word.

G. Depth and Breadth of Processing:

1. Another determinant of retention is the elaborateness of the analysis carried out.

2. Depth of processing is associated with the elaborateness of the stimulus analysis.

3. It is argued that stimuli receiving sufficient processing so that they are comprehended, rather than only recognized, will be remembered better.

V. Comprehension

A. Representation of Knowledge:

1. Comprehension is seen as totally dependent on long term memory as perceptual information is transformed into meaningful ideas.

2. Information stored in long-term memory is accumulated as experiences and represents an individual's knowledge of the world.

3. Since retrieval of information stored in long-term memory is critical to the comprehension of auditory stimuli, two types of organization of semantic memory have been hypothesized:

   a. network models - vast representational systems consisting of conceptual structures and relationships among concepts and words;

   b. feature models - concepts are represented by features on a continuum from "most important" to "least important".

B. Models of Language Comprehension:

1. Language comprehension, the association of meaning with information abstracted from the acoustic signal, is the end product of the auditory process.

2. Information processing models attempt to delineate each storage and control process between the reception of stimuli and the meaning response.

3. Research has emphasized that auditory linguistic input is never into a static system but into one which is organized continuously by the functional state and previous experience of the individual.

4. Complete theory for language comprehension is not presently available.

**REVIEW QUESTIONS**

1. Atkinson and Shiffrin's comprehensive view of memory differentiates structural features of information processing from control processes. Structural features:

   A. Are voluntary strategies performed by the individual.
   B. Are influenced by the individual's history.
   C. Are variable features of the information processing system.
   D. Are fixed levels of storage.
   E. Are influenced by the demands of the situation.

2. Bottom-up processes are driven by:

   A. Sensory data received from external sources.
   B. Conceptual data generated from external sources.
   C. Sensory data received from internal sources.
   D. Perceptual data received from internal sources.
   E. Conceptual data generated from internal sources.

3. Speech perception theories which suggest that perceptual units are built up by combining previously analyzed fragments are considered:

   A. Comparatory systems.
   B. Passive systems.
   C. Parallel systems.
   D. Top-down systems.
   E. Active systems.

4. The nonspecific sensory system includes the:

   A. Thalamus.
   B. Reticular formation.
   C. Hippocampus.
   D. Limbic system.
   E. Inferior colliculus.

5. Neural correlates of long-term memory appear to be:

   A. The cingulate gyrus and hippocampus.
   B. Localized in particular regions of the cortex.
   C. Located in the brain-stem core.
   D. The hippocampus and associated structures.
   E. Distributed in the cortex.

6. Unilateral cortical lesions do not have an appreciable effect on:

   A. Identification of tone duration.
   B. Sound localization.
   C. Identification of changes in temporal patterns.
   D. Absolute pure tone thresholds.
   E. Dichotic listening scores.

7. Based on available data, it is generally accepted that in man:

   A. The left hemisphere predominates in processes requiring spatial capabilities.
   B. The two cerebral hemispheres are anatomically identical.
   C. The right hemisphere predominates in many linguistic processes.
   D. The two cerebral hemispheres are differentially involved in linguistic functions.
   E. The right hemisphere is capable of producing speech.

8. The angular and supramarginal gyri appear to subserve comprehension of selected components of language. They are:

   A. Phonetic, phonological, and lexical components.
   B. Phonetic and phonological components.
   C. Phoneme sequence components.
   D. Lexical, semantic and syntactic components.
   E. Syntactic and pragmatic components.

9. Speech perception theories are concerned most with:

   A. Analysis of acoustic patterns and recognition of phonemes.
   B. How language is understood by humans.
   C. Physical events in the auditory signal.
   D. Control processes.
   E. Analysis of the acoustic signal.

10. The first attempt at a complete model of human information processing abilities was made by:

   A. Deutsch
   B. Broadbent
   C. Norman
   D. Treisman
   E. Baddley

11. A comprehensive theory of information processing with incorporated top-down influences was developed by:

    A. Deutsch
    B. Broadbent
    C. Norman
    D. Treisman
    E. Baddley

12. Which of the following speech perception theories views pattern recognition as an active process?

    A. Selfridge's "Pandemonium".
    B. Abbs and Sussman's neurological theory.
    C. Steven and Halle's analysis–by–synthesis.
    D. Fant's auditory theory.
    E. Hughes' computer-based theory.

13. Recent studies of memory suggest:

    A. The long-term store is a "working memory".
    B. Different coding strategies for short- and long-term memory.
    C. The sensory register is the center of the control system.
    D. Different storage structures for short- and long-term memory.
    E. Information is held in the sensory register for 15 to 30 seconds.

14. Which of the following statements concerning attention is NOT true?

    A. Certain tasks can be carried out automatically, requiring little or no attention, while others require considerable attentional resources.
    B. Selection is necessary because of limitations on processing capacity.
    C. Alertness, the most basic aspect of attention, is a function of general level of arousal.
    D. Knowledge of conceptual and linguistic rule systems is utilized in selecting certain sensory input for further processing.
    E. Selection among various external inputs results in focus of attention on certain stimuli and total suppression of information in the irrelevant channels.

15. Compare and contrast network and feature models for the organization of semantic memory.

16. Develop your own model of auditory linguistic information processing.

# Chapter 13

# ISSUES IN CHILD LANGUAGE ACQUISITION

*Robin S. Chapman*

I. Description of the Child's Language System

    A. Three Aspects of Linguistic Development:

        1. **Syntax**: the rules for putting words together in sentences.

        2. **Semantics**: the mapping of meaning into words.

        3. **Pragmatics**: the reasons and rules of language use

    B. Language Universals vs. Individual Differences:

        1. 1970 – increased interest in language diversity.

        2. (Blount, 1970; Mitchell-Kernan, 1971; Bowerman, 1973) – anthropological linguistics have shifted from studying the similarities in acquisition across language and cultures to an increased emphasis on differing patterns of acquisition (Schieffelin, 1979).

        3. Individual differences in the interactive acquisition of content, form, and use have been the object of systematic exploration by Bloom and her colleagues.

        4. Nelson (1973) and Ramer (1976) have linked individual and dyadic differences in early acquisition to rate differences.

    C. Macrodevelopment vs. Microdevelopment:

        1. Bloom (1875b) and colleagues have traced differences in two versus three-word expressions containing locative action verbs to whether the verb is new in the child's repertoire (utterance is shorter) or old (longer).

2. Reich (1977), Menn (1978), and Bates (1979) describe the changing contextual support required for comprehension and production in the one-word period.

3. Greenfield (1972) for recognition of the Peekaboo game in the first year of life.

D. Becoming Aware of Language: Metalinguistic Development:

1. (Flavell, 1977) - body of work on children's conscious knowledge about learning and thinking.

2. (Sinclair et al., 1978) - children's conscious reflections on language.

II. Learning to Talk: What Are the Child's Rules?

A. Major Developmental Changes:

1. Infancy - 8 months: babble repeated consonant-vowel syllables
   10 months: gestures, vocalization
   12 months: first recognizable word

2. Preschool - sentence length increases.

3. School-age - by 5 years of age most sentence structures of the language are present in speech.

B. Pragmatics: Early Communicative Intents:

1. Actions.

2. Vocalizations.

3. Halliday (1975) - early functions:

   a. instrumental;

   b. regulatory;

   c. interactional;

   d. personal;

   e. imaginative;

   f. heuristic;

   g. informative.

C. Older Children: Increased Diversity of Communicative Intent:

1. Chapman (1981) and Rees (1978) summaries.

2. Dore's (1978) analysis.

3. Moerk's (1975) categories.

4. Keenan's (1977) report.

5. Fough's (1977) study of use of language in peer play.

D. Semantics: Word Meaning

1. Early word uses.

   a. refer to people and objects or play a role in a communication game.

2. Nelson (1973) points out that object words in the child's first 50 spoken words refer primarily to things that move or that the child can act upon.

3. Clark (1973) demonstrated that one- to two-year-olds overgeneralized word uses on the basis of perceptual similarity.

4. Pragmatic Limits:

   a. Greenfield (Greenfield and Smith, 1976; Greenfield, 1980) argues that children choose to talk about what is most salient to them; what is new, changing, or most informative.

5. Phonological Limits:

   a. Swartz and Leonard (1980) suggest that children's early production vocabularies are further limited to those words for which they can achieve reasonable phonetic approximations.

6. Conceptual and Experiential Limits:

   a. vocabulary restriction in comprehension, as well as production, arises from restrictions in the child's experience, input, and conceptual representation of the world.

7. Modeling the "Mental Dictionary": Semantic Features:

   a. 16 months - when a child can understand a word in the absence of context (Nelson et al., 1978; Miller et al., 1980) it becomes appropriate to ask what form his "mental dictionary" takes;

        b. Clark's semantic feature hypothesis was an important
           focus for semantic research in the 1970's.

    8. Developmental Changes in Dictionary Organization:

        a. researchers have speculated that not only does the
           entry for a single word change over time, but also
           that the organization of entries changes as well;

        b. Bowerman (1978) details changes in children's word
           use over the 2 to 4 year span, which suggest that
           a reorganization of the system is gradually taking place;

        c. Petrey (1977) – shifts in word associations between ages
           5 and 7.

E. Semantics:   Changing Semantic Roles

    1. Holophrase position – McCarthy, 1954.

    2. Bloom (1973) "empty pivot".

    3. Branigan (1979) – single word utterances have phonetic
       properties suggesting that they are parts of a single
       intended string in the sense that early elements anticipate
       later ones.

III. Early Sentences: What Are the Child's Rules?

A. Shifts in Theoretical Accounts:

    1. Early accounts (Braine, 1964; Miller and Ervin, 1964;
       Brown et al., 1964) – pivot grammars.

    2. Class categories (noun/verb) Bloom, 1970.

    3. Intensive attempts to fit particular adult grammars to the
       data – Chompky's (1965) transformational grammar
       (Brown, 1973) and Fillmore's (1968) case–relational grammar
       (Bowerman, 1973) led to rejection in favor of categories
       similar to case relations that captured semantic roles
       (Schlesinger, 1971; Brown, 1973; Bloom, 1973; Bowerman,
       1973).

    4. Braine, 1976 – restricted and idiosyncratic semantic
       categories often with lexical and pragmatic restrictions
       (Ervin-Tripp, 1977).

    5. Syntactic categories for rule writing.

    6. Semantic categories for rules.

    7. Braine's limited-scope formulas for first word combinations.

B. Pragmatic Constraints or Production Rules:

    1. A role for communicative function.

    2. A role for prior discourse.

    3. Lexical constructs.

    4. A role for the conversational histories of objects and activities.

C. Later Semantic Sequences:

    1. Semantic aspects of WH-Questions.

    2. Semantic aspects of conjoined sentences.

IV. Developmental Sequences in Syntax: Brown's (1973) Stages

A. Stages:

    1. Stage I: (MLV 1.1 to 2.0) marked by emergence of the early word combinations.

    2. Stage II: additions of grammatical elements.

    3. Stage III: increasing differentiation of sentence type.

B. The syntax of sentence negation.

C. The syntax of questions.

D. Problems in sequence identification for negatives and questions.

E. Complex sentences.

F. Accounting for syntactic development.

V. The Role of Cognition

A. Strong form of cognition hypothesis.

B. Weak form of cognition hypothesis.

C. Correlational hypothesis.

D. Problems in assessing cognition.

E. The role of input in determining acquisition.

VI. Individual Differences in Acquisition

1. Research has focused on three different aspects of linguistics – identify these areas from the definitions provided below:

   A. _SYNTAX_ : the rules for putting words together into sentences.

   B. _semantics_ : the mapping of meaning into words.

   C. _pragmatics_ : the reasons and rules of language use.

2. During infancy, children begin to babble repeated consonant-vowel syllables at approximately (A) _8_ months of age; communicate intention with conventionalized gesture or vocalization at (B) _10_ months, and use a first recognizable word at (C) _12_ months. By (D) _20_ months of age most children have acquired a 50-word speaking vocabulary.

3. As children grow older, increasingly more information is included into each spoken utterance. The proportion of utterances in a narrative containing dependent clauses increases from approximately 16% in first grade to _70_% at the end of high school.

4. What is meant by the term "holophrase"?

   _one word utterances stand for whole sentences_

5. What is <u>pivot</u> <u>grammar</u>? _two word combinations - such word is high frequency use, combined with others while in fixed position_

6. Mothers alter their speech from adult conversation patterns when talking to language-learning children. List six ways in which this is accomplished:

   A. _____

   B. _____

   C. _____

   D. _____

   E. _____

   F. _____

7. What 2 factors interact to bring about the changes in mother's speech to language-learning children?

   A. _desire to make herself understood_
   B. _____ _to express affection___

8. Match these negations with the appropriate children's age ranges:

   _1_ A. denial of truth-value          1. 19-23 months
   _2_ B. rejection words                2. 13-15 months
   _3_ C. unfulfilled expectations       3. 16-19 months

9. Put in proper chronological and developmental sequence the following phases for learning to request action:

   _4_ A. Variation in Form
   _3_ B. Locutionary
   _1_ C. Perlocutionary
   _6_ D. Variation in Justification
   _5_ E. Variation in Explicit Content
   _2_ F. Illocutionary

10. Average sentence length increases throughout the preschool years, from just above 1 word sentences at 20 months to (A) __4__ word sentences at 3 1/2 years and to (B) __8__ word sentences at age 6 years.

# Chapter 14

# TOWARD AN UNDERSTANDING OF COMMUNICATIVE DISORDERS

*William M. Diedrich*

I.  Introduction

   A.  The terms <u>hearing</u>, <u>language</u> and <u>speech</u> are subsumed under
       the more generic term <u>communication</u>.

       1.  The field of speech pathology has been considered a
           "borrower" – from neuroanatomy, psychoacoustics, child
           development and linguistics, engineering, psychology,
           education and medicine.

       2.  Word descriptions and classifications used in our field
           may have actually had restrictive effect on our understanding
           of communicative disorders.

       3.  Through better use of labels, we might better understand
           communication and communicative disorders.

II.  Historical Perspective

   A.  Official beginning of the American Speech and Hearing
       Association was in 1925 under the name Academy of Speech
       Correction.

       1.  The early roots of the profession go back to Europeans
           who described language and speech problems in systematic
           fashion.

   B.  Historical Review of Textbooks in Speech Pathology:

       1.  First American textbook to describe disorders of speech
           as "speech pathology" written by Travis (1931).

       2.  Another early text titled <u>Rehabilitation of Speech</u>
           (West et al., 1937, 1947, 1957).

3. Van Riper's <u>Speech</u> <u>Correction</u> (1939–1963) classified speech disorders into four categories:

    a. articulation;

    b. time (or rhythm);

    c. voice;

    d. symbolization (or language).

4. Berry and Eisenson wrote <u>The Defective in Speech</u> (1942) and <u>Speech Disorders</u> (1956).

5. The use of the word "pathology" retained by Travis in 1957 – <u>Handbook of Speech Pathology</u>.

6. Rieber and Brubaker edited <u>Speech Pathology</u> (1966).

7. Van Riper served as editor for 14 volumes entitled <u>Foundations of Speech Pathology Series</u> (1964).

8. A similar series, <u>Studies in Communication Disorders</u>, was undertaken by Halpern (1972).

C. Influence of behavioral studies from psychology reached our field in the 1960's.

D. Recent authors have attempted to incorporate other terms in book titles to describe the field.

1. Mysak's <u>Pathologies of Speech Systems</u> (1976).

2. Minifie et al. edited <u>Normal Aspects of Speech, Hearing and Language</u> (1973).

3. Skinner and Shelton edited <u>Speech, Language and Hearing: Normal Processes and Disorders</u> (1978).

4. Main direction of change is toward use of the label "communication".

    a. Byrne and Shervanian (1977), <u>Introduction to Communicative Disorders</u>.

    b. Curtis (1978), <u>Processes and Disorders of Human Communication</u>.

E. In 1978, the American Speech and Hearing Association officially changed its name to the American Speech-Language-Hearing Association.

III. Component Descriptions of Language and Speech

    A. The study of classification in speech pathology indicates that the field has moved from the early cataloguing of descriptive etiologic classifications such as mongoloid speech and cerebral palsy speech to a nonquantitative comparative system.

        1. Linguistic components of language include:

            a. pragmatic;

            b. semantic;

            c. syntactic;

            d. phonologic categories acting in synergistic fashion.

        2. Speech includes:

            a. respiration;

            b. phonation;

            c. resonance;

            d. articulation;

            e. prosody.

        3. The label "prosody" includes the constructs of:

            a. pitch;

            b. loudness;

            c. duration;

            d. tempo;

            e. rhythm;

            f. voice quality.

IV. Speech

    A. Relationship of speech to language:

        1. Speech and language are duplicates of one another.

        2. Speech is the spoken vehicle for language.

        3. Speech and language are separate entities in a symbiotic partnership.

V.   Motor Speech

A.   In order to diagnose a communicative disorder and establish
     therapeutic measures  the clinician must understand how
     speech is heard, language understood and formulated, and how
     a speech response is uttered (motor).

B.   Some questions about the use of the term "motor speech".

     1.   If speech is a motor act, the use of "motor speech"
          is redundant.

     2.   Historic classifications of sensory vs. motor in
          neuroanatomic models is not clear.

     3    Treatment procedures for motor and non-motor speech
          disorders are more alike than unalike - the term "motor
          speech disorders" has not resulted in clearly different
          treatment paradigms.

          a. motor system is part of the central and peripheral
             nervous system and functions under the influence
             of sensory, cognitive, affective and linguistic
             processes;

          b. speech is the concurrent motor functions of respiration,
             phonation, resonance, articulation and prosody;

          c. articulation, respiration, phonation, resonance
             and prosody disorders result from disturbances
             in the nervous system;

          d. apraxia is a speech planning disorder that results
             from an impaired central nervous system;

          e. dysarthria is a neuromuscular disorder that results
             from an impaired central or peripheral nervous
             system affecting singularly or in combination
             elements of (c) above.

VI.   Emotional Speech

A.   Must consider the psychologic dynamics in speech development.

     1.   In order to better understand normal communication and
          management of communicative disorders, we must be
          aware of "...the biological, sociological and psychological
          interplay of forces" during human communication.

VII. Critique of Treatment in Communicative Disorders

    A. Darley (1978) stated that "...it should be understood that there is no absolute division between diagnosis and therapy".

        1. Identification of a speech or language problem is generally not difficult; determination of the cause of the problem is another matter.

    B. Medical Model:

        1. Symptoms and causal relationships are investigated.

        2. Focus of attention is on the presumed underlying cause of the disorder.

        3. Therapy is often "hope therapy" or perhaps "shotgun therapy" in which treatment is attempted without absolute determination of cause.

        4. Few speech and language disorders have a single, specific cause.

        5. Patient in medical model is a passive recipient of treatment; in communicative disorders therapy the patient is an active participant interacting with someone.

    C. Symptomatic Treatment:

        1. Refers to treating the problem and disregards the cause of the distress.

        2. "Good behavior" management is literally not symptomatic treatment.

        3. Irwin (1971) is not sure that symptom substitution (extinguishment of one behavior followed by eruption of some other behavior) is present in remedial speech therapy.

    D. Process Analysis:

        1. Attempts to draw attention to the multiple factors operating in communication:

            a. speech production;

            b. speech planning;

            c. perceptual, cognitive and linguistic aspects;

            d. biological, psychological and sociological aspects.

E.  What makes therapy different?

1.  The clinician's philosophy (bias) determines which treatments will be used for a specified disorder.

2.  Notions can be generated which describe any treatment encounter as "different".

F.  What are the similarities in therapy management?

1.  There exist general principles of therapy management:

    a. therapy mode (dyad or group);

    b. patient concerns;

    c. clinician management decisions.

2.  After a given treatment regimen has been determined, the general therapy procedures are similar.

3.  Clinicians therapy approaches are summarized as:

    a. immediate modeling of the clinician's stimuli;

    b. recalling from memory a previously learned response;

    c. response building.

4.  To get the patient to initiate the response is the crucial step in the diagnosis-therapy analysis.

1. Match the authors and their books:

    _4_ A. Rehabilitation of Speech          1. Travis

    _2_ B. Speech Correction              2. Van Riper

    _1_ C. Handbook of Speech Pathology    3. Minifie et al.

    _5_ D. The Defective in Speech         4. West et al.

    _6_ E. Speech Pathology: An Applied      5. Berry and Eisenson
            Behavioral Science
                                            6. Perkins

    _3_ F. Normal Aspects of Speech,        7. Darley et al.
            Hearing and Language

    _2_ G. Foundations of Speech Pathology
            Series

    _7_ H. Motor Speech Disorders

2. Identify three different approaches used to evaluate speech and language problems:

    A. _Medical_
    B. _Symptomatical_
    C. _Process analysis_

3. Darley et al. (1975) defined three basic <u>processes</u> useful to the building of a conceptual understanding of speech and language; to what process does each definition below refer?

    A. _language_ the organization of concepts and their symbolic formulation and expression.

    B. _speech_ the externalization of thought through the concurrent motor functions of respiration, phonation, resonance, articulation and prosody.

    C. _motor speech planning_ the programming of these motor skills in the volitional production of individual speech sounds and their combination into sequences to form words.

# Chapter 15

# THE DIAGNOSTIC PROCESS

*James E. Nation and Dorothy M. Aram*

I.  Diagnosis:  A Professional Activity

    A.  Goals of Diagnosis:

        1.  Diagnosis of speech and language disorders is central to all activities of the speech pathologist.

        2.  Diagnosis results in:

            a. descriptions of communication disorders;

            b. information regarding causal factors;

            c. decisions regarding management alternatives.

    B.  Testing is not diagnosis:

        1.  Testing is the clinician's tool, and only one aspect of diagnosis of speech and language disorders.

    C.  Some disagreement exists among professionals about the speech pathologists' and other behavioral scientists' role in diagnosis because of infringement upon extraprofessional territory.

    D.  Speech pathologists do not make medical diagnoses, psychological diagnoses or dental diagnoses - only speech and language diagnoses.

II.  The Diagnostician as a Problem-Solver

    A.  The diagnostician must have a systematic way of thinking:

        1.  Must have funds of knowledge organized into a framework for retrieval, use and change

        2.  A scientific orientation to problem-solving.

B. Organized Funds of Knowledge:

    1. Incorporates accumulated facts as well as theories and frameworks that have been developed.

    2. Diagnostician in speech and language should work from a framework that stresses integration rather than a separation of subject matter.

C. A number of models and frameworks exist to help in understanding the processing underlying observed behavior.

D. The Speech and Language Processing Model (SLPM):

    1. Speech and language environment component.

    2. The internal speech and language processing component.

    3. The speech and language product component.

E. Problem-Solving Orientation:

    1. The diagnostician uses the scientific method as a problem-solving tool:

        a. develops clinical hypotheses;

        b. selects and administers appropriate measurement procedures;

        c. analyzes and interprets the information gathered;

        d. arrives at conclusions.

    2. Each client is a "mini-research project" and each diagnosis is "tailor-made" for each client.

III. The Diagnostic Process

A. Model represents seven steps in diagnosis:

    1. Constituent analysis – also called the case study; an analysis of the client's background relative to his disorder:

        a. from referral information;

        b. from interviews;

        c. from case history questionnaires;

        d. from reports from other professionals;

e. reports from other agencies;

f. purpose is to uncover potential cause–effect relationships and organize client information.

2. Clinical hypothesis:

   a. the derivation of a cause–effect clinical hypothesis;

   b. a form of prediction that requires examination;

   c. and provides a tentative solution to the problem;

   d. it may be necessary to reformulate or modify the hypothesis during the diagnostic process.

3. Clinical design:

   a. careful planning for testing the clinical hypotheses cannot be overemphasized;

   b. the clinician must decide what he wants to measure, the specificity of the measurements, and what could facilitate or prevent his obtaining the measurements;

   c. the diagnostician must not be tied to any particular test or test battery;

   d. care taken in the selection of appropriate measurement tools may determine the success or failure of the diagnostic session;

   e. the diagnostician must plan the testing strategy and put into order the procedures, which usually flow from effect to cause, from general to specific, from easy to hard.

4. Clinical testing:

   a. the clinician must prepare the test room, materials and self;

   b. meet the client and proceed with clinical testing;

   c. close the clinical testing session when enough appropriate information has been obtained.

5. Clinical analysis:

   a. nonjudgemental, objective organization of the results of testing;

b. the diagnostician must objectify the data for comparative analysis against norms or other standards of performance;

c. the clinician inventories; orders and organizes data with regard to the cause-effect relationship expressed in the clinical hypothesis.

6. Clinical interpretation:

a. the clinician brings together the clinical testing results and the constituent analysis of data;

b. interprets the information carefully;

c. confirms or rejects the original hypotheses - is prepared to formulate a new hypothesis if necessary;

d. formalizes the interpretation into a precisely thought-out diagnostic statement that can lead to management decisions;

e. critically evaluates the quality of the diagnosis.

7. Conclusions:

a. the clinician translates diagnostic findings into a management proposal for the client;

b. holds an interpretive conference with the client;

c. prepares professional reports;

d. completes all administrative details relative to the "disposition" of the client.

IV. Modifications of the Diagnostic Process

A. The diagnostician's work setting often specifies the diagnostic responsibilities.

B. Responses to referral requests may alter specific steps of the diagnostic model.

C. Clinician's main concern must remain with the client, not with a cause or symptom.

D. Diagnosis is not a detailed specification of procedures, but a process requiring the pinnacle of professional knowledge and expertise.

**REVIEW QUESTIONS**

1. Which of the following is not a goal of diagnosis?

   A. Describing symptomatology.
   B. Understanding the causal basis for the speech-language disorder.
   C. Selecting testing instruments for assessment.
   D. Establishing cause-effect relationships.
   E. Providing management alternatives.

2. The concept of causation in diagnosis requires:

   A. Knowing the specific cause of the disorder.
   B. Determining the original cause for the disorder.
   C. Establishing a single cause-effect relationship.
   D. Understanding historical and contemporary causal factors in relationship to the presented symptoms.
   E. Focusing on contemporary behavioral events.

3. The scientific method adapted for diagnosis requires that the speech-language pathologist:

   A. Bring a problem-solving orientation to the process.
   B. Know all possible testing instruments used in the profession.
   C. Focus on a behavioral description of the disorder.
   D. Emphasize quantitative data.
   E. Adopt a single framework for viewing speech-language disorders.

4. The diagnostic model developed in this chapter:

   A. Is a rigid interpretation of the scientific method.
   B. Allows the speech-language pathologist to focus on different aspects of the diagnostic process.
   C. Emphasizes assessment and testing.
   D. Does not incorporate management and treatment goals.
   E. Emphasizes the technical skills of the speech-language pathologist.

5. The constituent analysis step of the diagnostic process:

   A. Always requires case history information prior to the appointment.
   B. Emphasizes historical information.
   C. Focuses on causation.
   D. Focuses on symptomatology.
   E. Allows for the establishment of a tentative cause-effect relationship.

6.  Which of the following clinical hypotheses would lead to the most specific clinical design?

    A.  John is mentally retarded.
    B.  James' language disorder is related to a maturational delay.
    C.  Bob's semantic disorder interacts with his pragmatic and syntactic problems.
    D.  Alex has a severe language formulation disorder at all language levels stemming from an emotional disturbance.
    E.  Mrs. Smith has Broca's aphasia resulting from a cerebrovascular accident.

7.  Measurement of speech and language disorders implies:

    A.  Only the use of "formal" testing instruments.
    B.  Descriptions of both causal factors and symptoms.
    C.  The use of quantitative data over qualitative data.
    D.  Focus on behavioral description.
    E.  Developing a battery of tests that measure all aspects of speech and language.

8.  During clinical testing the speech-language pathologist:

    A.  Alters his testing strategy as data is collected.
    B.  Adheres exactly to the clinical design.
    C.  Emphasizes interpersonal skills over technical skills.
    D.  Does not introduce new tests into the diagnosis.
    E.  Does not alter the standardized instructions of the tests being used.

9.  Which of the following is not primary to clinical interpretation?

    A.  Integration and synthesis of the constituent analysis information with the clinical testing information.
    B.  Analyzing the clinical testing information.
    C.  Utilization of knowledge of speech and language disorders apart from that collected on the client.
    D.  Determination of the accuracy of the clinical hypothesis.
    E.  Development of a diagnostic statement.

10. Which of the following is a diagnostic statement ?

    A.  Betty has a language disorder.
    B.  Alex has severe hypernasality.
    C.  Bob is mentally retarded.
    D.  Jim's comprehension and formulation disorder is related to his degree of mental retardation.
    E.  Pat's short palate is causing her problem.

11.  Is a diagnosis complete that does not address causation?

12.  What distinctions are drawn when considering historical and contemporary causation?

13.  What are the essential tasks formalized at each step of the diagnostic process?

14.  If a client is referred to determine the effects of a short lingual frenum on speech how would you modify the diagnostic process?

15.  What steps should be taken if the speech-language pathologist does not arrive at a cause-effect relationship at the end of the diagnostic process?

# Chapter 16

# MANAGEMENT OF SPEECH AND LANGUAGE DISORDERS

*James E. Nation*

I. Management Decisions

    A. Definition of <u>management plan</u>: a directed, controlled overall plan of action designed to ameliorate the client's problem.

    B. Decisions based on total set of environmental, social, educational, physical and other circumstances surrounding client.

II. Management Objectives

    A. Objectives rest on three fundamental sources:

        1. Well-reasoned philosophy about rehabilitation.

        2. Must be aware of professional literature.

        3. Must know the specifics of each client's speech and language disorder.

    B. Rehabilitation Philosophy:

        1. Speech pathology does not always have a consistent rehabilitation philosophy to guide decisions about management objectives.

        2. We need clearer focus on management objectives.

        3. Must know:

            a. what speech and language disorders are amenable to change;

            b. the extent of the change that can be expected;

            c. the variables upon which this change is dependent.

        4. Must be aware of specific environmental factors that operate on the learning process.

C. Can the Client Change?

    1. Must predict if each client has the ability to change his speech and language disorder.

    2. Our tools for predicting a client's ability to change are in their infancy.

III. Professional Services Required

    A. Must determine the need for speech pathology services as well as the need for other professional services.

    B. Management of speech and language disorders is generally a long-term process.

IV. Client-Complex Role

    A. Must be sensitive to opinions and preferences of the client-complex:

        1. Personal concerns.

        2. Communicative needs and problems.

        3. Sociocultural concerns.

        4. Aspirations of the client.

    B. Need for the systematic imparting of information to the client-complex members.

V. Implementation

    A. How all aspects of the management plan come together to meet management objectives:

        1. Focuses on the professional who is to monitor the plan.

        2. Use and availability of services.

    B. Roles of the speech pathologist:

        1. Primary manager.

        2. Shared management.

        3. Team management.

        4. Speech pathology is a related service.

C. Must know how to go about obtaining needed professional services:

    1. When a referral is needed.

    2. The referral choice.

    3. How to make the referral.

    4. What to expect from the referral.

VI. Speech Pathology Services

A. State of the art and science of speech pathology is still in need of knowledge, theory and organization.

B. Therapy decisions:

    1. Why therapy is offered.

    2. What therapy is available.

    3. How therapy is done.

C. Therapy principles:

    1. Principles: a rule of action.

    2. Method: an orderly, systematic manner of instruction.

    3. Most therapy methods have developed from a pragmatic, educated trial-and-error framework.

D. Need for a Therapy Model:

    1. Requires that we organize theories, the funds of knowledge, the subject matter into a systematic framework that will allow us to formulate principles of therapy from which methods can be derived and applied:

        a. principles derived from learning theory;

        b. principles inherent to the speech, language and communication processes.

E. How therapy is to be done:

    1. Must determine the most appropriate therapy schedule to accomplish the therapy objectives in the shortest amount of time.

    2. Specific operational goals (long-term or short-term) must be established over time.

3. Techniques and procedures that will accomplish the operational goals must be selected.

4. Progress must be measured and evaluated and goals revised and restated as needed.

5. Must determine when maximum benefit has been derived from therapy; termination criteria must be established.

6. Follow-up of clients to determine if therapy effects are being maintained.

F. The Therapy Process:

1. Therapists are strategists who utilize clinical judgement to make the best decision from limited evidence in the face of uncertain outcomes (Perkins, 1977).

2. Therapist must have "clinical competence", with appropriate <u>technical skills</u>.

3. Interpersonal skills are important because therapy is a reciprocal relationship between client and clinician.

4. Clients perceive the technical skills of the clinician and the interpersonal dimensions as important to therapeutic effectiveness.

## REVIEW QUESTIONS

1. Management of clients with speech and language disorders requires the speech-language pathologist to address a series of issues. Which of the following is not considered a major management issue?

   A. Determination of needed professional services.
   B. Evaluation of the speech-language pathologist's interpersonal skills.
   C. Implementation of the management plan.
   D. Determination of the objectives of the management plan.
   E. Consideration of the role the client-complex will play in management.

2. In establishing management objectives for a 62 year old woman who recently sustained a cerebral vascular accident which of the following should receive the highest priority?

A. The site of the lesion.
B. A rehabilitation framework.
C. The presence of a right hemiplegia.
D. Emotional lability of the client.
E. An understanding of aphasia therapy.

3. A rehabilitation framework is necessary in arriving at appropriate management decisions because:

A. Patients will often need physical and occupational therapy.
B. The client-complex is more concerned about other needs than speech-language services.
C. Speech pathology services may not be the highest priority for professional services.
D. Management objectives are based on answers to a set of complex issues.
E. Some speech and language disorders cannot be changed.

4. Knowing what speech and language disorders can be changed and whether individual patients can change is important if we are to:

A. Implement appropriate professional services.
B. Determine the best treatment schedule.
C. Know what referrals to make.
D. Offer precise prognostic statements.
E. Assist the client-complex through their emotional reactions to the problem.

5. In determining if a 7 year old boy with hypernasality can change his disorder which of the following variables would be most important to consider?

A. Significant academic difficulties.
B. An anterior cross bite.
C. A short lingual frenum.
D. Lives in a foster home.
E. A short palate that otherwise functions adequately.

6. The role of the client-complex in management is essential:

A. If we are to provide the services wanted by the client-complex.
B. To keep the client-complex from rejecting needed services.
C. To determine if they are able to pay for the services.
D. If the management and treatment plans are to be implemented.
E. To determine appropriate referrals for service.

7. In development of a treatment plan for speech-language services the first concern is to:

A. Locate a competent speech-language pathologist.
B. Determine if the client is able to pay for the services.
C. Understand why services are being offered in relation to the management objectives.
D. Have the client-complex obtain a second opinion.
E. Arrive at a method of therapy.

8. The treatment method chosen for each patient's speech-language disorder is only as good as:

    A. The speech-language pathologists' ability to carry it out.
    B. The underlying theoretical orientation and supporting research from which it derives.
    C. The activities and materials that support the method.
    D. The amount of structure inherent in the method.
    E. Its applicability across a wide range of clients.

9. To implement speech and language therapy the competent clinician must:

    A. Not use a method he/she has not used before.
    B. Develop rapport with the client.
    C. Determine within the first session whether the client will respond to the method.
    D. Have a complete understanding of the disorder.
    E. Demonstrate a high level of technical and interpersonal skills.

10. Therapy principles:

    A. Are well established in speech-language pathology.
    B. Cannot be established across all speech-language disorders.
    C. Must be established based upon management objectives.
    D. Are not well established in the profession of speech-language pathology.
    E. Are available that guide the major methods of treatment in our profession.

11. Which of the following causal variables is most crucial in determining if speech and language disorders can be changed?

    A. Biologic abnormality.
    B. Environmental disruption.
    C. Poor interpersonal relations.
    D. Maturational lag.
    E. Age of onset of the disorder.

12. In what circumstances might the speech-language pathologist not be the primary manager of a client with a speech-language disorder?

13. What professional advantages are there to maintaining a conceptual distinction between management and treatment of clients with speech-language disorders?

14. How might clinicians add to the derivation of therapy principles for the profession of speech-language pathology?

15. How can the material in this chapter assist the speech-language pathologist in evaluating his own development of clinical competence?

# Chapter 17

# PHONATION: ASSESSMENT

*Thomas Murry*

I.  Introduction

    A.  Phonation is specialized activity of the larynx.

        1.  Larynx is the organ of phonation.

        2.  Respiratory and phonatory systems act in synchrony to obtain appropriate voice pitch and loudness.

        3.  When voice is abused, a phonatory problem is likely to occur.

        4.  Voice disorders may or may not accompany abnormalities of larynx.

    B.  Voice disorder incidence is on the increase.

        1.  3-5% of school-age children have voice disorders, or 1,750,000 children in U.S.

        2.  5-10% of adult population estimated to have voice disorders.

        3.  Incidence greater in men than in women.

        4.  American Cancer Society indicates laryngeal trauma and malignant lesions are increasing faster in women than in men.

        5.  In 1955, 14 male laryngeal cancer victims for each female; in 1975, ratio changed to 10:1.

II. Model for Assessment

    A. Dysphonia:

        1. Voice disorder that results in abnormal vocal output.

        2. Dysphonia may occur from behavioral dysfunction.

        3. Dysphonia may be due to an organic disorder.

        4. Caused by certain predisposing conditions:

            a. excessive talking;

            b. talking above background noises;

            c. misuse of voice;

            d. environmental pollutants;

            e. anxiety-related stress.

    B. Role of speech pathologist:

        1. Detailed analysis of the physiology of the laryngeal mechanism.

        2. Analyze the behavior of laryngeal mechanism and the patient's general speech/voice production.

        3. Sources of information - case history:

            a. all voice patients need evaluation by speech pathologist and an otolaryngologist prior to initiation of voice therapy;

            b. speech pathologist may be trained to do indirect laryngoscopy to examine vocal folds;

            c. must provide calm, concerned and knowledgeable counseling for patient;

            d. encourage patient to do most talking during initial interview so therapist can evaluate behavioral symptoms during use of normal conversational voice;

            e. obtain diagnostic information according to Moore (1971):

                (1) description of patient's voice and speech;

                (2) history of voice problem;

                (3) assessment of speech and voice mechanism;

(4) audiometric evaluation;

(5) determine need for additional referral;

(6) prepare summary of findings;

(7) determine tentative or specific diagnosis;

(8) written recommendations to be discussed with patient.

f. Boone's (1971) voice evaluation form:

(1) patient's name, date of birth, age, occupation;

(2) description of problem and possible causes;

(3) onset and duration of problem;

(4) variation in consistency of the problem;

(5) description of vocal abuse;

(6) pertinent surgical information;

(7) family voice and speech problems;

(8) previous voice therapy;

(9) general health statements.

g. clinician should also obtain standard voice sample:

(1) name, age, date;

(2) spontaneous speech;

(3) sample of reading;

(4) samples of sustained vocalization.

4. Parameters of the clinical evaluation:

a. areas of specific assessment procedures:

(1) respiratory evaluation;

(2) peripheral oral examination;

(3) phonatory evaluation;

(4) resonance;

(5) loudness;

149

(6) clinical impressions;

(7) summary and recommendations.

b. experienced clinician may prefer open interview format;

c. less experienced clinician may prefer prepared form check-list.

C. Evaluation of Respiration:

1. Important because vocal folds are activated during exhalation.

2. Two measures of respiration function related to vocal phonation:

a. subglottic pressure - difficult to measure since device must be placed below glottis in trachea;

b. as subglottic pressure increases, speaking fundamental frequency increases;

c. mild relationship exists between increases of subglottic pressure and voice intensity;

d. rate of airflow - rate at which air is expelled from oral/nasal cavities during phonation;

e. normal airflow rate for males is approximately 150 cc/sec; normal female airflow rate less than males; children's rate less than adult females;

f. airflow rate measured with pneumotachograph;

g. also measured with wet or dry spirometer: measure volume of air in lungs at start of phonation and volume of air at end of phonation; find difference of volume and divide by time of sustained phonation;

h. high airflow rate usually associated with lack of complete vocal fold closure, such as shown by patients with vocal fold paralysis;

i. spastic dysphonia - characterized by over-adduction of vocal folds - results in lower than normal airflow rate;

j. Hollien (1974) has shown relationships between airflow rates, frequency of phonation, and vocal registers;

k. clinician should observe stability of exhalation and general mode of breathing.

3. <u>Clavicular breathing</u> exhibits prominent shoulder movement and may cause strained exhalation.

4. <u>Abdominal-diaphragmatic</u> breathing shows little activity in upper chest – most activity in lower thorax (ideal breathing posture).

5. <u>Thoracic breathing</u> – most common breathing style – somewhat between other two types of breathing activity.

6. Some patients speak on "residual air" – they do not attempt to speak until most of their air is exhaled; creates strain on vocal mechanism; patient may need referral to pulmonary specialist or neurologist.

D. Structural Observations:

1. Clinician must follow local policy regarding examination of oral and laryngeal structures.

2. Clinicians must be properly trained and experienced to conduct peripheral-oral examination.

   a. begins with exterior organs – face, lips, head and neck; notes breathing style;

   b. observe mouth and oropharynx for malocclusion, dental defects, articulatory defects;

   c. tongue and tongue movement observed;

   d. inspection of vocal folds typically done by otolaryngologist.

E. Assessment of Vocal Production:

1. Frequency or pitch:

   a. easiest parameter of phonation to measure – pitch is a subjective judgement by clinician;

   b. <u>habitual modal pitch level</u> – patient's comfortable pitch level or pitch level he uses most often;

   c. determination of fundamental frequency requires specialized equipment;

   d. <u>phonational range</u> – range of frequencies the patient is able to produce (including falsetto); may extend three octaves;

e. important relationship between phonational range and patient's comfortable level of pitch: optimum voice usage is pitch that is 25-30% above the lowest frequency which can be phonated (Fairbanks, 1960);

f. speaking pitch is a function of sex and age – male and female children have approximately same speaking pitch until age 8 or 9; by age 14 or 15, male voice is about 1 octave lower than that of female through adulthood.

2. Loudness:

a. appropriate vocal loudness is a difficult subjective assessment:

   (1) is overall voice too loud or too soft?

   (2) is there rapid onset or sudden bursts of loudness?

   (3) is patient forcing without loudness?

   (4) are loudness changes smooth?

   (5) does patient show increased tension when loudness changes?

   (6) does change in loudness cause change in voice quality?

b. no accurate method to assess vocal loudness clinically;

c. excessive loudness may lead to a voice problem; voice that is too soft may be due to a voice problem;

d. breathy voice related to failure of vocal folds to approximate correctly;

e. soft voice may be characteristic of certain personality types – not pathological;

f. another cause of a voice that is too soft may be overapproximated vocal folds – as in spastic dysphonia – strained, yet quiet, voice;

g. if vocal loudness is inappropriate for environment, suspect hearing problem – refer for audiogram.

3. Voice Quality:

a. difficult to quantify; no standard terminology to describe voice quality:

(1) <u>breathiness</u> – denotes audible airflow during phonation – similar to whisper; vocal folds fail to approximate correctly owing to unilateral paralysis or asynchronous vibration;

(2) <u>vocal roughness</u> – or "hoarseness"; associated with imagery or huskiness, throatiness, coarseness – or closely allied to harshness or raspy voice; vocal folds are typically not functioning correctly.

  b. Murphy (1964) indicated more than 40 terms used to describe abnormal phonation.

F.  Additional Considerations:

1.  Clinician should describe phonatory disorders in physiological terms supplemented by acoustic descriptions.

2.  Successful voice therapy requires good patient motivation and determination.

3.  Non-organic voice disorders may require psychiatric evaluation prior to recommending voice therapy.

**REVIEW QUESTIONS**

1.  Identify the following statements True (T) or False (F):

  T A.  When the voice is abused by excessive or improper use a phonatory problem may occur.
  T B.  Voice disorders may be present in the larynx with no anatomic anomalies.
  F C.  The laryngeal disorder always precedes the vocal disorder.
  T D.  The laryngeal disorder may be related to the cause of the vocal disorder.
  F E.  The larynx is accessible to easy, direct observation and assessment.

2. The generally accepted incidence of voice disorders is:

   A.  All children _____ to _____%
   B.  School-age children _____ to _____%
   C.  Adults _____ to _____%

3. There is increasing concern that voice disorders are on the increase owing to several predisposing conditions.  Identify 3 such conditions:

   A. _____

   B. _____

   C. _____

4. Moore (1971) describes eight specific types of information which should be obtained during the diagnostic session.  How many of these can you identify?

   A. _____

   B. _____

   C. _____

   D. _____

   E. _____

   F. _____

   G. _____

   H. _____

5. What areas should be evaluated in the assessment process?

   A. _____

   B. _____

   C. _____

   D. _____

   E. _____

6. Fill in the blanks:

   "In general, as subglottic pressure _____,
   speaking fundamental frequency _____.

   "...as subglottic pressure pulse is reduced in amplitude there is a concomitant _____ of vocal fold closure".

   High airflow rates have generally been associated with _____ of complete vocal fold closure.

154

7. Match the following types of breathing with their proper description:

___A. clavicular
___B. abdominal-diaphragmatic
___C. Thoracic breathing

1. Uses very little upper chest and shoulders.
2. Activity exists in lower thorax.
3. Prominent shoulder movement.

8. Put the following into proper sequence of structural observations and examinations:

vocal folds _____
tongue _____
mouth _____
oropharynx _____
malocclusion ___
lips _____
face _____

9. The three aspects of the voice evaluation are:

A. _____

B. _____

C. _____

10. The two key patient characteristics for successful voice therapy are:

A. _____

B. _____

# Chapter 18

# PHONATION: REMEDIATION

*Thomas Murry*

I. Introduction

    A.  Speech pathologist responsible for remediation of voice problems.

    B.  Must have good relationship with patient and allied medical personnel.

    C.  Presence of laryngeal pathology ususally requires medical intervention and voice therapy.

        1.  Vocal polyps or nodules in children usually require voice therapy prior to surgical treatment.

        2.  Goal of treatment is to reduce vocal abuse.

        3.  Fractures of larynx, cysts, structural abnormalities of vocal organs, congenital airway obstructions and growths on vocal folds require surgical care. Surgery often followed by voice therapy.

    D.  Cancer of larynx usually treated with radiation or surgery, followed by esophageal speech instruction or other appropriate training in communication.

    E.  Following surgical correction of vocal apparatus, improvement in vocal fold vibration and glottic closure will increase chance of successful speech therapy.

II. Approaches to Therapy

    A.  Therapist's approach depends on background, level of training, orientation and client rapport.

        1.  Auditory system important for positive reinforcement as patient attempts to imitate a model voice.

2. With adults the use of vocal recordings of prominent speakers as models is worthwhile.

3. Therapist and patient must agree on definitions of "good quality," "pleasant," or "efficient" voice model.

4. Not unusual for a voice disorder to be a single symptom of a more extensive problem:

   a. therapist must approach the voice problem as a problem of self-image;

   b. technique is valuable with children who develop vocal nodules from shouting; the treatment is to change the vocal habits that result in misuse.

5. Ultimate goal of remediation is to alleviate poor vocal habits to develop a clear, efficient, nonabusive voice.

6. Regardless of the type of therapy, a positive approach and strong motivation of patient are essential.

III. Establishing Goals in Therapy

A. Necessary to set realistic goals and plan therapy to achieve desired results.

B. General long-term goals in treatment of all voice disorders:

   1. Improvement in overall communication.

   2. Healthy use of laryngeal structures.

C. Specific long-term goals in treatment of voice disorders:

   1. Improve vocal hygiene.

   2. Reduce sources of vocal abuse and excessive loudness.

   3. Develop easy, relaxed phonation.

   4. Increase stability of respiratory and phonatory systems.

   5. Reduce situational stresses.

   6. Establish appropriate pitch and intonation characteristics.

   7. Improve patient's ability to monitor his vocal output.

D. Goals for each patient must be individualized.

E.  Develop short-term goals for voice disorder patients:

   1.  Auditory recognition skills.

   2.  Kinesthetic feedback skills.

F.  Primary goal for voice disorder patient is to reduce vocal abuse.

   1.  Must control need for excessive throat clearing or coughing with "silent cough".

   2.  Patient must learn to recognize negative environmental influences:

      a. noisy background conditions;

      b. conversational distance;

      c. exposure to dust;

      d. inhalation of certain gases;

      e. smoking control program.

   3.  Excessive vocal loudness is treated directly with exercises for more effective auditory-kinesthetic feedback loop.

      a. loudness may also be controlled by visual monitoring of face for proper mouth opening, forced wrinkles on forehead, or facial grimace.

G.  Vocal Loudness in Children:

   1.  Control of vocal abuse in children centers on reduction of voice usage and reduction of loudness.

   2.  Requires cooperation from family and school teacher.

IV.  Relaxation

A.  Relaxation is an integral part of every voice therapy session.

   1.  Majority of voice disorders result from misuse of vocal folds.

   2.  Hyperfunctional voice means person speaks with excess effort, loudness or force.

3. Goals of relaxation therapy:

   a. change patient's overall activity level;

   b. disassociate environmental stresses from therapy session;

   c. reduce tension in muscles of respiration, phonation and articulation.

4. Relaxation is not a passive activity to provide relief from habitual tension.

5. "Progressive relaxation" requires relaxation of successive muscle groups.

6. Improvement in phonatory parameters, especially vocal onset and vocal roughness; often follows successful program of relaxation.

V. Respiration

A. Brodnitz (1953) feels most voice disorders with hyperfunctional basis result from excessive force or incorrect breathing habits.

B. Physiology for normal phonation:

   1. As vocal folds approximate, air pressure builds up in trachea until it exceeds resistance of the closed folds.

   2. As folds open, air is expelled and subglottic air pressure lowers.

   3. Gravity and elasticity of laryngeal muscles cause folds to close again.

   4. Cycle repeats - as long as the air is expelled, the tone will sound normal in frequency and intensity.

   5. Aperiodicity in the glottal pulses, incomplete closure of the glottis, or asymmetry in vocal fold motion, will create dysphonia.

C. Breathing for speech:

   1. Considerable misunderstanding exists about the type of breathing needed to control respiratory system during speech.

   2. "Deep breathing" with small amount of air is more efficient than inhaling a large amount of air in upper chest cavity only.

3. Maximal inhalation is smooth, abdominally supported, followed by slow, continuous exhalation.

4. According to Eisenson (1974) breathing for speech should:

   a. provide adequate supply of air with least expenditure of energy;

   b. allow for easy control of the expiratory air;

   c. not interfere with the speech utterance.

5. Respiration should be controlled by the abdominal muscles rather than those of the upper rib cage and shoulder girdle.

6. Inhalation should be rapid and free, but not excessive or forced.

7. Exhalation must be smooth and controlled if voice is to function normally.

VI. Phonatory Features

   A. Vocal Pitch:

   1. While hyperfunctional dysphonia may be accompanied by lower voice pitch, not all people with lower pitch have voice disorders.

   2. Clinical judgement of lowered pitch in dysphonia may be confounded by other voice features, i.e., loudness, effort, quality, etc.

   3. Changing pitch to higher frequency may temporarily create straining of the vocal folds.

   4. Increasing pitch may reduce breathiness or hoarseness, but usually at the expense of requiring additional effort.

   5. May be better to work for loudness reduction rather than increase in pitch.

   6. Indications for need of pitch change:

      a. when pitch is so deviant as to cause incorrect judgement of gender;

      b. when phonation occurs at or near vocal fry or falsetto pitch range.

B. Voice Quality:

1. Normal phonation is result of symmetrical vocal fold vibration, closed, opening and closing phases of vocal fold vibration, and a balance between oral and nasal air emission.

2. Goal of vocal rehabilitation is achieved when a clear tone is produced with minimum effort.

C. Hypofunctional Voice Disorders:

1. Defined as dysphonias that result from insufficient vocal fold adduction.

2. Characterized by lack of glottic closure or sluggish, flaccid movement of vocal folds.

3. Disorders include:

   a. paralysis of superior laryngeal nerve;

   b. bowing of vocal cords;

   c. vocal fold paralysis;

   d. multiple sclerosis;

   e. certain psychogenic disorders;

   f. habitual voice disorders.

4. Hypokinetic dysphonia usually accompanied by hypotonicity of laryngeal muscles.

   a. may be due to withdrawn personality trait or atrophic laryngitis.

5. While hypofunction implies lack of complete glottic closure or weak, flaccid vocal fold movement, the patient's overall behavior must be considered.

D. Voice Disorders and Behavior:

1. Necessary to treat voice patient in a holistic manner because voice production is a behavioral manifestation of emotion as well as a series of adjustments of muscles and ligaments.

2. Deviation in voice production is a deviation from normal behavior.

3. Role of therapist is to help patient understand relationships between certain behaviors and voice production.

**REVIEW QUESTIONS**

1. Vocal cord stripping in children is usually deferred as long as possible unless there exists:

   A. Inspiratory stridor.
   B. Heavy snoring.
   C. Interference in respiration.
   D. Shortness of breath.
   E. All of the above.

2. The ultimate goal of the remediation process is to alleviate poor vocal habits in order to:

   A. _____
   B. _____
   C. _____
   D. _____

3. When treatment goals are being established, the therapist should take into account:

   A. _____
   B. _____
   C. _____

4. True or False:

   __ A. It is unusual for a voice disorder to be a single symptom of a more extensive problem.
   __ B. A passive personality is often associated with someone who speaks too loud.
   __ C. Role-playing may be necessary to generate a new image for an improved voice.
   __ D. Positive reinforcement is useful in order to strengthen self-confidence.
   __ E. In many cases, the voice patient suffers from some type of personality maladjustment which causes him to resist vocal change.

5. Specific goals in the treatment of voice disorders may be divided into seven categories:

A. _____

B. _____

C. _____

D. _____

E. _____

F. _____

G. _____

6. How can patient loudness be controlled by visual observation of the face?

_____

_____

_____

7. Hyperfunctional voice usage implies that the patient is speaking with excessive effort, loudness or force. Therefore, it is important to include exercises in _____ during each therapy session.

8. In order to achieve normal phonation, the respiratory and phonation systems must work in concert. Number the following actions in appropriate sequence:

___A. air pressure below vocal folds lowers
___B. air pressure exceeds resistance of closed folds
___C. air is expelled
___D. vocal folds approximate
___E. vocal folds are parted by air pressure
___F. air pressure builds up in trachea
___G. gravity and elasticity causes folds to close again

9. The hypofunctional voice disorder is characterized by:

A. Sluggish, flaccid movement of the vocal folds.
B. High squeaky vocalization.
C. Lack of glottic closure.
D. A, B and C
E. A and C

10. If the therapist suspects an emotional behavior problem which extends beyond the normal relationships between voice and personality, he should:

A. Initiate relaxation therapy.
B. Start intensive therapy immediately.
C. Refer the patient for psychiatric/psychologic assessment.

D. Investigate the patient's family relationships.
E. Create short-term behavioral adjustments.

# Chapter 19

# ASSESSMENT OF RESONANCE DISORDERS

*David P. Kuehn*

I. Disorders in Vocal Shaping

    A. Anatomic defects of the orofacial region.

        1. Congenital:

           a. alters shape or size of structures;

           b. has potential for disrupting the learning of normal resonance patterns.

    B. Congenital Malformations.

        1. Approximately 3% of all children are born with congenital malformation (Warkany, 1978).

        2. Syndromes which include malformations of the cranio-facial region:

           a. Pierre Robin syndrome;

           b. mandibulofacial dysostosis;

           c. Apert syndrome;

           d. Crouzon disease.

        3. Potentially affecting vocal tract resonances are the ones which affect the following:

           a. tongue:

               (1) microglossia;

               (2) macroglossia;

               (3) aglossia;

               (4) ankyloglossia.

b. mouth opening malformations:

    (1) microstomia;

    (2) macrostomia.

c. maxillary and mandibular deformities:

    (1) improper jaw relationships;

    (2) micrognathia;

    (3) abnormal palatal arch configuration and palatal swellings.

d. congenital nasal deformities involving distortions of the nose:

    (1) atresia;

    (2) deviated septum;

    (3) enlarged turbinates;

    (4) adenoids.

C.   Anatomic Defects Acquired after Birth:

    1.   Trauma:

       a. accidentally imposed;

       b. surgically imposed.

    2.   Growth aberrations.

D.   Physiologic defects of the orofacial region.

    1.   Dysarthria and apraxia of speech; Darley et al. (1969a and b, 1975).

    2.   Speech of the deaf; Nickerson (1975) has reviewed characteristics of deaf individuals.

    3.   Nonorganic disorders.

II.   Disorders in Nasal Coupling

    A.   Hypernasality.

    B.   Hyponasality.

    C.   Mixed hyper-hyponasality.

D. Disorders in timing of velopharyngeal closure.

III. Assessment of Resonance Disorders

    A. Perceptual Assessment:

        1. Standard reference:

            a. single listener (clinical evaluations):

                (1) test tools;

                (2) articulation tests;

                (3) test battery.

            b. group evaluation and scaling procedures:

                (1) increases reliability of judgements compared with single-observer situation (Cullinan and Counhan, 1971).

        2. Factors affecting the perception of hypernasality:

            a. phonetic aspects;

            b. pitch level;

            c. loudness level;

            d. articulatory proficiency and overall intelligibility.

    B. Structural Assessment:

        1. Visual inspection:

            a. individual;

            b. group (several examiners may assess structural adequacy in a clinical staffing).

        2. Examination of the speech mechanism is described in an appendix to this chapter prepared by Dr. Sally Peterson-Falzone.

    C. Acoustic Assessment:

        1. Spectrographic Methods:

            a. sound spectrograph (Koenig et al., 1946; Polter et al., 1947);

b. investigators have attempted to identify acoustic correlates of nasality using spectrographic techniques (Joos, 1948; Smith, 1951; Bloomer and Peterson, 1955; Hattori et al., 1958; Dickson, 1962; Hanson, 1964; Ericsson et al., 1973).

2. Acoustic effects of nasal coupling are complex (Funt, 1960; Curtis, 1968).

3. The more prevalent acoustic effects of nasal coupling have been described by Funt (1960), Curtis (1968), and Schwartz (1971).

4. Spectrographic analyses may be utilized for the assessment of resonance disorders other than hypernasality.

D. Linear Predictive Coding:

1. Determines fundamental frequencies as well as format frequencies and their bandwidths.

2. Analyzes speech spectra containing only resonances and not antiresonances.

3. Inexpensive.

4. Effective.

5. Simple.

6. Raw speech waveform is transformed into a simpler smooth spectral waveform.

E. Spectral Comparison Technique:

1. Lindblom et al. (1977) have described a technique for assessing resonance disorders which rests on the basic premise that certain speech sounds are perceptually less distinct than others.

a. determine overall acoustic differences between pairs of acoustic signals.

2. Technique avoids having to identify specific acoustic correlates of a resonance disorder.

3. Inexpensive.

4. Provides a single numerical index of the resonance disorder.

IV.  Nasal Versus Oral Sound Pressure Levels (see Counihan, 1971a, for review of the literature)

   A.  Conventional Methods:

      1.  Insertion of a probe-tube microphone inside the nostril and a second microphone positioned in front of the lips.

      2.  Tonar II (Fletcher, 1970, 1972).

      3.  Accelerometers.

      4.  Ultrasound.

V.  Nonacoustic Instrumental Assessment

   A.  Aerodynamic Methods – Comprehension reviews have been published previously (Lubker, 1970; Warren, 1973, 1975).

      1.  Simple devices:

         a. U-tube manometers;

         b. mirrors;

         c. various blowing devices.

      2.  Oral manometer.

      3.  Flow meters and pressure transducers:

         a. warm-wire anemometer;

         b. pneumotachograph;

         c. pressure transducers.

      4.  Airflow balancing technique:

         a. T-shaped tube.

      5.  Vocal tract damping time.

   B.  Radiographic Methods:

      1.  X-ray procedures:

         a. still x-ray;

         b. tomography;

         c. cinefluorography.

2. Radiographic projections:

   a. lateral;

   b. frontal;

   c. bare.

3. Quantification:

   a. good visualization of the structures of interest;

   b. scaling dimensions.

C. Endoscopic and photoelectric methods:

   1. Nasal endoscope.

   2. Oral panendoscope.

   3. "Nasograph".

   4. "Velograph".

**REVIEW QUESTIONS**

1. An example of a congenital anatomic defect which may lead to a resonance disorder is:

   A. Dysarthria
   B. Apoplexy
   C. Microglossia
   D. Dacryorrhea
   E. Ophryosis

2. Which of the following may render vowel formant frequencies abnormally low?

   A. Ankyloglossia
   B. Cleft palate
   C. Deafness
   D. Microstomia
   E. Nasal atresia

3. Which of the following statements concerning ablative surgery of the face, mouth, and pharynx is true?

   A. In most patients receiving this surgery, speech is rendered totally unintelligible.
   B. Prosthetic devices may help to restore the normal shape and size of a resonance cavity.
   C. Prosthetic devices cannot be used to reclose a resonance chamber.
   D. Unilateral nasal excisions will have no effect on nasal resonances as long as the contralateral nasal cavity is undisturbed.
   E. Ablative surgery of the pharynx is less deleterious for speech than ablative surgery of the oral cavity since fewer formants are affected.

4. A characteristic quality involving abnormal resonatory patterns often is associated with the speech of the deaf. Acoustic studies of the speech of the deaf have indicated which of the following compared with normal?

   A. Lower formant frequencies.
   B. Higher formant frequencies.
   C. Wider spacing between the first and second formant frequencies.
   D. Smaller spacing between the first and second formant frequencies.
   E. Absence of the second formant frequency.

5. Which of the following types of resonance disorders is the most prevalent?

   A. Hypernasality
   B. Hyponasality
   C. Mixed hyper–hyponasality
   D. Dyspnea
   E. Dysgnosia

6. Which of the following would most likely be related to an enlarged adenoid mass?

   A. Distorted fricative consonants.
   B. Distorted stop consonants.
   C. Distorted vowels.
   D. Distorted sibilants.
   E. Distorted nasal consonants.

7. Compared with listener judgements, one of the major advantages of instrumental techniques for assessing resonance disorders is that:

A. Instrumental techniques are more valid.
B. Instrumental techniques can be calibrated to function equivalently in different laboratories or clinics.
C. Instrumental techniques are reliable, whereas listener judgements have been shown to be unreliable.
D. Instrumental techniques are less expensive in the long run.
E. Instrumental techniques are amenable to computer analysis, whereas listener judgements are not.

8. Of the following factors, which is the least likely to affect judgements of nasality?

A. Phonetic aspects.
B. Loudness level.
C. Pitch level.
D. Articulatory precision.
E. Experience of the listener.

9. Spectrographic studies have shown that the most consistent acoustic effect of nasal coupling is:

A. An increase in amplitude of all formants.
B. A reduction in the bandwidth of the first three formants.
C. A lowering of the fundamental frequency.
D. A reduction in amplitude of the first formant.
E. The elimination of antiresonances in the spectrum.

10. Of the following, the major disadvantage in utilizing spectrographic techniques to assess hypernasality is:

A. The sound spectrograph is not readily available because of its extremely high cost.
B. The sound spectrograph must be used only by highly trained technicians.
C. The sound spectrograph is not sensitive in the frequency range in which nasal coupling has its major effect.
D. The sound spectrograph gives spurious results if antiresonances are not present in the acoustic spectrum.
E. The acoustic characteristics of nasalized speech vary both with the speaker and with the speech sound produced.

11. Vibration of the alar cartilage of the nose provides a measure of nasalization. Which of the following devices has been used to record this activity?

A. Strain gauge.
B. "Nasograph".
C. "Velograph".
D. Accelerometer.
E. High-speed photography.

172

12. In relation to resonance disorders, ultrasound has been used most frequently to assess movement of which of the following structures?

   A. Tongue
   B. Lips
   C. Jaw
   D. Pharynx
   E. Larynx

13. The major disadvantage of the pneumotachograph compared with the warm-wire anemometer and the thermistor in measuring nasal and/or oral airflow is:

   A. It requires the use of a mask.
   B. It is insensitive to the direction of airflow.
   C. It is difficult to calibrate.
   D. Its output is nonlinear in the range of speech airflows.
   E. Its risk of producing asphyxiation.

14. The advantage of videofluorography compared with computer assisted tomography (CAT) in assessing resonance disorders is that:

   A. CAT scans are less sensitive to small differences in tissue density.
   B. Structural movements can be recorded using videofluorography but not CAT scans.
   C. Internal structures such as the soft palate cannot be visualized using CAT scans.
   D. Videofluorography provides a clearer image of soft tissue structures.
   E. Videofluorography is not limited by a fixed recording speed.

15. Internal structures may be visualized by using endoscopic as well as radiographic techniques. Compared with endoscopy, radiography has the following major advantages:

   A. Immediate diagnostic information may be provided.
   B. Less expensive.
   C. Quantification of images is easier.
   D. Images more sharply focused.
   E. Less blurring due to rapid movements.

# Chapter 20

# RESONANCE DISORDERS IN STRUCTURAL DEFECTS

*Sally J. Peterson-Falzone*

I. Working Definitions

    A. Hypernasality: the resonance alteration of vowels and voiced consonants which results from:

        1. Abnormal coupling between the oral and nasal cavities, and/or

        2. Increased oral impedance relative to nasal impedance of the resonated airstream.

    B. Nasal Emission: denotes emission of air through the nose during production of pressure consonants.

    C. Hyponasality: resonance alteration resulting from decreased coupling of nasal and oral tracts.

    D. Cul-De-Sac Resonance: the result of air flowing into the nasal cavities but being blocked from escape by obstruction of the nasal passage.

II. Clinical Entities Presenting Structural Hazards to Normal Resonance

    A. Hypertrophic Tonsils and Adenoids.

        1. May result in forward displacement of tongue to maintain a patent airway.

        2. May cause resonance resembling hyponasality or cul-de-sac.

        3. Or hypernasality if the upper poles of the tonsils limit palatal elevation.

4. Inflamed adenoids can result in hyponasality:

   a. surgical removal should be preceded by physical examination to insure adequate palatal length and thickness, pharyngeal depth and velar elevation.

B. Nasal deformities such as nasal polyps or inflamed nasal mucosa may result in hyponasality or cul-de-sac resonance.

   1. Nasal deformities common in cleft lip and palate patients.

C. Ablative surgery defects include partial removal of lips, tongue, mandible, soft and hard palate, maxilla, nose, larynx, etc.

D. Cleft palate often causes disturbances of resonance, phonation, articulation, rate, loudness and pitch.

   1. Hypo and hypernasality and cul-de-sac resonance -- even in combination -- are heard in cleft palate patients.

E. Congenital Palatopharyngeal Incompetency (CPI) is a condition characterized by hypernasality and nasal emission in the absence of an overt cleft.

   1. Inadequacy of palatal length.

   2. Deficiency in bulk of soft palate.

   3. Absent or reduced palatal elevation.

   4. Insufficient motion of pharyngeal walls.

   5. Abnormally large pharyngeal dimensions.

F. Craniofacial Malformation Syndrome may involve abnormal configuration of the supralaryngeal vocal tract and/or incompetency of the velopharyngeal mechanism may cause resonance problems.

III. Responsibilities of the Speech Pathologist

A. Assessment of the speech mechanism and speech itself.

B. Those cases in which a minimal deficit or inconsistent problem may prove remediable through therapy.

C. Teach the patient to maximize use of a physically adequate mechanism.

D.  Minimize the defects of a physically inadequate system.

IV.  Assessing the Etiology of Resonance Problems

    A.  Supplemental procedures may include:

        1.  Multiview videofluoroscopy.

        2.  Oral or nasal endoscopy.

        3.  Ultrasonography.

        4.  Aerodynamic studies.

        5.  Acoustical studies.

    B.  Clinician begins with his eye and ear:

        1.  Examine resonance properties of the patient's voice by exploring changes in the configuration of the vocal tract.

        2.  With minimal or inconsistent nasality, a high-quality tape recording may provide the speaker with his/her initial accurate auditory impression of the problem.

V.  Focal Points of Therapy

    A.  Respiratory and Laryngeal Behavior.

        1.  In the presence of incompetency, increased volume rate of respiratory flow may result in increased nasal emission and hypernasality.

        2.  Some speakers become more nasal when they increase loudness.

        3.  Pitch-intensity relationships in cleft palate speakers varies with vowel sample and speaker sex, so clinicians are advised to explore effects of pitch and vocal effort level in each individual patient.

    B.  Tongue Carriage and Mouth Opening.

        1.  The relationship between tongue position and nasality is not simple:

           a. high tongue position appears to be correlated with increased oral impedance but firmer velopharyngeal closure;

b. low tongue position offers lower impedance but may mean less firm closure;

c. thus, benefits derived from changes in mouth opening and tongue position will be affected by:

(1) size of the velopharyngeal opening;

(2) vocal effort level;

(3) relative nasal impedance to the air stream.

C. Velopharyngeal Mechanism.

1. Focus of concern when:

a. post-op hypernasality persists following adenoidectomy;

b. hypernasality persists following prosthetic or surgical treatment;

c. prosthetic or surgical treatment has resulted in hyponasality.

2. Hypernasality should disappear following surgery within a few days; depending upon the severity of the nasality, additional diagnostic studies should be conducted at one month post-op, and if hypernasality persists for two months, recommend physical management.

3. The patient who presents with persistent post-op hypernasality usually falls into one of two categories:

a. minimal or inconsistent hypernasality, early in the post-treatment period, which may yield to therapy;

b. moderate hypernasality, probably combined with nasal emission, which cannot be altered by further physical management, and is unlikely to be improved with further behavioral therapy.

VI. Behavioral Approaches to Modifying Velopharyngeal Closure

A. Behavioral approaches are undergoing change, but still valuable for patients with minimal deficit or the patient who does not make maximum use of a treated velopharyngeal mechanism.

1. Current behavioral approaches are based on:

a. a physiological similarity in closure for blowing, whistling, and speech;

b. videoendoscopic feedback -- allowing a patient a direct view of his velopharyngeal mechanism in operation.

VII. Orofacial Ablative Surgery

A. Initial concern following orofacial ablative surgery include the negative functions of <u>mastication</u>, <u>sucking</u> and <u>swallowing</u>.

1. Early involvement of the speech pathologist offers dual benefits:

a. gaining the patient's confidence;

b. observation of the altered speech mechanism pre- and post-surgical/prosthetic reconstruction.

2. Types of ablation:

a. ablation of lip:

(1) 25% of oral malignancies;

(2) usually involves lower lip --- pertinent to articulation problems.

b. supramaxillary excisions:

(1) excisions in area of the antrum, ethmoid and nasal cavities should have minor effect on intelligibility and resonance if the maxilla remains intact and the velopharyngeal mechanism functions satisfactorily.

c. maxillectomy:

(1) partial or total removal presents a severe threat to articulation and resonance.

d. ablation of the soft palate:

(1) may destroy points of attachment for the palate on one or both sides;

(2) may affect palatopharyngeal valve function through coincident denervation of palatal muscles;

(3) may have problems due to relative shrinkage and immobilization of the palate through formation of scar tissue.

e. glossectomy:

(1) carcinoma of tongue is the second most frequent form of oral cancer and usually involves both the tongue and floor of mouth;

(2) may require prosthetic tongue.

    f. mandibulectomy:

        (1) usually involves parts or all of tongue as well as varying amounts of the mandible.

3. Prosthetic and surgical rehabilitation.

    a. prosthetic replacement of mandibular structures, including the tongue, is frequently described;

    b. prostheses for maxillary patients are designed to replace missing alveolar and palatal structures and to re-establish the division between oral and nasal cavities;

    c. special efforts are made to attain close fit between the prosthesis and surrounding tissue to preclude leakage of air into nasal cavity during speech.

4. Guidelines for therapy:

    a. therapy usually limited to those patients who are adapting to prosthetic obturation;

    b. if there is little or no motion of the pharyngeal walls on phonation, it is difficult to prevent hypernasality without totally obstructing the nasopharynx;

    c. the speech pathologist should work with the prosthodontist <u>on site</u> in the fitting of a pharyngeal bulb;

    d. therapy should be based on:

        (1) thorough and continuing patient assessment;

        (2) exploration of changes in resonance and intelligibility produced by altering mouth opening, vocal effort level, rate of speech, exaggerated articulation and pitch usage;

        (3) need for the clinician to be honest, sensitive and compassionate in care of such patients.

VIII. Cleft Palate and Congenital Palatopharyngeal Incompetency

   A. Incidence.

      1. Cleft lip and/or palate occurs about 1:1000 live births in Caucasians.

      2. Incidence is double in Mongolian races; halved in blacks.

   B. Ascertainment.

      1. Unlike overt cleft, congenital palatopharyngeal incompetency (CPI) is not discovered until the child begins to talk or until adenoidectomy.

   C. Nomenclature.

      1. Patient may show bifid uvula, muscular diastasis of soft palate, and a submucous defect of hard palate.

      2. However, a person may show any, or all, of these stigmata and not be hypernasal.

   D. Types of Cleft.

      1. Clefts of the primary palate vary from a unilateral or bilateral notch of the lip to a complete unilateral or bilateral cleft extending back to the incisive foramen.

      2. Median or midline clefts of lip and alveolus are extremely rare.

      3. Failure in fusion of the secondary palate varies from a bifid uvula to a complete cleft.

      4. A complete unilateral cleft of the lip and palate combines:

         a. a cleft through the lip and alveolar ridge;

         b. a cleft through the soft palate and portion of the hard palate.

      5. In summary, clefts vary along the four dimensions of complete-incomplete, unilateral-bilateral, anterior to posterior extent, and width.

   E. Types of Congenital Palatopharyngeal Incompetency (CPI).

      1. No agreement on what physical findings should be included in CPI.

2. Some patients present with hypernasality and one or more of the oral stigmata of bifid uvula, submucous defect of the hard palate, and muscular diastasis of the soft palate.

3. Speakers with one or more of the triad of visible stigmata do not necessarily demonstrate incompetency.

4. Some patients present with hypernasal speech in the absence of any visible stigmata.

5. Some normal speakers are in fact CPI speakers, without visible stigmata but with congenitally short palates and/or reduced mobility of the velopharyngeal mechanism.

F. Velopharyngeal Incompetence in Cleft Palate and CPI: Prosthetic Management.

   1. Prosthetic care usually falls into one of four categories:

      a. in an unrepaired cleft, an appliance with a palatal section and a pharyngeal section;

      b. in a repaired cleft, a "palatal plate" resembling an orthodontic retainer;

      c. in case of a short palate, a "speech bulb" or pharyngeal section attached to an anterior supporting structure;

      d. in case of a palate with deficiency in elevation upon phonation, a palatal lift may be used.

G. Velopharyngeal Incompetency in Cleft Palate and CPI: Surgical Treatment.

   1. Surgery is basically of two types:

      a. attempts to bring the pharyngeal wall forward;

      b. a variety of "pharyngeal flaps" designed to reduce the size of the velopharyngeal port.

H. Guidelines for Therapy.

   1. Small percentage of patients do not achieve normal speech following a pharyngeal flap or prosthetic care.

   2. Persistent hypernasality requires repeated consultation between the speech pathologist and surgeon or prosthodontist.

3.  Therapy involves:

    a. instrument monitoring if available;

    b. exploration of changes induced by altering pitch, rate, effort level, mouth opening, etc.;

    c. if hypernasality persists, exploration of further physical management.

IX.  Craniofacial Malformation Syndromes

A.  Background.

    1.  Most craniofacial malformation syndromes vary greatly in expressivity.

    2.  Assessment and treatment of resonance and articulation problems is complicated by associated problems such as hearing loss and mental retardation.

    3.  General knowledge of the syndrome is requisite to intelligent and thorough diagnosis.

B.  Physical Hazards to Resonance Balance in Craniofacial Malformation Syndromes.

    1.  Abnormal laryngeal structure and/or behavior.

    2.  Aberrant supralaryngeal vocal tract.

    3.  Abnormalities in tongue size, mobility or carriage.

    4.  Cleft palate.

    5.  CPI.

C.  Pierre Robin Syndrome.

    1.  Occurs 1:30,000 live births.

    2.  Characterized by mandibular micrognathia which produces in utero, glossoptosis and cleft palate.

    3.  Speech problems include cleft palate considerations and residual velopharyngeal incompetency after palatoplasty.

    4.  Associated defects include hearing loss and possible laryngeal damage consequent to tracheostomy and/or intubation.

D. Mandibular Dysostosis (MFD).

   1. Also known as Treacher-Collins Syndrome.

   2. Includes hypoplasia of the malar bones, antimongoloid slant of palpebral fissures, lower eye lid defects, bilateral malformations of auricle and middle ear, and hypoplasia of the maxilla and mandible.

   3. 30% incidence of cleft palate.

   4. Dramatic range of expressivity.

   5. Hazards to resonance include:

      a. cleft or CPI;

      b. altered tongue posture;

      c. hearing loss;

      d. anomalous supralaryngeal vocal tract;

      e. possible aberrant laryngeal function.

   6. Abnormal resonance is often unremediable in MFD due to problems faced in physical management.

E. Hemifacial Microsomia.

   1. Combines, in varying degrees, hypoplasia of the mandible, maxilla, auricle and middle ear, and sometimes the eye.

   2. Minimal diagnostic criteria are ear abnormalities and hypoplasia of the mandibular condyle and ramus.

   3. Severity of involvement may vary from one structure to another on the same side of the face.

   4. Although the syndrome is unilateral, it can occur in bilateral asymmetric form.

   5. The bony asymmetry of the face is usually accompanied by some degree of muscular asymmetry -- which may be noted in mild cases only in palatal elevation.

   6. Potential threats to resonance include:

      a. hearing loss;

      b. asymmetry of tongue posture and function.

F.  Oral-Facial-Digital Syndrome, Type I (OFD).

1.  Includes broad nasal root, hypoplasia of the malar bones, variable median cleft of the upper lip, and a short philtrum. The hands show a variety of abnormalities including clinodactyly, syndactyly and brachydactyly.

2.  Associated CNS findings include median defects, cysts, hydrocephalus and mental retardation.

3.  Extensive oral findings including multiple buccal frena, multilobulated tongue poorly differentiated from mouth floor, alveolar clefts, "irregular" cleft palate, early loss of teeth, etc.

4.  Hazards to intelligible speech are nearly insurmountable in OFD.

G.  Ectrodactyly-Ectodermal Dysplasia-Cleft (EEC).

1.  Includes lobster claw deformity of the hands and feet, ectodermal dysplasia, and cleft of lip and palate.

2.  Extensive clinical findings -- face is characterized by midface hypoplasia, prominent supraorbital ridges, and typically a bilateral cleft lip and palate.

3.  As in OFD-Type I, palatal repair and secondary pharyngoplasty may produce less than optimal results.

4.  Additional problem is breathy or somewhat hoarse voice.

H.  Apert Syndrome.

1.  Premature closure of several cranial sutures (most often those in the coronal complex) results in a skull which is vertically long but shortened in the anteroposterior dimension.

2.  Hypoplasia of the middle third of face, including the maxilla, contribute in part to exophthalmus and relative prognathism.

3.  Mental retardation of varying severity is commonly associated.

4.  These patients often have syndactyly of the hands and feet.

5.  The combination of a long, thick soft palate and a shallow oropharynx leads to mouth breathing, denasality, and forward carriage of the tongue with minimal palate elevation.

6.  Hazards to normal resonance are many and complex.

I.  Crouzon Disease.

1.  Also known as craniofacial dysostosis involving premature cranial synostosis.

2.  The cranial deformity is similar to that noted in Alpert syndrome.

3.  Similar in symptoms, intellectual development and speech problems as Apert syndrome patients.

4.  Denasality and mouth breathing, velopharyngeal incompetency postoperatively with high incidence of middle ear disease.

J.  Guidelines for Therapy.

1.  Clinician faces a multitude of interacting structural hazards, language function problems, poor intellectual function and emotional factors.

2.  Many of the physical hazards are unremediable.

3.  Carryover of newly learned behavioral therapy depends on patient's own ability to monitor.

4.  Goals and techniques of therapy must be individually adjusted.

## REVIEW QUESTIONS

1.  What would be the most likely effect on resonance in a speaker with velopharyngeal incompetency but bilateral obstruction of the nares?

A.  Cul de sac.
B.  Hypernasality.
C.  Hyponasality.
D.  Alternating hypernasality-denasality.
E.  No effect due to counteraction of velopharyngeal incompetency.

2.   Reports in the literature to date indicate that the success of
     prosthetic obturation in anatomic velopharyngeal deficits
     (e.g., surgical ablation of the soft palate, congenitally short
     soft palate) depends primarily upon:

     A.   Extent of the anatomic deficit.
     B.   Amount of pharyngeal wall motion.
     C.   Articulatory competency prior to fitting of the prosthesis.
     D.   Vertical size of the prosthesis.
     E.   Etiology:  congenital versus acquired defects.

3.   Which of the following is likely to go undetected except by nasal
     endoscopy?

     A.   Webbing of the posterior faucial pillars.
     B.   Bifid uvula.
     C.   Submucous defect of the soft palate.
     D.   Submucous defect of the hard palate.
     E.   Deficiency in bulk of the musculus uvulae.

4.   Pierre Robin includes what type of cleft?

     A.   May be any type.
     B.   Cleft lip only.
     C.   Cleft palate only.
     D.   Unilateral lip and palate.
     E.   Bilateral lip and palate.

5.   A patient with mandibulofacial dysostosis will, in theory, pass
     this syndrome on to what percentage of his or her offspring?

     A.   10%
     B.   25%
     C.   50%
     D.   75%
     E.   Risk unknown

6.   Which two features are likely to be mistakenly diagnosed (e.g.,
     identified as present when they are not) in Apert syndrome?

     A.   Malocclusion and macroglossia.
     B.   Macroglossia and cleft palate.
     C.   Hearing loss and malocclusion.
     D.   Ear deformities and cleft palate.
     E.   Ear deformities and midface hypoplasia.

7.   Which syndrome includes poor differentiation of the tongue from the
     floor of the mouth?

     A.   Ectodermal dysplasia–ectrodactyly–cleft palate (EEC).
     B.   Crouzon disease.
     C.   Mandibulofacial dysostosis.
     D.   Congenital palatopharyngeal incompetency.
     E.   Oral-facial-digital syndrome (OFD), Type I.

8.  Which two syndromes are most likely to include external and middle ear deformities?

    A.  Hemifacial microsomia and mandibulofacial dysostosis.
    B.  Mandibulofacial dysostosis and oral-facial-digital syndrome Type I.
    C.  Ectodermal dysplasia-ectrodactyly-cleft palate (EEC) and hemifacial microsomia.
    D.  Apert and oral-facial-digital syndrome (OFD), Type I.
    E.  Crouzon and ectodermal dysplasia-ectrodactyly-cleft palate (EEC).

9.  In which syndrome are limited oral opening and pharyngeal hypoplasia likely to complicate treatment for velopharyngeal incompetency?

    A.  Apert syndrome.
    B.  Oral-facial-digital syndrome (OFD), Type I.
    C.  Pierre Robin.
    D.  Mandibulofacial dysostosis.
    E.  Congenital palatopharyngeal incompetency.

10.  Which two syndromes fall in the general category of premature cranial synostosis?

    A.  Apert and Crouzon.
    B.  Oral-facial-digital syndrome (OFD), Type I and ectodermal dysplasia-ectrodactyly-cleft palate (EEC).
    C.  Crouzon and Pierre Robin.
    D.  Apert and ectodermal dysplasia-ectrodactyly-cleft palate (EEC).
    E.  Mandibulofacial dysostosis and hemifacial microsomia.

11.  According to the research of Warren and associates, what factors besides actual size of the velopharyngeal port determine nasal airflow?

12.  Explain the term "CPI unmasked by adenoidectomy".

13.  Aerodynamic and perceptual studies suggest one relationship between tongue height and severity of "nasality," while radiographic studies suggest the opposite relationship.  Explain.

14.  What are the anatomic/physiologic (not behavioral) factors which may produce velopharyngeal incompetency in a patient who does not have an overt, unrepaired cleft palate?

15.  What are the causal factors underlying the increased appearance of patients with craniofacial malformation syndromes in our schools, university and hospital clinics, etc.?

# Chapter 21

# REMEDIATION OF IMPAIRED RESONANCE AMONG PATIENTS WITH NEUROPATHOLOGIES OF SPEECH

*J. Douglas Noll*

I.  Vocal Resonance

    A.  <u>Definition</u> – selective reinforcement of certain components of the laryngeal tone due to the acoustic properties of the air-filled cavities in the vocal tract.

        1.  Impairment of vocal resonance can be any condition in which there is an abnormal acoustical signal due to inappropriate modification of the laryngeal tone.

            a. from a clinical point of view – we usually limit the notion of a vocal resonance problem to that of <u>excessive</u> <u>nasality</u> and/or <u>nasal</u> <u>emission</u>.

II. Neuropathologies of Speech

    A.  <u>Definitions</u>:

        1.  If <u>language</u> is disrupted because of a neurologic deficit, then the result is an aphasia.

        2.  If <u>speech</u> is impaired from a neurologic deficit, then the result is a transmission disorder of motor production – a <u>dysarthria</u> or an <u>apraxia</u>.

        3.  <u>Dysarthria</u> is defined as an impairment of the motor functions of speech resulting from lesions of the central or peripheral efferent nervous system.

        4.  <u>Apraxia</u> of speech is a disorder due to impairment of programming articulatory movements – no loss of muscle function, <u>per</u> <u>se</u>.

        5.  <u>Dysarthria</u> results from specific damage to motor nerve tracts.

6. Apraxia of speech is attributed to a cortical lesion of the inferior frontal convolution in the dominant hemisphere.

B. Neuropathologies of speech refers to dysarthria and/or apraxia of speech.

III. Hypernasality as a Feature of Dysarthria

A. Occurs when the nasal cavity is coupled to the vocal tract by means of opening the velopharyngeal port during speech.

1. Some dysarthric patients have velopharyngeal dysfunction due to reduced mobility of the soft palate, and in some patients, hypernasality manifests itself only at specified speaking rates, or during specific variations in phonetic context.

2. Excessive nasality does not appear to be a cardinal feature of apraxia of speech, even though apraxic patients may have difficulty in motor control of their soft palate.

B. Hypernasality is common feature of dysarthric patients with bulbar paralysis:

1. May also occur in disorders such as myasthenia gravis or myotonic dystrophy, or Moebius syndrome.

C. Thus, hypernasality is frequently noted with certain lesions of the motor nerve nuclei in the medulla, of the cranial nerves supplying the velopharyngeal musculature, or the muscles themselves.

D. Hypernasality may also occur from lesions to the upper motor neurons - as in pseudobulbar palsy.

E. But hypernasality is not a distinct problem in all types of neuromotor disorders:

1. Not a problem in ataxia or other types of movement disorders (Parkinson's disease, dystonia, chorea-athetosis).

F. The dysarthric patient is likely to have more than one speech deviation in addition to being hypernasal:

1. Defective articulation.

2. Defective voice quality.

3. Defective speech rate.

IV. Surgical Management

    A. Most common surgical procedure on the velopharyngeal mechanism among dysarthric patients is a <u>pharyngeal flap procedure</u>.

    B. Some question exists about the function of the pharyngeal flap itself during speech:

        1. It may act as a passive band of tissue tethering the soft palate to the posterior pharyngeal wall, thereby constricting the velopharyngeal opening.

        2. The flap may simply occupy space, narrowing the opening through which air can escape into the nasal cavity.

        3. The flap may retain muscle contractility as a functional neuromuscular unit.

    C. Review of surgical reports suggests that any form of surgical treatment of the velopharyngeal system for dysarthric patients is less than totally successful.

        1. It appears that neurologic integrity is probably necessary for any kind of palatopharyngeal surgery to achieve its optimal results.

        2. Have been surgical attempts for direct intervention of the central nervous system to improve neuromuscular control with chronic electrical stimulation of the anterior cerebellum.

V. Prosthetic Management

    A. Use of a palatal lift prosthesis is an appliance to assist in velopharyngeal closure for dysarthric speakers.

        1. Purpose is to elevate the soft palate in an upward and backward direction to approximately the level of the palatal plane – to the position one would expect the velum to take during speech.

        2. Proved to be quite useful in reducing excessive nasality for those speakers who have anatomically normal but physiologically inadequate velopharyngeal system.

    B. The palatal lift prosthesis is better for the dysarthric speaker who has some motor control of the velopharyngeal mechanism than for those dysarthric speakers with severe paralysis of this musculature.

C.  Gonzales and Aronson (1970) report that the palatal lift prosthesis can achieve the following:

   1.  Correct or considerably improve velopharyngeal closure.

   2.  Stimulate the pharyngeal musculature.

   3.  Provide a supportive function until the musculature achieves adequate strength and activity.

VI.  Speech Therapy Principles

   A.  The only way to modify hypernasality problem is to improve the apposition of the soft palate with the pharyngeal walls – regardless of the cause.

      1.  If structural defect is of such a degree that insufficient anatomical tissue exists to accomplish closure – no amount of speech therapy will alter the problem of hypernasality.

      2.  Same situation for patients with severe neuromuscular involvement so that closure cannot be accomplished.

   B.  Goals of direct muscle training activities:

      1.  Bring palatopharyngeal activity to conscious awareness.

      2.  Bring it under voluntary control.

      3.  Develop greater muscle tone and strength.

      4.  Improve range of motion, flexibility and efficiency of movement.

   C.  Some question exists, however, whether direct muscle exercises show any carry-over to speech or result in improved velopharyngeal function or decrease excessive nasality.

      1.  Much disagreement exists as to the usefulness of "non-speech" activities as a therapeutic method in modifying hypernasality.

   D.  The following are examples of various self-monitoring devices used by dysarthric patients as adjuncts in speech therapy to reduce hypernasality.

      1.  TONAR – displays nasal/oral acoustic ratio.

      2.  Speech Indicator – registers the level of vibration.

3. Nasopharyngolaryngofiberoptiscope – videotape system that enables patient to view his own velopharyngeal mechanism during speech.

E. The clinician should encourage and instruct patients to use an open-mouth position with low tongue carriage during all utterances.

   1. Exaggerated oral activity rather than a clenched, tight oral posture should be reinforced.

VII. Conclusions

A. There are few reports on speech therapy specifically for patients with neuromuscular problems of the velopharyngeal system.

B. There is no single therapeutic procedure which is universally recognized as the procedure of choice in working with patients exhibiting hypernasality.

C. Many factors operate to influence whether a patient will improve or not from a therapeutic program:

   1. Patient's age, intelligence, socioeconomic level, and personality characteristics.

   2. Motivation.

   3. Clinician's skill.

   4. Severity and extent of the problem.

   5. Etiology of the disorder.

   6. Clinician's and patient's attitudes toward therapy.

   7. Presence of associated disabilities.

**REVIEW QUESTIONS**

1. What is the usual type of surgical procedure on the velopharyngeal mechanism for dysarthric patients?

   A. Palatal pushback.
   B. Electrical stimulation of the cerebellum.
   C. Surgical manipulation of the tensor palatini muscle.
   D. Pharyngeal wall implants.
   E. Pharyngeal flap.

2. Hypernasality is a common feature of:

   A. Bulbar paralysis.
   B. Apraxia of speech.
   C. Aphasia.
   D. Parkinson's disease.
   E. Ataxic dysarthria.

3. Which type of dysarthric patient would probably benefit most from a palatal lift prosthesis?

   A. One with a flaccid paresis.
   B. One with amyotrophic lateral sclerosis.
   C. One with an upper motor neuron lesion.
   D. One with spasticity of the velopharyngeal system.
   E. One with severe neuromuscular involvement.

4. Myasthenia gravis is a disease of the:

   A. Brain
   B. Neuromuscular juncture
   C. Myelin sheath
   D. Temporal lobe
   E. Spinal cord

5.  Damage to which of the following cranial nerves is most likely
    to result in hypernasality?

    A.  I
    B.  II
    C.  VII
    D.  VIII
    E.  XI

6.  If someone has a minimal velopharyngeal gap, he will tend to
    sound more nasal on which sound?

    A.  /ʃ/
    B.  /i/
    C.  /j/
    D.  /o/
    E.  /r/

7.  Pseudobulbar palsy is a disease of the:

    A.  Upper motor neuron.
    B.  Spinal cord.
    C.  Cranial nerve nuclei.
    D.  Lower motor neuron.
    E.  Musculature.

8.  Coupling and uncoupling of the nasal cavity from the rest of
    the vocal tract is a result of:

    A.  Vocal intensity changes.
    B.  Laryngeal control.
    C.  Muscular atrophy.
    D.  Movements of the velopharyngeal mechanism.
    E.  Positioning of the mandible, lips, and tongue.

9.  The acoustic reinforcement of particular components of the sound
    generated at the larynx by dynamic changes in the shape of the
    vocal tract is referred to as:

    A.  Phonation
    B.  Prosody
    C.  Speech
    D.  Palatal insufficiency
    E.  Resonation

10. The following is a reproduction of Figure 17-25, showing the palatal lift prosthesis. Which portion of the prosthesis is in direct contact with the under-surface of the soft palate?

    A.  1
    B.  2
    C.  3
    D.  4
    E.  No part of the prosthesis touches the soft palate.

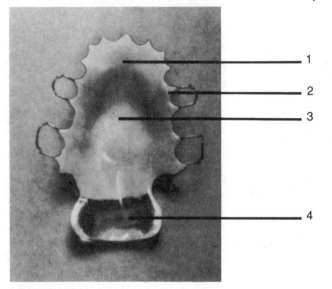

11. The term "bulb" or "bulbar" refers to:

    A.  Cortex
    B.  Medulla
    C.  Axons
    D.  Upper motor neurons
    E.  Muscular dystrophy

12. Give a complete definition of "dysarthria".

13. Differentiate between the probable site of lesion for dysarthria and that for apraxia of speech.

14. What are the probable goals of direct muscle training techniques in therapy for dysarthric patients?

15. One researcher (Misurya) observed that the eustachian tube continues to open regularly in patients with palatal paralysis. How does he explain the phenomenon?

# Chapter 22

# ARTICULATION ASSESSMENT

*Nicholas W. Bankson and John E. Bernthal*

I. Assessment Methodology

    A. Articulation assessment is the almost exclusive domain of the speech pathologist.

    B. Articulation screening – short speech sample is elicited to determine whether or not a detailed articulation assessment is advised.

    C. Articulation assessment should be done with a battery of evaluation instruments.

        1. Speech sound inventory in which picture stimuli are used to elicit consonant productions in initial, medial and final word positions.

        2. Elicitation of spontaneous conversation.

        3. Measure of stimulability (ability to imitate the correct form of error sounds at different levels of complexity).

        4. A systematic sampling of target sounds in various phonetic contexts (deep testing).

    D. Nature of the speech sample(s) used to analyze articulation disorders:

        1. With severe problems, the speech sample may be almost unintelligible.

        2. Child may be reluctant to engage in conversation with an unknown adult.

3. Spontaneous speech seldom contains a representative sample of English phonemes.

4. Because of limitations associated with the spontaneous speech sample, other speech sampling tasks are also used.

E. Speech sound inventories:

1. Usually structured to sample all of the sounds in English language.

2. Using single words to make inferences about performance during connected speech is questionable.

3. Inability to evaluate the effect of coarticulation on speech sound productions with single word utterances.

4. Single production of a stimulus item may not reflect customary phonologic patterns.

5. Syllable structure may affect pronunciation, but stimulus items in speech sound inventories include words which differ in syllable structure.

6. Sound inventories alone do not provide a comprehensive view of articulation status because of:

   a. phonetic context;

   b. syllable structure and stress pattern;

   c. word familiarity.

F. Recording samples:

1. Audio tapes should be routine procedure for permanent record of utterances.

2. Difficult to transcribe sibilants and other high frequency sounds from tape recordings.

G. Scoring Samples:

1. Scoring system varies according to test purpose, transcription skills and personal preference.

2. Traditional scoring method classifies errors as either substitutions, distortions or omissions (SDO).

3. In order to describe speech sound error productions, it is necessary to utilize a speech sound transcription system such as the International Phonetic Alphabet (IPA).

4. "Narrow transcription system" permits more refined details of articulatory productions.

H. Reliability:

1. Accuracy of transcription judgements is determined by comparing independent judgements of one speech clinician with another.

2. Interjudge reliability can be determined by:

a. comparing total number of agreements;

b. comparison of agreement on item-by-item basis.

II. Test Battery

A. Case History:

1. Possible etiologic factors.

2. Family and/or client's perception of problem.

3. The academic/work, home and social environment of the client.

4. Medical, developmental and social history.

B. Hearing, language, voice and fluency screening.

C. Phonetic Inventories:

1. Utilization of standard speech sound inventories has the following advantages:

a. reduces time used in selecting test items, developing test stimuli, and preparing recording forms;

b. lends itself readily for comparisons of data collected;

c. allows comparison of scores with normative data;

d. contains features that are difficult to replicate in self-constructed tests;

e. may include screening items.

2. Four of the most frequently utilized articulation inventories:

a. The Templin-Darley Test of Articulation (1969);

b. The Goldman-Fristoe Test of Articulation (1969);

c. The Fisher-Logemann Test of Articulation Competence (1971);

d. The Arizona Articulation Proficiency Scale (1974).

3. Reading passages are available which include all the phonemes of English:

a. "Rainbow Passage";

b. "My Grandfather".

D. Continuous Speech Samples:

1. Measure of connected speech should be a spontaneous sample.

2. Engage client in conversation about hobbies, TV, travel, etc., and tape record speech samples to be transcribed later.

E. Stimulability Testing:

1. Knowing if phonetic integrity exists for a particular sound, and at what level it exists (i.e., isolation, syllables, words).

2. Important information for planning remediation program.

3. Clinician can make some guesses about future articulatory status if the child can or cannot self-correct sound errors.

F. Phonetic Context Assessment:

1. Need for deep testing based on following premises:

a. that three-position inventories are representative of the location of sounds in written words rather than connected speech;

b. that articulation errors, especially in children, are highly variable and inconsistent.

2. The McDonald Deep Test of Articulation (1946).

3. Sound Production Tasks (Shelton et al., 1967).

4. It is well documented that adjacent sounds influence each other during speech production, and thus, as contexts change, production variability is observed.

G. Oral Peripheral Examination:

1. Observations of the structure and function of the speech mechanism:

a. appearance;

b. symmetry;

c. rate, extent and movement of articulators;

d. dentition is checked for occlusion and missing teeth;

e. hard palate observed for palatal height;

f. soft palate examined for submucous clefts, fissures, mobility, and functional length.

2. Overall motor integrity is assessed by having the client imitate nonsense syllables and tongue movements at varying rates of speed.

3. Medical referral may be in order if the possibility for correction or treatment is available.

H. Auditory Testing:

1. Every client seen for articulation evaluation should also have his hearing tested.

2. Sound speech discrimination testing is also traditional part of the hearing evaluation:

a. Wepman Auditory Discrimination Test (1958);

b. Templin Test of Auditory Discrimination (1957);

c. Goldman-Fristoe-Woodcock Test of Discrimination (1970).

3. Main question is the client's ability to discriminate the correct form of his error sound from other sounds, including the incorrect form.

III. Analysis of Test Data

A. Traditional Analysis Procedures:

1. Clinician notes the level of intelligibility reflected in the client's speech.

a. frequency with which the correct form of the error sound(s) occurs in the language;

b. consistency with which individual sounds are misarticulated;

c. similarity of error production to target sounds.

2. Traditional procedures which analyze sound errors on a sound-by-sound basis.

   a. should include a determination of the consistency of sound errors;

   b. stimulability analysis can look at phonemes on a sound-by-sound basis;

   c. selection of sounds for treatment should focus upon frequently occurring sounds;

   d. compare level of phoneme mastery with chronologic age norms:

      (1) guideline for initiating intervention is that the child is at least one standard deviation below his age norm in number of sounds produced correctly.

   e. must give consideration of "linguistic culture" – language used in the client's environment.

      (1) one cannot use norm data based on general American English for phonologic disability in subcultures;

      (2) one should not assume that subcultures have homogeneous linguistic patterns.

3. Error analysis can be done by reviewing articulation test data to determine the presence of error patterns.

   a. place, voice and manner analysis (Van Riper and Irwin, 1958);

   b. distinctive feature analysis;

   c. phonologic process analysis.

      (1) <u>Phonological Process Analysis Test</u> (Weiner, 1978).

4. Clinician must take into account the special characteristics of the articulatory patterns of certain populations.

1.  It is recommended that articulation evaluation should be accomplished through a battery of tests because:

    A.  The tester wants to check his reliability by using more than one test.
    B.  Different types of information are necessary in order to obtain a more complete picture of a client's articulatory status.
    C.  Articulation tests have their weaknesses and it's best to use more than one.
    D.  Giving only one test is tedious for the client.
    E.  One is more likely to "catch" errors through a battery of tests.

2.  The most important measures of a battery for describing articulation include:

    A.  Voice, articulation, language
    B.  Auditory discrimination, language, articulation
    C.  Sound inventory, conversation, stimulability, contextual
    D.  Oral peripheral, inventory, conversation
    E.  Distinctive features, phonological processes

3.  Samples of continuous speech:

    A.  Are usually impossible to obtain.
    B.  May require follow-up because of the lack of intelligibility.
    C.  May not provide a representative sample of English phonemes.
    D.  Represent the level of articulatory performance of ultimate importance to the clinician.
    E.  B, C, D

4.  The most refined method for "scoring" errors is through:

    A.  Broad transcription.
    B.  Right/Wrong categorization.
    C.  Substitution, distortion, omission categorization.
    D.  Narrow transcription.
    E.  English orthography.

5.  Which of the following is not a reason for utilizing a published test:

    A.  Reduces the time required to select items.
    B.  Lends itself to cross-clinician comparison of data.
    C.  May allow comparison of scores with normative data.
    D.  Contain features difficult to replicate in self-constructed tests.
    E.  Have been demonstrated to be more "accurate" than self-constructed measures.

6. A factor <u>not</u> considered to be important when selecting a sound inventory is:

   A. Sample adequacy.
   B. Number of years the test has been in use.
   C. Normative data.
   D. Material presentation.
   E. Scoring and analysis procedures.

7. Assessing articulation in more than single words is important because:

   A. There is a very low correlation between sound production in single words and running speech.
   B. Speech does not occur in single words.
   C. Single words do not allow for the effects of coarticulation.
   D. Picture naming has proved to be a successful testing technique.
   E. B and C.

8. When analyzing test results, the most important clinical observation for a school age child with multiple sounds in error is:

   A. The number of sounds in error.
   B. The developmental lag in sound productions.
   C. Stimulability.
   D. Patterns among the errors.
   E. The number of omissions.

9. Information reviewed when analyzing test findings includes all but the following:

   A. Case history.
   B. Speech sound discrimination skills.
   C. Language screening.
   D. Hearing acuity.
   E. Handedness.

10. The reliability of one's observations is ultimately important because:

    A. Testing results can't be published without it.
    B. Test manuals suggest one obtain it.
    C. The tester has more confidence in himself when he has good reliability.
    D. Clinical decisions are based on accuracy of the tester's perceptions.
    E. It means the tester has done everything properly.

11. Match each of the articulation tests with an outstanding characteristic:

    __ A. Arizona                1. Variety of sub-tests
    __ B. Templin-Darley         2. Facilitates pattern analysis
    __ C. Fisher-Logemann        3. Large colored pictures
    __ D. Goldman-Fristoe        4. Intelligibility index

12. Match the following analysis procedures with one of the two types of analysis:

   A. Sound by sound analysis ___, ___, ___
   B. Pattern analysis ___, ___, ___

   1. Distinctive Features
   2. Stimulability
   3. Age Comparison
   4. Phonological Process
   5. Place, Manner, Voicing
   6. Consistency

13. What is the purpose of articulation screening?

14. Why are minority group "dialects" not considered articulatory disorders?

15. What are the two important questions that are to be answered based on an articulation evaluation?

   (1)

   (2)

Chapter 23

# ARTICULATION DISORDERS OF UNKNOWN ETIOLOGY AND THEIR REMEDIATION

*Leija V. McReynolds and Mary F. Elbert*

I. Definition of Functional Articulation Disorders

    A. An articulation error traditionally has been defined as <u>omission</u>, <u>substitution</u>, <u>distortion</u> or <u>addition</u> of a sound or sounds.

        1. <u>Functional articulation disorders</u> have no obvious etiological factors present.

    B. Research has studied many variables, but most have not been related to articulation problems.

        1. Perhaps no common factor operates within all articulatory defective individuals.

        2. Factors may be too subtle to be studied with the methods used.

        3. Our methodology may be inadequate.

        4. Maybe the wrong variables were studied for causal relationships.

    C. Variables to be considered in describing articulatory problems:

        1. <u>Articulatory Error Pattern</u> – number of error sounds and type of error.

        2. <u>Stimulability</u> – the difference in ability to imitate sounds and to produce the same sounds spontaneously.

        3. <u>Context</u> – search for specific contexts for individual misarticulating children.

        4. <u>Language and Articulation</u> – articulation cannot be considered apart from the language of a child with an articulation deficit.

5. Speech Sound Discrimination – ability to discriminate error sounds in own production may be a variable in articulation disorders.

D. Functional Articulation Disorders:

1. Functional articulatory problems have no apparent organic basis.

2. "Functional" may be a wastebasket term for articulation problems which seem to arise from unknown causation.

3. "Functional" should carry no inference of either organic or nonorganic cause.

4. McDonald (1964) suggests four possible sources for functional articulation disorders:

   a. certain gross structural problems or severe dysfunction which cannot be successfully counteracted with compensatory abilities;

   b. various combinations of coexistent anomalies or dysfunctions, any one of which would not prevent development of normal articulation, but in combination creates a pattern of detrimental influences;

   c. extended plateaus in the learning of articulatory skills which result in the habituation of immature sensorimotor patterns.

   d. breakdown in the monitoring process which results in the development of inadequate sensorimotor patterns.

5. Multiple variables may be present and responsible for the articulation disorder.

6. The articulation of individuals with organic involvement and that of individuals without organic involvement are not extremely different.

7. The word "functional" added to the term "articulation disorder" adds little except to indicate that etiologic factors are unidentified.

II. Models of Articulation and Articulation Disorders

A. Discrimination Model:

1. Servo-system composed of a source of energy, a motor, a regulator, and a circuit connecting the three in a continuous loop.

2. Regulator scans the acoustic signal produced by the mouth, compares this product with a standard, and modifies the product until it matches the standard.

3. Rationale in treatment is that the articulatory defective individual does not use the feedback he receives to control production automatically.

4. "Ear training" for client is the focus of treatment:

   a. isolated sound level;

   b. sound in syllable level;

   c. sound in word level;

   d. sound in meaningful sentences.

B. Sensorimotor Model:

   1. Articulation is viewed as a sensorimotor skill.

   2. Emphasis is placed on the movements in production;

   3. Information processing and decision-making pertaining to how sounds are produced are important concepts.

   4. Attention to therapy is directed toward sound production rather than sound discrimination.

   5. Automatization is attained when the client produces the sound correctly without deliberate or conscious effort.

C. Operant Conditioning Model:

   1. "Faulty learning" is basis of development of articulation errors.

   2. Proponents acknowledge that identification of the variables responsible for faulty learning is not necessary.

   3. Treatment effort is directed toward specifying procedures necessary to modify articulation.

D. Psychological Models:

   1. Few complete psychological models exist.

   2. Offer the viewpoint of psychoanalytic theory and/or interpersonal relationships.

3.   Initially indirect treatment is offered to help the child appreciate the need to communicate, feel worthwhile and gradually to help him or her be motivated to change speech patterns.

4.   In psychoanalytic theory errors in articulation reflect developmental failures in personality rather than stops in normal maturation of speech articulation.

E.   Phonologic Disorders Model:

1.   Developmentally, children produce errors as they attempt to articulate adult forms.

2.   Similar simplification patterns can be identified in the error production of misarticulating children.

3.   Two training goals:

a. elimination of the simplification processes responsible for the errors;

b. establishing or increasing the number of linguistic contrasts in the child's repertoire.

F.   Diverse Variables Model:

1.   Developed from learning theory, linguistics, child development, verbal learning and studies of physiological and acoustic dimensions of speech.

2.   Articulation errors represent learned behavior, such as approximation efforts before the child's phonetic mastery is complete.

3.   Winitz (1975) divides the learning of articulatory reponses into four principles:

a. discrimination training;

b. production practice;

c. transfer of training;

d. retention.

G.   Most clinicians do not adhere closely to any specific model, electing instead to use an eclectic approach to selecting the best from various theories.

III. Remediation Plans

   A.  Development of a remediation plan demands that articulation
       samples obtained during assessment be scanned to decide
       which procedure will provide the most accurate profile
       of the disorder and which target sounds need training.

   B.  Basic Analysis:

       1.  If the client misarticulates only a few sounds a DSO
           (distortion, substitution, omission) analysis may be
           sufficient.

       2.  The viewpoint of the clinician regarding the nature of
           the functional disorder will also partially determine
           the analyses procedure.

       3.  Examination of articulation errors for consistency,
           stimulability, frequency of occurrence, error type
           and developmental norms is often the only analysis
           applied.

   C.  Place, Voice and Manner Analysis:

       1.  Utilizes a classification system of describing English
           consonant sounds according to the three parameters.

       2.  The advantages of this system of analysis are time
           saving and identification of the more obvious error
           patterns.

       3.  Possible disadvantage is that such a large array of
           error patterns may exist so that no significant specific
           patterns emerge.

   D.  Distinctive Feature Analysis:

       1.  Utilizes linguistic feature systems, and compares
           substituted error productions with targets to determine
           particular features which account for the misarticulations.

       2.  Time consuming analysis.

       3.  Advantage is that training on a feature in a few sounds
           revealed changes across several error phonemes containing
           the feature, thus maximizing efficiency of training.

   E.  Phonologic Process Analysis:

       1.  Identifies the number and consistency of simplification
           processes present in the child's articulation sample.

2. Training is directed toward the process involving the sounds.

3. Assumption is that errors are systematic, and each sound does not have to be taught separately.

4. Disadvantages include large amount of time needed for analysis, and the requirement that the clinician have knowledge concerning linguistics and linguistic analysis procedures.

IV. General Treatment Principles

A. Structured treatment programs are more prevalent than unstructured ones.

1. Selection of the target sound is followed by preparation of a treatment program.

2. Principles of reinforcement operate in all types of treatment programs.

B. Acquisition Training:

1. Training usually involves two phases:

a. imitation;

b. spontaneous production.

2. Correct production is shaped gradually by reinforcement of approximations produced by the child during imitation.

3. Goal is to teach the client to produce a sound and to use the sound in:

a. different phonetic contexts;

b. in utterances of various lengths;

c. in different materials;

d. other environmental settings.

C. Generalization:

1. Generalization is the ultimate goal in treatment.

2. At the unit level, generalization is quite dependable.

3. Transfer at the second level (new materials and situations) has been noted in research studies.

4. Exploration of generalization to the <u>third level</u> (different individuals and settings) has not been extensive.

5. Research in identification of variables that influence generalization is limited.

V. Retrospection

A. Articulation disorders constitute the largest segment in the population of speech disorders.

1. Need for research in remediation procedures and variables related to generalization.

2. Not a simple disorder, but rather, a complex one.

**REVIEW QUESTIONS**

1. Functional articulation problems are caused by:

A. Poor discrimination
B. Motor incoordination
C. Unknown factors
D. Phonological disability
E. Psychological problems

2. A variable with predictive power for prognosis in articulation learning is:

A. Stimulability
B. Oral and facial motor skills
C. Speech sound discrimination
D. Laterality
E. Kinesthetic sensitivity

3. The most useful information for planning articulation remediation can be gained from examining the client's:

   A. Physical status
   B. Related skills
   C. Environment
   D. Articulatory behavior
   E. Mental status

4. In the sensorimotor model of articulation disorders emphasis in treatment is placed on:

   A. Fine motor coordination
   B. Memory skills
   C. Oral stereognosis
   D. Language training
   E. Facial postures

5. Within a phonologic disability model the child is thought to:

   A. Produce adult forms
   B. Use simplification processes
   C. Be unable to use language
   D. Produce syntactic errors
   E. Not exhibit rule governed behavior

6. Reopening the self-hearing circuit is one of the goals in treatment in the:

   A. Phonologic Disorders Model
   B. Psychological Model
   C. Discrimination Model
   D. Operant Conditioning Model
   E. Diverse Variables Model

7. Inconsistent error productions are attributed mainly to:

   A. Poor auditory memory
   B. Motor incoordination
   C. Discrimination problems
   D. Faulty learning
   E. Contextual influences

8. Identification of etiological factors is not important in the:

   A. Sensorimotor Model
   B. Discrimination Model
   C. Phonologic Disorders Model
   D. Psychoanalytic Model
   E. Operant Conditioning Model

9. Phonological processes apply to:

A. A single sound
B. A single feature
C. Sentences
D. Groups of sounds
E. Paragraphs

10. Analysis of the articulation behavior obtained in assessment is completed for the purpose of:

A. Determining the cause of the problem.
B. Selecting the target sound or sounds for treatment.
C. Deciding the length of treatment.
D. Determining the relevance of environmental events to the problem.
E. Determining the presence of a language problem.

11. Relationships between error sounds are best revealed in an analysis based on:

A. Linguistic principles
B. Developmental norms
C. Stimulability
D. Contextual effects
E. Severity and consistency of errors

12. A recent version of a sensorimotor approach to articulation disorders includes:

A. A discrimination component
B. A language component
C. A memory component
D. A decision making component
E. An organizational component

13. Most treatment programs are structured and utilize particularly:

A. Operant learning principles
B. Interpersonal relationships
C. Group training
D. Discrimination learning
E. A natural approach

14. Treatment derived from linguistically based analyses places emphasis on training:

A. One phoneme at a time.
B. Sounds in contexts in which they are produced correctly.
C. Phonemic contrasts.
D. Stimulable sounds.
E. Inconsistently produced sounds.

15. According to research studies generalization is obtained most readily to:

   A. Other settings
   B. Untrained words containing the target sound
   C. Other individuals besides the clinician
   D. Other error sounds
   E. Conversational speech

# Chapter 24

# ARTICULATION DISORDERS IN OROFACIAL ANOMALIES

*Sally Peterson-Falzone*

I.  Clinical Entities Presenting Structural Hazards to Articulation

   A.  Isolated Problems of Single Structures:

       1.  Lips – problems in labial articulation are most often found in:

           a. ablative surgery patients;

           b. facial paresis;

           c. post-op cleft lip.

       2.  Tongue – abnormal lingual structure is usually accompanied by other structural hazards to speech.

           a. lingual frenulum "clipping" is usually unnecessary if proper tongue mobility exists;

           b. "tongue-thrust" – may be found in children in a normal developmental stage between 6 and 9; can coexist with normal speech; "myofunctional therapy" a controversial topic.

       3.  Teeth – good articulation can exist in the presence of severe dental deviations.

       4.  Velopharyngeal mechanism – least "modifiable" of the articulators.

           a. does not provide any appreciable tactile or kinesthetic feedback to the speaker.

5. Ablative surgery defects - each case is a unique combination of problems.

6. Cleft lip and palate and congenital palatopharyngeal incompetency (CPI) have the same possible articulation problems.

7. Craniofacial malformation syndromes - hazards to speech are many:

   a. dental and occlusal anomalies;

   b. aberrant structure or limited tongue mobility;

   c. cleft palate or CPI;

   d. hearing loss;

   e. mental retardation;

   f. learning disabilities;

   g. emotional overlay.

II. Responsibilities of the Speech Pathologist in Dealing with Articulation Problems Associated with Structural Defects

   A. Responsibilities include:

   1. Accurate diagnosis.

   2. Consultation with medical and dental specialists and referral when appropriate.

   3. Selection of appropriate goals for therapy.

   B. Need for continual testing throughout the therapy process.

   C. Pitfalls for the speech pathologist dealing with patients with orofacial anomalies:

   1. Assumption of a one-to-one relationship between structural defect and a given articulation problem.

   2. Effects of nonvisible factors.

   3. Effects of visible facial deformity.

   4. Effects of past defects.

   5. Presumably nonorganic problems.

III. Articulation Problems in Dental and Occlusal Anomalies

    A. Missing teeth:

        1. Research indicates that adjustment to edentulous spaces is highly variable.

        2. Effect of edentulousness on speech and success of prosthetic treatment is dependent upon other factors such as age, hearing acuity, oral health, adjustment to dentures, etc.

    B. Verted and Malpositioned Teeth:

        1. Anomalies of individual tooth position may prevent normal valving contacts of the articulators.

    C. Open Bite:

        1. Most common associated speech problem is interdentalization of the sibilants and possibly the affricatives.

    D. Crossbite:

        1. Extreme crossbite may appear in conjunction with lateral lisp.

        2. Tongue may be in unfavorable position for production of sibilants and affricatives.

    E. Neutroclusion (Angle Class I):

        1. Implies normal molar relationships with anomalies of individual tooth position which may affect articulation.

    F. Distoclusion (Angle Class II, Maxillary Protrusion, Mandibular Retrusion).

    G. Mesioclusion (Angle Class II, Maxillary Retrusion, Mandibular Protrusion).

    H. Guidelines for Therapy:

        1. Relationship between tongue, lip and lower incisors appears to be critical factor in articulation.

        2. Individual adjustments to verted, mixing, or malpositioned teeth and open bite or crossbite vary.

        3. Class II malocclusions are not necessarily associated with defective articulation - except in extreme cases.

        4. Class III malocclusions may coexist with acceptable articulation

IV. Ablative Surgery Defects

  A.  Ablation of the Lip:

      1.  Patient with upper lip ablation may substitute labiodental
          approximations with moderately intelligible speech.

  B.  Maxillectomy:

      1.  Impairs speech by removal of teeth, alveolar ridge and
          the structural division between the oral and nasal
          cavities.

  C.  Ablation of Soft Palate:

      1.  Prosthetic restoration of missing structures results in
          normal speech if adequate pharyngeal wall motion is
          present.

  D.  Mandibulectomy:

      1.  Usually involves partial or total ablation of the tongue.

  E.  Glossectomy:

      1.  Generally, the extent and location of extirpation of
          lingual tissue are the main factors in determining
          postoperative speech ability.

      2.  Needs of the total glossectomy patient include:

          a. rehabilitation of vegetative functions;

          b. compensatory articulation assistance in development
             of gestures;

          c. prosthetic or surgical reconstruction.

      3.  Skelley et al. (1972) indicate that usable gains in
          compensatory articulation require six to eight months
          in total glossectomy cases.

  F.  Guidelines for Therapy:

      1.  Lip ablation patients may develop their own articulatory
          gestures for speech maintenance.

      2.  Rehabilitation for maxillectomy patients is primarily
          prosthetic.

      3.  Rehabilitation for soft palate ablation is also prosthetic.

4.  Partial glossectomy patients may have articulation problems.

5.  Therapy for the total glossectomy patient includes speech, as well as techniques for feeding and control of saliva – may benefit from prosthesis to facilitate "tongue-palate" contact.

6.  "Compensatory physiologic phonetics" is a reasonable goal for partial and total glossectomies.

V.  Cleft Palate and Congenital Palatopharyngeal Incompetence (CPI)

A.  Problems include hypernasality, hyponasality, nasal emission, and maladaptive compensatory articulations.

B.  Extensive literature exists on generalizations regarding the speech problems of these patients.

C.  Etiologic basis for articulation problems:

1.  Repaired cleft lip may be deficient in length and mobility – particularly in bilateral clefts.

2.  Relationships between articulation and dentition cannot be delineated until articulation skills are well advanced.

3.  Recent studies have interpreted aberrant lingual posture or contacts as directly consequent to velopharyngeal incompetency, rather than as a primary defect of the craniofacial complex.

4.  Velopharyngeal incompetency for speech is a primary cause of:

a.  hypernasal resonance;

b.  articulation problems in the form of nasal emission, nasal "snort" or posterior nasal friction and a variety of compensatory maladaptive gestures.

5.  Velopharyngeal incompetency may also affect articulation through:

a.  influence upon tongue posture or movements;

b.  otitis media and fluctuating hearing loss.

D.  Oral Sensory Function:

1.  Research of the 1960's and 1970's represented interest in the role of oral sensory function in the acquisition and maintenance of articulation skills.

2. Some studies of experimentally induced oral sensory deprivation report speech results similar to the articulation characteristics of cleft palate speakers.

3. No data have been reported to date which allow establishment of a cause-effect pattern among the factors of severity of cleft (and/or inadequacy of repair), orosensory deficit and articulation problems.

E. Hearing Loss:

1. Common occurrence of ear disease and hearing loss in children with disruption of the velopharyngeal mechanism.

F. Presumably "Nonorganic":

1. Errors on nonpressure consonants in cleft palate patients are often termed "functional" or "learned".

G. Guidelines for Therapy:

1. Be certain the patient is physically capable of the changes you are asking him to make.

2. Lack of evidence exists to support the use of strengthening exercises for awareness or control of the velopharyngeal mechanism in speech.

3. "Ear training" – Bzoch (1971) indicates the direct teaching of articulatory placement is more appropriate than "ear training".

4. Application of "distinctive features" theory to the analysis of misarticulation in cleft palate patients has received only limited study.

5. Data on "coarticulation" suggest that a target sound in therapy should be practiced in a variety of phonetic contexts.

6. Shelton et al. (1968) pointed out that intelligibility in cleft palate speakers can be increased by:

   a. correct phonetic placement, even in the presence of nasality, omissions, distortions and glottal stops;

   b. light, quick contacts for stops and light, quick constriction of the oral breath flow for fricatives.

7. Use of successive approximations to correct sound production is valuable.

8.  Early language stimulation programs for cleft palate infants.

VI.  Craniofacial Malformation Syndromes

A.  Possible hazards to articulation include:

1.  Cleft palate.

2.  Hearing loss and anomalies of ear.

3.  Maxillary/mandibular disproportions in early childhood.

4.  Glossoptosis in early childhood.

5.  Impaired tongue function.

6.  Limitations in early communication and socialization experiences.

B.  Selected craniofacial malformations and syndromes associated with speech problems:

1.  Mandibular dysostosis.

2.  Hemifacial microsomia.

3.  Oral-facial-digital syndrome, Type I.

4.  Ectrodactyly - ectodermal dysplasia - cleft.

5.  Apert syndrome.

6.  Crouzon disease.

C.  Guidelines for Therapy:

1.  Therapy similar to treatment of articulation problems related to the specific deformity or deviation.

2.  Effects of concomitant ear disease or ear malformation must be considered.

3.  Limitation of intellectual development may be integral to the syndrome.

**REVIEW QUESTIONS**

1.  Angle Class II, Division 1 malocclusion is characterized by:

    A.  Mandibular retrusion with the maxillary incisors in labioversion.
    B.  Mandibular retrusion with the maxillary incisors in linguoversion.
    C.  Mandibular protrusion with the mandibular incisors in labioversion.
    D.  Mandibular protrusion with the mandibular incisors in linguoversion.
    E.  Pseudoprognathism.

2.  From previous studies and from his own research, Starr concluded that the single dental factor most likely to affect articulation was:

    A.  The relationship between the upper and lower incisors.
    B.  The relationship between the upper incisors and the tongue.
    C.  The relationship between the lower incisors and the tongue.
    D.  Alignment of the upper incisors.
    E.  Alignment of the lower incisors.

3.  In case of "total" glossectomy, which muscle may serve to imitate lingual movements?

    A.  Geniohyoid
    B.  Genioglossus
    C.  Glossopharyngeus
    D.  Mylohyoid
    E.  Stylohyoid

4.  According to Fletcher et al. (1961), many children showing concurrent abnormal swallow, speech defects and malocclusion are in a developmental stage between:

    A.  3 to 6 years
    B.  6 to 9 years
    C.  9 to 11 years
    D.  11 to 13 years
    E.  13 to 15 years

5. The fundamental problem in modifying velopharyngeal behavior appears to be:

   A. Insufficient bulk of the levator palati.
   B. Insufficient bulk of the musculus uvulae.
   C. Insufficient bulk of the palatopharyngeus.
   D. Insufficient efferent innervation.
   E. Insufficient kinesthetic feedback.

6. "Buccal crossbite" refers to a dental relationship in which:

   A. The maxillary incisors are distal to the mandibular incisors.
   B. The maxillary incisors are medial to the mandibular incisors.
   C. The maxillary first molar is distal to the mandibular first molar.
   D. The maxillary first molar is medial to the mandibular first molar.
   E. The maxillary third molar is medial to the mandibular third molar.

7. Articulation in the patient with velopharyngeal incompetency tends to be shifted:

   A. Superiorly
   B. Inferiorly
   C. Anteriorly
   D. Posteriorly
   E. Laterally

8. Research of Warren and associates has indicated what size velopharyngeal opening as the critical difference between competency and incompetency for speech?

   A. $.02 \text{ cm}^2$
   B. $.10 \text{ cm}^2$
   C. $.20 \text{ cm}^2$
   D. $.50 \text{ cm}^2$
   E. $1.00 \text{ cm}^2$

9. In general, what appears to be the major deciding factor in adequacy of speech production in a patient with a cleft palate?

   A. Type of cleft.
   B. Width of cleft.
   C. Age at which the cleft was closed.
   D. Presence or absence of velopharyngeal closure.
   E. Presence or absence of dental/occlusal hazards to speech.

10. Which articulatory gesture tends to sound equally like a /t/ and a /k/?

    A. Glottal stop
    B. Mid-dorsum palatal stop
    C. Pharyngeal stop
    D. Labio-lingual stop
    E. Tip-alveolar stop

# Chapter 25

# ARTICULATION AND HEARING IMPAIRMENT

*Donald R. Calvert*

I. Observations Relating Hearing and Speech

    A. As hearing loss increases, one of the initial deficits to occur involves information about the place and manner of articulating consonants.

        1. As severity of loss further increases, information is reduced concerning the voice and rhythm of speech.

    B. Delayed Auditory Feedback: the serious interruption of articulation and the flow of connected speech occurs when speech is delayed by .2 seconds and fed into the speaker's ears.

    C. Lombard effect: when background noise is increased in loudness, a speaker automatically increases the volume of his voice proportionally to hear it over the masking noise.

    D. Paracusis Willisi: decrease in voice volume when background noise at the usual level is blocked from entering the ear (reverse phenomenon from the Lombard effect).

        1. Under normal circumstances we monitor our own voices by air conduction and bone-conduction hearing pathways.

    E. Age-related hearing loss – the older a child is when he loses hearing, the better his speech is likely to remain.

    F. Audiometric configuration: the flatter the audiogram, and the broader the residual frequency sensitivity, the better his speech is likely to be.

        1. Higher incidence of minor articulation deviations is noted in individuals with pre-lingual unilateral hearing loss.

II. Influence of Voice, Rhythm and Language on Articulation

A. Voice - "deaf voice" has been described as tense, flat, breathy, harsh and throaty.

1. Judgements about "deaf voice" probably depend heavily on articulatory information.

B. Rhythm:

1. Severe congenital hearing loss seriously impairs control of the rhythm features of speech - which in turn adversely affect articulation.

2. Abnormal use of stress for accent also influences articulation.

3. Normal phrasing, which groups words together as units of meaning, may be disrupted in deaf speakers.

C. Language:

1. Deaf persons deprived of opportunity to hear the spoken language of others with sufficient regularity to learn syntax and semantics.

III. Misarticulations of Prelingually Severely Deaf

A. Following variables contribute to a deaf person's accuracy in articulation:

1. Degree and type of hearing loss.

2. Use of amplification.

3. Facility with rapid, synergistic movements necessary for articulation.

4. Ability to use oral, tactile and kinesthetic feedback for monitoring speech.

5. Interference by abnormal voice quality, irregular speech rhythm and deficient language.

6. Teaching methods used to develop, improve and maintain speech.

7. Reinforcement and opportunity to use speech.

B. Errors of articulation of deaf children are not limited to production of individual phonemes; they can occur because of the phonetic context in which the phonemes are embedded.

C. Errors of Omission:

1. The /s/ sound ranks low in visibility and internal feedback and is a prominent deviation in the speech of the adult whose hearing is failing.

2. Omission of final consonants is a common error because of:

    a. reduced force of articulation on final consonants;

    b. lack of coarticulation effect on preceding vowels;

    c. abnormal duration of preceding vowels in relation to final consonants.

D. Errors of Substitution:

1. Error is really distorted production of intended consonants, but heard by the listener as a substituted consonant.

2. Typical error of deaf speakers is the "surd- sonant," or substitution of sounds which have the same place of articulation but differ in the voiced-voiceless feature due to:

    a. inadequate coordination of voicing and articulation;

    b. inappropriate force of articulation causing duration distortion of the consonant;

    c. distortion of the duration of vowels preceding consonants.

3. Nasal consonant may be substituted for its oral cognate.

4. A sound may be substituted because it provides more perceivable tactile and kinesthetic feedback.

5. Substitution of vowels is caused largely by imprecision in the fine movements of the mouth opening, rounding of lips, place or height of tongue.

E. Errors of Distortion:

1. Degree of force - too little force gives the listener short duration and reduced intensity; too much force gives the listener abnormally long duration and increased intensity.

2. Hypernasality - deaf speakers who have difficulty with the fine coordination of rapid, oral-nasal resonance changes in connected speech produce hypernasal sounds.

3.  Imprecision and indefiniteness – deaf speakers may be slightly off target with production of certain vowels, particularly those with low kinesthetic feedback.

4.  Duration of vowels – the duration of vowels in connected speech should vary according to context; deaf speakers tend to produce vowels with undifferentiated duration (usually excess duration).

5.  Temporal values in diphthongs – diphthongs combine two continuously phonated vowels with the first portion (the nucleus) longer than the second (the glide); deaf speakers tend to make the second portion longer than it needs to be.

F.  Errors of Addition:

1.  Deaf speakers may insert a superfluous vowel between consonants that gives the listener a misleading syllabic cue.

2.  Unnecessary release of final stop consonants.

3.  Diphthongization of vowels giving rise to what appears to be a bisyllabic utterance.

4.  Superfluous breath before a vowel so that listener perceives the added aspiration as /h/ sound.

IV.  Misarticulations of the Postlingually Deafened

A.  Defects of articulation are usually the first change in speech for postlingually deafened individuals.

B.  Distortion or omission is typical of speech sounds characterized by low intensities and high frequency.

C.  Consonants in final position in words are particularly vulnerable to erosion – they are usually produced with less force so that the tactile and kinesthetic pattern is not strong.

V.  The Congenitally Hard of Hearing

A.  This population is very heterogeneous.

B.  Effective production of certain sounds may plague the hard of hearing person throughout his life.

C. Cause of misarticulations in this population is three-fold:

    1. Hard of hearing person is liable to hear from others a distorted auditory pattern to associate with phonemes.

    2. His hearing loss reduces the number of examples of the sound he will perceive from the speech of others.

    3. Pattern of total speech feedback may give him inaccurate or inadequate information for monitoring his articulation.

VI. Implications for Assessment

A. Articulation of deaf persons should never be assessed as an independent feature.

    1. Scales and tests used for articulation of normal hearing persons are usually inadequate for use with the deaf.

    2. Need to look at deaf speech assessment as follows:

        a. articulation and other speech skills;

        b. intelligibility;

        c. speech usage.

    3. Measurement of speech intelligibility must consider:

        a. the listener;

        b. the material;

        c. the context.

VII. Speech Conservation and Insurance

A. The best technique to use for avoiding deterioration of speech patterns, established prior to loss of hearing, is to work to prevent the deterioration that is liable to occur.

B. When partial hearing loss occurs, techniques necessary to achieve speech conservation depend on the degree and pattern of hearing impairment.

    1. Exploiting use of auditory amplification for control of speech.

C. When hearing loss is complete, or nearly so, speech work must depend on learning to use tactile and kinesthetic cues for speech feedback.

1. Speech conservation should be part of a total aural rehabilitation approach.

VIII. Methods of Articulation Development for Deaf Children

A. The Auditory Global Method:

1. Principal feature is that the channel for speech development is auditory and the input is fluent connected speech.

2. Also known as "auditory-oral," "aural-oral," "acoupedic" and "unisensory".

3. Essential characteristics of this method:

a. maximum emphasis on early and consistent use of hearing;

b. comprehensive intervention toward developing speech;

c. emphasis on connected speech.

4. Correction of speech errors is always attempted first through the auditory channel.

B. The Multisensory Syllable Unit Method:

1. Distinctive characteristics of this approach:

a. multisensory stimulation for speech;

b. focus on development of articulating speech sounds;

c. the syllable is the basic unit for speech instruction.

2. Progression follows babbled syllables at the phonetic level, putting sounds into syllable-unit drills, then advancing to the phonological level to connect articulation to meaning.

C. The Association Phoneme Unit Method:

1. Technique developed for children who were not learning to talk with other methods.

2. Distinctive characteristics of method:

a. speech production is associated with other language modalitie

b. the phoneme is the basic unit of instruction;

c. speech development progresses in small increments;

3. Basic to this method is the concept that speech perception is strongly influenced by speech production.

1. The following class of speech sounds is especially vulnerable to deterioration in the articulation of a post-lingually deafened person:

   A. Stop consonants
   B. Front vowels
   C. Final consonants
   D. Diphthongs
   E. Initial consonants

2. Articulation errors of substitution by congenitally hearing-impaired children are most likely to occur because the child:

   A. Has not yet learned the correct sound.
   B. Talks too fast.
   C. Mistakenly confuses the substituted sound for the intended sound.
   D. Doesn't know how the word is correctly spelled.
   E. Distorts the intended sound so that listeners judge it to be another sound.

3. The following group of phonemes is most likely to be misarticulated by hearing-impaired persons:

   A. [p b m]
   B. [s ʃ tʃ ]
   C. [u i a ]
   D. [m n ŋ ]
   E. [f v θ ʒ ]

4. A common vowel substitution by severely hearing-impaired children is the following:

   A. [ɪ [ for [ i ]
   B. [ æ ] for [ u ]
   C. [ u ] for [ i ]
   D. [ ʌ ] for [ æ ]
   E. [ ɔ ] for [ ɛ ]

5. The following statement best describes congenitally hard of hearing children:

   A. They are usually educated in regular school classes.
   B. They have significant impairment of language.
   C. They have normal articulation if they use acoustic amplification.
   D. They are an extremely heterogeneous group.
   E. They have a "U" shaped audiogram.

6. The following statements describe why the usual tests of articulation developed for children with normal hearing are not likely to be appropriate for severely hearing-impaired children EXCEPT:

   A. The tests do not take into account the influence of language ability on judgements of articulation.
   B. The tests do not take into account the influence of speech rhythm on judgements of articulation.
   C. The tests do not include a number of errors of articulation commonly made by severely hearing-impaired children.
   D. The tests do not take into account the influence of voice quality on judgements of articulation.
   E. The tests are not familiar to teachers of severely hearing-impaired children.

7. The following statements are applicable to the speech of hearing-impaired persons EXCEPT:

   A. The speech problems of prelingually deaf children, post-lingually deafened adults, and congenitally hard of hearing persons are different not only in degree but in kind.
   B. Even if articulation is very good, a deaf child's speech may be hard to understand because of other problems.
   C. Judgements about "deaf voice" quality are likely to be based on spectral information concerning fundamental frequency and resonance of vowel sounds.
   D. The broader the frequency range of hearing and the flatter the audiogram, the better a hearing-impaired person's speech is likely to be.
   E. Conscious development of tactile-kinesthetic control over articulation can help maintain speech for a person with progressive hearing loss.

8. In considering the teaching of speech to severely deaf children:

   A. Different methods of teaching speech should be selected according to each child's abilities.
   B. Speech should be taught in special speech clinics.
   C. If an oral-aural approach is not successful, the child will not be able to learn to speak.
   D. There is a single best method of teaching available.
   E. The effort is futile if everyone does not understand the child's speech.

9.  The following observations relating hearing loss and speech can be made EXCEPT:

    A.  Use of hearing aids helps a person with decreasing hearing maintain his speech.
    B.  The better the child's hearing level, the better his speech is likely to be and the easier to develop.
    C.  Use of hearing aids helps a deaf child develop, improve, and maintain speech.
    D.  A child born severely or profoundly deaf cannot learn to speak.
    E.  The child with mild to moderate hearing loss will have speech deviations primarily of articulation.

10. When a person experiences a sudden, complete, post-lingual hearing loss:

    A.  He will not develop normal language.
    B.  Professional intervention should begin immediately.
    C.  His speech will not deteriorate for many years if he continues talking.
    D.  His speech will deteriorate immediately.
    E.  He should have professional intervention in a year or so.

# Chapter 26

# PROSODY IN PERCEPTION, PRODUCTION, AND PATHOLOGIES

*Frances Jackson Freeman*

I. Every major category of disordered speech is characterized by some degree of disrupted prosody.

    A. Prosodic Disorders include:

        1. Stuttering.

        2. Cluttering.

        3. Speech of deaf.

        4. All of the dysarthrias.

        5. Speech apraxia.

        6. Some language disorders.

    B. Successful treatment methods are infrequent in the literature.

        1. We tend to hold the view that prosody functions only to make speech more aesthetically pleasing.

        2. However, prosody is <u>intrinsic</u> and <u>critical</u> in both perception and production of speech.

II. Background

    A. Previous lack of substantive research in this area.

    B. 1980's will be characterized by expansion of our knowledge of suprasegmental features of speech.

    C. Any critical aspect of the speech and language process (including prosody) should be considered both in production and perception of the acoustic signal.

D. Human listeners are normally not aware of the complexity of the transformation of acoustic signals into a speech-language coding system.

E. Three assumptions are basic to current speech information processing models:

1. Perception is not immediate but results from direct operations distributed over time.

2. There are "capacity limitations" at various stages during the processing.

3. Perception necessarily involves various types of memorial processes.

F. Most models of speech perception describe at least four stages of processing:

1. Auditory analysis.

2. Phonological analysis.

3. Syntactic analysis.

4. Semantic analysis.

G. Role of prosody.

1. May serve as the interface between low-level segmental information and higher levels of grammatical structure in speech.

2. Carries direct phonetic cues to certain semantic and grammatical classes.

a. prosody information may be additive to the information processing;

b. may influence the allocation of processing capacity in terms of power, temporal location and duration.

3. Thus, reduced prosody may significantly reduce processing efficiency.

H. Current investigations suggest two interrelated ways in which prosody may function:

1. "Chunking" or "parsing" - divides the incoming flow of speech into coherent auditory structures suitable for further processing.

2. "Predictive device" to allow the listener to anticipate arrival of potentially important speech material.

III. Prosodic Features

A. The terms "prosodic features" and "suprasegmental features" are herein used to refer to speech events that are of longer duration than segmental events.

B. The Acoustical Level.

1. Fundamental <u>frequency</u> and <u>intensity</u> are closely related to the perceptions of <u>pitch</u> and <u>loudness</u>.

2. $F_o$ (fundamental frequency) is determined by glottal state and transglottal pressure differential:

a. vibration rate can be altered by:

(1) increasing or decreasing vocal fold tension;

(2) increasing or decreasing subglottal air pressures;

(3) increasing or decreasing supraglottal air pressures.

3. Intensity is determined by subglottal air pressure and degree of constriction and length of the subglottal vocal tract.

4. While some speakers vary $F_o$ and Intensity independently, the tendency is for one parameter change to alter the other parameter.

5. <u>Duration</u> of brief signals can alter the perceived loudness.

6. $F_o$ is a stronger cue than intensity.

7. Another important acoustic cue is "temporal spacing of acoustic events":

a. brief timing differences are relevant to the perception of voicing, place and manner.

8. Most current research in the time domain has focused on <u>duration</u> and <u>rate</u> measurement and their exceedingly <u>complex</u> relationship.

9. Many factors influence segment durations:

a. semantic factors;

b. syntactic factors;

c. stress;

d. word and utterance length;

e. phonetic factors.

10. "Temporal compensation" is hypothesized as a means of achieving approximately equal temporal spacing between stressed syllables even though the intervening syllables are composed of segments of differing lengths.

11. Important to note that real-time durations and rates are not equivalent to perceived durations and perceived rates.

C. The Perceptual Level.

1. Prosodic features are linguistic abstractions that exist in the mind of the competent speaker-listener.

2. Prosodic features are essentially perception of patterns.

3. Specific events directly cue some prosodic features.

4. Acoustic events may cue perceptions - and the variations in these percepts give rise to the perception of prosodic features.

5. Intonation is the perceived patterned rise and fall of pitch over linguistic units.

6. Stress is the perception of some linguistic unit as emphasized or prominent in contrast to surrounding units.

a. stressed or accented syllables are perceived as louder, longer and higher in pitch than unstressed syllables.

7. Prosodic rhythm may be defined as the perception of a patterned time program underlying sequences of speech.

8. Our perceptions of tempo and rhythm, as well as stress, are directly linked to perception of segment duration.

9. Juncture plays a prominent role in written language - as spaces and marks of punctuation.

a. the percept of word juncture has been found to be dependent in large part on segmental acoustic cues - such as the perception of a pause (silent period in the acoustic signal).

IV.  Functions of Prosody

    A.  Integration and Segementation.

        1.  The perceptual system must be able to:

            a. integrate related events into a single perceptual whole or unit and;

            b. segment meaningfully related units from the continuous flow of events.

    B.  Whether one stimulus will be integrated with another depends on:

        1.  The intervening interval.

        2.  Similarity of the stimulus.

        3.  Whether the nature of the task requires that they be integrated

    C.  Silent intervals play a critical role in determining whether acoustic events will be integrated or separated.

    D.  The breath group is a physiologically based universal organizational unit in speech production.

    E.  The "word" is, in fact, a natural linguistic unit.

        1.  Stress pattern and rhythm of speech are used as primary prosodic cues for word perception.

        2.  Anticipation or Expectancy.

            a. words excised from fluent speech are significantly less intelligible than words spoken in isolation;

            b. it is hypothesized that when a listener hears the first portion of an utterance he begins generating expectancies based on prosodic features;

            c. prosodic features are also useful for generating expectancies about the length or form of an utterance.

        3.  Developmental Functions of Prosody:

            a. children learn and produce intonation patterns of the input language during the first year of life;

            b. speech addressed to infants and young children differs from that addressed to older children and adults;

            c. "special speech routines", that involve definite rhythmic structure, are found in all cultures in interactions with babies;

d. speakers also modify prosodic patterns in speech addressed to individuals they perceive as limited in comprehension.

4. Hemispheric Specialization in Prosody:

a. in recent years, neurolinguists have suggested that the right hemisphere may have specialized functions in speech perception and production.

V. Clinical Consideration of Prosody

A. Perception of Suprasegmentals.

1. We know almost nothing about how individuals with "speech processing" disorders use, or fail to use, prosodic cues in message decoding.

2. If we do not know how to evaluate competence in perception of suprasegmental features, we are far from developing treatment strategies.

B. Production of Suprasegmentals.

1. We have no standardized tests for appraisal of suprasegmental production.

2. Acoustic analyses offer a means for increasing our understanding both of pathological conditions and of individual clients.

3. Kent (1979) describes 3 types of prosodic disturbance including:

a. hyperprosody – excessive or exaggerated prosody;

b. dysprosody – distorted prosody – noted in cerebellar ataxia, aphasia and speech apraxia;

(1) three patterns of dysprosody:

sweeping – exaggerated $F_o$ glides

scanning – marked dissociation of syllables in time

blurring – short rushed syllables with monotone $F_o$ and tendency toward continuous voicing

c. aprosody – attenuation, reduction or lack of normal prosody – Parkinson patients and right hemisphere lesion patients.

## REVIEW QUESTIONS

1. Identify the four stages of processing included in most models of speech perception:

   A. _____

   B. _____

   C. _____

   D. _____

2. The acoustic cues for prosodic features which have received the most research attention are:

   A. _____

   B. _____

   C. _____

3. The acoustic cues of fundamental frequency ($F_o$) and intensity have been experimentally demonstrated to be closely related to perceptions of _____ and _____.

4. Timing differences as brief as _____ to _____ msec are relevant and significant cues to the perception of voicing, place and manner features in some contexts.

5. Identify five factors that are known to influence segmental durations:

   A. _____

   B. _____

   C. _____

   D. _____

   E. _____

6. The perceived patterned rise and fall of pitch over linguistic units is the critical prosodic feature known as _____.

7. Huggins (1974, 1975, 1977) has discussed the basic principles underlying the perceptual integration of successive events. Whether one stimulus will be integrated with another depends on which three of the following factors?

   A. Word content
   B. Intervening interval
   C. Similarity of stimulus
   D. Nature of the task
   E. Unnatural processors

8. Studies indicate that prosodic features are used to generate expectancies about the arrival time of acoustic events, as well as generating expectancies about the _____ and _____ of an utterance.

9. True or False:

   __ Normal neonates 24 hours old respond to heard speech rhythms by synchronizing their movements to those speech rhythms.
   __ Infants between 1 and 2 days of age discriminate between rising and falling speech intonation patterns.
   __ Children between the ages of 3 and 8 years are generally unable to produce and make perceptual use of temporal cues in speech.

10. Align the following disorders with the appropriate category or prosodic disturbance:

    __ (1) ataxic dysarthria
    __ (2) speech apraxia
    __ (3) Parkinson syndrome
    __ (4) manic state
    __ (5) right hemisphere lesion
    __ (6) aphasia
    __ (7) cerebellar ataxia
    __ (8) drunk speech

    A. hyperprosody
    B. dysprosody
    C. sweeping
    D. scanning
    E. blurring
    F. aprosody

241

# Chapter 27

# STUTTERING

*Frances Jackson Freeman*

I.  Introduction

    A.  Van Riper (1974) described stuttering as the most fascinating and the most frustrating of the communicative disorders.

    B.  Literature on stuttering dates back 20 centuries of accumulated "theories" of stuttering.

        1.  Hebrew writers viewed stuttering as a punishment or testing imposed by God.

        2.  Greeks, Romans perceived stuttering as a result from a humoral imbalance of four elements -- heat, cold, moisture, and dryness.

        3.  Victorian England viewed stuttering as the result of a weak or diseased morality.

        4.  Modern medical sciences developed biochemical and/or neurophysiologic theories of stuttering.

        5.  Freudian theory was applied to stuttering; a number of intriguing psychoanalytic theories resulted.

        6.  Korzybiski (1933), Sapir (1921), and Whorf (1956), altered Wendall Johnson's (1946, 1958) perception of the world and led to his semantogenic theory of stuttering.

        7.  Pavlov (1927), Thorndike (1898), and Skinner (1938) viewed stuttering as "behavior" and therapy as "modification".

II. Fluency, Dysfluency, and Stuttering.

    A. Two views regarding the relationship between fluency, dysfluency, and stuttering.

        1. Individual speakers rank somewhere between very fluent and severe stutterers.

        2. Two discrete groups: normal speakers and stutterers.

    B. Types of dysfluencies:

        1. Voelker (1944), Boehmler (1958), Williams and Kent (1958) and Johnson (1961) have demonstrated that the types of dysfluencies associated with stuttering are syllable or sound repetitions, sound prolongations, and broken words.

        2. Interjections, word repetitions, phrase repetitions, revisions and incomplete phrases are commonly associated with "normal dysfluencies".

        3. Dysfluencies that break the flow of speech between words are apparently perceived as normal.

        4. Dysfluencies that break or fragment the word are perceived as abnormal, or stuttering.

    C. The Stuttering Block is defined as momentary occlusion of the airway (Van Riper, 1971).

        1. From exterior observation (outside the vocal tract) and reports of stutterers, many blocks do involve occlusion of the vocal tract at one or more points.

        2. Many studies are available:

           a. Aerodynamic patterns (Hutchinson, 1974);

           b. Fiberoptic observations (Conture et al., 1977; Freeman et al., 1976);

           c. EMG recordings by Freeman and Ushijima (1978), raised the possibility that some blocking may involve an open vocal tract in which voiced sound production is prevented by abducted rather than adducted vocal folds.

    D. "Blocking" can be defined as a momentary inability to move forward in the speech production sequence.

        1. Identifying the point of the block is the audible dysfluency.

a. Priori - the sound repeated or prolonged; the sound on which the block occurred;

b. Van Riper (1971), Stromstra (1965), and Freeman (1979) have proposed that the stutterer is not blocked on the sound repeated or prolonged, but on the transition from one sound to the next.

2. Monitoring devices for vocal tract events:

a. Guitar's (1975) use of EMG biofeedback;

b. Webster's (1977) use of the voice monitor.

E. Authorities agree that stuttered speech and particular moments of stuttering are characterized by "tension".

1. Bluemel, 1935; Foreschels, 1943; Weiss, 1964; Bloodstein, 1975, cite that the presence or degree of "tension" is useful in distinguishing between normal dysfluencies and stuttering; between the early and more advanced stages of the disorder; between different degrees of severity; or between stuttering and cluttering.

2. Many stutterers report "muscular tensions" associated with stuttering (Snidecoi, 1955).

3. Treatment approaches have emphasized relaxation as a means of reducing "tensions" and promoting fluency (Bluemel, 1913, Brutten and Shoemaker, 1967; Lanyon, 1969; Wolpe, 1969; Lander, 1970).

4. "Tensions" are described as very high or excessive levels of muscle activity.

a. electromyograph has been used to study the level of muscle activity in stuttered and fluent speech (Sheehan and Vaos, 1954; Freeman and Ushijima, 1978);

b. use of EMG biofeedback devices for stuttering therapy has accelerated.

5. Observable features of stuttering such as prolonged articulatory contacts, hard attacks, vocal tremors, vocal fry, sound prolongations, lengthened stops, and overaspirated stop releases are the direct consequences of high levels of muscle activity (Bloodstein, 1975).

F. Conditions under which stuttering is markedly reduced or absent:

1. Singing, whispering, choral speaking, shadowing, speaking in rhythm, speaking under delayed auditory feedback, and speaking in the presence of a loud voiced-masking noise.

2. Columbat, 1830; Moll, 1939; Dantzig, 1940; Cherry and Sayers, 1959; Marland, 1957; Parker and Christopherson, 1963; Andrews and Harris, 1964; Fransella, 1967; Barr and Carmel, 1969; Donovan, 1971, have formed a basis for therapy techniques while using fluency-evoked conditions.

3. Stutterers have also been observed to be fluent while speaking in an affected manner (accent or dialect, ventriloquism or impersonation), speaking to infants or animals, and shouting.

4. Fluency-evoked conditions are labeled as distraction devices.

    a. the distraction hypothesis predicts that once the device becomes habitual it will cease to inhibit stuttering (Bloodstein, 1975);

    b. communication responsibility is reduced, stutterer is no longer under communicative interpersonal pressures and may speak freely, (Erenson and Wells, 1942; and Lisenson and Horowitz, 1945; and challenged by Pattie and Knight, 1944).

5. Experimental studies of speech fluency effects of masking and delayed auditory feedback led to the conceptualization of stuttering as a disorder of disturbed feedback.

6. Wingate (1969, 1970) reviewed the literature on fluency-evoking conditions and offered a new hypothesis. He proposed the following:

    a. fluency-evoking conditions have the common property of effecting changes in the manner of vocalization;

    b. "In these circumstances which improve fluency, the stutterer is induced in one way or another to do something with his voice that he does not ordinarily do."

    c. this hypotheis added a shift in emphasis from articulation to phonation, from the lips, jaw, and tongue to the larynx (Freeman, 1979).

III. Concepts of "Cause" in Stuttering

A. Levels of cause:

1. The underlying cause(s) – the genetic, neurological, physiological and psychological factors that may predispose a child to fluency disruption.

    a. underlying organic causes in stuttering is an old theory and was conducted prior to 1945;

    b. current research design and data interpretation have become more sophisticated;

    c. Kidd (1977) investigated the relationship between environmental and developmental factors and genetic predisposition, and the theory and methods used for investigating behavioral problems in a genetic model.

B. The environmental cause(s) – the environmental factors associated with the onset and the development of stuttering symptoms.

    1. Bloodstein (1960, 1961, 1975); Van Riper (1971); Sheehan (1970); Travis (1957); Lemert (1970); Brulten and Shoemaker (1967, 1969) and Brulten (1975) have studied the factors or conditions that contribute or accompany, cause, or maintain the onset and development of stuttering.

    2. Interest is increasing in the linguistic development and speech production characteristics of young children who are dysfluent or in the early stages of stuttering.

    3. Stromstra's (1965) finding that spectrograms of the dysfluencies of children who continued to stutter showed "a lack of format transition and abrupt phonatory stoppages" which were absent in the dysfluencies of the children who later developed normal fluency.

    4. Wall (1977) exemplified the potential of linguistic analyses based on new psycholinguistic models.

C. The precipitating cause(s) – when, where, and under what conditions moments of stuttering are likely to occur.

    1. 90% of stuttering blocks involve the initial sound of the word (Johnson and Brown, 1935; Hahn, 1942).

    2. When stuttering occurs within a polysyllabic word it usually involves the initial sound of the stressed syllable (Brown, 1938; Hejan, 1972).

3. Stuttering occurs more often in England on words with initial consonants than on words with initial vowels.

D. The vocal tract cause(s) – the vocal tract events that generate the disrupted speech patterns.

    1. Holds great potential for treatment; however, there is limited research.

        a. knowledge of the behaviors (vocal tract dynamics) of stuttering and how to assess, measure, and/or monitor these component behaviors is at present lacking but potentially available;

        b. criticism has been leveled at descriptive physiological studies of the dynamics of stuttering on the grounds that these events are peripheral and do not deal directly with underlying causes;

        c. for purposes of treatment, the vocal tract is the most accessible part of the disordered system.

IV. Treatment for the Two Million Stutterers in the U.S.

A. Different approaches (views) of fluency, dysfluency, and stuttering carry over into the realm of treatment.

    1. The first approach assumes that any stutterer properly treated can achieve normal fluency.

    2. If fluency is not achieved, it is assumed that:

        a. stutterer did not work hard enough;

        b. lacks motivation;

        c. treatment was not properly administered or is not appropriate for individual.

    3. Second view assumes that a real stutterer can never expect to achieve the effort-free fluency of normal speakers.

B. Treatment procedures:

    1. Requires specialized training with clinical experience in the field of stuttering.

    2. All good treatment must be based on recognition of and respect for each individual's uniqueness, his special circumstances, current and future needs, and his perception of his problem and needs.

3. Treatment must include differential diagnosis and an individualized treatment plan with goals, emphasis and follow-up appropriate to this problems, and needs.

C. Treatment approaches:

1. Approaches for young children beginning to stutter:

   a. eliminate physical stress;

   b. reduce sources of emotional stress;

   c. create rewarding communicative situations;

   d. initiate appropriate therapy to facilitate development speech motor problems.

2. Approaches for children aware of their stuttering:

   a. help child understand what he is experiencing;

   b. environmental modification;

   c. direct treatment through fluency enhancement.

3. Approaches for older children and adults to generalize, habituate, and maintain fluency:

   a. recognize the effort that stutterers must exert in order to maintain fluency;

   b. free feelings of guilt, failure and depression that accompany periods of relapse;

   c. continuing sources of support and assistance;

   d. stutterer and clinician must appreciate the dramatic alterations in self-concept, lifestyle, in personal adjustment, and in interpersonal relationships that a stutterer must face when he becomes "fluent" speaker;

   e. choice of method used to shape and modify the stutterer's speech.

D. Modification Techniques:

1. Phonatory emphasis techniques:

   a. altering phonatory pattern:

      (1) lower levels of activity in laryngeal muscles;

(2) slower rates of vocal fold abduction and adduction;

(3) loose rather than tight vocal fold closure.

E.  Treatment in the Future.

    1.  Synthesization of a number of existing therapy programs.

    2.  Humanistic and individualized with behavior shaping and modification techniques.

    3.  Differential diagnosis, ongoing in therapy, will be used to determine each stutterer's treatment needs.

    4.  Follow-up support built into treatment.

    5.  Carry-over and maintenance.

F.  Vocal tract dynamics of stuttering:

    1.  Analysis of speech production:

        a. Freeman (1979) reported using sound spectrograms to diagnose phonatory failure in stutterers;

        b. Hutchinson (1974) discussed using aerodynamic patterns for diagnosis.

    2.  Biofeedback in treatment:

        a. Webster (1978) monitors rise-time for teaching gentle onset of production;

        b. Guitar (1975) illustrates both the potential of the approach and the need for research.

G.  Related fluency disorders:

    1.  Cluttering:

        a. Weiss (1964) stated that the basis of cluttering is a central language imbalance.

        (1) grammatical difficulties;

        (2) hyperactivity;

        (3) poor concentration;

        (4) poorly integrated thought processes;

        (5) lack of musical abilities;

        (6) reading and writing disorders.

H.  Neurological disorders with dysfluency components:

1.  A number of neurological disorders including chorea, Parkinsonism, Gilles de la Tourette's disease, aphasia, apraxia, presenile dementia, head injury, ataxic and hypokinetic dysarthria, and spastic dysphonia may be associated with speech dysfluencies.

2.  Shtremel (1963) and Frost (1971) have viewed stuttering as apraxia, proposing that dysfluencies, and articulator errors may "derive from breakdown or disturbance in some aspect(s) of verbal apraxis" (Frost, 1971).

3.  Canter (1971) and Frost (1971) hypothesize that dysfluencies occur as patients grope or search for articulatory postures for words.

4.  Rosenbek (1978) views stuttering as a neurological disorder which might be regarded as an interrupted, saccadic production of sounds, words, or phrases which can be spontaneous, provoked, facilitated, or inhibited.

5.  Additional research in this area includes observations of the relationship between spastic dysphonia and stuttering (McCall, 1974), observation of laryngeal activity in Parkinsonism (Fenton and Numi, 1976), observations in stuttering and cerebral ischemia (Rosenfield, 1972), observations of stuttering in aphasic and nonaphasic brain damaged adults (Farmer, 1975).

## REVIEW QUESTIONS

1.  Match the following theories of stuttering with their proponents:

    A.  Hebrews
    B.  Greeks-Romans
    C.  Wendall Johnson
    D.  Skinner
    E.  Victorian England

    1.  weak or diseased morality
    2.  learned behavior
    3.  numeral imbalance of elements
    4.  punishment from God
    5.  semantogenic theory

2.  Which of the following types of dysfluencies are associated with
    stuttering (not "normal dysfluencies"):

    A.  Sound prolongation
    B.  Incomplete phrases
    C.  Syllable or sound repetitions
    D.  Interjections
    E.  Broken words

3.  Dysfluencies that break the flow of speech between words are
    apparently perceived as _____, whereas dysfluencies
    that break or fragment the word are perceived as _____.

4.  The momentary inability to move forward in the speech production
    sequence is the definition of _____.

5.  The theory that "anything that diverts the stutterer from careful,
    conscious attention to his speech will lead to natural, automatic
    and therefore fluent speech" is known as the _____
    _____.

6.  Identify the four levels that Freeman proposes as "cause" in
    stuttering:

    A.  _____

    B.  _____

    C.  _____

    D.  _____

7.  Mark each statement "True" or "False".

    __ A.  Over 90% of stuttering blocks involve the final sound of a word.
    __ B.  When stuttering occurs within a polysyllabic word it usually
           involves the initial sound of the stressed syllable.
    __ C.  In English, stuttering occurs more often on words with initial
           consonants than on words with initial vowels.

8.  The desired model for speech pattern to reduce dysfluencies in
    young children beginning to stutter is:

    A.  Normal rate; quick vowel sounds, crisp consonants.
    B.  Slightly faster than normal rate, hard vocal attacks.
    C.  Slightly faster than normal rate; loud and clear.
    D.  Slow in rate, slightly lengthened vowels; slightly breathy.
    E.  Slow in rate; shortened vowels; hard vocal attacks.

9.  The major problem in our present clinical management of stuttering
    is not in teaching the stutterer to speak without audible dysfluencies,
    but in helping him to _____, _____ and
    _____ fluency.

10. Identify three techniques of phonatory modification that may produce improvement in fluency.

A. _____

B. _____

C. _____

11. The onset of stuttering, like dysfluencies in older children and adults, can be an early symptom of neurological dysfunction. Six of these neurological disorders that the therapist should consider in such patients might include:

A. _____

B. _____

C. _____

D. _____

E. _____

F. _____

# Chapter 28

# THE NATURE OF
# APHASIA IN ADULTS

*Malcolm R. McNeil*

I. A Philosophical Perspective

    A. The study of aphasia is undertaken in order to:

        1. Gain insight into basic and universal properties of man.

        2. Infer brain-behavior relationships.

        3. Better treat the symptoms.

    B. Approaches to aphasia must be broad (multiform) and changeable (protean), in order to synthesize information from divergent disciplines.

II. Definitions of Aphasia

    A. Schuell, Jenkins, Jimenez-Pabon: aphasia is a general language deficit that crosses all language modalities and may or may not be complicated by other sequelae of brain damage.

    B. Benson: the loss or impairment of language caused by brain damage.

    C. Definitions of exclusion are common, e.g., aphasia is not.....

    D. McNeil: Aphasia is a multimodality physiological inefficiency with verbal symbolic manipulations. In isolated form it is caused by focal damage to cortical and/or subcortical structures of the hemisphere(s) dominant for such symbolic manipulations. It is affected by and affects other physiological information processing and cognitive processes to the degree that they support, interact with, or are supported by symbolic deficits.

III. Classification Systems and Neural Substrates of Aphasia

    A. Numerous classification systems have appeared in the literature over the past 120 years (see Table 28-1 in text).

    B. Classical systems correlate a lesion in a particular location with a particular type of aphasia.

    C. Some aphasiologists follow the view of Marie (1906) and Schuell et al. (1964) that there is a "single aphasia," one underlying verbal deficit in all aphasic adults, and reject the notion of different types of aphasia with differing underlying neuroanatomic mechanisms.

    D. The Boston Classification System of aphasic syndromes is clear and currently used by many aphasiologists (Benson, 1979) including neurologists, psychologists, linguists and speech-language pathologists.

        1. Broca's Aphasia:

            a. conversational speech – nonfluent;

            b. auditory comprehension – good;

            c. repetition – abnormal;

            d. reading comprehension – good or abnormal;

            e. writing – abnormal.

        2. Wernicke's Aphasia:

            a. conversational speech – fluent, paraphasic;

            b. auditory comprehension – abnormal;

            c. repetition – abnormal;

            d. reading comprehension – abnormal;

            e. writing – abnormal.

        3. Conduction Aphasia:

            a. conversational speech – fluent, paraphasic;

            b. auditory comprehension – good;

            c. repetition – abnormal;

            d. reading comprehension – good;

            e. writing – abnormal.

4. Transcortical Motor Aphasia:

    a. conversational speech - nonfluent;

    b. auditory comprehension - good;

    c. repetition - good;

    d. reading comprehension - often good;

    e. writing - abnormal.

5. Transcortical Sensory Aphasia:

    a. conversational speech - fluent, paraphasic, echolalic;

    b. auditory comprehension - severely abnormal;

    c. repetition - good;

    d. reading comprehension - abnormal;

    e. writing - abnormal.

6. Mixed Transcortical Aphasia:

    a. conversational speech - nonfluent with echolalia;

    b. auditory comprehension - severely abnormal;

    c. repetition - good;

    d. reading comprehension - abnormal;

    e. writing - abnormal.

E. The Boston Classification System has demonstrated correlations between behavior complexes and sites of lesions based on autopsy and neuroradiological studies; however, this cannot be used as strong evidence to support a simplistic brain-behavior relationship (centers-pathways models).

F. Classification of aphasic patients should be done with awareness of the temptation to see what is not there, to miss what is there, and to ignore individual differences.

IV.  Approaches to the Study of Adults with Aphasia

   A.  Aphasia has been viewed from a variety of frameworks, including a cybernetic perspective.

   B.  Jenkins et al. (1975) have provided a useful interactive schema for evaluating the levels and processes disordered in aphasia.

   C.  Aphasia should be viewed from three perspectives:

      1.  The processes, levels or functions that are essential disturbances of the disorder.

      2.  The secondary processes, levels or functions that are disturbed because of the primary disturbances.

      3.  The undisturbed processes, levels, or functions that can be used to facilitate or circumvent the disturbed ones.

   D.  More psycho-sociolinguistic research is needed in aphasia to integrate understanding of cognition, linguistics, and communication.

V.  Intelligence

   A.  Do persons with aphasia have a reduced intelligence?  The question remains incompletely answered.

      1.  On nonverbal classification tests, aphasics are generally deficient compared to normals, but not more so than brain-injured patients without aphasia.

      2.  There is no conclusive evidence from tests of drawing that aphasics display a generally reduced intelligence.

      3.  Standardized intelligence tests have shown a significant difference between deficits on verbal and nonverbal tests, with poorer performance on verbal tests by aphasics when compared to nonaphasic brain damaged groups.

   B.  Intelligence functions, in general, are insufficient to describe or explain the nature of aphasia or the person with aphasia.

VI.  Memory Processes in Aphasia

   A.  Memory tasks differ as a function of hemisphere:

      1.  The left temporal lobe is specialized for short-term verbal memory.

2. The right temporal lobe is specialized for short-term nonverbal memory.

B. Language dominant lesions produce verbal memory deficits in aphasic persons; however, nonverbal memory tasks also appear to be reduced. A reduced rate and amount of information processed in memory has been suggested as a cause for both findings.

C. Ichonic and echoic memory literature in aphasia is sparse. There is some evidence that ichonic memory is intact.

D. Short-Term Memory (STM):

1. STM has been investigated in a number of ways in aphasic adults.

2. STM is disturbed in aphasics to a greater extent than in normal or brain-injured nonaphasics, in terms of total number of units stored and in sequence.

3. Perceptual problems (slow processing time) as well as reversal, naming and capacity deficits may be responsible for STM deficits in aphasic adults.

4. While aphasics are slower than normals, conflicting results exist concerning the qualitative strategies used by aphasic and normal persons in the search of memory for recently acquired information. Like normals, the style of the search appears to be an exhaustive one in aphasics; however, some patients may adopt a self-terminating search strategy.

5. Aphasics appear inefficient at employing top-down clustering and organizing strategies.

6. Long-term memory in aphasic persons is usually regarded as normal unless the aphasia is complicated by other factors.

VII. Loss (Competence) Vs. Interference (Performance)

A. Has the aphasic adult lost the ability to manipulate verbal symbols (competence) or become unable to assess these abilities (performance)?

B. Evidence to answer this question comes from four facts:

1. Aphasia can be transient.

a. epileptogenic aphasia. Aphasia due to epilepsy or seizure activity is evidence that aphasia can be caused by interference of verbal symbolic processes, and that a lesion of a center/pathway is not necessary to cause it;

b. <u>Migraine-Induced Aphasia</u>;

c. <u>Structural Cerebral Lesions</u>:

   (1) transient ischemic attack (TIA);

   (2) lacunar infarcts;

   (3) reversable ischemic neurological deficits (RIND).

2. Aphasia is variable.

   a. an almost infinitely large number of factors affect an aphasic person's communicative abilities and their variability;

   b. to detect this variability, measuring instruments must have four characteristics:

      (1) homogeneous test items used to assess function at a single level of difficulty within a subtest;

      (2) an adequate number of homogeneous items within a given subtest;

      (3) test-retest (instrument), intrajudge (same judge) and interjudge (different judges) reliability;

      (4) a sensitive, valid scoring system, e.g., a multidimensional system.

   c. aphasic adults demonstrate variability in performance which is attributable to internal state factors to a striking degree, more than decreased performance due to lost ability;

   d. performance deficits and variability appear to be due to:

      (1) an inefficiency or reduction of efficiency in the system(s); these have been described as "generalized reduction of efficiency after brain damage" and "change in dynamic neurophysiological processes";

      (2) altered perceptual thresholds and altered temporal processes;

      (3) increased inertia -- the time required by the system to process information and recover from preceding stimulation (increased response time, inability to shift tasks, slow rise time, noise buildup, perseveration);

(4) increased fatigability;

(5) disordered attentional processes:

    (a) aphasics have lower speed in working than normal subjects;

    (b) aphasics are impaired in focused attention.

3. The aphasic is <u>stimulable</u>.

    a. aphasic patients can be stimulated or manipulated to perform at any increased level of efficiency and accuracy;

    b. eight categories of stimulation discussed by Darley in his summary of 20 years of research include:

        (1) stimulus characteristics, e.g., saliency-redundancy;

        (2) linguistic factors of stimulus and response, e.g., word frequency, syntactic complexity;

        (3) stimulus and response length;

        (4) linguistic context;

        (5) time dimension variations;

        (6) scheduling of stimuli presentations;

        (7) attitude;

        (8) content of treatment.

4. Aphasia resides on a <u>continuum</u> from aphasic to normal.

    a. aphasic adults are qualitatively similar to normals, but quantitatively different; thus, they make the same kind of errors but with greater frequency;

    b. the mechanism for understanding language appears to be much the same for normals and aphasics; however, aphasics seem to operate the mechanism with reduced efficiency;

c. other dimensions which reflect the same pattern include:

   (1) perceptual speed;

   (2) several linguistic levels:

      (a) semantic-lexical;

      (b) syntactic;

      (c) pragmatic.

d. this continuum provides further evidence that aphasia reflects a reduction in efficiency rather than a loss of function.

VIII. Recovery, Prognosis and Efficacy of Treatment

A. Recovery of function after brain damage is the process by which a particular behavior is reinstated that has been disturbed and involves the utilization of that part of the system which was spared. The most popular explanation for improvement of abilities following aphasia is physiological recovery.

B. Prognostic variables include:

   1. Type of aphasia.

   2. Familial left handedness in right handers.

   3. Specific linguistic abilities.

   4. Nonlinguistic speech abilities.

   5. Age.

   6. Sex.

   7. Severity at onset.

   8. Etiology of the aphasia producing lesion.

   9. Size and location of lesion.

   10. Initiation of aphasia therapy.

   11. Early initiation of treatment following onset.

   12. Psychosocial factors.

C. Assessment of Aphasia:

1. Tests or assessment procedures for aphasia must be judged against psychometric considerations.

   a. the reasons to use a test designed for aphasia are varied:

      (1) detection of suspected aphasia;

      (2) differential diagnosis;

      (3) classification of aphasia;

      (4) prognosis;

      (5) candidacy and focus of treatment;

      (6) termination of treatment;

      (7) determination of site of lesion.

   b. technical problems in aphasia testing include four types of validity and three types of reliability.

2. The standardization of a test for aphasia requires that:

   a. the population from which the sample was drawn be clearly defined;

   b. the task and item instructions be clearly specified;

   c. the procedures used in evaluation of each response be described and objective scored:

      (1) descriptive;

      (2) plus-minus;

      (3) rating scales;

      (4) category scores;

      (5) multidimensional scales.

   d. the criteria for deriving normative data be presented;

   e. validity be addressed including: construct validity, predictive validity, and content validity;

   f. reliability be addressed including test-retest, interjudge, and intrajudge reliability.

3.  No single current published aphasia test meets all of the psychometric requirements. Most clinical aphasiologists use a battery of tests.

4.  Table 28-7 (pg. 708) lists the published tests for aphasia, along with a list of primary assets and limitations of the tests.

5.  The instrument chosen will depend upon:

    a. the conceptual framework on which the test is built;

    b. the specific purposes for giving

       (1) psychometric considerations - PICA and RTT;

       (2) prognostic considerations - PICA and MTDDA;

       (3) prediction of functional communication - CADL and FCP;

       (4) categorizing types of aphasia - BDAE and WAB.

D.  Treatment of Aphasia:

    1.  Treatment can be effective for individuals and/or groups of patients.

    2.  The exact approach to treatment varies with the patient's specific deficits, severity, assets, personality, etc.

    3.  Treatment approaches have been directed at:

        a. the areas of deficit;

        b. effect on patient.

    4.  Treatment may be classified as:

        a. direct;

        b. semidirect;

        c. indirect;

        d. compensatory.

    5.  Summary of specific treatment techniques:  see Table 28-8.

    6.  Important factors relative to treatment (Darley, 1977) include:

a. intensive therapy has a decisive, positive effect on recovery from aphasia in patients in whom spontaneous recovery has run its course;

b. beneficial effects are maximized if treatment is started early and is prolonged for a period of several months;

c. the gains that result from aphasia therapy are not confined to changes in listening, reading, speaking and writing, but are also observed in attitude, appropriateness of affect, morale, and maintenance of social contact.

7. Little is known about what type of therapy is efficacious and for whom.


## REVIEW QUESTIONS


1. Broca's area is concerned with:

   A. Conscious emotional activities.
   B. Regulation of hormonal systems.
   C. Motor organization of speech.
   D. Auditory organization of language.
   E. Short-term memory skills.

2. Disturbances in execution of the motor speech act due to muscular uncoordination or paresis are called:

   A. Diplalia
   B. Apraxia
   C. Aphasia
   D. Dysarthria
   E. Anomia

3. Identify the two areas shown below as A and B named for two early aphasiologists.

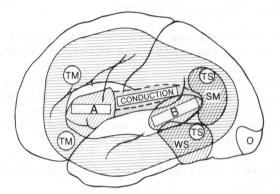

In questions 4-7, use the terms nonfluent, good, abnormal, usually good, normal, paraphasic.

4. Fill in the expected symptoms for a patient with Broca's aphasia:

   A.  Conversational speech _____

   B.  Auditory Comprehension _____

   C.  Auditory Speech Reception _____

   D.  Confrontation Naming _____

5. Fill in the expected symptoms for a patient with Wernicke's aphasia:

   A.  Conversational speech _____

   B.  Auditory Comprehension _____

   C.  Auditory Speech Reception _____

   D.  Confrontation Naming _____

6. Fill in the expected symptoms for a patient with conduction aphasia:

   A.  Conversational speech _____

   B.  Auditory Comprehension _____

   C.  Auditory Speech Reception _____

   D.  Confrontation Naming _____

Circle the normal or abnormal in each blank in the following sentence:

7. In the Mixed Transcortical Aphasic, his reading aloud abilities are (normal) (abnormal), reading comprehension is (normal) (abnormal) and his writing abilities would be (normal) (abnormal).

8. The left temporal lobe (language dominant) is specialized for short-term _____ memory, while the right temporal lobe is specialized for _____ short-term memory.

9. Recovery from aphasia is a function of many interacting factors. Give the prognostic value (good, mixed, poor or unknown) of each of the following isolated factors:

    A. Global aphasia _____

    B. Severe onset _____

    C. Small, single lesion in language area _____

    D. Early initiation of treatment _____

    E. Broca's aphasia (as compared to other types of aphasia)_____

10. Intelligence in the aphasic adult:

    A. Is always related to the severity of the language impairment.
    B. Is generally normal.
    C. Is not related to the symptoms.
    D. Has resulted in controversial research findings.
    E. A and D

11. Long-term memory in persons with aphasia is usually regarded as _____ unless the aphasic is more than simply aphasic.

12. Aphasia can be transient. Identify three causes of transient aphasia:

    A. _____

    B. _____

    C. _____

13. Name the tests for aphasia associated with the following persons:

    A. Holland _____

    B. Eisenson _____

    C. Schnell _____

    D. Porch _____

# Chapter 29

# THE ELEPHANT IS SOFT AND MUSHY: PROBLEMS IN ASSESSING CHILDREN'S LANGUAGE

*Judith Felson Duchan*

I. What the Language Pathologist Wants To Know

   A. Does the child have a language problem?

      1. This question often presupposes that the answer is to be found by comparing the child to a normal population.

      2. If the child deviates significantly from the comparison group, the child is declared to be language impaired.

      3. The problem of test validity is a difficult issue:

         a. one must select tests which are valid for identifying not only language impaired children but also their areas of language impairment;

         b. the areas of language competence deemed significant are different for different clinicians.

      4. We lack a sense of whether formal tests will answer questions about the identification as well as the nature of the language problem.

      5. Problems exist as to what constitutes "normal"?

         a. the "normalcy" approach disregards individual differences even among those who speak standard English.

      6. Comparable scores cannot always be used to assume comparable competencies.

      7. Children's use of language is highly context-bound, thus their normal language use will not be like that found in standardized tests.

a. this fact raises question with the reliability aspect of tests;

b. the idea that language requires context appropriateness is not examined in formal language tests -- and in fact is violated by the nature of the tests.

B. What is causing the child's language problem?

1. Disease Syndromes:

   a. aphasia;

   b. hearing impairment;

   c. emotional disturbance;

   d. designation of the syndrome is often not on anatomical or physiological evidence, but rather on the lack of language development;

   e. once diagnosed as a syndrome, language abilities are often no longer examined;

   f. we now de-emphasize labelling children in terms of their syndromes, and instead, <u>describe</u> their problems.

2. Psychological Mechanisms:

   a. another approach to explaining language problems is to look for difficulties in various kinds of processing that could have led to the child's language problems;

   b. <u>processing</u> <u>tests</u> usually test one modality at a time with emphasis on distinguishing visual from auditory processing deficits;

   c. considerable controversy still exists about auditory processing as a source of language problems;

   d. it is inevitable that some children with language problems will also do poorly on auditory processing measures.

3. Social Contexts:

   a. social and cultural categories used to blame language problems include social deprivation, troubled family, lack of environmental stimulation, disadvantaged, maternal overprotection, etc.;

b. causes are applied too easily and imply only what we assume to be the case for a particular child;

c. the question is whether the child has a language learning problem or is just speaking the language of the dialect of those around him?

d. therapy programs that teach the value of standard English over nonstandard English have generally failed.

C. What is the child's language like?

   1. Child-to-Adult Comparison:

      a. the clinician simply matches the child's utterance to the form in which the adult would say it and considers the answer right or wrong depending upon the exactness of the match.

   2. Child-to-Normal Child Comparison:

      a. generally a checklist approach to identify what the child knows about preselected categories found in normal children at different developmental stages;

      b. results may be used in a three-pronged approach:

         (1) does the child have normal performance in various linguistic areas?

         (2) how does the child's knowledge compare with that of normally developing children at the same stage?

         (3) can these results be used as a guide for directing therapy?

   3. Checklist approaches are not really geared to analyzing what the child knows or is doing in his or her own terms.

   4. Structural Analysis:

      a. a non-checklist approach to reduce data to the underlying regularities;

      b. commits the diagnostician to determine what it is that makes a particular child seem unusual and then to postulate what kinds of processes may be leading the child to that difference.

II. Structural Analysis as an Assessment Approach

    A. The purpose of structural analysis is to determine the basic structures or units a child is thinking in as he or she understands and produces language.

        1. Follows the effects of structural linguistics in doing analyses of children with language disorders.

            a. uses structural categories such as "categories", "contextual rules", "underlying structures" and "surface structures".

        2. Deciding what to analyze:

            a. those aspects of the child's language that are most debilitating and communicatively interfering;

            b. another approach is to determine a small subset of related structures within a linguistic level and to delve more deeply into analyzing those;

            c. the three stages of working with a child (the initial period, getting into the data, and the therapy phase) will offer different perspectives on what to analyze for.

        3. Determining appropriate units:

            a. relevant structures in a child's language not only describe patterns in the surface production but should also give insight into the underlying structures;

            b. debate exists in linguistics concerning the question, "...how abstract phonology needs to be?"

                (1) generative phonologists -- advocate a multilevel abstraction;

                (2) natural phonologists -- underlying representations are closer to the surface productions;

            c. do the explanatory categories assume knowledge on the part of the child which it is not necessary to assume?

            d. whether the categories are sufficiently rich to explain all significant elements of the child's behavior;

            e. one test of a good analysis could be that it comes up with a new set of categories rather than an evaluation of children's knowledge in terms of the clinician's mental checklist derived from adult or normal child models;

f. four errors in determining structural units:

    (1) over-representation of knowledge;

    (2) under-representation of knowledge;

    (3) mis-representation of knowledge;

    (4) not to see what is there.

g. how do we devise guidelines for testing whether the structures we think we are finding are relevant to the child?

    (1) study surface features carefully for unexpected clues to structural categories;

    (2) test hypothesized structures for their psychological reality for the child.

h. after being delineated, the units' relevance to the child can be tested by making predictions from the rule about how the child would say something new;

    (1) a weaker test for psychological reality is to see whether the structures are used in different syntactic contexts;

    (2) another test is to observe the units' change over time to see if the entities within the proposed category change together;

    (3) design the structures so that they predict degrees of complexity, then make predictions about the child's performance from the complexity dimension.

4. Considering the Role of Context:

a. we often see "unexplained inconsistencies" in the behavior of units ;

b. the study of these inconsistencies is considered "pragmatics";

c. pragmatics will help us <u>not</u> focus on the child's language as being the source of communication breakdown, but will begin assessing communication breakdown <u>contextually</u>;

d. we will begin to diagnose language impairment as violations of cultural expectations rather than deviations from an average score on a text.

5. Developing an integrated understanding of the child:

   a. we must avoid a fragmented view of the child's language;

   b. the "synergistic approach" to the child's language involves looking at how the child performs on different tasks across different language levels;

   c. the psycholinguistic processing model is a means of integrating our assessment approach:

      (1) assumes that language knowledge is important and that it is the same in both comprehension and production;

      (2) any model of comprehension knowledge should contain a section of strategies that reflect the short cuts the child uses in language comprehensions;

      (3) in the production model is the set of phonological processes that convert the abstract lexical elements to the phonetic levels of production.

   d. memory constraints also undoubtedly affect comprehension and production differently;

   e. "cognitive load" factors also affect both comprehension and production differently;

   f. recent emphasis on <u>cognition</u> shows that ideation and knowledge of the world are very important to language comprehension and production.

III. Conclusion

   A. Author presents a fine summary of this chapter -- which is an excellent review of material and well-worth re-reading (see pages 757-758).

**REVIEW QUESTIONS**

1. The normative approach in assessing children's language is:

   A. A cultural viewpoint.
   B. Of questionable validity.
   C. Of questionable reliability.
   D. Crucial for borderline children.
   E. All of the above.
   F. A and D.

2. Identify four "disease syndromes" commonly identified with language problems in children.

   A. _____

   B. _____

   C. _____

   D. _____

3. Identify five "social-cultural factors" often associated with language problems:

   A. _____

   B. _____

   C. _____

   D. _____

   E. _____

4. The purpose of the structure analysis approach is to determine

   _____

   _____.

5. The four steps of structural analysis are:

   A. _____

   B. _____

   C. _____

   D. _____

# Chapter 30

# LANGUAGE DELAY

*Carol Lynn Waryas and Thomas A. Crowe*

I.  Theories of Normal Language Development

    A.  The Behavioral Approach:

        1.  Emphasizes the predominant effect of the environment on the organism through the mechanism of events consequent on behavior.

        2.  Language is assumed to be a learned behavior which develops through the establishment of stimulus-response (S-R) connections.

        3.  Posits that there is no necessary association between the development of language and the emergence of other cognitive or motor skills.

    B.  The Nativist Approach:

        1.  Also known as the "linguistic" or "content" approach.

        2.  View is that language is totally different from all other behaviors and the search for a common set of learning principles to account for its acquisition is meaningless.

        3.  States the existence of some "pre-wired" linguistic knowledge.

    C.  The Neurologic Approach:

        1.  Language is assumed to be contingent upon neuronal patterns established and linked with cortical integration areas.

        2.  Language development is viewed as being consequential to gradual differentiation and specialization of the central neurologic substratum.

D. Process Approaches:

    1. Suggests that an innate set of general cognitive mechanisms, inference rules, or processes exist that are not specific to language.

    2. Posits the existence of a biologic foundation in the form of a neurologically determined cognitive mechanism capable of receiving and processing information in certain specified ways.

    3. The Cognitive Approach:

        a. language development occurs to express what the child has already learned about his environment;

        b. language is a form of representational ability and, as such, is related to other cognitive skills.

    4. The Social Approach:

        a. states that language is a social tool used to coordinate and correlate our actions with those of others;

        b. assumes man is genetically predisposed to learning language and there is an isomorphism between the genetic substrates for language and the structure of language.

II. Organism-Environment Interactions

A. Biologic Correlates:

    1. Lenneberg (1966) states that language is precipitated by internal organismic changes rather than external stimulation or socially induced needs.

    2. From the neurological position, this maturation process represents the "track" by which neurologic milestones requisite to language acquisition are attained.

B. Cerebral Dominance:

    1. Studies of its ontogeny represent one attempt to establish the neurophysiological requisites of language.

    2. Some researchers have concluded that in early childhood there is perfect equipotentiality existing between the two hemispheres which signifies cerebral plasticity of speech and language.

3. Period of perfect hemisphere equipotentiality usually ends around the start of the second year of life; onset of language acquisition involves a right-to-left lateralization and anterior-to-posterior polarization of function.

C. Myelogenesis:

1. Assumption is that specific asymptotes of chemical maturation of the brain roughly correlate with specific speech and language milestones.

2. Myelinization of the corticothalamic networks (associated with language) begins during early developmental periods (cooing and babbling stages), and continues to increase in density throughout the language acquisition period.

D. Rationale for Assumed Neurologic Correlates:

1. The idea persists that language development depends upon the precondition of biologic maturation involving the synchrony of linguistic, motoric, and perceptual maturation schedules.

2. Postulates that with the achievement of language-specific biologic milestones, the individual enters successive states of neurophysiologic "readiness", which in turn bear upon his environment.

3. Maturation of the neurologic substratum "pulls" the organism along through environmental interactions involving the various components of the language system.

E. Environmental Correlates:

1. Three types of environmental interactions - linguistic, cognitive and social - all related to neurologic maturation.

2. As interactions between the maturing organism and the environment unfold across time, the environmental demands and opportunities begin to increase at least semi-independently of the behavior the child emits.

III. Language Delays Within the Proposed Developmental Framework

A. "Traditional" definition of language delay: failure to develop language at the expected age.

1. May mean that development of language begins at a later age.

2.  May mean that the language development proceeds more slowly.

3.  Or that the final level of development reached is lower than that of normal children.

4.  Implies a "stretching out in time of the normal sequence of development" (Menyuk, 1972).

B.  It is in the pragmatic aspects of language that language delayed and normal children appear to be the most different.

1.  It is probably the "performance" factors rather than "competence" factors which result in a child's being identified as language delayed.

2.  Language deficiencies seem to have a profound effect on the development of social, cognitive, and affective behaviors.

C.  The concept of "language delay" implies, probably incorrectly:

1.  That such a notion exists as a distinct, definable entity different than disordered language.

2.  That language is "slowed down", which in turn implies that the child's language system is developing, rather than static.

D.  "Delay" is generally spoken about in terms of temporal discrepancy between chronological age and expected language skills.

E.  Leonard (1972) differentiates between "language delay" and language disorders to determine whether or not the child is likely to develop more appropriate language without clinical attention, albeit at a slower rate.

F.  Minimal brain damage and minimal brain dysfunction implies characteristics often not observed in the language delayed child.

1.  Minimal brain damage syndrome children demonstrate poor attention span, memory deficits, lability, perseverative behavior and the severe language delay - usually the term language disorder is applied (Eisenson, 1972).

2.  Weiner (1974) points out that in cases of language delay when no intellectual, emotional or sensorimotor involvement is apparent, cerebral dysfunction is indicated.

G.  It may be concluded that language delay and language
    disorder should fall together into one category of communicative
    disorders characterized by the inappropriate development of a
    culturally determined language system for the purposes of
    interpersonal, referential communication.

IV.  Implications for Assessment and Intervention

   A.  Assessment/Diagnosis:

      1.  Aram and Nation (1975) classify linguistic disorders
          into three forms:

          a. etiologic category;

          b. a single homogeneous category;

          c. based on language patterns demonstrated by the child.

      2.  Language delay classification represents a "differential
          diagnosis" and assumes that all such individuals possess
          the same language characteristics.

      3.  "Developmental Process Approach" of Miller (1978):

          a. most relevant criterion for making decisions regarding
             goals is a description of the child's actual receptive
             and expressive linguistic behaviors;

          b. within this framework, the only necessary label is
             "language deviant";

          c. language delay is often considered an "etiology-less
             etiology".

      4.  It is necessary to determine if neurologic factors are
          causally indicated.

      5.  The initial categorization need involve only the term
          "language disordered" – any co-existing problems (such
          as mental retardation) should be identified as secondary
          categories.

   B.  Intervention Strategies:

      1.  No child should be denied language therapy on the assumption
          his problem is "only delay".

      2.  Language stimulation, especially early intervention for the
          "language delayed" child, is essential.

      3.  A promising approach is to initially teach the child to express
          and comprehend a wide range of semantic relations and
          pragmatic functions, paralleling those of normal children.

277

**REVIEW QUESTIONS**

1. In the behavioral approach, language acquisition is viewed as:

   A. Interdependent with other forms of behavior.
   B. A behavior learned through the establishment of stimulus-response connections.
   C. Heavily dependent on the biologic structure of the organism.
   D. An example of "stimulus-bound" behavior.
   E. Best characterized as the acquisition of an internalized grammar.

2. In the nativist approach to language acquisition, it is necessary to posit:

   A. A common set of learning principles to account for the acquisition of language and other behaviors.
   B. A "Black Box" approach to the language acquisition process.
   C. A neurophysiologic basis for language development.
   D. The existence of a linguistic auditory detection system.
   E. An inherent knowledge of the linguistic system.

3. Language development from the neurologic perspective is viewed as involving all of the following processes EXCEPT:

   A. Gradual differentiation of the CNS.
   B. Linguistic input from the environment.
   C. Innate linguistic universals.
   D. Successive stages of neurologic instability.
   E. Biologic courses of maturation.

4. In Figure 30-1, from page 765, the following is true:

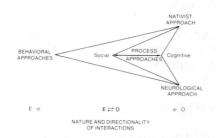

   A. Only the neurologic approach is represented by O→e.
   B. The cognitive approach is an aspect of the Nativist position.
   C. E→o represents a unidirectional effect of the organism on the environment.
   D. E⇄O indicates an equal role for biologic and environmental factors.
   E. O→e indicates a greater role for environmental factors than E→o.

278

5. All of the following are characteristic of process approaches to language

A. Language and cognition are clearly separated processes.
B. The assumption of some innate, biologically determined structures.
C. Language development is viewed as an aspect of social behavior.
D. They represent a mid-ground theoretically to the nativist, neurologic, and behavioral approaches.
E. They are divisible into social and cognitive emphases.

6. While the role of cerebral localization in language development is, at present, not completely understood, it could conceivably be relevant in cases of language delay where:

A. Cerebral plasticity extends through the preschool years.
B. A sinistral tendency is demonstrated by the child.
C. Hemispheric equipotentiality exists after two years of age.
D. Cerebral localization occurs during the first two years of life.
E. An anterior-to-posterior polarization of function is involved.

7. Myelinization of the corticothalamic networks associated with language:

A. Occurs during the first two years of life.
B. Occurs throughout early childhood.
C. Is initiated at approximately five years of age.
D. Is initiated during puberty.
E. Is essentially complete at birth.

8. The presumed neurologic substrates of language imply:

A. The independence of the various biologic processes underlying language.
B. The importance of brain weight to language acquisition.
C. An increase in CNS maturation subsequent to language acquisition.
D. Neurologic asymptotes achieved during infancy.
E. The synchrony of reciprocally-linked maturation schedules.

9. The three main components of the language system--form, content, and use--emerge from three types of environmental interactions discussed in this chapter. The corresponding environmental interactions for these three components are:

A. Cognitive, neurologic, and social.
B. Linguistic, cognitive, and social.
C. Linguistic, cognitive, and neurologic.
D. Social, cognitive, and linguistic.
E. Neurologic, linguistic, and social.

10. In Figure 30-2 the neurologic projection at the bottom represents:

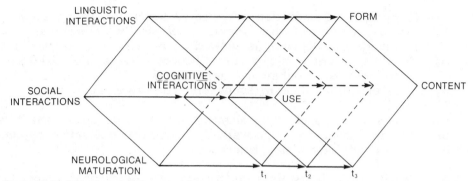

**Figure 30-2** Projection of environmental interactions through time as determined by neurological maturation.

A. Feedback mechanisms.
B. A means of gauging the child's cognitive development.
C. An index of social interactions.
D. Successive states of neurologic readiness which bear upon the environment.
E. The <u>primum</u> <u>mobile</u> of the developmental process.

11. In studies comparing the language development of language delayed and normal children, the following was found:

A. Some studies have indicated the presence of quantitative differences between the two groups when matched on MLU.
B. The pragmatic aspect of language appears to be the least disturbed in cases of language delay.
C. When the language skills of retarded children are adjusted for slowness, no differences from normals are noted.
D. Once a language delayed child acquires a given aspect of language, he/she uses it with the same general frequency and in the same contexts as normals.
E. The language delayed child has the same basic symbolic representation abilities as the normal child.

12. All of the following statements regarding language delay are probably true EXCEPT:

A. The distinction between "language knowledge" and "language use" is very important.
B. Social and cognitive skills may be greatly affected during adolescence.
C. Language delay is often differentiated from language disorder in clinical practice based on the degree of deviance from environmental expectations.
D. It may represent a lack of synergy between the components of form, content, and use.
E. Many forms of environmental interactions may be affected.

13. Research studies on language delay have indicated that:

A. "Dysphasic" children show good prognosis for language development.
B. Spontaneous remission of language delay has never been documented.
C. In the majority of cases, neurologic, psychiatric, and environmental factors do not appear adequate for language learning.
D. The age of the child has little relevance in relation to the amount of delay relative to normal development.
E. The presence of minimal brain damage symptoms clearly differentiates between cases of language delay and language disorders.

14. In the diagnosis/assessment of language disorders, the following are true EXCEPT:

A. "Differential diagnosis" results in etiological classification.
B. The "developmental process approach" involves describing the child's actual language, social, and cognitive behaviors.
C. The use of homogeneous categories tends to obscure differences.
D. Clinical labels such as "language delayed" are useful since children who are labeled differently differ from each other in specific ways with respect to the language system.
E. It is important to attempt to determine the causes of language delay.

15. In regard to intervention procedures, the authors suggested that:

A. Language intervention is probably not necessary in most cases of language delay.
B. "Language disordered" children should be given precedence in a caseload over "language delayed" children.
C. Therapy is probably useless in cases that have a neurologic basis.
D. The initial focus of all therapy should be the development of language structures, rather than social or cognitive skills.
E. Early intervention for all children is essential.

# Chapter 31

# THE LANGUAGE
# DISORDERED CHILD

*Judith R. Johnston*

I. Introduction

   Definition: Impairment of language acquisition and function other
   than that associated with mental retardation, hearing impairment,
   psychosis, damage to peripheral speech mechanism, and social/
   environmental deprivation.

II. Perceptual Functions

   A. Studies of Auditory Perception

      1. Language disordered children show greater signal detection
         threshold variation and have difficulty identifying brief
         signals.

      2. Language disordered children require longer ISI's to
         determine order of acoustic events. This appears to
         be a function of signal duration, not order per se.

   B. Studies of Visual Perception and Memory

      1. It is not clear whether language disordered children have
         difficulty judging the order of visual events.

      2. Preliminary studies of memory reveal no abnormalities in
         pattern of recall but latencies may be longer.

   C. Efferent Perceptual Deficits

      1. Perceptual difficulties in language disordered children
         may result from general, non-modality-specific dysfunctions,
         e.g., failure to adjust scanning mechanisms rapidly enough.

      2. Language disordered children show abnormal patterns of
         attention.

D. Implications for Intervention

1. The relationship of perceptual dysfunction to language learning is as yet unclear and it is premature to conclude that such dysfunctions are the primary cause of language disorders.

2. Since shared attention is necessary to language learning, clinicians should create events with maximal attention-getting properties or follow the child's own attentional focus.

3. Visualization techniques such as the simultaneous use of sign and oral language may assist child to learn language patterns because the visual signal is more static and slower than the auditory signal.

III. Language Acquisition Patterns

A. Experimental and Observational Studies of Language Use

1. Syntax:

   a. the language disordered child's knowledge of major syntactic categories and combinational rules resembles that of a younger, normal child;

   b. order of acquisition and relative frequencies of use for sentence patterns appear to be normal.

2. Grammatical Morphology: Inflectional morphemes and syntactic functions appear to be learned in the normal order but over a protracted span of stages.

3. Relational Semantics: Preliminary studies indicate no abnormal patterns of acquisition despite the fact that language disordered children are chronologically older at each language stage. This could indicate:

   a. relational meanings are all expressed early and thus analyses of this sort fail to capture developmental trends;

   b. pragmatic factors as well as cognitive maturity influence learning of relational expressions.

4. Lexical Semantics: Preliminary studies fail to show the expected lexical advancement of language disordered children.

5. Pragmatics: Language disordered children appear to use their limited grammatical knowledge in a responsive and communicatively effective manner.

B.   Although research to date indicates that language disordered children follow normal patterns of acquisition <u>within</u> each linguistic domain, i.e., syntax, semantics, pragmatics, it remains possible that the developmental relationships <u>between</u> these systems is abnormal.

C.   Implications for Assessment and Intervention

1.   Linguistic profiles of competence across different areas of language knowledge may distinguish different subgroups of language disordered children.

2.   Although normal patterns of acquisition can provide a useful starting point for intervention programming, it may be possible to deviate from the normal model in areas where the language disordered child shows cognitively determined language learning strengths.

IV.  Emotional and Social Health

A.   Language disordered children are by definition non-psychotic, but they evidence a higher than normal incidence of emotional and social disorders.

B.   The question as to whether these emotional/social problems are causes or sequelae of language disorder is essentially moot since in either case they influence the learning of language.

C.   Intervention programs may facilitate language growth both by helping parents provide more appropriate language models and by helping them to interact non-verbally in ways that promote social/emotional health.

V.   Intellectual Development

A.   Preliminary studies suggest that language disordered children:

1.   May be delayed in their acquisition of means-ends schemes.

2.   May be delayed non-verbal conceptual development.

3.   May have poor non-verbal symbolic abilities as evidenced by immature pretend play and difficulty on visual imagery tasks.

B.   Conceptual deficits may directly result from language deficiencies or may stem from underlying information processing dysfunctions that lead to language disorders.

C. Implications for Assessment and Intervention

    1. Non-verbal IQ scores may not reflect a sufficient range of cognitive abilities and thus may not be reliable indices of mental growth.

    2. Conceptual deficits, if present, may place constraints on the content of language therapy and indicate a need for non-verbal training activities.

VI. Central Nervous System Integrity

A. EEGs, neurological examinations, autopsies and studies of dichotic listening indicate neurological pathology in some, but not all language disordered children.

    1. Improved diagnostic techniques may document higher proportions of neuropathology in the future.

    2. The fact of language disorder is taken by some theorists to be evidence of neuropathology.

    3. Some language disorders may represent normal variation in language ability rather than neuropathology.

B. Studies of CNS integrity highlight the heterogeneity of the language disordered population.

VII. We now have sufficient information about language disordered children to develop training techniques which are uniquely suited to this group, but experimental training studies remain to be done.

## REVIEW QUESTIONS

1. Which of the following areas of linguistic knowledge seems to present the greatest difficulties for the language disordered child?

    A. Phrase structure rules.
    B. Lexical meaning.
    C. Grammatical morphology.
    D. Relational semantics.
    E. Conversational rules.

2. Language disordered children are necessarily communicatively-handicapped because:

   A. Their lack of grammatical skill prevents them from being responsive conversationalists.
   B. Their lack of grammatical skill prevents them from using language to accomplish social purposes.
   C. They lack the knowledge that language is a conventional symbolic code.
   D. They have few grammatical options to use in constructing conversational repairs or context-sensitive utterances.
   E. They have a restricted non-verbal symbolic repertoire.

3. Children with language disorders frequently evidence emotional-social disturbances:

   A. Since these problems can be expected to resolve with improvement in language skills, they need not be a focus of intervention.
   B. Since these problems may influence the amount and quality of linguistic input to the child, they should be considered a legitimate focus of language intervention.
   C. The language clinician must somehow work around these problems since he/she is not professionally qualified to address emotional-social growth, however important it may be.
   D. Since these problems may well disrupt language learning, language intervention should not begin until the child achieves emotional-social health.
   E. Such problems are the consequence of hyperactivity and are hence best treated by medication.

4. Tallal's research with language disordered children suggests that:

   A. They have difficulty identifying rapid auditory stimuli.
   B. They have difficulty determining the order of auditory events.
   C. They have difficulty recognizing auditory patterns which incorporate frequency change.
   D. They have difficulty with auditory verbal association processes.
   E. They have no difficulties in the area of auditory perception.

5. If a child bears a normal range IQ on a performance scale such as the Leiter, Columbia or Ravens we know that:

   A. The child's intellectual development in nonverbal areas is age-appropriate.
   B. The child's intellectual potential is normal.
   C. Certain of the child's cognitive skills are age-appropriate.
   D. The child should be capable of age-appropriate academic achievement in mathematics and logic as long as these subjects are taught nonverbally.
   E. The child's rate of learning is age-appropriate.

6. If a normal child typically learns language form X before form Y, the clinician should "teach" the language disordered child form X before form Y:

   A. If there are evident linguistic rule dependencies between the forms.
   B. To insure that pre-requisite knowledge is available.
   C. As a conservative strategy when the dependency relationships between forms is unclear.
   D. Only if the child appears to have normal nonverbal intelligence.
   E. A and C.
   F. B and D.

7. Children with language disorders evidence language skills which:

   A. Are below expectations for their mental age.
   B. Are below expectations for their chronological age.
   C. Are not due to the influence of motor impairment, hearing loss, retardation, environmental deprivation or psychosis.
   D. A and C.
   E. B and C.

8. Research with language disordered children has demonstrated that their proficiency with grammatical morphemes is typically below that which would be predicted on the basis of utterance length. This suggests that:

   A. The rules which are typically used for determining utterance length are inappropriate for use with language disordered children.
   B. Mean length of utterance is a better index of phrase structure complexity than of morphological knowledge.
   C. Language disordered children learn grammatical morphology more slowly than do normal children.
   D. Grammatical morphology is a relatively unimportant aspect of linguistic competence.
   E. Language disordered children acquire language in patterns of development which are different than those seen in normal children.

9. Most research studies which have looked at the language disordered children have:

   A. Investigated a single aspect of language knowledge such as vocabulary or sentence structure.
   B. Compared knowledge across different aspects of language.
   C. Concluded that their language acquisition patterns differ from those of normal children.
   D. Examined the effects of specific intervention techniques.
   E. Utilized both mental-age and language-level control groups.

10. Language intervention techniques which make use of signed English or other visual analogues of English may assist the language disordered child in learning to speak because:

A. They circumvent the auditory modality.
B. They introduce the concept of language in a less demanding fashion.
C. They present a slower, more static correlate to the auditory signal.
D. They provide the child with a communication tool which may be used while oral language is being learned.
E. They simplify the decontextualization process.

11. Based on current research, which of the following factors appear to be viable as "explanations" of developmental language disorders? (You may choose more than one.)

A. Difficulties with the attentional control and fine-tuning aspects of perceptual processing.
B. Symbolic deficits.
C. Neurological dysfunction.
D. Restricted exposure to the physical environment.
E. Inadequate body image.

# Chapter 32

# SOCIOLINGUISTICS AND COMMUNICATION DISORDERS

*Orlando L. Taylor and Cassandra A. Peters*

I.  Introduction

    A.  Classic definitions of communication disorders claim that speech and/or language or both are disordered when they deviate sufficiently from a <u>norm</u>.

        1.  In the U.S., the norm is defined as the phonological, semantic, grammatical and pragmatic features of "standard" English.

        2.  Actually "normal" language varies as a function of interactions among several sociocultural variables.

        3.  Pathological communication within a specified group of speakers can be measured only against the language norms for their community.

        4.  A perfectly normal speaker of a particular dialect of a language will be inaccurately labeled as having a <u>pathology</u> -- when the real difference is only in language use.

    B.  <u>Dialect</u> is used as a term to mean a variety of a language.

    C.  Contrary to popular belief, Standard English is not one way of speaking, nor is it an intrinsically better way of speaking.

    D.  In the U.S., several varieties of Standard English are spoken, all of which are identified with specific regions of the country or with certain racial, ethnic, or language groups.

    E.  All varieties of Standard English share a common set of grammatical rules.

II. Social and Cultural Factors Which Influence Language Acquisition and Behavior

A. Basic Sociolinguistic Concepts and Terminology

1. Social and cultural factors influence all dimensions of language.

2. Sociolinguistics studies the structure and use of language in its social and cultural context.

3. Pragmatics investigates language use in interactional communicative settings employing the speech act as the fundamental unit of analysis.

4. Ethnography of speaking/communication refers to the characteristics of the language as used by a particular speech community.

5. Linguistic competence is the intuitive knowledge that a speaker/listener possesses of the grammatical rules of the language.

6. Conversational postulates are the rules for interaction.

7. The linguistic repertoire of a speech community may consist of several mutually intelligible dialects.

8. A vernacular or colloquial variety of a language is more informal, casual and intimate.

9. Sociolinguistic variables identify the nonlinguistic dimensions of the social context which influence the selection of a particular language variety.

B. Race and Ethnicity.

1. Racial and ethnic background can influence language patterns that are not genetic or biological.

2. Related to transmission and/or preservation of cultural attitudes and values.

3. Racial or ethnic membership alone does not preclude one from acquiring or using a number of other language codes.

C. Social Class/Education/Occupation.

1. Historically, linguistic differences have served to identify and separate social classes.

2. Many dimensions of language variation are attributed to social class influences:

   a. poverty and home environment;

   b. child-rearing practices and maternal teaching;

   c. family interaction patterns;

   d. travel and experience;

   e. code switching.

D. Region.

   1. Regional dialects are defined by geographic boundaries.

   2. There are at least 10 regional dialects in U.S.

   3. Regional dialects are marked by specific linguistic patterns.

E. Gender.

   1. Major differences in the speech of men and women result from contrasting physical and psychological characteristics of the voice.

   2. Certain differences exist between the "characteristic language uses of men and women".

   3. As sex roles become less differentiated, it is likely that these will be fewer surface differences between male and female speech.

F. Situation/Context.

   1. Several important situational and contextual variables that may influence all dimensions of language behavior:

      a. dyadic interactions;

      b. role relationships;

      c. linguistic code.

G. Age.

   1. Age-grading refers to differences in speech relative to the age of the speaker and listener.

   2. Includes the importance of peer pressure on language during adolescence.

3. Language is a fairly good indicator of a person's age.

H. First Language Community/Culture.

    1. <u>Bilingual</u> persons usually have distinct vestiges of their first language remaining.

    2. Bilingual persons typically code-switch from one language to another depending on the social situation.

    3. The frequency with which one hears and interacts within the second language code typically determines one's skill in the use of a second language.

III. Descriptions of Selected Dialects of American English

A. Background.

    1. In U.S. the variety of spoken English is related to:

        a. languages brought by various cultural groups;

        b. indigenous native American languages;

        c. cultural mix of various communities and regions;

        d. political and economic forces;

        e. migration patterns of various cultural groups;

        f. social stratification.

B. Black English.

    1. Most controversial and most written about dialect of American English.

    2. Defined as the set of phonological, grammatical and pragmatic rules used by working class black people, especially for communication in informal situations within the speech community.

    3. Black English has considerable overlap with several other dialects, notably Southern English and Southern White Nonstandard English.

    4. <u>Creolist theory</u> - holds that Black English is an outgrowth of a complex history of language hybridization involving several African languages and four main European languages.

5. <u>Pidgin</u> – develops when peoples speaking different languages come in contact with each other and have need for a common language.

    a. typically from nondominant cultural groups;

    b. usually informal, consisting of single word utterances and many gestures.

6. Some dispute over the validity of the concept of Black English based on semantics.

C. Spanish-Influenced English.

    1. One's acquisition of a new language is influenced by the phonology and grammar of the native language -- <u>linguistic interference</u>.

    2. Spanish-Influenced English is the best U.S. example of language interference.

IV. Application of Sociolinguistic Data and Theory to the Practice of Speech/Language Pathology

A. Attitudes – the speech/language pathologist needs to view language variety as a normal phenomenon and not as an indicator of communication pathology.

B. Definitions – contemporary views permit defining pathology from the perspective of language norms.

C. Most tests in current use in speech/language pathology are based on linguistics presuppositions consistent with Northern Midland Standard English.

    1. Taylor (1979) lists 7 sources of possible bias in standardized tests:

        a. social situational bias;

        b. value bias;

        c. phonological bias;

        d. grammatical bias;

        e. vocabulary bias;

        f. pragmatic bias;

        g. directional/format bias.

D. Management and Education.

   1. Guidelines for the speech/language pathologist who must provide instruction in Standard English to speakers of nonstandard dialects:

      a. highlight distinguishing characteristics between the two dialects;

      b. discrimination drills;

      c. identification drills;

      d. translation drills;

      e. response drills.

## REVIEW QUESTIONS

Define the following terms:

1. speech community _____

_____

_____

2. linguistic competence _____

_____

_____

3. linguistic repertoire _____

_____

_____

4. conversational postulates _____
   _____
   _____

5. vernacular or colloquial _____
   _____
   _____

6. language markers _____
   _____
   _____

7. code switching _____
   _____
   _____

8. dyadic interactions _____
   _____
   _____

9. age-grading _____
   _____
   _____

10. pidgin language _____
   _____
   _____

11. There are at least  (how many?) dialects recognized in the United States.

    A.  4
    B.  6
    C.  8
    D.  10
    E.  12

12. Distribution of linguistic forms is related to several factors including:

    A. _____
    B. _____
    C. _____
    D. _____
    E. _____

# Chapter 33

# LANGUAGE PROCESSING AND READING DEFICIENCIES: ASSESSMENT AND REMEDIATION OF CHILDREN WITH SPECIAL LEARNING PROBLEMS

*Geraldine P. Wallach*

I. Introduction

    A. Recent psycholinguistic research has had great influence on management of children with language and learning disabilities.

        1. Such as the nature of auditory perception on reading acquisition and reading problems.

        2. Influence of a listener's current knowledge, the particular situation and the relatedness of sentences are all part of the comprehension process.

        3. A discussion of reading comprehension is really a discussion about language comprehension.

II. Historical Perspective

    A. Children with special learning problems have been described as minimally brain-damaged, perceptually impaired, dyslexic, emotionally disturbed, slow, language-learning disabled or "poorly taught".

    B. Visual and Auditory Perceptual Orientations:

        1. Terms <u>perceptually</u> <u>impaired</u> (visually) and <u>learning impaired</u> frequently were used as synonyms for each other.

            a. early researchers emphasized the training of visual processes as a forerunner for higher level learning;

            b. other researchers emphasized auditory perceptual processing training through skills such as discrimination of isolated sounds and words, listening, etc.;

c. more recently authors have pointed out the inadequacies of both visual and auditory "perceptual deficit" as a global educational concept of learning disabilities;

d. current theories involve the examination of speech and reading relationships, the integration of semantic and syntactic cues with visual information, etc., etc.

C. The Endless Terminology

1. Whatever we call them, there clearly exists a population of children who are having difficulty learning in regular classroom settings, who frequently fall behind in their work (around grades 2 and 3) and who are becoming increasingly frustrated by peer, parent and teacher pressure.

2. Difficult to subgroup learning disabled youngsters at this time – perhaps better to specify the patterns of abilities and deficits exhibited by different types of learning disabled children.

III. The Language System (Phonology-Syntax-Semantics) and the Language Medium (Auditory-Visual)

A. Proficient language users and fluent readers scan and predict, attending to meaning and not to the isolated components within the message.

B. Phonemic Segmentation and Early Reading:

1. The beginning reader must construct "a link between speech and the arbitrary signs of script".

2. "Phonetic recoding" is how many letter segments must be taken into account to arrive at a correct pronunciation or proper "phonetic rendition".

a. an important skill in the acquisition of reading.

3. Complexity of the problem associating speech with reading increases when the acoustic structure of speech is considered, i.e., "bat" has 3 phonemes but only 1 acoustic segment.

a. Savin (1972) found that even adults have difficulty analyzing syllables into phonemes;

b. Liberman et al. (1977) found a developmental progression of segmentation skills in children:

297

（1）perception of larger, undifferentiated units
(sentences/phrases) of speech;

(2) individual word discrimination from the speech stream;

(3) ability to segment words into syllables;

(4) ability to segment words/syllables into phonemes.

C.   Use of Semantics and Syntax in Early Reading:

1.   Even in early reading stages, children try to derive
meaning from what they read.

2.   At next level, child gets idea that what is said must be
related to what is seen; if not, the child remains silent
in "no response" phase of reading.

3.   Children's Comprehensive Strategies for Individual
Sentences:

a. Bever (1970) – the canonical order strategy:
segment initial noun-verb-noun sequence to correspond
to the actor-action-recipient;

b. Clark and Clark (1968) – order of mention strategy:
clause order in sentences corresponds to order of events;

c. Amidon and Carey (1972) – pay attention to the main
clause strategy:   attend to main clause regardless
of clause order within the sentence;

d. Sheldon (1977) – the parallel function strategy:
assumes that the relative pronoun has the same
grammatical function as its antecedent.

4.   Strategies for the Integration of Sentences:

a. Bransford and Franks (1972) demonstrated that adult
listeners integrate sentences to obtain a complete idea;

b. another important aspect of comprehension is the ability
to draw inferences, i.e., to add to given information –
inferential strategies;

c. discourse strategies – abilities to relate old and new
information, utilize themes around which to organize
other information, and influence of titles.

IV. Formal and Informal Assessment Procedures

    A. Wiig and Semel (1976) state that "...language and communication problems in children are multi-faceted, defying unitary description".

        1. Assessment of children with special learning problems is difficult because:

            a. data from standardized tests must be related to meaningful theoretical framework;

            b. many cognitive processes may not be sampled by standardized tools at this time;

            c. test scores and information must be related to the real world of the child.

        2. Caution should be exercised in making too strong a case for any single process being the cause of a child's difficulties.

    B. Comprehension of Individual Sentences Assessment:

        1. Rees and Shulman (1978) state that many standardized tests probably only measure literal comprehension, e.g.:

            a. the Assessment of Children's Language Comprehension (ACLC, Foster et al., 1972);

            b. the Northwestern Syntax Screening Test (NSST, Lee, 1971);

            c. the Test for Auditory Comprehension of Language (TACL, Carrow, 1973);

            d. the Token Test for Children (Hahn and Weiss, 1973).

    C. Knowledge and Logical Reasoning Assessment:

        1. Developmental Test of Language Comprehension (DTLC, Weiner-Mayster, 1975).

        2. Test of Linguistic Concepts (Wiig and Semel, 1976).

        3. Detroit Tests of Learning Aptitude (Baker and Leland, 1959).

D.  Individual Sentences in Listening and Reading:

1.  Children unskilled in reading are unskilled in encoding linguistic information.

2.  Fluent readers seem to go from print to meaning without conscious effort.

3.  Poor readers take too long to process.

4.  Assessment of strategies used by good and poor readers needs to be incorporated into future evaluation and teaching programs.

V.  Beyond Individual Sentences

A.  Recent research shows that normal children integrate short sentences into whole new ideas, while learning disabled children could only integrate up to two ideas at one time – they tended to recall individual sentences.

B.  Information about the way children integrate (and/or abstract) can be obtained from:

1.  Durrell Analysis of Reading Difficulty Test (Durrell, 1955).

2.  Gates–MacGintie Test (1968).

C.  Braun and Froese (1977) suggest the following scheme for assessment and remediation:

1.  Literal – recognizes details, main ideas, and relationships.

2.  Inferential – predicts outcomes, cause–effect, etc.

3.  Evaluative – distinguishes fact from fiction, makes judgements, recognizes purposes.

4.  Interpretive – uses information to draw conclusions.

VI.  Auditory Processing

A.  One of the most critical factors for early reading acquisition is phonemic segmentation and identification.

1.  Assessment of speech segmentation might include the following:

a. can the child tell how many words are in a sentence?

b. can the child segment words into syllables?

c. can the child segment syllables into sounds?

VII. Guidelines for Remediation in Children with Special Learning Problems

    A. Teaching the child to organize information means developing strategies for language and learning.

        1. Implementing techniques for comprehension and general discourse of:

            a. individual sentences;

            b. sentence pairs;

            c. paragraphs and stories.

    B. Linguistic Awareness and Reading:

        1. Regarding the specific development of reading, Gibson and Levin (1975) offer the following:

            a. consider individual differences among children;

            b. make relationship between reading and language clear from the beginning;

            c. consider simultaneous training using phonologic, syntactic, and semantic information;

            d. child must develop a "set for diversity" as English language is not a phonetically regular language.

        2. Strategies for chunking, scanning and predicting are as important for the listener as they are for the reader.

VIII. From Theory to Theory:   The Final Word

    A. Any standardized test or program is only as good as the teacher using it.

    B. The three fields, learning disabilities, psycholinguistics and reading should be viewed as intersecting areas.

    C. Research and curriculum development must be mutually dependent matters.

**REVIEW QUESTIONS**

True or False:

1. ___ Written information is presented visually, and thus reading is essentially a simple visual process.

2. ___ Normal and learning disabled children have a knowledge of spoken language which interacts with the development of reading.

3. ___ To learn to read is to learn a system of rules and strategies for extracting information from text.

4. Describe the 3 levels of comprehension discussed by Perfetti (1977):

   Level 1: _____

   _____

   _____

   Level 2: _____

   _____

   _____

   Level 3: _____

   _____

   _____

5. Identify the following standard tests from their common abbreviations:

   A. ACLC _____

   B. NSST _____

   C. TACL _____

6. Name 3 tests that might be used to evaluate knowledge and logical reasoning assessment:

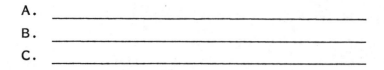

   A. _____

   B. _____

   C. _____

7. Name 2 tests that would be useful in assessing a child's ability to integrate and/or abstract information:

   A. _____

   B. _____

8. One of the most critical factors for early reading acquisition is phonemic segmentation and identification. How might you assess speech segmentation ability?

   A. _____

   B. _____

   C. _____

# Chapter 34

# PROBLEMS OF MATHEMATICS IN CHILDREN WITH LANGUAGE DISORDERS

*Doris J. Johnson and Jane W. Blalock*

I.  Mathematics is a highly complex symbol system that requires the acquisition, integration and use of many subskills including the abstraction and application of rules.

   A.  Differential Diagnosis:

   1.  First task is to determine as much as possible about the child's basic abilities and background of experience.

   2.  Assessment of hearing and vision is essential; also assessment of mental ability.

   3.  Children with language disorders often score below average on verbal intelligence measures.

   4.  Must be alert for perceptual or perceptual-motor difficulties.

   5.  Child's background or experience is important since lack of stimulation or instruction history may contribute to underachievement.

   6.  Rarely does a problem exist in isolation; thus a child with an auditory verbal comprehension disorder typically will have difficulty with reading comprehension, written language and some aspects of numerical reasoning.

   7.  Child will need a comprehensive study of language and all areas of academic achievement.

   B.  In order to plan a specific remedial program, further investigation of the child's learning processes is necessary.

   1.  Must determine if problems exist at any level of input in any system, or in integration of information, or in conveying what is known.

2. The real task of the diagnostician is to determine whether the child has some problem in mathematics or whether a processing deficit interferes with performance:

    a. <u>level</u> of the disturbance is important – attention, perception, memory, symbolization or conceptualization?

    b. verbal vs. nonverbal information processing.

II. Mathematics and Cognitive Disturbance

    A. Four cognitive factors occur frequently with problems of mathematics (according to Guttman, 1936 and Cohn, 1971):

        1. Language.

        2. Memory.

        3. Logical reasoning.

        4. Visual-spatial difficulties.

    B. Gerstmann (1940) observed a different set of behaviors:

        1. Disturbances in calculation.

        2. Agraphia.

        3. Right-left disorientation.

        4. Finger agnosia.

    C. Children with language problems tend to have problems with word problems in arithmetic.

III. Language Problems

    A. Verbal Comprehension.

        1. The Boehm Test of Basic Concepts is very useful in assessing some of the vocabulary needed during the early school years.

        2. School readiness tests are also valuable in studying language comprehension in relation to mathematics achievement.

        3. The understanding of comparative and superlative terms is important for many aspects of mathematics.

        4. Child should understand and use waves of geometric designs.

B. Auditory Memory Span.

1. Children with limited memory spans have difficulty in many areas of learning.

2. The language impaired child should be given auditory memory span tests that require both nonverbal and verbal responses.

C. Sequencing.

1. Perception, retention and reproduction of material in a specified sequence is necessary for many facets of learning.

2. Sequencing is critical for meaningful counting and many aspects of problem solving.

3. The clinician should attempt to determine whether cognitive sequencing problems occur primarily in intrasensory or intersensory learning.

D. Word Retrieval.

1. Word retrieval problems have been noted in many language impaired and learning disabled children.

2. Some have difficulty with the quick recall of numbers.

E. Syntax.

1. Several studies show a relationship between syntactic complexity and the ability to solve verbal mathematics problems.

2. Math is a specialized language form and there is high conceptual density in problems to be solved.

3. Vocabulary and syntax are both important factors in math.

4. Verbalization of principles and generalizations is important to transfer after nonverbal experience and awareness.

F. Oral Formulation.

1. Language impaired children use an overabundance of nonspecific words that do not convey meaning to the listener.

2. These children often know more than they can convey.

3. They need help and encouragement to ask appropriate questions to the subject matter.

4. Some language impaired children may use vague, ambiguous explanations because they have a limited sense of audience.

IV. Related Learning Problems

A. Meaning.

1. Generalized disturbances of meaning and conceptualization are very debilitating for they interfere with both academic and social learning.

2. Students with meaning disorders need an abundance of concrete experience that is simultaneously presented with the symbols.

B. Rule Acquisition and Application.

1. Children with language and learning disorders have difficulty abstracting and applying rules.

2. In remediation, the teacher should attempt to clarify the child's understanding of principles and provide practice that will foster automatic rule usage.

C. Reading.

1. It is important to evaluate both decoding and reading comprehension skills before giving the child word problems in math.

2. Mathematics vocabulary contains many words with multiple meanings, requiring the child to select the appropriate meaning from context.

D. Attention.

1. Children with attention disorders have a variety of problems in the area of mathematics.

2. Information overloading may also be considered part of an attention disorder – as when children are unable to integrate multiple messages and to monitor their own performance.

3. Attention is best when the material is in keeping with the child's cognitive structure.

E. Organization.

    1. Lack of self-organization is a problem that is of concern to many young adults with language and learning disorders.

    2. Lack of self-organization is often evident in mathematics – students fail to determine what is relevant and cannot decide which numbers to use in what way.

F. Nonverbal Visual Skills.

    1. A diagnostic study should include an investigation of many aspects of visual perception.

        a. perception of sequence;

        b. attention to details;

        c. rotation or inversion of figures;

        d. disturbance of visual memory and imagery;

        e. generalized problems of representation;

        f. failure to comprehend meanings of gesture, pantomime or pictures.

## REVIEW QUESTIONS

1. What general areas must be considered in the differential diagnosis of problems in mathematics from children with language disorders?

A. _____

B. _____

C. _____

D. _____

E. _____

F. _____

2. Identify the four cognitive factors that occur frequently in conjunction with problems of mathematics according to Guttman (1936) and Cohn (1971):

   A. _____

   B. _____

   C. _____

   D. _____

3. Identify six areas of language problems that may be investigated as potentially related to mathematics disability:

   A. _____

   B. _____

   C. _____

   D. _____

   E. _____

   F. _____

4. Identify areas of learning problems that may interfere with various aspects of symbolic behavior – including mathematics:

   A. _____

   B. _____

   C. _____

   D. _____

   E. _____

   F. _____

5. Rarely does a problem exist in isolation. Therefore, it is necessary to investigate interrelationships between various symbol systems. A child with auditory verbal comprehension disorder may have difficulty with what other academic areas?

   A. _____

   B. _____

   C. _____

   D. _____

6. The role of verbalization in the acquisition and application of concepts is very important. However, verbalization of principles and generalizations is important in transfer after _____ and _____.

# Chapter 35

# COMMUNICATION AND LANGUAGE INSTRUCTION FOR SEVERELY HANDICAPPED CHILDREN AND YOUTH

*Lawrence J. Turton*

I. Introduction

    A. <u>Severely handicapped</u> student, by definition, manifests severe developmental disabilities, i.e., retarded, neurologically or sensorily handicapped, severely emotionally disturbed, or severely multiply handicapped.

    B. All severely handicapped students must also be taught how to learn and how to use normal developmental processes.

    C. A communication system is one of the highest priority developmental domains for the severely developmentally disabled student.

II. Principles of Assessment

    A. Content and strategies of training program should follow the sequence of normal development and functions.

    B. The selection of an assessment procedure for any specific student is a function of the student's developmental level and the behavior domain being assessed.

    C. <u>Observational Procedures</u>:

        1. Data obtained under "naturalistic" conditions.

        2. Responses are primary biological reflexes, elicited only be environmental stimuli.

        3. Purpose of the assessment is to specify the conditions that control emission of the behavior.

        4. Specific assessment of the frequency of occurrence of a response is needed as pre- or post-intervention data.

5. Goal is to determine whether changes in environmental conditions will precipitate a change in the responses or behaviors of a student.

6. Observational procedures include:

   a. narrative recordings;

   b. structural observations.

D. Criterion-Referenced Procedures:

   1. Criterion-referenced testing procedure bases decisions upon the performance of an individual relative to the objectives of a teaching sequence.

   2. In this approach to language treatment (curriculum concept of treatment), the clinician must conform to the following sequence:

      a. specification of the developmental model;

      b. identification of the teaching strategies to be used;

      c. modification of the developmental sequence into a set of teaching objectives and procedures;

      d. design and implementation of the assessment procedures for gathering pre- and post-intervention data and teaching data.

E. Formal Instruments:

   1. Purpose of most formal tests is to obtain responses to items so that a student's raw score can be converted to some form of a transformed value according to a table of norms.

      a. this goal is virtually meaningless with the severely handicapped population.

   2. Content of the items and the required responses can provide screening data to determine a priority sequence for informal procedure.

   3. Every formal test implicitly demands that the student being tested must be able to attend to the relevant stimulus, to comprehend the instructions, and emit a specific verbal or motor response.

4. Rating scales – instruments for rating the behavior of severely handicapped students in lieu of testing them:

   a. not really measures of a student's developmental level – they are scaled measures of the perceptions of another person regarding the student's functional level;

   b. often attempt to screen a wide range of behaviors in as few items as possible;

   c. few rating scales for the severely handicapped have been subjected to vigorous psychometric procedures for test development;

   d. rating scales are a poor substitute for direct observation and measurement of the student.

5. Teaching Program Data:

   a. most important data set is that which is accumulated during teaching activities;

   b. help in decisions regarding appropriateness and validity of pre-intervention measures;

   c. monitors student progress in communication development;

   d. evaluates student's use of learning strategies;

   e. evaluates the effectiveness of the teaching procedures;

   f. continuous recording, i.e., the scoring of every response by the student, provides valuable data.

III. Developmental Prerequisites

   A. Recent research has specified a sequential pattern of sensorimotor, cognitive and semantic prerequisites for the development of social interactions necessary for human communication.

   B. "Prerequisite" is different than "maturation":

      1. Prerequisite is a specific skill, behavior or response system that is necessary for acquisition of subsequent skills.

      2. Maturation suggests readiness based upon cumulative factors and indicated by a general term such as chronological age.

3. Prerequisites can be taught or experimentally manipulated; maturation cannot be.

C. Developmental Learning Skills (a set of prerequisites which have specific functions in the teaching sequence):

1. Attention.

2. Matching.

3. Imitation.

4. Discrimination.

5. Following directions.

D. Cognitive Prerequisites – relative to language acquisition, the following prerequisites can be isolated:

1. Early social communication and sentence prototype behaviors.

2. Object permanence and functional use.

3. Symbolic use and play.

4. Specific attributes and functions.

5. Conversational postulates.

E. Teaching Basic Prerequisites:

1. Basic teaching concept is that the process is cumulative; initially responses are taught in separate tracks and then merged at the appropriate points in time.

2. Visual tracking and reflex motor movements are the two most basic responses of students to permit entrance into virtually all developmental programs.

3. Early social communication is enhanced by attending to objects and gross motor imitation.

4. Subsequently, the student is engaged in object matching and functional use instruction using objects common to daily activities.

IV. Principles of Communication and Language Instruction

A. Teaching Procedures:

1. Communication instruction for severely handicapped students should reflect the normal developmental process.

2. "Errorless teaching" - each time the student is presented with a stimulus, the prompting system should insure that a correct response will be emitted.

3. Effective teaching is a combination of careful sequencing of content and a consistent format and utilization of prompts.

4. Instructional format follows the paradigm:

   a. recognition (comprehension);

   b. imitation;

   c. labeling (or spontaneous production);

   d. in conjunction with objects, pictures, verbal or signed instructions.

B. Response Modes:

1. Significant progress in the domain of communication training for all handicapped children has been the development of "non-vocal" or "alternative" response modes.

2. The clinician must identify the nonoral motor responses that will enhance the student's ability to interact with persons and objects in the environment.

   a. pointing, touching, manipulating objects, etc.

3. Manual sign language systems are especially valuable for use with the severely handicapped.

   a. potent teaching strategy for presenting materials;

   b. signs can be used as linguistic cues;

   c. sign cues increase correct response probabilities;

   d. signs can be used as a prompt during the shaping component of the language program.

C. Vocabulary Instruction:

1. The fundamental language forms are vocabulary items.

2. Vocabulary acquisition is both "developmental" and "functional".

3.   Principles for selecting the initial vocabulary:

   a. words selected should reflect early semantic forms;

   b. words should reflect syntactic categories used in early phrase structures for children;

   c. words should reflect high frequency persons, objects and events that have functional relevance.

D.   Vocabulary Expansion:

1.   Limited only by the innovativeness and ingenuity of the clinician.

2.   Curriculum integration is very relevant to vocabulary instruction.

E.   Vocabulary and Shaping:

1.   Vocabulary instruction is the appropriate point to introduce the notion of response shaping.

2.   Through approximations the student is taught, principally through imitation, to combine phonetic movements into more acceptable forms.

F.   Syntax Teaching:

1.   Syntax is predicted upon the cognitive prerequisite of symbolic use or play.

2.   One of the principal semantic forms in syntactic structures of young children is the form Agent-Action-Object.

3.   Another important form is the Experiencer-State such as "I want.....".

4.   Format for syntactic instruction follows the sequence outlined for vocabulary:

   a. recognition;

   b. imitation;

   c. spontaneous production - with shaping when necessary.

G.  Generalization:

1.  Ultimate test of any teaching program is the degree to which the content is transferred (or generalized) to nonteaching contexts.

2.  In case of language – the final criterion is demonstration by the student that he can produce appropriate, meaningful, and grammatical linguistic responses in any enivronmental context.

**REVIEW QUESTIONS**

1.  Which of the following assessment procedures does <u>not</u> measure a student's behavior in a direct fashion:

A.  Rating Scales.
B.  Criterion-referenced procedures.
C.  Formal procedures.
D.  Informal procedures.
E.  Narrative Recordings.

2.  The assessment procedure which provides the clinician with the most viable information for program decisions for the severely handicapped is

A.  Frequency of occurrence measures.
B.  Teaching ratings of performance.
C.  Teaching data.
D.  Structured observations.
E.  Formal tests.

3.  Criterion-referenced procedures have construct validity when they are:

A.  Compared to standardized tests.
B.  Consistent in determining program placement for students.
C.  Derived from structured classroom observations.
D.  Comprised of effective probe procedures.
E.  Consistent in obtaining the same scores.

4. Developmental learning skills are those response systems which:

   A. Cannot be taught or experimentally manipulated.
   B. Serve as prerequisites for the developmental process.
   C. Serve as the basis for teaching programs.
   D. Are used to generate motor behavior.
   E. Are unique to language acquisition.

5. Of the five developmental learning skills discussed, the most basic is:

   A. Imitation.
   B. Matching.
   C. Following directions.
   D. Discrimination.
   E. Attention.

6. The specific cognitive prerequisites for early vocabulary are:

   A. Static attributes and functions.
   B. Social communication and behaviors.
   C. Object permanence and functional use.
   D. Symbolic use and play.
   E. Conversational and sentence postulates.

7. The acquisition of attention as a prerequisite is determined by:

   A. Visual fixation to stimuli.
   B. Auditory localization.
   C. Eye contact with an adult.
   D. Remaining seated in front of the teacher.
   E. Auditory localization and fixation.

8. Once a student acquires a prerequisite, the clinician:

   A. Assumes that it is available for subsequent programs.
   B. Assumes that it generalizes to other response systems.
   C. Uses it to obtain attention for other responses.
   D. Uses it as a prompt for subsequent responses.
   E. Assumes that it is integrated with other response systems.

9. Response shaping for oral and manual responses is implemented primarily through:

   A. Articulation therapy.
   B. Recognition teaching.
   C. Physical manipulation.
   D. Visual cues.
   E. Imitation as a prompt.

10. Nonoral or alternative response modes are employed:

    A. When the student cannot use speech.
    B. With physically handicapped students.
    C. As an integral part of all language training.
    D. As a secondary system for the severely hearing impaired child.
    E. When other response modes are unavailable to the student.

11. Initial vocabulary teaching includes words that are:

    A. Functional in the classroom and home.
    B. Functional, developmental and semantically appropriate.
    C. Primarily nouns that refer to objects and items in the environment.
    D. Phonetically similar to facilitate articulatory movements.
    E. Restricted in syllable and phonetic characteristics.

12. Two semantic forms that serve as the bases for early syntax teaching are:

    A. Nonexistence and Experience-State.
    B. Agent-Action and Recurrence.
    C. Agent-Action-Object and Nonexistence.
    D. Nonexistence and Recurrence.
    E. Agent-Action-Object and Experience-State.

13. When scoring syntactic responses, the clinician must maintain a distinction between:

    A. Stimulus-correct and developmentally-correct patterns.
    B. Phonetically-correct and phonologically-correct patterns.
    C. Semantically-correct and syntactically-correct patterns.
    D. Semantically-correct and stimulus-correct patterns.
    E. Phonetically-correct and developmentally-correct patterns.

14. Vocabulary teaching and syntax teaching are:

    A. Independent activities.
    B. Taught in a sequential pattern.
    C. Taught through different formats.
    D. Taught in parallel, but integrated programs.
    E. Taught at different development points.

15. Generalization is viewed as:

    A. A natural sequel to the teaching program.
    B. A product of an effective measurement system.
    C. A function of the teacher.
    D. A function of the clinician.
    E. A skill to be taught by the school and home.

# Chapter 36

# AN OVERVIEW OF AUGMENTATIVE COMMUNICATION

*Carol G. Cohen and Howard C. Shane*

I. Model of Communication (Shane, 1980)

    A.  Purpose:

        1.  To provide a framework for classifying diverse forms of human communication.

        2.  To provide a foundation for assessing communicative behavior in severely communicatively handicapped persons.

        3.  To provide a foundation for the implementation of a non-speech communication program.

    B.  Integration (Forms of Expression):

        1.  Vocal, Nonlinguistic:

            a. crying;

            b. grunting;

            c. laughing;

            d. pleasure sounds.

        2.  Vocal, Linguistic:

            a. speaking;

            b. listening.

        3.  Representational:

            a. line drawings;

            b. pictures;

            c. photographs;

            d. models.

4. Nonvocal, Nonlinguistic:

    a. affect;

    b. gestures;

    c. physiological reactions.

5. Nonvocal, Linguistic Traditional Orthography Initial Teaching Alphabet:

    a. blissymbols;

    b. sign language;

    c. non-SLP;

    d. Morse code.

C. Transmission (Mode of Expression):

  1. Vocal Structures:

    a. respiratory;

    b. phonatory;

    c. resonatory;

    d. articulatory.

  2. Nonvocal Structures:

    a. head;

    b. body;

    c. upper extremities;

    d. face;

    e. eyes.

II. Review of Nonspeech Literature

A. Unaided:

  1. Manual Modes:

    a. American Sign Language (Amslan);

    b. American Indian Sign (Amerind);

          c. signed English;

          d. pantomime;

          e. gesture.

     2.   Employment of Manual Systems:

          a. autism;

          b. mental retardation;

          c. apraxia of speech;

          d. aphasia;

          e. glossectomy;

          f. dysphonia and laryngectomy;

          g. dysarthria.

B.   Aided:

     1.   Augmentative content.

     2.   Augmentative hardware:

          a. automated;

          b. nonautomated.

III.   Selecting Aids and Systems

     A.   Unaided Methods:

          1.   Expressed through upper extremity movement:

               a. fingerspelling;

               b. sign;

               c. gesticulation (ASHA, 1980).

     B.   Aided Methods:

          1.   Not a natural part of communicator's body (ASHA, 1980):

               a. language boards;

               b. electronic instrumentation.

C. Factors to consider before deciding between aided and unaided methods:

1. Neuromotor factors.

2. Portability.

3. Acquisition rate.

4. Picture orientation.

5. Gesture orientation.

6. Environmental considerations.

7. Interaction - integration.

8. Preference (both user's and his family).

**REVIEW QUESTIONS**

1. In 1980, ASHA presented a system of common terminology for non-speech communication. Fill in the recommended terms below:

   A. _____ refers to communication techniques which require some physical medium (in addition to one's body) in order to display symbols or symbol sets.

   B. _____ techniques refer to those methods that utilize manual, body and/or facial movements in order to express information.

2. According to Birdwhistle (1970) ___% of information exchange is oral language, while ___% is nonverbal language.

3. Give four examples of vocal, nonlinguistic expression:

   A. _____

   B. _____

   C. _____

   D. _____

4. Name eight conditions that typically lead to implementation of an augmentative communication system.

A. _____

B. _____

C. _____

D. _____

E. _____

F. _____

G. _____

H. _____

5. When certain brain circuits devoted specifically to the programming of articulatory movements are impaired, the resulting articulatory disorder is called _____.

6. When there is impairment in the cerebral hemisphere that has as its primary function the processing of the language code, the resulting language disorder is _____.

7. The surgical excision or removal of all or part of the tongue is referred to as _____.

8. The collective name for a group of related speech disorders that are due to disturbances in muscular control of the speech mechanism resulting from impairment of any of the basic motor processes involved in the execution of speech is _____.

9. The most common non-automated hardware or augmentative display is the _____.

10. Logographs are graphic representations of words or concepts which have some possible pictographic similarity to the meanings. Identify three common logographic systems:

A. _____

B. _____

C. _____

11. Recent investigations estimate that approximately _____ million nonspeaking children and adults currently reside in the United States.

# Chapter 37

# HEARING DISORDERS: AUDIOLOGIC MANIFESTATIONS

*Janet M. Zarnoch*

I.  Impedance Audiometry

    A.  Impedance Test Battery:

        1.  Tympanometry;

        2.  Static compliance;

        3.  Acoustic reflex thresholds.

    B.  Tympanometry is an objective measure of the mobility (or compliar of the tympanic membrane as air pressure is varied in the externa ear canal.

    C.  Static Compliance determines the compliance of the middle ear syst while at rest.  Normal range of test values is .30 cc to 1.6 cc:

        1.  PVT – Physical Volume Test:  part of the static compliance te: which tells whether the eardrum is intact or not.

        2.  Normal ear canal PVT is 1.4 cc or less; if perforation is preser or patent ventilation tube is in place in the tympanic membran PVT may be as large as 4.0 or 5.0 cc or greater.

    D.  Acoustic Reflex Thresholds are normally obtained between 70 and 100 dB HTL.

II.  Electronystagmography (ENG)

    A.  Definition of ENG:  clinical test of vestibular function which evaluates only the function of the semicircular canals:

        1.  ENG is an electrical recording, obtained with electrodes placec around the eyes, of nystagmus measured from the corneoretin potential.

        2.  Nystagmus is defined as a rhythmic back-and-forth movement of the eyeball.

3. Nystagmus is characterized by a slow and fast phase; named for direction of the <u>fast</u> <u>phase</u>:

   a. slow phase is a slow conjugate deviation of eyes to right or left and is initiated by the vestibular system;

   b. fast phase is the quick return of the eyes to the midline, initiated by a central mechanism.

4. ENG results do not provide specific diagnosis, but provide additional objective information about a patient's vestibular function:

   a. <u>peripheral</u> site-of-lesion refers to the vestibular end organs and/or the vestibular portion of the VIIIth nerve;

   b. <u>central</u> site-of-lesion refers to any of the vestibular neural connections in the brain stem or higher up in the central nervous system;

   c. <u>nystagmus</u> is the normal response during optokinetic portion of ocular tests;

   d. <u>positional nystagmus</u> is nystagmus which occurs when the head is placed in specific positions - normal patients should not show positional nystagmus;

   e. <u>spontaneous nystagmus</u> is abnormal and present constantly, regardless of head or body position - it does not vary in intensity, does not change direction, and does not disappear with repeated positioning.

5. Bithermal Caloric Test:

   a. each ear is irrigated with warm ($44^{o}C$) and cold ($30^{o}C$) water for 30-40 seconds, with a 5-minute rest between each of the four irrigations;

   b. the warm irrigations produce nystagmus which beats toward the irrigated ear;

   c. the cold irrigations produce nystagmus which beats toward the opposite side of the irrigated ear;

   d. "COWS" - cold-opposite; warm-same.

6. ENG Results:

   a. comparison between right and left ear responses to determine if a <u>unilateral</u> <u>weakness</u> exists;

   b. comparison between all right beating nystagmic responses ($R44^{o}C$ and $L30^{o}C$) and all left beating nystagmic responses ($R30^{o}C$ and $L44^{o}C$) to determine if a <u>directional</u> <u>preponderance</u> of right or left beats is present;

c. normal caloric responses should show symmetry between ear;

d. difference between ears of 20% or greater represents "unilateral weakness" associated with peripheral vestibular end organ lesions;

e. if all four caloric responses are depressed or absent, "bilateral weakness" is present which can be related to peripheral or central vestibular lesion;

f. "directional preponderance" exists if a 30% or greater difference exists between the two right beating responses and the two left beating responses – nonlocalizing finding that has little clinical significance.

7. ENG is used to evaluate persons complaining of dizziness, dysequilibrium, vertigo, imbalance:

a. provides quantitative information of vestibular function;

b. objective documentation of subjective symptoms;

c. used to monitor vestibular function;

d. evaluates each vestibular system independently through caloric irrigations;

e. performed with eyes closed to eliminate patient's visual fixation which could suppress nystagmus;

f. lengthy, expensive test which causes discomfort to some patients.

III. Conductive Hearing Loss

A. Cerumen Impaction of external ear canal:

1. Degree of conductive hearing loss is variable – from 25 dB to 45 dB; hearing returns to normal when cerumen is removed.

2. May produce type A or B tympanogram with small PVT.

3. ENG may show erroneous unilateral or bilateral weakness if wax is not removed prior to the ENG test.

B. Otitis Externa – infection of external ear canal skin:

1. Usually mild conductive hearing loss of 20 to 30 dB.

2. Impedance testing not advised if patient is in pain.

3. ENG usually not required.

C. Congenital Anomalies of the External Ear:

1. Microtia – deformation which may range from a small deformed pinna to a totally absent pinna and closed ear canal:

   a. unilateral microtia is six times more common than bilateral; more common in males; affects right ear most often;

   b. if ear canal is totally closed with the microtic pinna, a maximum 60 dB conductive loss will be present.

2. Atresia – complete closure or absence of the external ear canal; may occur with microtic pinna or normal pinna:

   a. often associated with congenital middle ear defects;

   b. usually produces maximum 60 dB conductive hearing loss;

   c. usually not possible to perform impedance test battery or ENG.

D. Otitis Media/Middle Ear Effusion (middle ear filled with serous fluid):

1. Inflammation of the middle ear which occurs frequently in children.

2. Serous otitis media – shows pure conductive loss of 15 dB to 30 or 40 dB depending on thickness of fluid, amount of negative middle ear pressure and degree of eardrum retraction:

   a. tympanograms are typically Type B or C; acoustic reflexes generally absent from probe ear and/or elevated in earphone ear.

3. Acute otitis media – sudden onset of suppurative or purulent middle ear fluid:

   a. conductive hearing loss of 15–40 dB; may show low-frequency "stiffness" audiogram or high-frequency "mass" type audiogram pattern;

   b. tympanograms Type B or C; acoustic reflex absent from probe ear and elevated or absent from earphone ear.

4. Chronic otitis media – characterized by a permanent perforation of tympanic membrane:

   a. perforations involving less than 20% of pars tensa cause hearing loss of less than 15 dB; larger perforations cause up to 30 dB conductive loss; if ossicular chain is involved the hearing loss may be as great as 45 dB;

b. sensorineural hearing loss may develop in patients with long-term, severe, chronic otitis media;

c. tympanogram – Type B with large PVT;

d. ENG is usually done with an air caloric stimulus rather than water because of tympanic membrane perforation.

E. Cholesteatoma – skin tumor of middle ear created from epithelium ingrown from the external ear canal:

    1. Degree of conductive loss varies as a function of severity and location of cholesteatoma growth.

    2. Tympanogram type will also vary depending on extent of ossicular involvement.

F. Mastoiditis – dangerous inflammation of the mastoid air cells which can spread to meninges of the brain causing meningitis:

    1. Usually significant conductive hearing loss.

    2. Tympanogram type will depend upon status of tympanic membrane and middle ear ossicles.

G. Otosclerosis – disease of bony capsule of inner ear:

    1. Creates progressive conductive hearing loss characterized by "stiffness tilt" audiogram with "Carhart's notch".

    2. Mild to maximum conductive hearing loss.

    3. Tympanograms are usually a shallow Type A or a normal Type with absent acoustic reflexes bilaterally.

H. Ossicular Discontinuity – disruption of the middle ear ossicular chain due to disease, trauma or congenital defect:

    1. Usually shows maximum conductive hearing loss of 60 dB.

    2. High, flaccid Type A pattern with bilateral absence of acoustic reflexes.

I. Longitudinal Temporal Bone Fracture:

    1. Hearing loss may be conductive, sensorineural or mixed in nature ranging in degree from mild to severe.

    2. Tympanogram type will vary as function of middle ear conditions; acoustic reflex pattern also variable.

    3. 50% have positional nystagmus toward involved ear, or rotatory in pattern.

IV. Sensorineural Hearing Loss

    A. Transverse Temporal Bone Fracture:

        1. Usually result in "dead ear" with permanent, total loss of hearing.

        2. Type A tympanogram with no acoustic reflex from earphone ear.

        3. May show spontaneous nystagmus with absent vestibular caloric response on involved side.

    B. Presbycusis – hearing loss due to aging:

        1. Schuknecht's (1964) four basic processes which lead to presbycusis:

            a. sensory;

            b. neural;

            c. metabolic;

            d. mechanical processes.

        2. Hearing loss is sensorineural and variable in degree and configuration.

        3. Many patients complain of inability to understand speech.

        4. Amplification is not always helpful.

        5. Tympanograms usually Type A; acoustic reflex often at lower sensation level suggesting presence of recruitment.

        6. Often have symptoms of dysequilibrium associated with old age, as described by Schuknecht (1974):

            a. cupulolithiasis;

            b. ampullary dysequilibrium;

            c. macular dysequilibrium;

            d. vestibular ataxia.

    C. Ototoxicity – drug-induced hearing loss and/or vestibular damage:

        1. Ototoxicity usually causes bilaterally symmetrical permanent sensorineural hearing loss.

        2. Many exceptions to (1) above; loss usually accompanied by tinnitus.

3. Type A tympanograms with acoustic reflexes present at reduced sensation levels.

4. Vestibular damage may be documented with ENG; often shows bilaterally depressed responses to bithermal caloric stimulation :

    a. some patients may have spontaneous or positional nystagmus following vestibular ototoxicity.

D. <u>Noise-Induced Hearing Loss</u> – results from exposure to loud noise

1. <u>Temporary threshold shift</u> (TTS) – occurs when a person is exposed to loud noise for a short period of time; depressed auditory thresholds slowly return to normal within a short period of time.

2. <u>Permanent threshold shift</u> (PTS) – permanent hearing loss as a result of long history of chronic noise exposure.

3. Noise-induced hearing loss has a "notch" in audiogram at 4000 Hz, which deepens and widens with continued exposure to noise.

4. Noise exposure usually results in severe tinnitus which may be relieved with biofeedback therapy or "tinnitus masker" technique.

E. <u>Labyrinthitis</u> – infection of the inner ear labyrinth system :

1. Schuknecht (1974) has four categories:

    a. acute toxic labyrinthitis;

    b. acute suppurative labyrinthitis;

    c. chronic labyrinthitis;

    d. labyrinthine sclerosis.

2. English (1976) reports four clinical types:

    a. circumscribed labyrinthitis;

    b. diffuse serous labyrinthitis;

    c. acute suppurative labyrinthitis;

    d. chronic suppurative labyrinthitis.

F. <u>Meniere's Disease</u> – classic triad of symptoms which include fluctuating hearing loss, vertigo and tinnitus:

1. Audiogram configuration is flat, or rising curve, with sensorineural low frequency unilateral hearing loss.

2. May have <u>phonemic regression</u>: abnormally poor speech discrimination - worse than expected from degree of hearing loss.

3. Type A tympanograms with acoustic reflexes present bilaterally at normal hearing levels.

4. ENG useful in differential diagnosis of Meniere's disease - positional nystagmus is usually present; bithermal calorics typically show reduced vestibular response on the involved side.

G. <u>Measles</u> - type of viral labyrinthitis:

1. Classic audiogram shows bilaterally symmetrical high frequency sensorineural hearing loss ranging from 40-60 dB.

2. 50% of maternal rubella children will have hearing impairment.

3. Impedance audiometry shows type A tympanograms and acoustic reflexes consistent with degree of loss.

4. ENG usually results in reduced or absent responses to calorics bilaterally.

H. <u>Mumps</u> - also a type of viral labyrinthitis:

1. Hearing loss is usually unilateral, sudden onset, and complete.

2. ENG may show impaired caloric responses.

I. <u>Syphilis of Temporal Bone</u> - also known as "lues":

1. Sudden sensorineural hearing loss that progresses over months or years.

2. Degree of loss usually becomes quite severe, and usually affects both ears.

3. Speech discrimination is usually very poor.

4. Vertigo is a common complaint, but subsides as damage to the labyrinth increases.

5. ENG may show abnormal caloric responses.

J. <u>Acoustic Tumor</u> - benign tumor that arises from vestibular portion of the VIIIth nerve:

1. Requires complete differential diagnosis battery of audiological tests.

2.  Johnson (1966) reports that approximately 50% of tumor patients "pass" special audiometric tests.

3.  Typical patient has unilateral sensorineural hearing loss with extremely poor speech discrimination.

4.  Vertigo is common complaint.

5.  ENG shows reduced vestibular response to caloric stimulation on the involved side.

**REVIEW QUESTIONS**

1.  Electronystagmography (ENG) can best be described as:

    A.  An instrument for testing vision.
    B.  A specialized branch of electronics.
    C.  An electrical recording of eye movements.
    D.  An electrical recording of vision and hearing.
    E.  A test to screen vision in newborns.

2.  Which of the following is <u>NOT</u> a part of the standard ENG procedure?

    A.  Bithermal calorics
    B.  Past pointing
    C.  Calibration
    D.  Optokinetic
    E.  Pendulum tracking

3.  What is the most diagnostic finding that ENG can yield?

    A.  Positional nystagmus
    B.  Directional preponderance
    C.  Spontaneous nystagmus
    D.  Bilateral weakness
    E.  Unilateral weakness

4.  Which of the following ENG findings has the least clinical significance in differential diagnosis?

    A.  Positional nystagmus
    B.  Directional preponderance
    C.  Spontaneous nystagmus
    D.  Bilateral weakness
    E.  Unilateral weakness

5.  The hearing loss associated with impacted cerumen is:

    A.  Sensorineural in nature with a 45 dB pure tone average.
    B.  Sensorineural in nature with a variable pure tone average from
        25 to 45 dB.
    C.  Sensorineural in nature with a 25 dB pure tone average.
    D.  Conductive in nature with a 25 dB pure tone average.
    E.  Conductive in nature with a variable pure tone average from
        25 dB to 45 dB.

6.  Which of the following statements is NOT characteristic of microtia?

    A.  Unilateral involvement more frequent than bilateral.
    B.  More common in females than males.
    C.  Often associated with atresia.
    D.  Affects the right ear more than the left.
    E.  May be result of chromosomal defects, hereditary, or maternal rubella.

7.  Which of the following conductive disorders will NEVER reveal a
    normal Type A tympanogram?

    A.  Chronic otitis media
    B.  Cholesteatoma
    C.  Cerumen
    D.  Otosclerosis
    E.  Mastoiditis

8.  Which of the following conductive disorders will most likely demonstrate
    a normal Type A tympanogram with absent acoustic reflexes?

    A.  Chronic otitis media
    B.  Tympanic membrane perforation
    C.  Cerumen
    D.  Otosclerosis
    E.  Microtia/Atresia

9.  Which of the following conductive disorders is most likely to produce
    a finding of unilateral weakness on ENG?

    A.  Chronic otitis media
    B.  Cholesteatoma
    C.  Cerumen impaction
    D.  Otosclerosis
    E.  Mastoiditis

10. Schuknecht (1974) discusses four types of dysequilibrium associated
    with old age.  Which of the following is NOT one of the 4 types?

    A.  Cupulolithiasis
    B.  Ampullary dysequilibrium
    C.  Macular dysequilibrium
    D.  Presby-vestibulo dysequilibrium
    E.  Vestibular ataxia

11. Which of the following statements best describes the patient who sustains inner ear damage from ototoxic drugs?

    A. Bilateral conductive hearing loss; severe vertigo, bilateral tinnitus
    B. Bilateral symmetrical sensorineural hearing loss, high frequencies affected first; tinnitus
    C. Bilateral asymmetrical sensorineural hearing loss; vertigo; tinnitus
    D. Unilateral sensorineural hearing loss; high frequencies affected first; tinnitus
    E. Unilateral mixed hearing loss; tinnitus; vertigo

12. Which of the following is NOT a treatment procedure for the relief of tinnitus?

    A. Sudafed
    B. Actifed
    C. Tinnitus masker
    D. Biofeedback therapy
    E. Hearing aid

13. When speech discrimination scores are sometimes considerably poorer than one would expect from the degree of pure tone hearing loss, this phenomenon is known as:

    A. Regression toward the mean
    B. Phonemic relapse
    C. Phonemic backslide
    D. Phonemic regression
    E. Phonemic continuation

14. The ENG results obtained from a patient with long-standing unilateral Meniere's Disease will most likely reveal:

    A. Unilateral weakness with a failure fixation suppression
    B. Directional preponderance toward the involved side
    C. Directional preponderance with direction-changing positional nystagmus in one or more positions
    D. Unilateral weakness on the involved side with concurrent directional preponderance
    E. Unilateral weakness on the involved side with possible positional nystagmus in one or more positions

15. Choose the answer below which best identifies three disorders typically associated with unilateral audiologic and unilateral electronystagmograph abnormalities:

    A. Acoustic tumor; Meniere's Disease; presbycusis
    B. Acoustic tumor; mumps; Meniere's Disease
    C. Acoustic tumor; measles; mumps
    D. Mumps; syphilis; presbycusis
    E. Mumps; syphilis; Meniere's Disease

# Chapter 38

# BASIC HEARING MEASUREMENT

*Fred H. Bess*

I. Pure Tone Measures

  A. Thirty-five years ago C.C. Bunch published his classic textbook, Clinical Audiometry.

  B. Pure tone measurements are used to:

   1. Aid in identification of different auditory lesions.

   2. Monitor hearing sensitivity following surgery or medical treatment.

   3. As a screening device for identifying hearing loss in young children.

   4. Assist in the identification of educational and social needs, and in the selection of appropriate rehabilitative procedures.

  C. The Audiometer:

   1. Historically:

      a. 1878 - Hartmann's "acoumeter";

      b. 1879 - Hughes "electric genometer";

      c. big change because of advent of vacuum tubes in 1920's - precise control of audio signals;

      d. today: solid-state electronics capable of delivering a variety of audio signals via any of several types of transducers.

  D. Reference Levels in Audiometry:

1. Human ear does not perceive all frequency sounds at the same sound pressure level. Thus, expedient to build audiometers so that zero on the dial is automatically presented at a normative threshold for each test frequency.

2. Initial hearing threshold levels established by Sivian and White in 1933 under carefully controlled laboratory conditions.

3. In 1938, Beasley conducted a United States Health survey on normal listeners which later became first audiometric zero standard. Hearing levels were 15-20 dB higher than those reported by Sivian and White.

4. Beasley results adopted by American Standards Association in 1951 for calibration of audiometers.

5. International Standards Organization (ISO) recommended audiometer standard levels in 1964 that were closer to Sivian and White's data than Beasley's data.

6. Current audiometer standard was established by American National Standards Institute (ANSI) in 1969.

7. Definition of hearing threshold level (HTL) is the amount of decibel loss for a given ear as it relates to a standard audiometric threshold.

8. Definition of sensation level (SL) is the number of decibels by which the intensity of a sound exceeds the threshold of a particular ear.

E. The Audiogram:

1. The audiogram is a graph to represent hearing thresholds as a function of frequency (in Hertz) and hearing levels (in dB).

2. In 1974, standard audiometric symbols for use on audiograms recommended by ASHA.

   a. in 1976, Jerger recommended a more lucid standardized symbol system using separate audiograms for each ear.

F. Classification of Hearing Impairment:

1. Audiogram is an excellent means for predicting the actual threshold for speech reception by averaging pure tone thresholds at 500, 1000 and 2000 Hz.

2. Normal hearing is usually considered to be auditory thresholds between -10 dB and 26 dB -- should be no significant difficulty in hearing and understanding faint speech.

    a. Downs (1977) suggests more stringent normal range of hearing for children to be better than 15 dB.

G. Air and Bone Conduction Hearing:

1. Threshold is the minimum effective sound pressure that a listener can detect approximately 50% of the time.

2. Hearing loss by air conduction implies the pressure of an auditory disorder anywhere along the standard conductive and sensorineural pathways.

3. Occlusion effect refers to the enhanced loudness of a bone-conducted signal following occlusion of the ear canal.

H. Audiogram Interpretation:

1. Comparison of air conduction hearing thresholds with bone conduction sensitivity provides the basis for differentiating middle ear (conductive) disorders from sensorineural disorders.

    a. air-bone threshold gap implies that some obstruction is impeding the transmission of air conducted sound to the inner ear.

2. Johansen (1948) showed that mass-dominated ear disorders impair the transmission of high frequency energy, while stiffness-dominated disorders impair transmission of low frequencies.

3. When both air and bone conduction thresholds are abnormal, but the bone conduction is better than air conduction, the condition is classified as a "mixed hearing loss".

4. In sensorineural hearing impairment, air conduction and bone conduction thresholds are nearly equivalent at all test frequencies.

I. Clinical Measurement of Threshold:

1. Basic pure tone audiometry begins with air conducted measurements at octave intervals ranging from 250 to 8000 Hz, followed by bone conduction measurements at octave intervals from 250 to 4000 Hz.

2. Threshold determination incorporates a modification of the method of limits, where the testor controls the intensity of the signal.

   a. familiarization (practice) phase, followed by;

   b. threshold seeking phase.

J. Important Variables in Threshold Measurement:

   1. Appropriate calibration of the audiometer.

   2. Appropriate test environment.

   3. Instructions to the patients.

   4. Personal patient factors (i.e., age, motivation, intelligence, etc.).

   5. Accurate positioning of the earphones.

   6. Placement of bone vibrator on skull:

      a. bone vibrator application force.

K. Masking:

   1. Important that the ear under test is not influenced directly by the auditory sensitivity of the non-test ear:

      a. introduction of noise (masking) to the contralateral ear prevents the non-test ear from participating in the test.

   2. The loss of intensity that occurs as the signal is transmitted across the skull from one ear to the other is called interaural attenuation:

      a. interaural attenuation for air conducted signals is conservatively figured as 40 dB;

      b. interaural attenuation for bone conducted signals is considered to be zero dB.

   3. Two main types of masking noise found in current audiometers:

      a. white noise or broad-band noise;

      b. narrow-band noise.

4. Effective masking refers to the amount of threshold shift in dB produced by a given amount of noise.

5. Most popular technique of masking is the Hood "plateau" method (1960).

II. Speech Measures

A. Speech audiometry is designed to assess a person's ability to hear and understand speech stimuli:

1. Requires speech audiometer, or speech circuit in a diagnostic audiometer.

2. Generally conducted live-voice with microphone or with pre-recorded tapes.

3. Calibration for speech under earphones is 0 dB HTL is equivalent to 20 dB SPL.

4. Calibration for speech through a loudspeaker is approximately 12 dB SPL.

B. Speech Reception Threshold (SRT):

1. Defined as the intensity at which an individual is able to identify simple speech materials approximately 50% of the time:

a. excellent reliability check against the pure tone audiogram;

b. serves as reference for conducting speech discrimination tests;

c. conducted with spondaic words – two syllables spoken with equal stress on both syllables.

C. Speech Reception Procedures:

1. Recommended ASHA procedure (1977) uses most of 36 spondaic words from the CID W-1, W-2 lists.

2. Uses ascending technique with blocks of four words presented in 5 dB increments. Threshold is lowest level at which half or more of the words are repeated correctly.

3. Minimum of 2 ascending series is required.

4. May use exploration (or familiarization) phase followed by threshold-seeking phase.

D. Assessment of Speech Discrimination:

1. Speech discrimination tests estimate a person's ability to understand conversational speech. Numerous tests available for the speech discrimination task.

2. Phonetically Balanced Word Lists (PB lists):

   a. basis for developing word discrimination tests described by Egan (1948) at Harvard Psychoacoustics Laboratories (PAL):

      (1) monosyllabic structure;

      (2) equal average difficulty;

      (3) equal range of difficulty;

      (4) equal composition of phonetic classes;

      (5) phonetic composition representative of English speech;

      (6) words in common use.

   b. initial lists known as PAL PB-50's; 20 lists of 50 monosyllabic each;

   c. Hirsh (1952) developed standardized recordings of modified lists to be known as CID-W-22's;

   d. Lehiste and Peterson (1959) proposed sets of lists using phonemic rather than phonetic balancing. Used consonant-nucleus-consonant words, so lists are known as CNC lists;

   e. Tillman and Carhart (1966) refined the CNC lists to form 50-word lists now known as Northwestern University Auditory Test No. 6.

3. Multiple-Choice Tests:

   a. most widely recognized multiple-choice speech discrimination test is the Modified Rhyme Hearing Test (MRHT) from Stanford Research Institute, 1968:

      (1) composed of six 50-word lists, with each list composed of 50 six-word ensembles. Each ensemble of words varies relative to initial consonant or final consonant;

      (2) tapes available with words in noise levels adjusted so that normal hearers perceive the test items with 96.83 or 75% accuracy.

b. recent introduction of the California Consonant Test (CCT), developed by Owens and Schubert, 1977:

(1) composed of two different scramblings of 100 test items, each of which was arranged within an ensemble of four CVC monosyllabic words;

(2) scores from this test are correlated to degree of high-frequency sensorineural hearing loss.

4. Sentence Tests:

a. several speech identification tests have been developed using sentences as the basic test item;

b. initial sentence test developed at CID, Silverman and Hirsh, 1955:

(1) not much in use today.

c. in 1965, Jerger and Speaks developed a set of synthetic sentences for use in research, but now used in clinical practice. Known as Synthetic Sentence Identification (SSI) test:

(1) comprised of different randomizations of 10 synthetic sentences, of similar length;

(2) patient selects perceived sentence from a closed-set format;

(3) easily used with competing message set at any message-to-competition ratio.

d. recent discrimination sentence identification test, referred to as SPIN (Speech Perception in Noise) proposed by Kalikow et al., 1977:

(1) 8 lists of 50 sentences each; last word of each sentence is the test item;

(2) pre-recorded with a background of babble-type competition composed of 12 voices reading continually - can be set for any message-to-competition ratio.

E. Clinical Strategies in Speech Discrimination Test Presentation:

1. Three issues of concern to audiologists in determination of speech discrimination test protocol:

a. whether to use recorded materials or employ monitored live-voice;

b. whether or not to use a carrier phrase;

c. determining the appropriate level for presentation of the test materials.

2. In order to reduce auditor bias (scoring verbal responses) – if the subject is able, and time permits, written responses should be employed.

3. Abbreviated Discrimination Tests:

a. several attempts have been made to shorten our present tests to reduce the overall evaluation time:

(1) use of 25-word half lists;

(2) in 1974, Rose developed a 10-word discrimination test to use as a screening tool in determining whether to use the full or half-list discrimination test.

b. the clinician is cautioned that test score variability will increase considerably as the number of test items is reduced.

4. Adverse Listening Conditions:

a. although several types of background noise have been used in speech discrimination testing, marked variability in scores will result as a function of level and type of background noise;

b. no standard technique for measuring speech discrimination in the presence of competing background noise.

5. Clinical Utilization of Speech Discrimination Tests:

a. attempts to predict extent of hearing handicap from speech discrimination scores have met with only limited success;

b. use of performance-intensity functions with speech discrimination tests can be used for general index of suspicion for peripheral hearing disorders;

c. word discrimination tests are widely used in hearing aid evaluation procedures;

d. clinicians must be aware that masking is often necessary in speech discrimination testing just as in testing with pure tones;

e. attempts at establishing a uniform relationship between pure tone thresholds and speech intelligibility at suprathreshold levels have met with only limited success;

f. some investigators have advocated the use of bone conducted speech audiometry as part of the basic hearing evaluation;

(1) usefulness of this technique seems limited because of the output capabilities of bone conduction vibrators - poor maximum output level and high harmonic distortion at high intensity levels.

III. Afterward

A. Of clinical concern is the insensitivity of the commonly used speech discrimination test, and the wide variability produced by using background noise.

B. Need for improved methods for assessing a hearing impaired person's ability to understand speech.

**REVIEW QUESTIONS**

1. Which three testing procedures are commonly employed in the basic hearing examination?

A. Evoked Response Audiometry.
B. Aural Reflexometry.
C. Pure Tone Measurements.
D. Impedance Audiometry.
E. Speech Audiometry.

2. Identify the name of the reference level for normal hearing associated with the following years:

1933 _____

1938 _____

1951 _____

1964 _____

1969 _____

3. Define <u>Sensation Level</u>:

4. Indicate on the table below, the hearing loss classification scheme by filling in the terms used to describe the severity of the hearing loss:

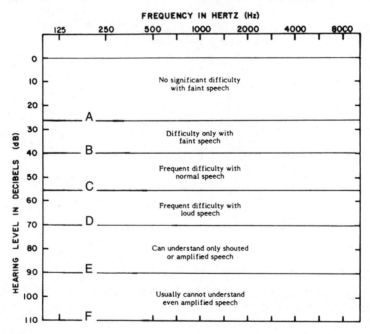

FREQUENCY IN HERTZ (Hz)

No significant difficulty with faint speech

Difficulty only with faint speech

Frequent difficulty with normal speech

Frequent difficulty with loud speech

Can understand only shouted or amplified speech

Usually cannot understand even amplified speech

HEARING LEVEL IN DECIBELS (dB)

5. Define <u>threshold</u> of audibility:

6. The "occlusion effect" refers to the enhanced loudness of a bone-conducted signal following the occlusion of the ear canal. The effect is seen predominantly in the _____ frequencies and may reach a magnitude of ____ to ____ dB.

344

7. An audiogram representing a hearing disorder to stiffness would show hearing loss in the _____ frequency range; an audiogram due to a mass-dominated lesion would show hearing loss in the _____ frequencies. The third component of impedance, _____, affects all frequencies.

8. Threshold determination in clinical audiometry incorporates which psychophysical method of measurement?

   A.  Method of Carhart-Jerger
   B.  Method of Fixed-Ratio Stimuli
   C.  Method of Limits
   D.  Method of Adjustments
   E.  Method of Constant Stimuli

9. Numerous variables may influence the threshold measurement. List four:

   A.  _____

   B.  _____

   C.  _____

   D.  _____

10. Complete the following sentences:

   "Generally speaking, masking should be used in air conduction audiometry whenever the level of the test tone minus the interaural attenuation is equal to or exceeds the _____ _____ _____ of the non-test ear."

   "Masking for bone-conduction, on the other hand, should be employed whenever there is an _____ - _____ _____ in the test ear, since the interaural attenuation rate is ____ dB."

11. Which are the two reasons presented below why the speech reception threshold (SRT) is included in the basic hearing evaluation?

   A.  Establish rapport with patient.
   B.  Reliability check for pure tone thresholds.
   C.  Check for auditory perception abilities.
   D.  Reference for conducting speech discrimination tests.
   E.  As indicator of patient cooperation.

12. The speech reception threshold (SRT) test is conducted with words that are:

   A. Bisyllabic
   B. Familiar
   C. Spondaic
   D. Equal stress on each syllable
   E. All of the above
   F. B and C

13. The words used in traditional speech discrimination tests are:

   A. Familiar
   B. Equal average difficulty
   C. Monosyllabic
   D. Phonetically balanced
   E. All of the above
   F. A, C and D

14. Identify the term(s) used to classify speech discrimination ability with the following scores:

   90–100% _____

   75–90% _____

   60–75% _____

   50–60% _____

   50% _____

15. Label the performance-intensity functions seen with normal hearing, conductive hearing loss, sensorineural impairments, and retrocochlear lesions.

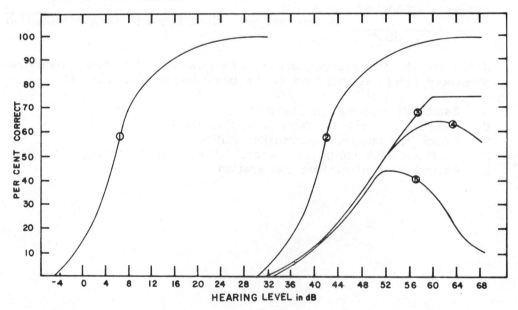

# Chapter 39

# DIAGNOSTIC AUDIOLOGY

*Jay W. Sanders*

I.  Introduction

   A.  Diagnostic Audiology – term used for special qualitative hearing test procedures:

   1.  The classic diagnostic test battery (1950's) included:

   a. loudness recruitment;

   b. differential sensitivity for intensity;

   c. abnormal auditory adaptation.

   2.  The special test battery distinguishes between cochlear and retrocochlear site of lesion in the sensorineural loss.

II.  Loudness Recruitment – a more rapid growth of loudness with increased intensity

   A.  ABLB – Alternate Binaural Loudness Balance – compares loudness growth between a normal and impaired ear; developed by Fowler (1936):

   1.  Stimulus is presented alternately to the two ears at a frequency at which the hearing is normal in one ear but a loss exists in the opposite ear.

   2.  Loudness level between the ears is matched by maintaining a constant level in one ear and varying the level in the other ear until the tones in both ears are at equal loudness levels.

   B.  MBL – Monaural Loudness Balance (or MBFLB – Monaural Bi-Frequency Loudness Balance) – compares loudness growth between two test frequencies in the same ear; developed by Reger (1936):

   1.  Stimulus is presented alternately to the same ear at one frequency at which hearing is normal and another frequency at which hearing is impaired.

2.   The loudness level between frequencies is matched by maintaining a constant level at one frequency and varying the level of the other frequency until the tones are at equal loudness levels.

C.   Interpretation - comparison of sensation levels of two ears in ABLB or at two frequencies in MBFLB for equal loudness:

1.   No recruitment - equal loudness at equal sensation levels.

2.   Complete recruitment - equal loudness at equal hearing levels.

3.   Partial recruitment - equal loudness at levels between no recruitment and complete recruitment.

4.   Decruitment - sensation level to the poor ear, at equal loudness, is significantly greater than that to the good ear.

D.   Results are recorded graphically on a laddergram or as a loudness growth function.

E.   Limitations of recruitment tests:

1.   Special equipment needed.

2.   Time consuming.

3.   Normal hearing is required either in opposite ear or at one frequency in the test ear.

III.   Differential Sensitivity to Intensity

A.   Difference limen for intensity (DLI) was first studied as a quicker and easier indirect test for recruitment.

1.   Rationale - if loudness growth is more rapid with increased intensity in a recruiting ear, then the just noticeable difference (jnd) in loudness would be abnormally small and indicated by a reduced DLI.

2.   Results of clinical application indicated that the DLI test distinguished between cochlear and retrocochlear pathologies but not in all cases between recruiting and non-recruiting ears.

B.   SISI - a test based on suprathreshold differential sensitivity to intensity was developed from DLI testing.

1.   Measures patient's ability to hear intensity differences of 1 dB at 20 dB sensation level.

2. The intensity differences are increments of short duration super-imposed on a continuous carrier tone.

3. The test consists of a series of 20 one dB increments with increments of two to five dB being used for patient conditioning and reorientation if necessary during the test.

4. Owen's modification to terminate the test after 10 increments if the response has been highly positive or negative if widely accepted (1965).

5. Because of the high presentation intensity, the cochlear pathology ear tends strongly toward a high score, and thus SISI scores (percentage of increments heard correctly) are interpreted as follows:

   a. positive for cochlear pathology (70-100%);

   b. negative for cochlear pathology (0-30%);

   c. questionable (35-65%).

6. SISI is used as a supplementary test to the loudness balance recruitment tests and is part of the classic special auditory test battery.

IV. Auditory Adaptation – a decrease in auditory sensitivity during auditory stimulation as a result of the stimulus

   A. Auditory adaptation was initially studied because of an assumed relationship to loudness recruitment.

   B. Threshold Tone Decay Test – (TDT) – developed by Carhart (1954) as a simple test of abnormal adaptation to be used as a supplement to the loudness balance tests for cochlear lesions.

      1. TDT – is an objective test to determine the least intensity at which the subject maintains a response for 60 seconds.

      2. The test stimulus is a continuous pure tone and the patient is asked to signal as long as he hears the tone.

      3. The tone is presented at hearing threshold level and the response is timed. If the response is discontinued in less than 60 seconds, the stimulus intensity is immediately increased by 5 dB without interrupting the tone and timing is begun again.

4. The difference between the least intensity to which subject maintains response for 60 seconds and his hearing threshold level is the amount of tone decay:

    a. moderate adaptation - cochlear pathology;

    b. excessive adaptation - indicates 8th nerve pathology.

C. Modifications of TDT:

1. Rosenberg (1958) - each time the patient no longer hears the tone the intensity is increased by 5 dB but the timing of the response is not restarted. The total test time is one minute and decay from threshold is measured over that 60-second period.

2. Green (1963) Modified Tone Decay Test (MTDT) - a one-minute test with specific instructions that the patient respond only to the original tonality of the stimulus and not to atonal noise.

3. Owens (1964) - measures tone decay only to a 20 dB sensation level with attention focused on the rate of decay:

    a. cochlear pathology - decay is progressively slower at higher sensation levels;

    b. 8th nerve lesion - little or no change in the decay rate with 5 dB intensity increases.

4. Olsen and Noffsinger (1974) - differs slightly from Carhart TDT in that the test is begun at 20 dB sensation level and not at threshold.

D. Studies indicate Carhart's TDT or Olsen and Noffsinger's modified version of TDT as being superior test of adaptation.

V. Bekesy Audiometry - a threshold tracking method to detect auditory adaptation using an automatic audiometer developed by Bekesy (1947).

A. Patient controls the attenuator and the machine provides a graphic readout of threshold response to a single pure tone fixed frequency stimulus or a pure tone sweep frequency (stimulus that constantly changes in frequency across the available range).

B. Jerger's classification of results (1960):

1. Type I – no adaptation; observed almost exclusively in normal ears and those with conductive loss as well as a few sensorineural impaired ears; hearing threshold levels were the same for interrupted and continuous tones.

2. Type II – characteristic of cochlear pathology; if adaptation is present it is less than that produced by a retrocochlear lesion; the continuous tone breaks away from the interrupted tone but stabilizes at a higher hearing threshold level and parallels the interrupted tone tracing throughout the remainder of the frequency range.

3. Type III – indicates excessive adaptation; observed in retrocochlear pathologies; hearing threshold levels for the interrupted tone were the same as those obtained by conventional audiometry but the continuous tone responses showed an immediate breakaway from that of the interrupted tone with no stabilization at any intensity.

4. Type IV – associated with retrocochlear pathology; demonstrates the same tracing as Type II but shows considerably more separation between interrupted and continuous tone tracings than that shown in Type II.

C. Some Bekesy results do not fit into any one of the classifications perfectly.

1. As an example – a Bekesy audiogram with a 25–30 dB difference between the interrupted and continuous tone tracing does not fit into any of the four classifications but it does indicate abnormal auditory adaptation.

VI. Test Battery Approach – Jerger formed the concept of diagnostic audiology; site of lesion in the peripheral auditory system is determined by interpretation of the pattern of test results of the test battery (i.e., tests of recruitment, adaptation, Bekesy, and SISI)

A. Cochlear Pathology – ears with sensorineural hearing loss from cochlear pathology have a high probability of diagnostic test results consistent with a cochlear lesion.

B. Eighth Nerve Pathology – mixed findings as to the predictive accuracy of the test battery results:

1. In ears with eighth nerve pathology the classic retrocochlear test results should be regarded as strong evidence of that pathology.

2. Negative results do not necessarily rule out eighth nerve lesions.

3. Even 1 or 2 test results that are indicative of eighth nerve pathology should be reason for suspicion.

4. Several studies show a correlation of tumor size and consistency of audiometric results with less accuracy in persons with small acoustic tumors.

5. Inverse relationship between successful surgery and tumor size places emphasis on early diagnosis and a more efficient test battery.

VII. Additional Test Procedures – a number of different tests have been proposed as supplements to the test battery or as replacements for some of the classic tests

A. Modified SISI – the SISI test is presented at a higher sensation level to obtain more consistent results from ears with a mild to moderate hearing loss from a cochlear lesion:

1. 70 dB HTL is recommended for the presentation level of the modified since a hearing level of greater than 70-75 dB can result in decreased predictive accuracy in retrocochlear pathologic ears.

2. 20 dB SL should be continued in ears with a hearing loss of 60 dB or greater.

B. Brief-Tone Audiometry – a diagnostic procedure to evaluate abnormal temporal auditory summation:

1. Test is based on psychoacoustic phenomenon of temporal summation – ability of the ear to accumulate acoustic energy over time in response to stimuli of extremely short duration:

a. a normal ear decreases in sensitivity for tones of short duration with decrease in duration;

b. linear function with a slope of approximately 10 dB per unit of duration change (i.e., pure tone at threshold in a normal ear is decreased in duration from 150 to 15 msec, the intensity must be increased approximately 10 dB to maintain a threshold response);

c. in a conductive pathology the slope of summation is unaffected;

d. cochlear pathologies show a reduced slope of summation;

e. ears with acoustic tumors display a slope of about 10 dB like that in a normal ear.

2. Useful addition to the special test battery:

a. applicable in patients with a severe hearing loss for whom suprathreshold tests (i.e., SISI, loudness balance, tone decay) are inconclusive or inapplicable; or for mild hearing loss when other tests give results consistent with a normal auditory system.

C. Brief-Tone Bekesy Audiometry - brief-tone audiometry performed with a Bekesy audiometer; proposed by Wright (1978):

1. Entire test can be given in three minutes and permits an assessment of abnormality in the areas of auditory response, temporal summation, and auditory adaptation.

2. Bekesy audiometer is used to track threshold response to three different stimuli:

a. pulsed tone of 500 msec duration;

b. pulsed tone of 20 msec duration;

c. continuous tone.

3. Separation between responses to the pulsed tones is the slope of temporal summation and the comparison of responses to the 500 msec pulsed tone and continuous tone is a fixed frequency Bekesy test of abnormal auditory adaptation.

D. Acoustic Reflex Test (ART) - measurement of the acoustic stapedial reflex threshold with an impedance bridge in an ear with a sensorineural impairment:

1. The earphone ear is the ear under examination since the concern is the hearing response.

2. ART consists of two parts and evaluates two different aspects of auditory response:

a. suprathreshold loudness - Metz test (1952):

(1) regarded by many as a direct test of loudness recruitment;

(2) reflex threshold at sensation levels of less than 60 dB are consistent with loudness recruitment and found in ears with cochlear pathology;

(3) reflex thresholds elevated hearing levels are consistent with retrocochlear pathology.

b. reflex decay test:

(1) 500 and 1000 Hz are the suggested frequencies at which to test reflex tone decay;

(2) decay of the reflex to one-half its original magnitude in five seconds or less is indicative of eighth nerve pathology.

3. Displays excellent promise as a diagnostic tool even though some overlap in the results between cochlear and retrocochlear pathology occurs.

E. Tests at High Intensity – modification of several existing test procedures to improve the predictive accuracy of eighth nerve pathology since the earlier signs of such a pathology appear at high intensities.

1. Performance – Intensity Speech Discrimination (PI-PB):

a. speech discrimination scores are obtained with half lists in steps of 10–20 dB up to 110 dB SPL to complete a performance intensity (PI) function;

b. results indicate:

(1) cochlear pathology – a strong tendency for scores to remain stable at a maximum score plateau even at high intensities;

(2) 8th nerve pathology – the scores at high intensity showed a "roll-over" effect; with increasing intensity the scores improved to a maximum score plateau but with further increases in intensity discrimination ability deteriorated markedly.

c. index is computed for each ear by subtracting the poorest score after "roll-over" from the best score and dividing by the best score (PB max – PB min/ PB max).

2. Synthetic Sentence Identification (SSI) – added to the PI-PB function by Jerger and Hayes (1977):

   a. scores are obtained for groups of 10 synthetic sentences at the same series of intensity levels used for PB word lists;

   b. this allows for a more detailed analysis of the site of lesion.

3. Bekesy Comfortable Loudness Tracings (BCL) – Bekesy tracings are obtained at the patient's maximum comfort level rather than threshold since abnormal adaptation of an eighth nerve pathology is more likely to occur at the higher intensity:

   a. results:

      (1) negative – 3 patterns of interrupted and continuous tones that are negative for eighth nerve pathology but consistent with normal hearing, conductive loss, or cochlear pathology;

      (2) positive – 3 response patterns for eighth nerve lesions showing excessive adaptation in part or all of the frequency range.

   b. results display a considerable improvement in diagnostic accuracy over Bekesy threshold audiometry.

4. Supra-Threshold Adaptation Test (STAT) – a high intensity test of auditory adaptation based on the patient's ability to maintain response to a continuous pure tone at 110 dB SPL for 60 seconds:

   a. failure to maintain response for 60 seconds indicates excessive adaptation and is positive for 8th nerve pathology;

   b. response for 60 seconds is negative for 8th nerve pathology.

5. The high intensity modifications of existing test procedures have resulted in improved predictive accuracy, but data with these methods are limited.

F. Electrophysiological Audiology – the assessment of the auditory system through electrophysiological measures is a promising new approach to diagnostic audiology.

1.  Electrocochleography (EcochG):

    a. records the computer-averaged electrical activity generated at the cochlea in response to acoustic stimulation;

    b. primary attention has been given to the compound action potential in the first order neuron;

    c. results can distinguish the recruiting ear, but data are limited for ears with 8th nerve pathology.

2.  Brain Stem Evoked Response Audiometry (BSERA):

    a. records the computer-averaged electrical activity generated in the acoustic nerve and brainstem in response to acoustic stimulation;

    b. the wave form and latencies and the inter-wave and inter-aural Wave V latency differences are extremely sensitive to retrocochlear pathology;

    c. the procedure is not an acoustic tumor test but rather is an assessment of the integrity of the auditory neural system from the acoustic nerve through the brain stem.

VIII. Loudness Tests: A Revised Concept

A. The original concept was that loudness recruitment and positive SISI scores were a result of an abnormally increased sensitivity to intensity brought about by cochlear pathology.

B. The original concept developed from comparisons of normal and cochlear pathology ears at equal sensation levels; whereas when comparisons are made at equal and high sound pressure levels, the results demonstrate that recruitment and positive SISI scores are normal loudness responses at high intensity.

C. The abnormal and pathological responses in an ear with sensorineural impairment are an absence of recruitment, or the presence of decruitment, and negative SISI scores, resulting from a transmission loss in an impaired 8th nerve.

D. In an ear with sensorineural impairment, recruitment and positive SISI scores are normal loudness responses at high intensity and thus are inconsistent with 8th nerve pathology; while the absence of recruitment and negative SISI scores should not be dismissed as "inconclusive" or "normal" but rather should be viewed as the abnormal, pathological effects of a transmission loss in an impaired 8th nerve.

IX. Revised Test Battery – additional procedures or alternatives and modification to Classic Test Battery are recommended.

  A. Brain Stem Evoked Response Audiometry (BSERA):

    1. The best single procedure in diagnostic audiology.

    2. It is an objective method that can be completed in a short period of time with excellent results in assessing a sensorineural disorder.

  B. Acoustic Reflex Test:

    1. Following BSERA this appears to be the most effective procedure available with good predictive accuracy for cochlear and eighth nerve pathologies.

    2. ART should include:

      a. examination of reflex threshold for reduced sensation level or elevated hearing level;

      b. evaluation of reflex decay at 500 and 1000 Hz.

  C. Tone Decay Test – most effective methods are Carhart's original procedure (1957) and Olsen and Noffsinger's modification (1974).

  D. Brief Tone Audiometry:

    1. Used for patients whose test results are inconclusive or inapplicable due to a very severe loss.

    2. In other patients another test at high intensity should be used instead.

  E. Tests at High Intensity:

    1. Performance-Intensity speech functions, Bekesy Comfortable Loudness Tracings, and Suprathreshold Adaptations Test should be used on a semi-experimental basis since data on eighth nerve pathology ears are limited.

  F. Modified SISI:

    1. Minimum hearing level should be 75 dB except for patients with a hearing threshold at 60 dB or greater for whom the test should be done at the standard 20 dB SL.

2. Far more weight should be given to the negative rather than the positive score.

3. Results – in a sensorineural loss a negative score on the SISI at high intensity is an abnormal response, demonstrating the pathologic effects of a transmission loss in an impaired eighth nerve.

X. Future Directions and Research Needs

A. The classic procedures are no longer adequate to evaluate the auditory system in a sensorineural loss.

1. As a battery they show good results and predictive accuracy in ears with cochlear pathology but show little consistency of results with eighth nerve pathology.

2. With the present battery even if only one test suggests an eighth nerve pathology it is necessary to suspect that pathology might exist.

3. It is necessary to develop tests that are more sensitive to minimal pathology of the eighth nerve.

4. More research is needed on the high intensity tests to increase our understanding of response of the impaired auditory system.

B. Diagnostic audiology should be redirected toward the advanced study of impaired auditory response for the purpose of total rehabilitation.

**REVIEW QUESTIONS**

1. The classic special auditory test battery developed in the 1950's was a set of auditory tests designed to assess auditory response in the following areas:

A. Tone decay and differential sensitivity for intensity.
B. Temporal auditory summation and acuity for speech.
C. Recruitment and Bekesy audiometry.
D. Supra-threshold loudness response and auditory adaptation.
E. Loudness recruitment and differential sensitivity for intensity.

2. The audiologist uses the special auditory test battery of the peripheral auditory system to:

   A. Arrive at a diagnosis of the hearing disorder.
   B. Gain a better understanding of the aberrant auditory behavior demonstrated by the patient.
   C. Rule out acoustic tumor.
   D. Provide further information for appropriate hearing aid selection.
   E. Make a decision regarding medical referral.

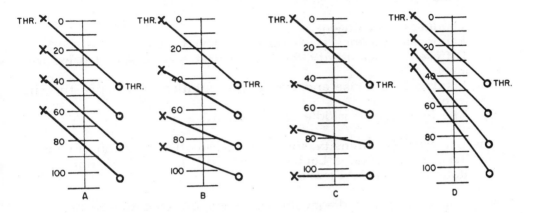

3. The results of the ABLB shown in the laddergram above indicate:

   A. No recruitment.
   B. Partial recruitment in the right ear.
   C. Complete recruitment in the right ear.
   D. Decruitment in the right ear.
   E. Decruitment in the left ear.

4. According to recent reports, which of the following tests is most accurate in the prediction of eighth nerve pathology?

   A. The Alternate Binaural Loudness Balance Test (ABLB).
   B. The acoustic reflex and reflex decay test.
   C. The Tone Decay Test (TDT).
   D. Bekesy audiometry.
   E. The Short Increment Sensitivity Index (SISI).

5. The basic purpose of modifying the SISI by presenting it at a high intensity is to:

   A. Insure a positive score from all ears with cochlear pathology.
   B. Insure a negative score from all ears with eighth nerve pathology.
   C. Make the test easier for the patient, since high intensity increments are easier to hear.
   D. Reduce the time required to take the test.
   E. Make the test more difficult.

6.  A number of studies of tests of auditory adaptation have indicated superior predictive accuracy for site of lesion for:

    A.  Bekesy sweep frequency audiometry.
    B.  Bekesy fixed frequency audiometry.
    C.  Bekesy sweep frequency audiometry combined with fixed frequency tests at a low, middle, and high frequency.
    D.  The Carhart Tone Decay Test (TDT).
    E.  The Modified Tone Decay Test (MTDT).

7.  The acoustic reflex and reflex decay test in the ear with sensorineural hearing loss is an assessment of:

    A.  Loudness recruitment.
    B.  Loudness response at a supra-threshold level.
    C.  Differential sensitivity for intensity at a high sound pressure level.
    D.  Loudness response and auditory adaptation at a supra-threshold level.
    E.  The integrity of middle ear function.

8.  The performance-intensity speech discrimination function (PI-PB), the Bekesy Comfortable Loudness test (BCL), and the Supra-Threshold Adaptation Test (STAT) are:

    A.  New concepts in diagnostic audiology directed toward areas of auditory response not tested by procedures in the classic special auditory test battery.
    B.  Modifications of previous diagnostic procedures based on the hypothesis that the earliest signs of eighth nerve pathology will occur at high intensity.
    C.  Modifications of previous diagnostic procedures based on the hypothesis that the earliest signs of cochlear pathology will occur at high intensity.
    D.  Modifications of previous diagnostic procedures in which testing is done at high intensity to make the task simpler for the patient.
    E.  New concepts in diagnostic audiology directed toward improving the sensitivity by making the tests more difficult.

9.  On the Supra-Threshold Adaptation Test (STAT), a failure to maintain response for 60 seconds to the high intensity pure tone stimulus is suggestive of:

    A.  The normal auditory adaptation of a normal ear.
    B.  The moderate auditory adaptation of a cochlear pathology ear.
    C.  The excessive adaptation of an eighth nerve pathology ear.
    D.  Loudness recruitment.
    E.  An abnormal differential sensitivity for intensity.

10. The Bekesy Comfortable Loudness test (BCL) is a test of:

A. Supra-threshold loudness growth.
B. Differential sensitivity for intensity at a supra-threshold level.
C. Temporal summation of acoustic energy.
D. The patient's most comfortable loudness level.
E. Supra-threshold auditory adaptation.

11. Brief Tone Audiometry is particularly useful in site-of-lesion testing in:

A. Patients with mild hearing loss.
B. Hard-to-test patients.
C. Patients with bilaterally symmetrical hearing loss.
D. Patients with bilateral asymmetrical hearing loss.
E. Patients with excessive auditory adaptation.

12. According to recent report, which of the following tests from the original classic special auditory test battery has continued to show a reasonably good predictive accuracy in patients with eighth nerve pathology?

A. The Alternate Binaural Loudness Balance test (ABLB).
B. The Carhart Tone Decay Test (TDT).
C. The Short Increment Sensitivity Index (SISI).
D. Bekesy audiometry.
E. Speech discrimination.

13. Recent reports of results obtained with the classic special auditory test battery have indicated:

A. A serious decline in predictive accuracy in both cochlear and eighth nerve pathology ears.
B. A continued high predictive accuracy in both cochlear and eighth nerve pathology ears.
C. A moderate decline in predictive accuracy in ears with eighth nerve pathology but a serious decline in predictive accuracy in cochlear pathology ears.
D. A serious decline in predictive accuracy in cochlear pathology ears but a continued high predictive accuracy in ears with eighth nerve pathology.
E. A continued high predictive accuracy in cochlear pathology ears but a serious decline in predictive accuracy in ears with eighth nerve pathology.

14. Special auditory test results that include a Type III Bekesy audiogram, 60 dB of decay on the Carhart Tone Decay Test, negative SISI scores, decruitment on the Alternate Binaural Loudness Balance Test, and a speech discrimination score of 92% are:

    A. Entirely consistent with eighth nerve pathology.
    B. Strongly suggestive of eighth nerve pathology.
    C. Strongly suggestive of cochlear pathology.
    D. Entirely consistent with cochlear pathology.
    E. Ambiguous and inconclusive.

15. Special auditory test results that include decay of 20 dB on the Carhart Tone Decay Test (TDT), acoustic reflexes at normal Hearing Levels and reduced Sensation Levels with no decay, no roll-over on the performance-intensity speech discrimination function (PI-PB), positive scores on the high intensity Short Increment Sensitivity Index (SISI) and a negative result on the Supra-Threshold Adaptation Test (STAT) are:

    A. Entirely consistent with eighth nerve pathology.
    B. Strongly suggestive of eighth nerve pathology.
    C. Strongly suggestive of cochlear pathology.
    D. Entirely consistent with cochlear pathology.
    E. Ambiguous and inconclusive.

# Chapter 40

# IMPEDANCE AUDIOMETRY

*James W. Hall and James F. Jerger*

I. Introduction

    A.  Metz (1946) initially described clinical utilization of acoustic impedance measurement.

    B.  Acoustic impedance used in variety of situations and for various purposes:

        1.  Hearing screening;

        2.  Differentiation of conductive vs. sensorineural hearing loss;

        3.  Differentiation of cochlear vs. retrocochlear hearing loss;

        4.  Identification and localization of central auditory disorders;

        5.  Prediction of hearing levels;

        6.  Hearing aid evaluations.

    C.  Impedance audiometry is objective, offers ease of administration and clinical versatility.

    D.  Impedance meter instrumentation uses three major components:

        1.  Impedance monitoring circuit with 220 Hz probe tone at 85 dB SPL:

            a. the greater the impedance of the middle ear mechanism, the greater the probe tone intensity in the external ear canal;

            b. impedance of the middle ear system is reported as the volume of air (in cubic centimeters) yielding equivalent compliance.

        2.  Air pressure system consists of pump and manometer – range of air pressure typically from +200 mm to –400 mm water pressure.

3. Acoustic reflex elicitation system includes pure tones from 250 to 4000 Hz; a broad band or white noise signal; and high pass and low-pass noise band signals:

   a. contralateral mode – the signal is presented to one ear through the earphone and the impedance change is measured with the probe assembly in the opposite ear;

   b. ipsilateral mode – signal is delivered by a small transducer located in the probe assembly, and the impedance change is measured in the same ear.

II. Impedance Measurements

   A. Tympanometry – reflects change in the compliance of the middle ear system and tympanic membrane as air pressure in the external ear canal is varied

      1. Tympanogram – a graph showing the mobility of the middle ear system.

      2. Requires an airtight seal between the probe and the external ear canal.

      3. Pressure is introduced into the canal from +200 to 0 mm and then to a negative pressure of –200 to –400 mm water pressure.

      4. Compliance of normal middle ear system increases as the ear canal pressure is decreased from +200 to 0 mm with decrease in air pressure compliance of the middle ear decreases.

      5. Classification of Tympanograms (Jerger, 1970):

         a. Type A – normal, has a peak at or near normal atmospheric pressure (0 to –100 mm $H_2O$);

         b. Type B – no point of maximum compliance, flat; reflects severe restriction of the middle ear – most common cause is middle ear fluid;

         c. Type C – peaks when air pressure in the canal exceeds –100 mm $H_2O$; precursor to middle ear disorder secondary to insufficient Eustachian tube function;

         d. Type $A_d$ – "deep" type A, reflecting high compliance or a flaccid tympanic membrane.

   B. Static Compliance – measures the compliance of the middle ear at rest:

      1. First measurement is taken at +200 mm; second measurement at the point of maximum compliance.

2. The difference between these two measurements is the equivalent volume or compliance of the middle ear mechanism - normal compliance ranges from 0.30 cc to 1.60 cc.

3. Compliance is influenced by age and sex:

   a. compliance increases with age from 1 to 35 years;

   b. above age 35 compliance decreases with age;

   c. average compliance value above age 70 approaches the lower limit of the normal range;

   d. in general static compliance is greater in males than in females.

4. Static compliance is useful in identification and differentiation of middle ear disorders:

   a. fixation of the ossicular chain such as otosclerosis:

      (1) static compliance is lower (0.35 cc);

      (2) otosclerotic ears cannot be identified by measurement of static compliance alone.

   b. otitis media - fluid in the middle ear:

      (1) static compliance is lower (0.29 cc).

   c. discontinuity of the ossicular chain:

      (1) static compliance is high - almost three times the normal value (1.93 cc);

      (2) a scarred tympanic membrane often produces similar increase in compliance.

5. Thus, static compliance must be used in conjunction with other audiometric findings.

C. Acoustic reflexes are due to bilateral contraction of the stapedius muscle in response to intense sound(s).

   1. Anatomy of the acoustic reflex:

      a. the cochlea transduces the signal to a neural correlate;

      b. the eighth nerve transmits the neural information to the CNS;

      c. the central portion of the reflex consists of auditory and facial nerve nuclei in the brain stem;

d. the facial nerve innervates the stapedius muscle;

e. the acoustic reflex arc is both crossed and uncrossed - producing contraction in the opposite ear and in the ear stimulated.

2. Contraction of the stapedius muscle tenses the ossicular chain, reducing the efficiency of sound transmission by the middle ear.

3. The altered impedance is detected at the plane of the tympanic membrane by the impedance bridge.

4. In normal ears the acoustic reflex is elicited at 85-95 dB HL.

5. Acoustic reflexes in conductive hearing loss follow two rules:

   a. with the probe in the involved ear there is a high likeliho of absent reflexes, even if the air-bone gap is only 5-10 dB;

   b. when sound is presented to the conductive ear and the impedance change is measured in the normal ear there is a direct relationship between the degree of conductive loss and the acoustic reflex threshold:

      (1) in a unilateral 30 dB conductive loss acoustic reflexes would probably not be measurable bilaterally;

      (2) with an air-bone gap of greater than 50 dB, there is a 90% chance that reflexes will be absent.

6. Acoustic reflex findings evaluated in isolation may be ambiguous.

III. Patterns of Impedance Audiometry Findings

   A. Conductive vs. Sensorineural:

      1. Conductive disorder - abnormal tympanogram, abnormal static compliance, elevated or absent reflexes:

         a. otosclerosis - a shallow Type A tympanogram, low static compliance (0.20 to 0.40 cc) and absent acoustic reflexes:

            (1) finding of a Type A tympanogram in an ear with a conductive loss is a distinct sign of fixation;

            (2) reflex may be characterized by a negative deflection at the onset and offset of the eliciting signal.

b. otitis media:

    (1) type C tympanogram – negative pressure develops due to insufficient Eustachian tube function;

    (2) flat, type B tympanogram – increased fluid restricts the mobility of the ossicular chain;

    (3) decreased static compliance;

    (4) acoustic reflexes are rarely present in ears with negative pressure greater than $-200$ mm $H_2O$;

    (5) impedance may be used to monitor the patient's recovery from otitis media;

    (6) ear canal volume measure ($C_1$) should be excessively large if the ventilating tubes used in treatment are patent and functioning;

    (7) normal Eustachian tube function can be assessed with patent ventilation tubes by introducing air pressure and having the patient swallow to see if he can equalize the pressure.

c. tympanic membrane perforation:

    (1) ear canal measure ($C_1$) – large volume;

    (2) no point of maximum compliance with tympanogram.

d. ossicular discontinuity:

    (1) type $A_d$ tympanogram – abnormally deep;

    (2) high static compliance (greater than 1.60 cc);

    (3) absent acoustic reflexes with the probe in the affected ear;

    (4) variations of ossicular discontinuity – total discontinuity vs. a functional connection between the stapedius muscle and a portion of the ossicular chain attached to the tympanic membrane results in inconsistent findings;

    (5) abnormally deep tympanograms are also associated with a scarred or monomeric tympanic membrane;

    (6) ossicular discontinuity results in a substantial air-bone gap (30 to 50 dB) while tympanic membrane abnormalities rarely produce a substantial air-bone gap.

2. Sensorineural disorders:

    a. cochlear loss:

        (1) normal type A tympanogram, normal static compliance;

        (2) <u>Sensitivity Prediction by the Acoustic Reflex (SPAR)</u> – comparison of reflex thresholds for pure tone vs. noise stimuli; reduced noise-tone difference (NTD).

    b. Eighth cranial nerve disorder:

        (1) normal type A tympanogram, normal static compliance;

        (2) absent or elevated acoustic reflexes;

        (3) acoustic reflex decay – a decrease in amplitude of greater than 50% during a 10-second sustained stimulation;

        (4) the degree of sensitivity loss is important in interpreting reflex findings – i.e., a purely cochlear loss exceeding 60 dB HL will probably result in absent reflexes since the signal may not be loud enough to elicit the reflex.

B. Peripheral vs. Central Auditory Disorder:

    1. Central disorders:

        a. crossed acoustic reflexes may be absent; uncrossed reflexes present and at normal levels;

        b. crossed amplitudes are usually decreased while uncrossed reflex amplitudes are unaffected;

        c. crossed and uncrossed acoustic reflex amplitudes decrease as a function of age;

        d. acoustic reflex thresholds and amplitudes may be affected by middle ear abnormalities; minor middle ear disorders must be considered in the interpretation of results.

IV. Impedance Audiometry in Speech Pathology

A. Three major applications:

    1. Hearing sensitivity can be predicted by the acoustic reflex – SPAR – particularly in difficult to test patients.

    2. To assess and monitor middle ear function, i.e., cleft palate and the mentally retarded.

    3. Used in the study of peripheral and central auditory function in stuttering and spastic dysphonia.

1. The dominant component of middle ear impedance is:

   A. mass
   B. stapes
   C. stiffness
   D. resistance
   E. tympanometry

2. Acoustic impedance is generally recorded in which of the following units:

   A. Millimeter (mm) of water pressure
   B. dB
   C. Cubic centimeters (cc) of equivalent volume
   D. Millimhos
   E. Hertz (cps)

3. The basis of hearing loss prediction by the acoustic reflex is the:

   A. Pure-tone average (PTA)
   B. Loudness recruitment phenomenon
   C. Critical band
   D. Noise-tone difference (NTD)
   E. Has not been determined

4. A popular method of hearing loss prediction by the acoustic reflex is referred to as the:

   A. SPAR
   B. SISI
   C. PTA
   D. SSW
   E. ABR

5. Acoustic reflexes for pure-tone signals are normally elicited at an intensity level of:

   A. 0 dB to 20 dB HL
   B. 25 to 40 dB HL
   C. 100 to 110 dB HL
   D. 85 to 95 dB HL
   E. 55 to 65 dB HL

6. The normal range for static compliance is:

   A. 0 to 20 dB
   B. 0.30 to 1.60 cc
   C. 0 to -100 mm water pressure
   D. 60 to 85 dB
   E. 1.00 to 2.00 cc

7. Each of the following is a measurement in impedance audiometry EXCEP

   A. Acoustic reflex threshold
   B. Tympanometry
   C. Static compliance
   D. Probe tone intensity
   E. Acoustic reflex decay

8. Which of the following is a normal TYPE tympanogram:

   A. Type E
   B. Type B
   C. Type A
   D. Type C
   E. Type W

9. A perforation of the tympanic membrane is typically suggested by:

   A. Absent acoustic reflexes
   B. Type A tympanogram
   C. Air-bone gap
   D. Ear canal volume measurement of 5.00 cc
   E. Abnormally low static compliance measurement

10. Which of the following factors is NOT considered a factor in acoustic reflex threshold measurement:

   A. Age of patient
   B. Hearing sensitivity level
   C. Middle ear dysfunction
   D. Central auditory dysfunction
   E. Patient's attention during test

11. Match the following:

   __A. Otitis Media
   __B. Central auditory dysfunction
   __C. Otosclerosis
   __D. Sudden deafness
   __E. Discontinuity of the ossicular chain

   1. Type B tympanogram
   2. Type A-deep tympanogram
   3. Type A-shallow tympanogram
   4. Type A-normal tympanogram

12. Which pattern of impedance findings best characterizes a moderate cochlear hearing loss:

A. Type B tympanogram, low static compliance, absent acoustic reflexes
B. Type A tympanogram, normal static compliance, absent acoustic reflexes
C. Type A tympanogram, reduced NTD, no reflex decay
D. Type C tympanogram, low static compliance, reduced NTD
E. Type A tympanogram, reduced NTD, abnormal reflex decay

13. Central auditory dysfunction (brain stem level) is best characterized by:

A. Type A tympanogram and absent acoustic reflexes
B. Type A tympanogram and normal static compliance
C. Type C tympanogram and acoustic reflex decay
D. Normal crossed reflexes, abnormal uncrossed reflexes
E. Normal uncrossed, abnormal crossed reflexes

14. A conductive auditory dysfunction is suspected by all of the following impedance findings EXCEPT:

A. Type B tympanogram
B. Static compliance of 3.00 cc
C. Absent acoustic reflexes
D. Type A-shallow tympanogram
E. Acoustic reflex decay

15. The three major components of impedance audiometry are:

A. _____

B. _____

C. _____

16. Which of the following auditory structures probably is not part of the acoustic reflex arc:

A. Stapes
B. Eighth cranial nerve
C. Temporal lobe
D. Cochlea
E. Superior olivary complex

# Chapter 41

# EARLY IDENTIFICATION OF HEARING LOSS

*Marion P. Downs*

I. The Need for Early Identification

    A. Critical Period Theory:

        1. Definition: at certain points in early life the infant is pre-programmed to learn certain activities.

        2. For higher intellectual skills such as learning to speak and listen critical periods may be extremely crucial.

        3. Wild Boy of Aveyron (1796) never learned to speak despite extensive therapy since critical periods for learning speech and language had passed.

        4. Proper exposure to stimulation during initial two years of life crucial to effective acquisition of speech and language at any time in later life.

        5. Helen Keller became deaf and blind after two years of normal family language environment.

        6. Two years where critical periods are most important:

            a. cognitive competence;

            b. auditory perception.

    B. Critical Periods and Language Learning:

        1. Failure of Head Start programs to produce permanent gains in achievement blamed on intervention therapies that are too late and inadequate.

        2. Delayed development is less amenable to modification with increasing age.

        3. Earlier identified hard-of-hearing children have improved speech and language skills.

4. Intervention should occur well before the age of two if it is to be successful.

5. The level of language development in hearing-impaired children is directly related to the age at which habilitation is begun.

C. Critical Periods and Early Auditory Deprivation:

1. Language and cognition are innate functions that are dependent on early experience.

2. Templin (1966) showed that language skills of deaf children showed no systematic improvement beyond age of 11 years – while normal hearing subjects continued to improve language skills until the age of 14.

3. Menyuk (1977) states that by age 40 days, infants can differentiate phonemic and intonation changes.

4. In terms of economics, congenitally deaf adults earn $1000 less per year than those deaf adults who lost hearing at age 6 (Schein and Delk, 1974).

D. Early Mild Conductive Hearing Loss and Language Deficiency:

1. Several studies have shown that children with mild conductive hearing loss, during first two years of life, show poorer language scores than matched children with no early conductive loss history (Needleman and Menyuk, 1977; Holm and Kunze, 1969; Quigley, 1970; Kaplan, 1969; Lewis, 1976).

2. Such studies prove the need for early identification of hearing loss in children.

3. Initial research with animals suggests irreversible organic central auditory pathway deficiencies due to early auditory deprivation.

E. Summary:

1. If sensory deprivation occurs during critical periods, permanent and irreversible deficits will be present in the perception of acoustic signals.

2. Prevention of such deficits rests with early identification before critical periods have occurred.

II. Methods of Identification

    A. Hearing screening meets public health criteria according to Frankenberg (1971):

        1. Frequency occurrence and serious consequences if not detected.

        2. Amenability to treatment.

        3. Availability of facilities for diagnosis and treatment.

        4. Reasonable cost with commensurate benefits.

        5. Validly differentiates diseased individuals from non-diseased individuals.

        6. Good public acceptance.

    B. Newborn Hearing Screening:

        1. Main goal in newborn screening is to identify all hearing losses present at birth so that training can be initiated for the hearing-impaired child.

        2. To identify infant hearing loss by 3 months of age, test procedures must be done in the newborn nursery.

        3. High-risk concept is that a small group of children with specific history or physical condition identifies them as possessing a high chance of having the handicap in question.

        4. Yield from high risk hearing register in intensive care newborn nursery is 1 in 67 babies.

        5. High risk hearing categories:

           a. family history of hereditary childhood deafness;

           b. maternal rubella or other intrauterine fetal infection (cytomegalovirus, herpes, etc.);

           c. anomalies of ear, nose, or throat at birth;

           d. birth weight less than 1500 grams;

           e. high serum bilirubin concentration.

        6. Some add neonatal meningitis to above list.

        7. High risk hearing register may be conducted by:

           a. trained volunteers;

           b. public health agency;

c. private or community agencies.

C. Infant Hearing Screening for Behavioral Testing:

1. 90 dB SPL stimulus with low frequency attenuation 30 dB/octave below 750 Hz.

2. Infant asleep with 15-seconds of no body movement prior to stimulus presentation.

3. Only acceptable response is generalized body movement involving more than one limb accompanied by some form of eye movement.

4. Scoring done by two independent observers - two (of eight maximum) stimulus responses constitute pass; failures should be retested at least once.

5. Technique identifies severe hearing loss greater than 75 dB HL, but misses mild-moderate hearing loss (Mencher, 1974).

D. Crib-O-Gram Technique:

1. Developed by Simmons (1975) at Stanford University.

2. Automated technique which utilizes motion-sensitive transducers underneath the infant bassinet in hospital nursery.

3. Automated high-frequency stimulus presentations of 92 dB SPL presented to infants at scheduled or random intervals.

4. Infant movements, time-locked to stimulus presentations, are recorded on automated strip chart recorder for daily review.

5. Technique is reported to be potentially low cost and identifies 1 in 1000 as deaf in regular nursery and 12 in 1000 in intensive care nursery.

E. Brain-Stem Evoked Response Infant Screening:

1. Advocated by Galambos (1978).

2. Uses computer-averaged electroencephalographic recordings with sedated infants (BSER).

3. Suspects deafness in intensive care nursery to be as high as 1 in 20 babies.

4. Galambos recommends 3-part infant screening program:

    a. BSER in intensive care nursery;

    b. high-risk register to entire newborn population;

    c. behavioral screening of entire newborn population.

III. Screening the Infant from Birth to Three Years

    A. Detecting Infant Hearing Loss:

        1. At every routine well-child visit, the infant's hearing should be rechecked.

        2. Need to detect deafness and mild hearing loss due to ear disease.

        3. Behavioral screening with noisemakers:

            a. five noisemakers recommended - two high-frequency, two low-frequency and one loud sound;

            b. child sits on mother's lap, and noisemakers used to elicit auditory reflexive localization behaviors;

            c. loud noisemaker is used as final test to elicit startle or jump.

        4. Expected age-related responses:

            a. birth to 4-months of age:

                (1) eyeblink or eyewidening;

                (2) only reliable response is a startle or eyeblink to the loud noisemaker;

                (3) at 3-4 months, head localization toward sound may occur.

            b. 4 to 7-months of age:

                (1) wobbly head turn toward sound source;

                (2) by 7-months, direct head turn to the side of sound.

            c. 7 to 9-months of age:

                (1) baby localizes sound source on correct side at lower plane level.

d. 9 to 13-months of age:

    (1) localizes directly to sounds in any plane - above, side or below eye level.

e. 13 to 36-months of age:

    (1) brisk localization in all planes;

    (2) 2 or 3-year-old may hear noisemaker, but inhibit localization behavior.

f. age-related auditory responses give rough estimate of child's developmental functional level;

g. children of 4-months or older who fail to localize as described above, or who fail to startle to loud noisemaker, should be referred for additional testing.

B. Impedance Tests with Infants:

    1. Impedance measurements, with some limitations, recommended to identify ear disease in infants:

        a. according to Paradise (1976), tympanometry has questionable validity in infants less than 7 months of age;

        b. however, tympanometry is 83% accurate with flat curves in infants.

IV. Hearing Screening at 3 to 5 Years of Age

A. Pure-Tone Screening:

    1. Play conditioning for 3-4 year-olds pairs some fun activity for child (building peg-board fences, or dropping pennies in bank) with presentation of pure-tone.

    2. Five-year-olds can do traditional finger-raising when pure tone sound is perceived.

    3. Any child who fails to respond to 15 dB HTL at any one test frequency, should be rescreened and referred if failure persists.

B. Non-Pure Tone Screening:

    1. VASC (Verbal Auditory Screening for Pre-School Children); child points to a picture corresponding to a word presented by tape through earphones.

2. Test consists of four randomized lists of 125 bisyllabic words, each presented 4 dB attenuation from previous word.

3. VASC useful with four and five-year-olds.

V. Minimal Auditory Deficiency Syndrome

A. Speech and language problems related to the problem of mild and fluctuating hearing loss due to otitis media during initial two years of life:

1. Questions whether or not extensive intervention after the age of two or three years can close achievement gap between normal children and early otitis media children (Needleman and Menyuk, 1977).

2. Eisen (1962) initially described auditory learning difficulties in a child with history of otitis media in early childhood - named the syndrome and called its effects irreversible.

3. Kaplan's study of nearly 500 Eskimo children from birth to 10 years, also showed that the gap in school achievement between early otitis media children and nonaffected children widened with each increasing grade level.

4. Howie (1976) found I.Q.'s of early otitis media children to be significantly lower than the I.Q.'s of non-otitis children.

5. Paradise (1976) observed cleft palate children as candidates for auditory learning problems and compared two groups - one treated "aggressively" with otologic management (ventilation tubes and myringotomies) with "standard" non-surgical treatment of otitis media. Mean I.Q. of children in "aggressive" care group was 110, compared with 98 in "standard" care group.

6. Holm and Kunze (1969) showed that experimental group of children with history of otitis media and mild conductive loss less than 25 dB; with a battery of tests requiring processing of auditory stimuli or production of verbal responses, the otitis media group had significantly lower scores than the control group.

7. Lewis (1976) studied socioeconomic level on the minimal auditory deficit syndrome by comparing a group of experimental otitis media aboriginal children, with non-disease history control groups of aboriginals and European children. Otitis media aboriginals did not perform as well on tests as either of the control groups.

8. Zinkus et al. (1978) showed that early severe otitis media was associated with central auditory processing disorders that interfere with development of reading, spelling and mathematical proficiency even in the presence of average or above-average intelligence.

VI. Acoustic Liabilities Associated with Minimal Auditory Deficiency

A. Effects of mild conductive loss on speech sounds:

1. Lack of constancy of auditory clues when acoustic information fluctuates.

2. Confusion of acoustic parameters with normal or rapidly spoken speech.

3. Confusion in segmentation and prosody.

4. Ambient noise masks intonation and stress patterns of speech.

5. Inability to perceive and discriminate speech sounds.

6. Breakdown in ability to abstract the meanings of sentences.

7. Faulty abstraction of grammatical rules.

8. Breakdown in the subtle stress patterns of speech.

B. Solution to the problem of acoustic liabilities:

1. Prevention:

a. identification of hearing loss;

b. aggressive medical treatment;

c. educational habilitation:

(1) home language stimulation program;

(2) placement of hearing aids.

2. Any child who has had three bouts of otitis media during the first year of life is at risk for language and cognitive problems.

**REVIEW QUESTIONS**

1.  Critical Period Theory suggests that the effective acquisition of speech
    and language is dependent upon appropriate stimulation and exposure
    during the _____.

    A.  Initial year of life
    B.  Initial two years of life
    C.  Initial three years of life
    D.  Initial four years of life
    E.  Preschool age years

2.  Two areas where critical periods are theorized to be most important
    are (choose two) _____ and _____.

    A.  Speech motor development
    B.  Cognitive competence
    C.  Psycholinguistics
    D.  Auditory competence
    E.  Hemispheric dominance

3.  The level of language development in hearing-impaired children has
    been shown to relate directly to:

    A.  Age of suspicion of hearing loss
    B.  Age of verification of hearing loss
    C.  Age at which habilitation is begun
    D.  Intelligence Quotient score
    E.  I.T.P.A. score

4.  Fill in the missing screening yield figure in the table below:

| Disease Screened | Yield |
|---|---|
| Phenylketonuria | 1 in 15,000 births |
| Maple Syrup Urine Disease | 1 in 300,000 births |
| Neonatal hyperthyroidism | 1 in 6,000 births |
| Neonatal Hearing Screening | _____ |

5. List the five high risk categories associated with profound congenital deafness:

A. _____
B. _____
C. _____
D. _____
E. _____

6. The recommended stimulus intensity for behavioral hearing screening testing is:

A. 100 dB HL
B. 100 dB SPL
C. 90 dB HL
D. 90 dB SPL
E. 95 dB SPL

7. By the end of this age period the normal hearing infant will be able to localize directly to sounds presented in any plane.

A. Birth to 4 months
B. 4 to 7 months
C. 7 to 9 months
D. 9 to 13 months
E. 13 to 36 months

8. By ____ months of age, the normal hearing infant will begin to turn his head toward the sound source.

A. Two
B. Three
C. Four
D. Five
E. Six

9. Recent research studies have shown that children who have a history of recurrent otitis media during the first two years of life are at risk of having (select two answers):

A. Central motor problems
B. Hyperactivity
C. Auditory learning problems
D. Dysfluency in speech
E. Reduced language skills

10. An automated technique for behavioral hearing screening of infants which utilizes a motion-sensitive transducer placed under the bassinet is known as:

A. Behavioral response testing
B. Crib-o-gram
C. BSER screening
D. Reflex orientation observation
E. Early infant detection system

# Chapter 42

# HEARING SCREENING

*Philip E. Rosenberg and Joanne Swogger-Rosenberg*

I.  Introduction

    A.  Hearing screening often misunderstood:

        1.  Not truly a "test".

        2.  Not a diagnostic audiology procedure.

        3.  "Passing" the screening in no way implies normality of structure or function.

        4.  Technique used to identify individuals easily, rapidly, economically, who may require additional attention because of an auditory problem.

    B.  Most hearing screening takes place in schools.

        1.  Goal is to identify children whose hearing poses a threat to their subsequent education.

II.  Increased Urgency for Hearing Adequacy

    A.  Moderate or severe bilateral hearing loss has a devastating effect on language development and educational achievement.

        1.  Recent research suggests that any auditory incompetence, even mild problems, may have a subtle but permanent influence on linguistic and intellectual achievement.

    B.  Physical examination of the "ear" tells little about "hearing".

        1.  Hearing conservation must consider both health, and educational implications.

III.  Neonatal Screening

    A.  Neonatal hearing screening programs seek to identify infants with severe-to-profound hearing loss so that early habilitative measures can be undertaken.

1. Behavioral <u>response</u> <u>observation</u> – high-frequency sound of 90-100 dB SPL presented to newborn. Typical responses include opening of eyes, gross body movements, full Moro reflex or the initiation or cessation of crying.

2. <u>Crib-O-Gram</u> – automatic technique which measures infant's <u>movements in</u> crib following the presentation of auditory stimulation.

3. Infant screening techniques always have had problems relative to false negative and false positive responses.

4. Decided that "at risk" infants be identified by physical examination and history for "in depth audiologic evaluation during their first two months of life".

5. Today, most deaf babies are identified before one year of age.

IV. Preschool and School Age Populations

A. In recent years the pre-school population has become the target for hearing screening programs:

1. Largest population to be subjected to hearing screening (pre-school and school-age).

2. Approximately 5% fail the hearing screening test.

3. Pittsburgh study indicated that 1.7% of children between ages of 5-10 years have some degree of hearing loss.

B. Group Hearing Screening:

1. Historically important:

a. fading number test;

b. group pure tone screening;

c. Massachusetts test.

2. Most group hearing tests proved unsatisfactory and are seldom used today.

C. Individual Hearing Screening:

1. Most commonly used today – the pure tone sweep test.

2. ASHA recommends the pure tone sweep test as the procedure of choice in hearing screening programs (1975).

3. Verbal Auditory Screening for Children (VASC) – speech hearing screening test utilizing 12 taped spondee words with pictures to which a child can point to when the word is heard.

   a. can be presented to two children simultaneously.

D. Test Environment:

   1. Noise levels in school test rooms make hearing testing difficult.

   2. Must attempt to find the quietest spot for screening.

   3. If it is just too noisy:

      a. eliminate test frequencies below 1000 Hz;

      b. adjust the screening test level upward (louder) to compensate for noise;

      c. equip earphones with special sound-isolating cushions;

      d. move the student to the examiner.

   4. Test equipment:

      a. screening air-conduction audiometer (must be portable and sturdy);

      b. spare set of earphones.

E. Personnel – probably doesn't matter who does the screening as long as they are thoroughly familiarized with the equipment and test procedure and rigorously supervised.

   1. Training should be conducted by an audiologist.

F. Follow-up – every screening program must have a plan for systematic follow-ups of those youngsters who do not pass the initial tests.

   1. Usually requires at least one additional re-screening.

   2. Then threshold air-conduction test.

   3. Referred to family physician.

   4. Reports sent to parents and school.

G. Special Populations – often difficult, if not impossible to "screen".

   1. Includes mentally retarded, emotionally disturbed, cerebral palsy, cleft palate, learning disabled, the blind, and the deaf.

2. Assume universal "failure" for hearing screening test and proceed with annual diagnostic hearing evaluation.

H. Inappropriate Populations – industrial audiology should never include "hearing screening".

1. Requires pre- and post threshold audiometry evaluations.

V. Ear Screening

A. Identification of middle ear disease in screening programs must be conducted in mass school populations.

1. Otoscopy and pneumatic otoscopy – excellent screening tools in <u>experienced</u> hands.

a. often not readily available, not inexpensive, nor precise enough to warrant being recommended as a routine procedure in a hearing screening program.

B. Impedance Screening:

1. Validity of tympanometry and acoustic reflex measurements for identifying middle ear effusion is extraordinarily good.

2. Questionable validity of tympanometry in infants less than 7-months of age.

3. Acoustic impedance referral criteria – Nashville Task Force of 1977 suggested:

a. combination of tympanometry and acoustic reflex measurements be used for screening.

4. ASHA Guidelines for Impedance Screening (1978) recommended annual testing of children nursery school age through grade 5 and to older children with history of middle ear problems.

a. seems to be a groundswell for school hearing screening programs to include acoustic impedance measurements;

b. impedance especially valuable in certain populations such as native Indian children, children with Down's syndrome, children with cleft palate, developmentally delayed children and children with known sensorineural hearing loss.

VI. Conclusion: Is Screening Obsolete?

A. It is apparent that screening, as it is currently carried out, fails to reveal a very large number of children who may be "at risk" for failure in achieving their educational and academic potential.

B.   The ideal hearing conservation program should be based on a <u>combination</u> of <u>impedance</u> <u>audiometry</u> and <u>pure</u> <u>tone</u> <u>air</u> <u>conduction</u> <u>threshold</u> <u>audiometry</u>

## REVIEW QUESTIONS

1.   Identify the following statements as true (T) or false (F):

___ A.   Hearing screening is a diagnostic procedure.
___ B.   Hearing screening is not truly a "test" which one passes or fails on an absolute basis.
___ C.   "Passing" a screening examination implies normality of structure and/or function.
___ D.   Screening of hearing is a set of compromises designed to produce maximum results at minimum expense.
___ E.   The main goal of hearing screening is the identification of thos children whose hearing loss poses a threat to their education.
___ F.   Most deaf infants are identified prior to the age of one year.

2.   Approximately ___ % of pre-school and school-age children will fail the hearing screening test.

A.   1%
B.   3%
C.   5%
D.   10%
E.   12%

3.   The classic Pittsburgh hearing study of 1967 indicated that ___ % of children between the ages of 5 and 10 will have some degree of hearing loss.

A.   1.0%
B.   1.7%
C.   2.3%
D.   2.7%
E.   3.7%

4.   The most popular current hearing screening technique is:

A.   Group pure tone test
B.   The Fading Numbers Test
C.   The Massachusetts Test
D.   Individual pure tone sweep test
E.   Western Electric speech test

5. Some hearing screening merely divides a large population into two groups, those children who "fail" should be:

   A. Retested
   B. Sent home
   C. Referred to the school principal
   D. Referred to a medical doctor
   E. Referred to the school nurse

6. Both sets of national guidelines for the use of impedance measurements in screening programs recommended the use of:

   A. The acoustic reflex
   B. Tympanometry
   C. Acoustic reflex and tympanometry
   D. Static compliance
   E. Acoustic reflex, tympanometry and static compliance

7. List five special children's populations for whom impedance screening is especially important:

   A. _____

   B. _____

   C. _____

   D. _____

   E. _____

8. "The ideal hearing conservation program would be based on a combination of _____ _____ and _____ _____ _____ audiometry".

9. The 1974 Infant Screening Joint Committee suggested that "at risk" children for hearing loss should be identified by means of:

   A. Physical examination
   B. History
   C. Hearing screening/audiometry
   D. Physical examination/history
   E. Physical examination/history/audiometry

10. The 1974 Infant Screening Joint Committee indicated that "at risk" children for hearing loss should be given in depth audiologic evaluation of hearing during...

    A. the first month of life
    B. the first two months of life
    C. the first three months of life
    D. the first four months of life
    E. the first five months of life

# Chapter 43

# CENTRAL AUDITORY TESTS

*Robert W. Keith*

I. Introduction

    A. Interest in evaluation of central auditory problems began in 1950's.

        1. Acceptance of the clinical importance of central hearing tests has come slowly.

    B. Central hearing tests serve several purposes:

        1. Basic investigation of central auditory system.

        2. Localization of disorders of auditory pathway.

        3. Determination of auditory perceptual problems in children and adults with learning difficulties.

II. Neuroanatomy of Auditory System

    A. Central auditory nervous system (CANS) is complex and diffuse.

        1. Electrical signals generated in hair cells of cochlea travel through auditory portion of VIIIth N. into medulla of brain stem into cochlear nucleus complex.

        2. Fibers from cochlear nuclei ascend to:

            a. opposite cochlear nucleus;

            b. contralateral inferior colliculus;

            c. contralateral superior olivary complex;

            d. ipsilateral superior olivary complex;

            e. cerebellar vermis.

        3. Superior olivary complex is the first place in ascending auditory pathway to receive information from both ears.

4. Lateral lemniscus pathway receives fibers from:

   a. contralateral cochlear nuceli;

   b. ipsilateral superior olivary complex;

   c. most of the above fibers terminate in the medial geniculate body;

   d. some fibers cross at the commissure of the inferior colliculus.

5. Main afferent flow from the medial geniculate body forms the thalamocortical connections with primary termination in the temporal lobe of the cortex.

6. Tonotopical organization (spatial frequency arrangement) is maintained at each level of the auditory system from cochlea to cortex.

7. Efferent auditory system exists with descending pathways which include:

   a. colliculocochlear bundle;

   b. olivocochlear bundle;

   c. and recurrent fiber tract.

8. Auditory cortex is involved in final analysis and interpretation of sound, associating meaning with sound, etc.

   a. language functions are related to left brain hemisphere;

   b. in some persons, especially if they are left-handed, it is normal for the right hemisphere to be dominant for speech.

III. Central Auditory Abilities

A. Binaural vs. monaural stimulation.

   1. Binaural reception has advantages over monaural reception for intelligibility of speech and spatial orientation.

   2. Binaural stimulation facilitates listening to speech in noise.

B. Central auditory abilities most frequently measured include:

   1. Localization.

   2. Binaural synthesis.

   3. Figure ground.

4. Binaural separation.

5. Memory.

6. Blending.

7. Discrimination.

8. Closure.

9. Attention.

10. Association.

11. Cognition.

C. Considerations Before Administration of Central Auditory Tests.

1. Current problem exists in definition of <u>central auditory function</u>:

   a. may imply from an inability to hear difference between phonemes to an inability to use proper verb tense;

   b. difficult to test central auditory abilities in isolation from each other.

IV. Principles of Diagnostic Testing

A. Principle of <u>redundancy</u>:

1. Most of speech measures that assess CANS attempt to reduce the redundancy of speech by:

   a. filtering;

   b. interrupting;

   c. time compression of the message;

   d. lowering signal-to-noise ratio.

B. <u>Subtlety</u> principle:

1. The subtlety of the auditory manifestation increases as the site of lesion progresses from peripheral to central.

C. <u>Bottleneck</u> principle:

1. Complex auditory stimuli encounter a point of neural congestion at the VIIIth N. and brainstem.

V.  Factors Affecting Central Auditory Tests

  A.  Numerous factors must be considered relative to their effect
      on central auditory tests to avoid false impression of central
      auditory dysfunction.

      1.  Peripheral hearing loss.

      2.  Age.

      3.  Intelligence.

      4.  Drugs.

      5.  Linguistic background.

VI.  Testing for Lesions of the Central Auditory Pathways

  A.  Physiological measures.

      1.  Stapedial reflex tests:

          a. elevated or absent acoustic reflexes;

          b. abnormal stapedial reflex decay;

          c. contralateral vs. ipsilateral acoustic reflex interpretation.

      2.  Auditory evoked potential measurements:

          a. fixed time relationship between "waves" generated
             at each neuroanatomical site in central auditory pathway;

          b. initial seven waves correspond to probable anatomic
             site in auditory nerve and brainstem;

          c. auditory pathway lesions result in latency delay of
             waves or loss of waveform.

  B.  Behavioral measures.

      1.  Require overt responses by subject – classified by the
          manner of stimulus presentation.

      2.  Includes monotic tests, diotic tests and binaural
          fusion tests.

      3.  Sensitized speech tests – monotic tests which include
          filtered, time-compressed and interrupted speech.

      4.  Filtered speech – speech intelligibility score is reduced
          in the ear contralateral to a temporal lobe lesion.

5.  Time-Compressed speech - reduction in total time duration of a speech message without a substantial change in the fundamental frequency of the voice.

6.  Interrupted Speech - uses electronic switch to interrupt speech at various rates; - results similar to filtered speech tests.

7.  Rush-Hughes PAL PB-50 - difficulty of this test makes it useful as a test of speech intelligibility.

8.  Synthetic Sentence Identification - administered with ipsilateral competing message (ICM) and contralateral competing message (CCM) with various signal-to-noise ratios.

C.  Summary of Sensitized Speech Tests:

1.  Normal patients have equivalent scores for each ear.

2.  When cortical auditory lesion is present, test scores are mild to moderately reduced in the ear contralateral to lesion.

3.  Brainstem lesions affect these tests more than cortical lesions.

4.  Reduced intelligibility score occurs on same or opposite side of lesion in brainstem problems depending on which neural pathways are involved.

D.  Dichotic Speech Tests:

1.  Conducted by presenting different stimuli simultaneously to the two ears.

2.  Dichotic CV Test developed by Berlin (1973) uses six stop-vowel syllables as consonants vowel syllables (CV).

    a. presents random series of dichotic pairs of the syllables with precise onset delays of the CV pairs.

3.  Staggered Spondaic Word Test (SSW):

    a. developed by Katz (1962); contains spondee words with two non-competing and one competing condition;

    b. lesion of central auditory reception area generally shows high percentage of errors in the competing condition of the ear contralateral to the lesion.

4. Competing Sentence Test:

   a. developed by Willeford (1974); ten sentence pairs are presented simultaneously with the primary message at 35 dB SL, and the competing message at 50 dB SL;

   b. results generally indicate the expected contralateral ear effect with decreased competing sentence scores by the ear opposite a temporal or parietal lobe lesion.

5. Binaural Fusion Tests:

   a. Matzker Test of Binaural Fusion; uses low-frequency speech pass to one ear and simultaneous high-frequency speech pass to opposite ear; neither pass is intelligible by itself, but normals can integrate both signals;

   b. reduction in binaural fusion scores resulting from lesions to the Olivary Complex but also result from cortical lesions remote from brain stem;

   c. test is especially affected by peripheral hearing loss and aging;

   d. Rapidly Alternating Speech (RASP) – test material is alternated between ears every 300 msec;

   e. Masking Level Differences (MLD) – based on masking phenomenon known as masking level difference or binaural release from masking; occurs when a binaurally presented stimulus is interaurally out of phase with itself when the other stimulus is in phase; results in a decrease of effective masking of the noise.

E. Summary of Dichotic Tests:

   1. These tests are useful in identification of the presence of a lesion but precise determination of lesion site is difficult.

VII. Central Hearing Testing With Children

A. Special interest because of educational emphasis on children with learning disabilities.

   1. Definition of learning disabilities: "disorders in one or more of the basic psychological processes involved in understanding or in using language, spoken or written, which disorders may manifest itself in imperfect ability to listen..."

2. Value of such tests is that they appear to indicate whether a child's auditory abilities are "normal" or "disordered", although how the results relate to functional behavior is not clear.

3. False assumptions are made that children who do poorly on these tasks will have a deficit in language, reading or learning.

4. Results of auditory perceptual testing obtained on children with language, reading or learning disabilities indicate that they <u>tend</u> to do poorer than normal children.

B. Remediation:

1. Assessment of central auditory abilities remains a controversial issue.

2. Disagreement exists whether disorders of auditory perception <u>cause</u> speech and language, reading, or learning disabilities or if they are just highly correlated.

3. Rees (1973, 1974) indicates that there is little foundation for the notion that most children with reading, speech and language disorders have a fundamental problem of auditory perception of speech.

4. No easy answer to the issue of remediation for "central auditory perceptual problems".

## REVIEW QUESTIONS

1. The primary auditory reception area of the brain is in the:

   A. Cochlear Nucleus
   B. Splenium of the Corpus Callosum
   C. Superior Olivary Complex
   D. Anterior Transverse Temporal Gyri
   E. Medial Geniculate Body

2. Tonotopic organization is:

   A. Present in the cochlea and more diffuse centrally.
   B. Necessary for localization of sound.
   C. Preserved from cochlea to cortex.
   D. A possible cause of periodicity pitch.
   E. The primary mechanism for encoding incoming stimuli.

3. Binaural auditory reception is necessary for:

   A. Understanding speech
   B. Monotic listening tasks
   C. Sensitized speech testing
   D. Brainstem evoked response audiometry
   E. Auditory localization

4. Match the following:

   A. The ability to identify a message in the presence of a background noise.
   B. The ability to form words from separately articulated phonemes.
   C. The ability to store and recall auditory stimuli.
   D. The ability to recognize fine differences that exist among phonemes.
   E. The ability to establish a correspondence between a linguistic sound and its meaning.

   1. Memory           _____
   2. Figure Ground    _____
   3. Discrimination   _____
   4. Blending         _____
   5. Cognition        _____

5. In audition, the principle of redundancy means that:

   A. It is preferable to do repeat auditory measures on a child.
   B. Speech discrimination will be poor in the presence of a central lesion.
   C. Increase in stimulus duration reduces the SPL necessary for absolute threshold.
   D. There are too many audiologists.
   E. There is excess acoustic energy and neurological mechanism available to the organism for understanding speech.

6. A 10-year old child demonstrates a 50 dB sensorineural hearing loss and poor central auditory test results. The most likely explanation of these results is:

   A. Sensory deprivation has caused failure of development of central auditory structures.
   B. Because of cochlear distortion, it is difficult to know about central auditory perceptual abilities.
   C. The child should be considered to have central auditory dysfunction.
   D. The child's limited language abilities caused him to yield poor central auditory test results.
   E. The child is too young to yield valid central auditory test results.

7. Considering the use of both physiological and behavioral test approaches, which of the following statements is most appropriate:

   A. Physiological tests are more valid than behavioral tests.
   B. Physiological and behavioral tests measure different aspects of audition.
   C. Physiological tests are more reliable than behavioral tests.
   D. Physiological tests are independent of patient cooperation.
   E. Physiological tests are more objective than behavioral tests.

8. Which of the following auditory tests are effective in identifying abnormalities of the central auditory pathways:

   A. Dichotic CV identification
   B. Pure-tone threshold configuration
   C. Sensitized speech tests
   D. Dichotic speech tests
   E. Hirsh recordings of CID W-22 word lists

9. Clinicians should be aware that:

   A. Sensitized speech test results can identify a specific site of lesion in the auditory cortex.
   B. Binaural fusion results are affected by brainstem lesions only.
   C. The Staggered Spondaic Word Test and the Dichotic CV Identification Test results are highly affected by brainstem pathology.
   D. Synthetic Sentence Identification tests are most useful in identifying cortical lesions.
   E. Many factors serve to confound test battery interpretation with regard to specific site of lesion.

10. Auditory perceptual skills of children as measured by a central auditory test battery are comparable to adults at approximately the age of:

    A. 4 years
    B. 8 years
    C. 12 years
    D. 16 years
    E. 20 years

11. Central auditory tests in young children are characterized by:

    A. Marked variability in results obtained from both ears.
    B. Marked variability from left ear scores.
    C. Marked variability from right ear scores.
    D. Bilaterally symmetrical test results.
    E. Increased variability with increasing age.

12. There is little consensus on auditory perceptual abilities of learning-disabled children. The <u>least</u> likely explanation of this fact is:

    A. The subject population is not homogeneous.
    B. There is poor definition of terminology of auditory perception and learning disability.
    C. Many test materials have been developed with insufficient considerations of children's special requirements.
    D. Learning-disabled children are not able to perform sufficiently well to give an adequate data base for forming an opinion.
    E. Results of various tests are often highly correlated.

13. What are the basic components of an auditory perceptual deficit hypothesis?

    A. _____

    B. _____

    C. _____

    D. _____

14. What are the basic components of a verbal mediation hypothesis?

    A. _____

    B. _____

    C. _____

15. Why is it not possible to say that intact auditory perceptual skills are necessary for the development of reading ability?

    A. _____

    _____

    _____

# Chapter 44

# MEDICAL AND SURGICAL TREATMENT OF HEARING LOSS

*Gerald M. English and Ruth S. Sargent*

I. Introduction

    A. Medical and surgical treatments are often integrated, and one therapy does not necessarily exclude the other.

    B. Treatment of a specific disease is not always the same -- based on the patient's age, sex, occupation, social status and general health.

II. Congenital and Hereditary Diseases of Hearing

    A. Definitions:

        1. <u>Congenital</u> - present at birth, but may be acquired.

        2. <u>Hereditary</u> - transmitted genetically from parents to child.

    B. External Ear:

        1. <u>Microtia</u>, <u>Anotia</u> and <u>Atresia</u> are anomalies of external ear (auricle and external auditory canal).

        2. Associated with conductive loss of 40-60 dB air-bone gap.

        3. Group I patients: have normal external and middle ear with <u>fixed</u> <u>stapes</u> footplate.

        4. Group II patients: absence of the external meatus, tympanic membrane and malformation of the stapes.

        5. Group III patients: without external meatus and tympanic membrane, stapedial deformities plus poor or absent pneumatization of mastoid air cells.

    C. Middle Ear:

        1. <u>Stapes</u> <u>footplate</u> <u>fixation</u> commonly associated with atresia of external ear canal.

2. Vascular anomalies in middle ear include anomalous carotid artery and prominent jugular bulb.

3. Eustachian tube atresia common in group III patients.

4. Congenital cholesteatoma usually creates conductive hearing loss best treated by surgery.

5. Otosclerosis is a bilateral hereditary disorder causing progressive fixation of the stapes footplate.

    a. candidates for surgery should show:

        (1) negative Rinne tuning fork test;

        (2) bilateral hearing loss;

        (3) may benefit from hearing aid;

        (4) risks and morbidity must be discussed prior to surgery;

        (5) mixed hearing loss treated with surgery may prove to be better hearing aid users following the operation.

    b. two basic methods of stapes surgery:

        (1) partial or total removal of stapes and replacement with a prosthesis;

        (2) repositioning of parts of the patient's stapes.

    c. reoccurrence of the conductive loss can occur following stapes surgery due to regrowth of otosclerotic bone.

6. Osteogenesis imperfecta is syndrome which includes blue eye sclera, fragile bones and conductive or mixed deafness due to fixed stapedial footplate.

    a. treatment generally the same surgical procedures used in otosclerosis.

7. Osteopetrosis – mixed-type hearing loss due to fixation of the ossicular chain; often accompanied by a recurrent facial paralysis.

D. Inner Ear:

1. Hereditary deafness is sensorineural and 90% recessive, 10% dominant inheritance.

2. Usually treated with aural rehabilitative techniques.

E.  Congenital Acquired Deafness:

   1.  Birth injuries.

   2.  Viral infections.

   3.  Drugs.

   4.  Rh incompatability (mother Rh negative and child Rh positive

   5.  Hypothyroidism.

III.  Inflammatory Diseases

   A.  External Ear:

   1.  External otitis is associated with pain, swelling, and
       drainage from ear.

   2.  Chronic external otitis due to complications of untreated
       acute infection.

   3.  Perichondritis and chondritis of the auricle is due to
       trauma or infection.

   B.  Tympanic Membrane, Middle Ear and Mastoid

   1.  Myringitis - inflammation of the tympanic membrane that
       usually occurs with infections of the middle ear or
       external ear canal.

   2.  Bullous myringitis - associated with influenza with blebs
       on the tympanic membrane; very painful with minimal
       hearing loss.

   3.  Tympanosclerosis - term applied to various forms of scar
       tissue that form in the tympanic membrane, middle ear,
       eustachian tube or mastoid.

   4.  Acute otitis media - pain, fever, hearing loss and
       vertigo; redness and swelling of the tympanic membrane
       as the pressure within the middle ear increases.

   5.  Serous otitis media - refers to an accumulation of fluid
       within the middle ear due to eustachian tube dysfunction.

       a. treatment may be medical (decongestants or antibiotics)
          or surgical (ventilation tubes in tympanic membrane).

   6.  Chronic otitis media - characterized by a permanent
       perforation of the tympanic membrane with or without
       associated middle ear or mastoid disease.

a. three types of perforations: central, marginal and attic.

7. Cholesteatoma - accumulation of desquamated skin cells within the mastoid or middle ear spaces.

8. Acute mastoiditis - occurs in conjunction with acute otitis media; symptoms of otitis media with pain and swelling in the mastoid area of the skull.

9. Chronic mastoiditis - associated with damage to the ossicles, otic capsule and mastoid bone commonly caused by cholesteatoma.

10. Acute labyrinthitis - results from agents (especially bacterial and viral) transmitted to the inner ear.

   a. four types of labyrinthitis that are not always distinct entities:

      (1) circumscribed;

      (2) diffuse serous;

      (3) acute;

      (4) chronic suppurative.

11. Syphilis - syphilis of the temporal bone, although rare, is characterized by progressive, sudden sensorineural hearing loss accompanied by vertigo.

IV. Trauma

A. External and Middle Ear

   1. Most common traumatic injuries to the auricle occur from accidents, wrestling or boxing, burns or frostbite.

   2. Barotitis occurs from sudden severe negative pressure in the middle ear and mastoid air system.

B. Inner Ear

   1. Fractures:

      a. longitudinal fracture - may cause lacerated tympanic membrane and ossicular discontinuity; may show temporary sensorineural hearing loss;

      b. transverse fracture - may lacerate facial nerve and usually results in permanent, complete loss of hearing, severe tinnitus and vertigo.

2. <u>Surgical trauma</u> – inner ear damage may occur during mastoid surgery.

3. <u>Noise deafness</u> – loss of hearing from exposure to high intensity noise.

4. <u>Labyrinthine concussion</u> – blow to head may cause deafness and dysequilibrium.

5. <u>Ototoxicity</u> – several drugs can create temporary or permanent hearing loss -- related to numerous factors:

   a. serum level of ototoxic drug;

   b. synergism (or combinations of ototoxic drugs);

   c. kidney function;

   d. congenital ototoxic hearing loss due to mother receiving ototoxic drugs during pregnancy.

V. Neoplasms

   A. External Ear

      1. Benign neoplasms – non-carcinogenic tumors on auricle or external ear canal.

      2. Malignant neoplasms – <u>epidermoid carcinomas</u> of external ears are common:

         a. <u>malignant melanomas</u> very aggressive epithelial tumors that require radical surgical excision.

   B. Middle Ear

      1. Benign neoplasms – usually <u>glomus jugulare</u> and <u>glomus tympanicum</u> tumors.

      2. Malignant neoplasms – <u>epidermal carcinomas</u> can arise in middle ear or invade middle ear from the external auditory canal.

         a. <u>sarcoma</u> – two types:

            (1) <u>rhabdomyosarcoma</u> – tumor of children -- nearly always fatal;

            (2) <u>chondrosarcoma</u> – malignant tumor in adults that arise from cartilage in the apex of the temporal bone.

C.  Inner Ear

   1.  Benign neoplasms – includes <u>acoustic neuromas,</u>
       <u>neurilemmomas,</u> and <u>neurofibromas</u> arise from sheaths
       of VIIIth cranial nerve.

   2.  Tumors of cerebellopontine angle include:

       a. <u>glioma</u> of pons;

       b. <u>astrocytomas;</u>

       c. <u>medulloblastomas;</u>

       d. <u>ependymomas;</u>

       e. <u>glioblastomas.</u>

   3.  Metastatic neoplasms – includes leukemia of the temporal bone.

   4.  <u>Multiple myelomas</u> – malignant disease of the skeletal
       system in adults with average survival of two years
       after diagnosis.

VI.  Vestibular Disorders

   A.  <u>Meniere's Disease</u> – triad of symptoms including episodic
       vertigo, low-frequency fluctuating unilateral hearing loss,
       and low-pitched unilateral tinnitus.

       1.  Subvarieties include cochlear and vestibular presentations.

       2.  May be initially treated medically, with surgical
           intervention reserved for severe cases.

   B.  Several vestibular disorders in which hearing is not
       ordinarily affected:

       1.  Benign paroxysmal positional vertigo.

       2.  Vestibular neuronitis.

       3.  Cervical vertigo.

VII.  Disorders of Aging and Metabolism

   A.  <u>Presbycusis</u> – hearing loss caused by the degenerative
       changes of aging.

       1.  <u>Sensory presbycusis</u> – degeneration of organ of Corti.

       2.  <u>Neural presbycusis</u> – degeneration of cochlear neurons
           in acoustic nerve.

3.  <u>Strial</u> <u>presbycusis</u> – due to atrophy of the stria vascularis.

4.  <u>Cochlear</u> <u>conductive</u> <u>presbycusis</u> – a mechanical problem resulting from stiffness of the basilar membrane.

B.  <u>Hypothyroidism</u> – general impression exists that decreased thyroid function is associated with hearing loss.

C.  <u>Diabetes</u> <u>Mellitus</u> – vascular changes may involve vessels of the inner ear.

D.  <u>Hypoglycemia</u> – has been correlated with hearing loss especially in patients with Meniere's Disease.

## REVIEW QUESTIONS

1.  Congenital diseases which may be responsible for hearing loss at birth:

    A.  Are always the same as hereditary diseases.
    B.  Are only transmitted genetically from parent to child.
    C.  May include maternal Rubella during pregnancy.
    D.  Include otosclerosis.
    E.  Are not identified or suspected through use of a High Risk Register.

2.  Stapedectomy surgery for patients with otosclerosis is usually recommended:

    A.  Only if a hearing aid is not beneficial.
    B.  When hearing tests reveal a significant air-bone gap.
    C.  Because it is a simple procedure without complications.
    D.  Only when optimum surgical benefit will alleviate need for a hearing aid.
    E.  To improve balance problems.

3.  Hyperbilirubinemia:

    A.  Cannot be treated medically.
    B.  Is increasing in incidence.
    C.  Occurs when the Rh factor in the blood of the mother and the child are incompatible.
    D.  Causes hearing loss without other associated problems.
    E.  Causes conductive hearing loss.

4.  External otitis:

    A.  Is characterized by painful swelling of the ear canal.
    B.  Is not accompanied by hearing loss.
    C.  Is more likely to occur in dry climates.
    D.  Should not be cleaned by an otologist if the canal is stenosed.
    E.  Cannot be effectively treated by antibiotics.

5.  Tympanosclerosis:

    A.  Affects the inner ear.
    B.  Is scar tissue resulting in the healing process in otitis media.
    C.  Should be removed surgically.
    D.  May be seen in the pinna.
    E.  Does not cause hearing loss.

6.  When acute otitis media causes a rupture of the tympanic membrane:

    A.  Increased pressure within the middle ear causes pain.
    B.  The fluid drains completely through the eustachian tube.
    C.  Otorrhea is usually followed by immediate resolution of fever and pain.
    D.  A polyethylene tube should be inserted.
    E.  A myringotomy will relieve the pressure and pain.

7.  "Glue-ear", a form of serous otitis media:

    A.  Is not likely to affect hearing enough to result in poor performance in school.
    B.  Is more likely to occur in adults than in children.
    C.  Cannot be treated medically.
    D.  Usually results from poor Eustachian tube function.
    E.  Commonly causes sensorineural hearing loss.

8.  Chronic otitis media is characterized by perforation of the tympanic membrane:

    A.  And usually causes pain in the ear.
    B.  Along with dizziness.
    C.  Which cannot heal without surgery.
    D.  Which may cause a conductive and/or sensorineural hearing loss.
    E.  Which may be either benign or malignant.

9. Traumatic injuries to the external ear:

   A. Always result in at least a temporary hearing loss.
   B. Cannot be tested audiometrically until the wound is healed.
   C. Should be repaired surgically if necessary to prevent stenosis or atresia of the external auditory canal.
   D. May result in a conductive loss of up to 20 dB if the external canal is completely closed.
   E. Do not usually also affect the middle or inner ear.

10. Barotitis:

    A. Occurs with weather changes.
    B. Usually produces a severe sensorineural hearing loss.
    C. Usually causes dizziness and air sickness.
    D. Cannot always be prevented by "popping" the ears during ascent and descent in an airplane.
    E. Cannot be treated medically or surgically.

11. A longitudinal fracture through the petrous pyramid of the temporal bone:

    A. May involve laceration of the tympanic membrane, ossicular dislocation, facial nerve paralysis, and spinal fluid otorrhea.
    B. Does not usually cause a hearing loss.
    C. Always causes a sensorineural hearing loss that is irreversible.
    D. Always results in a complete and permanent loss of cochlear and vestibular function.
    E. Follows the same fracture plane as a transverse fracture.

12. Ototoxic drugs:

    A. Always creates permanent damage to auditory and/or vestibular systems.
    B. Are carried through the bloodstream to the inner ear.
    C. Result in about the same degree of hearing loss whether one, two, or several such drugs are administered concurrently.
    D. Will not affect hearing because kidney function filters the drugs from the blood stream.
    E. Affect the hearing of patients regardless of age.

13. Malignant neoplasms:

    A. Occur only in the external ear.
    B. Are more common in children than adults.
    C. May occur in external, middle, or inner ear.
    D. Cannot be treated medically or surgically.
    E. Cause a reversible maximum conductive hearing loss.

14. Inner ear tumors:

    A. Are usually malignant.
    B. Often result in complaints of pain.
    C. Are suspected when audiometric tests reveal poor speech discrimination in relation to the configuration of pure tone thresholds.
    D. Cannot be treated medically.
    E. Cannot be seen on x-ray studies.

15. Meniere's disease:

    A. Is named after the man who discovered the cure for it.
    B. Is characterized by drainage from the middle ear.
    C. Is characterized by fluctuating hearing loss, episodic vertigo, tinnitus, and pressure or fullness in the ear(s).
    D. Should be suspected when a patient describes acute pain in the ear.
    E. Produces migraine headaches.

16. Presbycusis:

    A. Results in hearing losses in children as well as adults.
    B. May affect one ear but rarely both ears.
    C. Is characterized by bilateral mild hearing loss and relatively good or very poor speech discrimination ability.
    D. Responds to medical treatment in about 80% of the cases seen.
    E. May be treated with either non-destructive or destructive surgery.

# Chapter 45

# EDUCATION OF HEARING IMPAIRED LEARNERS

*Donald G. Ferguson, Doin E. Hicks,*
*and Glenn S. Pfau*

I.  A Point of Departure

   A.  Education of hearing-impaired learners is characterized
       by diversity in substance and form.

       1.  "The education of the deaf" implies that some sort of
           homogeneous group and that some single approach to
           teaching is applicable to all members of the group.

       2.  The more severe the handicap, the more specialized and
           individualized becomes the educational approach (Northcott,
           1978).

       3.  Must also consider important contribution of educational
           experiences outside the classroom.

       4.  For more than one century, the U.S. has experienced
           controversy regarding teaching methodologies.

           a. current movement is toward conciliation and avoidance
              of unilateral approaches.

       5.  "No single method of instruction and/or communication or
           educational setting can best serve the needs of all
           hearing-impaired children of school age".

II.  Communication Modalities

   A.  Oral Method - places reliance on a combination of residual
       hearing and speech reading.

       1.  Expressive language is achieved solely through speech.

   B.  Unisensory Method - places no emphasis on the acquisition
       of language through visual means - does not teach speechreading.

1. Singular attention to use of residual hearing.

C. Rochester Method – incorporates fingerspelling in conjunction with reliance on speechreading and residual hearing.

    1. No sign language – just rapid fingerspelling used concurrently with speech.

D. Total Communication – a combined method that makes use of modes of communication, including speechreading, speech, audition, fingerspelling, natural gestures, facial expression and manual sign language.

    1. Various modes used simultaneously.

E. Most agree on the following assets worthy of educational effort:

    1. Knowledge of one's native language.

    2. Clear oral speech.

    3. Understanding the oral speech of others.

    4. Ability to read with speed and comprehension.

    5. Ability to understand abstract concepts.

F. Conditions that influence education and result in different forms of specialized intervention (Reynolds and Birch, 1977):

    1. Nature of handicapping defect.

    2. Degree of loss.

    3. Age of onset.

    4. Cognitive level at which child functions.

    5. Nature and amount of sensory and intellectual stimulation.

III. Early Intervention

A. The most fruitful period to acquire and develop language is in infancy and during the pre-school years.

B. Significant legislation known as the Education for All Handicapped Children Act of 1975.

C. Program Emphasis on Early Childhood:

    1. All infant and pre-school programs place considerable emphasis on utilization of residual hearing.

2. Meadows (1969) cautions against too much stress on early intervention as it can lead to excessive expectations for verbal achievement.

3. The following factors in combination have contributed to recent improvement in early intervention programs:

   a. cognitive and academic training;

   b. use of combined oral and manual communication;

   c. improved utilization of residual hearing;

   d. more parental involvement.

4. Essential for parents to guard against development of overdependency through a highly protective, solicitous relationship.

IV. School Placement

A. Residential Schools:

1. At one time over 75% of hearing impaired students attended this type of live-in school; currently about 32% of the hearing-impaired children attend this type of school.

2. Some 15-20% of attendees actually live at home and use residential school as a day school.

B. Day Schools:

1. Have no overnight accommodations.

2. The typical day school is housed in a separate building but geared only for hearing impaired students.

C. Full-Time Classes:

1. Hearing-impaired students spend full-time in a special class housed in the local school.

2. In 1977, about 22% of hearing-impaired students were placed in a full-time special education class of this type.

D. Integrated:

1. The hearing-impaired child spends all or part of the day in regular classrooms with normal-hearing children.

2. This is also known as "mainstreaming".

3. These programs tend to enroll more postlingual hearing-impaired children than do the other programs.

V.  Mainstreaming

   A.  Considerable attention has been generated about this type of educational placement because of Public Law 94-142 (1975).

      1.  Such integration is a means of eliminating the deleterious effects of segregation and the stigma often attached to "the less successful" student.

      2.  Integration may create a more demanding environment to which the handicapped child must react.

      3.  Integration provides an environment rich in opportunities enabling children to learn by imitation.

      4.  Mainstreaming is not:

         a. wholesale return of all exceptional children in special classes to regular classes;

         b. permitting children with special needs to remain in regular classes without the support services they need;

         c. ignoring the need of some children for a specialized program that can be provided in the general education program;

         d. less costly than serving children in special contained classrooms.

VI.  Curriculum Planning

   A.  Curricula designed for use by general public schools are deemed applicable for the hearing impaired students - with some modification.

      1.  Language:  heavy emphasis on the teaching of language to hearing-impaired learners.

         a. informal approach - children are taught language spontaneously and naturally as need arises;

         b. formal approach - stresses grammatical principles using the process of memorization and various symbol systems to represent parts of sentences.

      2.  Visualization: children must learn to use vision and other senses to help overcome the hearing handicap.

3. <u>Individualization</u>: each child with special needs should have an individual educational program (IEP).

VII. Post-Secondary Education

A. Considerable growth nationally for post-secondary school programs for the hearing impaired.

1. Many such programs are technically-vocationally oriented.

2. Most programs serve regional rather than just local needs.

B. Over half of all post-secondary enrollment attend two national institutions:

1. Gallaudet College - Washington, D.C.

2. National Technical Institute for the Deaf - Rochester, N.Y.

VIII. In Summary

A. Education of hearing-impaired persons is not without controversy.

B. Language and communication remain the major nemesis for hearing-impaired learners.

**REVIEW QUESTIONS**

1. Education of the hearing impaired is currently characterized by all of the developments except one of the following:

A. Movement away from the notion of a single approach to education being applicable to all children.
B. Increase in residential school enrollments.
C. Added support by more states for educational programs at the pre-school level.
D. Expanded opportunities in post-secondary education for hearing-impaired students.
E. More applications of multi-media classroom approaches.

2. Of the following educational tasks which one poses the greatest challenge to the classroom teacher of hearing-impaired learners?

   A. Helping students become proficient in social graces.
   B. Developing pre-vocational skills.
   C. Developing an appreciation of rhythm and dance.
   D. Helping students use common everyday English.
   E. Developing reading readiness.

3. Match the following:

   A. Residential school
   B. Day school
   C. Full-time classroom
   D. Integrated classroom
   E. Resource classroom

   1. A school without dormitories which is geared totally to a special purpose such as deafness.
   2. A total care educational institution for a special population.
   3. A regular school in which hearing-impaired learners spend most of the day in a specialized situation.

4. Mainstreaming as a type of educational placement was given its greatest impetus by the:

   A. Council for Exceptional Children
   B. Alexander Graham Bell Association
   C. United State Congress
   D. American Instructors of the Deaf
   E. U.S. Department of Education

5. One of the following statements about mainstreaming as an educational placement is not true. Mainstreaming is:

   A. the judicious placement of exceptional children in regular classrooms.
   B. less expensive than serving children in special classrooms.
   C. successful in part depending upon the in-service education of regular teachers.
   D. dependent for its total effectiveness upon the provision of support services for regular teachers.
   E. possible by law for a special child only with parental approval.

6. The Fitzgerald Key is a term used to refer to a:

   A. System of teaching sentence structure.
   B. Set of rules for scientific reasoning.
   C. Manual for teaching geometry to young learners.
   D. Curriculum guide for vocational teachers.
   E. Central idea related to explaining idiomatic speech.

7. An IEP is an educational term used in all types of special education which refers to:

   A. Federal planning.
   B. Parental training.
   C. Programmed learning.
   D. Individualized instruction.
   E. Educational policy.

8. A formal approach to the acquisition of language which is common in many schools for hearing-impaired students stresses:

   A. Mastery of silent reading.
   B. The importance of observing children's language in formal settings.
   C. More written than oral exercises during language training.
   D. The importance of observing children at play as a medium for learning.
   E. Grammar principles through memorization.

9. A communications modality which incorporates fingerspelling along with speechreading and residual hearing is:

   A. Total Communication
   B. The Oral Method
   C. Manual Communication
   D. The Rochester Method
   E. The Acoupedic Method

10. The Captioned Films and Telecommunications Branch of the United States Department of Education has provided all the services below except one since its inception in 1958:

   A. Distribution of linotype equipment to schools for the hearing impaired.
   B. Project LIFE (Language Improvement to Facilitate Education).
   C. Distribution of entertainment films to adults.
   D. Workshops for teachers on utilization of educational films.
   E. Research on multisensory approaches to learning.

11. In all, there are about how many specialized programs for hearing-impaired learners in institutions of higher education in the United States?

   A. 6
   B. 16
   C. 60
   D. 160
   E. 600

12. The only liberal arts college in the world for hearing impaired students and limited to them at the undergraduate level is _____ College in _____.

13. What in brief is the century-long controversy regarding instructional methodologies in the education of hearing impaired youth?

14. Define what is meant by the unisensory method of communication. What other names does it go by? How does it differ from the use of the oral method of teaching children?

15. Which figure below is closest to the actual enrollment of hearing impaired students in special schools?

   A. 70,000
   B. 95,000
   C. 125,000
   D. 180,000
   E. 210,000

# Chapter 46

# AURAL REHABILITATION IN ADULTS

*Raymond H. Hull*

I. Introduction

    A. Hearing impairment can result in dramatic changes in the life of adults.

    B. No matter what the severity of the hearing disorder, all adults can benefit from aural rehabilitation services.

II. What is Aural Rehabilitation?

    A. <u>Definition</u>: aural rehabilitation refers to the restoration of communication skills which have become impaired because of a deficit in auditory function.

    B. Implies helping people with impaired hearing to reach their maximum potential in relation to their communicative needs.

        1. Vocational.

        2. Educational.

        3. Social.

        4. Personal.

    C. Provides the following services:

        1. Facilitates emotional adjustment.

        2. To use residual hearing as efficiently as possible in all environments.

        3. To use supplemental visual clues.

        4. Facilitate adjustment among family members.

        5. Generally includes speechreading and auditory training.

III. Lipreading vs. Speechreading/Auditory Training vs. Aural Rehabilitation

A. Lipreading:

1. Martha Bruhn introduced the Mueller-Walle method of lipreading in 1902.

   a. analytic approach which stressed kinesthetic awareness of movements involved in speech production, visible speech and rhythmic drill.

2. The Jena Method (Anna Bunger, 1932).

   a. also analytic approach; vowel and consonant charts were used to familiarize client with the formation of phonemes of speech.

3. The Nitchie approach introduced "whole thought" concept (1903).

   a. emphasis on "whole" message rather than the analytical pieces.

4. "Methods" of lipreading teaching in structured sequence are generally unacceptable because:

   a. clients generally emerge from the sequence of lessons as good or as poor in their skills at lipreading as they were when they began;

   b. lessons do not aid clients to cope within their daily communicative environments.

5. Lack of definitiveness in the visual-alone reception of speech is due to:

   a. similarity of some phonemes;

   b. some phonemes are not visible on the lips;

   c. general lack of redundancy of visible components of speech relative to the comprehension of messages.

B. Speechreading-Auditory Training:

1. Numerous studies affirm that the complement of vision to audition and audition to vision is an important factor in speech intelligibility.

C. Aural Rehabilitation:

1. Total client-oriented approach to aural rehabilitation involves more than speechreading and/or auditory training.

2.  Each client has special individual problems as a result of the hearing deficit.

3.  Group rehabilitation may be appropriate for general discussions of:

    a. causes of hearing impairment;

    b. increased difficulties experienced in certain environments;

    c. general listening skills;

    d. group sharing of common problems and frustrations.

4.  The process of aural rehabilitation involves:

    a. hearing aid orientation;

    b. program to increase communication efficiency;

    c. group and/or individual counseling;

    d. assessment of communicative gains.

IV.  The Client's Aural Rehabilitation Treatment Program

   A.  Counseling:

      1.  Motivational counseling to facilitate adjustment.

      2.  Assertiveness training.

      3.  Development of coping behavior.

      4.  Understanding the "whys" (the reasons).

      5.  Airing of concerns.

      6.  Development of understanding.

      7.  Adjustments to the hearing aid.

   B.  Planning the Treatment Program:

      1.  Client should be an integral part of the planning process.

      2.  Clients asked to list situations in which they experience the greatest communication difficulties.

      3.  Put situations into priority of importance.

      4.  Design program based on the client's information in items (2) and (3) above.

C. Treatment:

1. Further discussion of the effect of the shape and degree of hearing impairment as they relate to auditory function is important.

2. Solutions are discussed for each client's difficult communication experiences.

3. Development of coping behavior and assertiveness training is offered to help overcome tendency for social withdrawal.

4. Suggestions tactfully advising others to change their speech patterns, etc.

5. Provide clients with information about how they may derive clues pertaining to the content of verbal messages:

   a. linguistic redundancy: predictability and redundancy of English;

   b. content redundancy: predictability and redundancy of conversations;

   c. environmental redundancy: predictability and redundancy of verbal messages in certain environments;

   d. development in skill to grasp the meaning of verbal messages (closure techniques);

   e. development of skill in use of visual clues;

   f. development of communication skills and copying behavior in noisy environments.

V. Evaluation of Success in Treatment

A. Filmed lipreading tests were developed in the 1940's:

1. Mason (1943) had series of 30 films to teach lipreading.

2. Morkovin (1948) "real life situation" films.

3. Utley (1946) lipreading films in 3 parts.

B. Current approach is to have clients' express opinions of their own difficulties in communication.

C. Use of self-rating scales of communication handicap:

1. Hearing Handicap Scale (HHS).

2. Denver Scale of Communication Function.

3.   Hearing Measurement Scale.

4.   Profile Questionnaire for Rating Communication Performance.

5.   Scale of Communication Function for Senior Citizens Living in Retirement Centers.

D.   Following approaches to assessment are most reasonable:

1.   Observation of case history, etiology, duration of hearing loss, client's social and environmental needs.

2.   Use of all audiometric results, especially speech discrimination assessment.

3.   Hearing aid evaluation results.

4.   Assessment of client's ability to use visual clues with minimal audition.

5.   Use of scales or profiles of communication function.

6.   Plans and post-treatment assessment based only on client's needs and priorities.

## REVIEW QUESTIONS

1.   Which of the following terms do not refer to the restoration of skills which have become impaired as the result of hearing loss?

A.   Aural rehabilitation
B.   Aural habilitation
C.   Rehabilitative audiology
D.   Aural (Re) habilitation
E.   Habilitative audiology

2.   Which of the following are facets of the process of aural rehabilitation as discussed in this chapter?

A.   Facilitating emotional adjustment among hearing-impaired people.
B.   Aiding hearing-impaired people to utilize their residual hearing as efficiently as possible.
C.   Aiding hearing-impaired people to utilize their residual hearing in noisy or otherwise distracting environments.

D. Aiding hearing-impaired people to learn to utilize supplemental visual clues in communication.

E. Facilitating adjustment among family members and peers to the communicative difficulties the hearing-impaired person faces.

3. Studies on the strength of vision alone in speech perception have concluded that it contributes _____% to speech intelligibility.

   A. 50%
   B. 35%
   C. 40%
   D. 45%
   E. 60%

4. Which of the following ear practitioners of lipreading emphasized an analytic approach?

   A. Martha Bruhn (Mueller-Walle) – 1902
   B. Anna Bunger (Jena) – 1932
   C. Nitchie – 1903, 1950
   D. Kinzie sisters – 1931
   E. Ordman and Ralli – 1957

5. The concept of "speechreading" involves all of the factors presented below except:

   A. Facial expression.
   B. Gestures.
   C. Expression of the eyes.
   D. Formation of the articulators during speech production.
   E. Auditory function in degraded speech.

6. According to this author, one aspect of the aural rehabilitation treatment program is incorporated into all portions of the process. It is _____.

   A. Lipreading
   B. Speechreading
   C. Working through difficult listening environments.
   D. Counseling
   E. Hearing aid orientation

7. The process of counseling in aural rehabilitation treatment involves, according to these authors, which of the following?

   A. Facilitating adjustment
   B. Psychotherapy
   C. Assertiveness training
   D. Developing coping mechanisms
   E. Marital counseling

8. The most frustrating communicative environments faced by the majority of hearing-impaired adults are:

   A. At the theatre
   B. In churches
   C. Listening to children
   D. Noisy environments
   E. Visually distracting environments

9. Match the following:

   A. Linguistic Redundancies
   B. Content Redundancies
   C. Environmental Redundancies
   D. Making Closure
   E. Vision and Audition with Closure

   1. People generally say similar things on similar occasions.
   2. The English language is fairly stringently redundant in regard to its structure.
   3. Enhanced by being cognizant of the redundancies which exist within verbal and non-verbal communication.

10. Developing coping behaviors in noise environments in an effective way should not include which of the following:

    A. Learning about the physical make-up of noise per se.
    B. Use of high-fidelity record-playback equipment.
    C. Discussion of frustrations in noisy environments.
    D. Use of sympathy to evoke coping behaviors.
    E. Discussions on modifying noisy environments.

11. Differentiate between the terms Aural Rehabilitation and Aural Habilitation.

12. The author discussed two factors which have caused some professionals to question the use of strict methods of "lipreading". What are they?

13. Discuss: The complement of vision to audition and audition to vision is real and is an important factor in speech intelligibility.

14. A 42 year old male has been diagnosed as possessing a moderate sensorineural hearing loss bilaterally, sloping sharply into the high frequencies. Speech reception thresholds were found to be 35 dB in the right ear, and 40 dB in the left. Speech discrimination was confirmed at 52% in the right ear, and at 48% in the left. He describes himself as experiencing an extreme degree of difficulty functioning in his position as office manager with a large clothing firm. He also revealed that he has ceased going to parties and other social events since "I cannot understand a thing people are saying, and it's embarrassing to answer inappropriately when questions are asked". His office desk is located in an open-concept office environment. Four secretaries are located in the vicinity.

    Utilizing the information presented in this chapter, what would your approach to aural rehabilitation be for this person?

15. Support or negate the philosophy that, "For some hearing-impaired persons, the process of aural rehabilitation may involve only a session or two, while for others, an extensive aural rehabilitation program will be required which may last many weeks or months."

# Chapter 47

# THE DEAF

*William E. Castle*

I. Size of the Deaf Population

    A. In 1971, 0.87% of total U.S. population was deaf.

        1. 410,000 became deaf before age 19.

        2. 210,000 became deaf after age 3.

    B. Extrapolated to 1980 U.S. population statistics, the number of deaf persons = 1,914,000.

II. General Needs of Deaf Population

    A. Economic accommodation:

        1. In 1972 unemployment for deaf –6.5% while 5.7% in general population.

        2. Median deaf income was 84% of the average of U.S. families in general.

        3. Deaf generally underemployed and not trained for technical-professional jobs.

    B. Educational achievement:

        1. Only 34.7% of deaf had completed high school.

        2. Only 11.6% of deaf had any college education.

    C. Disabilities in communication skills:

        1. Schein and Delk (1974) interviewed deaf adults about their own communication skills:

            a. 31% felt their speech skills were "good";

            b. 9% felt they had "no speech";

c. 6.6% felt they had no speechreading skills;

d. only 41% felt their lipreading skills were good;

e. 66%-71% rated their manual signing and fingerspelling skills as "good";

f. 8%-9.3% rated their manual signing and fingerspelling reading skills as "poor".

D. Efforts to Satisfy Deaf Needs:

1. 1817 - first school for deaf in Hartford, Connecticut by Thomas Hopkins Gallaudet. School is now known as the American School for the Deaf.

2. Annual April issue of American Annals of the Deaf contains yearly statistics on deaf education programs. Represents extensive efforts to provide special education facilities for the deaf.

3. Gallaudet College for the deaf, only liberal arts college in world - established in 1864; currently has enrollment of 1100 deaf students.

4. National Technical Institute for Deaf currently serves 900 deaf students.

5. Education for All Handicapped Children (Public Law 94-142) established in 1973.

E. Unmet Needs of the Deaf:

1. Legislation is one thing, but fulfillment is another!

2. Observable trends for improved services for deaf:

a. early identification;

b. early intervention;

c. improved elementary and secondary education;

d. mainstreaming programs;

e. increasing postsecondary school opportunities.

3. Still lack of properly trained professionals, appropriate teaching techniques, and sufficient research.

4. Deaf still need equal educational opportunities.

III. Details of unmet Needs from PL 94-142, "Education for All Handicapped Children Act".

   A. Many handicapped children...do not have successful educational experiences because their handicaps go undetected.

   B. The law provides for all handicapped persons between the ages of 3 and 21 – not enough since education really does not stop at age 21.

   C. The law seeks to provide "appropriate" educational experiences for handicapped children at the preschool, elementary and secondary levels.

   D. Families of handicapped persons are forced to seek special educational services for them outside the public school system, often from agencies that are a great distance from their residence and at their own expense.

   E. The law provides that an individualized education program be designed for each handicapped child and indicates an assumption that this is feasible, with appropriate funding, based on existing approaches to teacher training and diagnostic and instructional procedures.

   F. The special educational needs of handicapped children are not being met adequately and at least 50% do not receive the special services required to assure them full equality of opportunity.

   G. Genuine implementation of PL 94-142 for elementary and secondary levels of education will require a drastic (but positive) revision of the teacher training programs designed to train persons to teach the deaf.

IV. Additional Unmet Needs for the Deaf

   A. Early detection:

      1. The U.S. lags behind such countries as Sweden, Holland, Israel, and Japan in efforts to detect deafness early in infancy.

   B. Early education:

      1. Home stimulation programs for deaf youngsters younger than three are very important for the adjustment of parents and the child, yet such programs are not readily available in the U.S.

C. Elementary and secondary education:

   1. Deaf students, in general, still do not reach elementary school and secondary school attainments which equal those of hearing students.

D. Graduate and continuing education:

   1. Although great strides have been made in these levels of education for the deaf, much more needs to be done.

E. Career education for the deaf:

   1. Deaf children and adolescents need more exposure to the world of work opportunities, and more educational experiences that are work or career oriented.

F. Teacher training programs for teachers of the deaf:

   1. Teachers at all three education levels should be technically qualified to teach both hearing and deaf students.

G. Other professionals in educational programs:

   1. The classroom teacher should not have to be all things to the deaf student.

   2. For example, audiologists at the National Technical Institute for the Deaf, who are specifically trained to work with deaf students have shown:

      a. non-users and seldom-users of hearing aids can be persuaded to become "users";

      b. good auditory training can improve listening skills and hearing aid use;

      c. speechreading abilities can be increased;

      d. with special instruction many of the deaf students can be taught techniques to permit them to use the regular telephone;

      e. audiologists, and other professionals who work with deaf students, must learn to use simultaneous communication.

H. Principles of technology:

   1. The deaf themselves need to become skilled in working with today's electronic teaching aids such as video tape, captioned films, television, behavior modification equipment, etc.

V.   Conclusion

   A.   The deaf population of the U.S. is sizable with diversified
        needs.  Although much has been done to meet those needs,
        it is evident that a great deal more needs to be done.

## REVIEW QUESTIONS

1.   The National Census of the Deaf Population of 1971 found what
     percentage of the total population of the United States to be deaf?

     A.   8.7
     B.   87
     C.   .087
     D.   .87
     E.   .0087

2.   The first school for the deaf in the United States was founded in
     what year?

     A.   1718
     B.   1778
     C.   1817
     D.   1877
     E.   1887

3.   Which of the following is true of Gallaudet College?

     A.   It was founded in 1901.
     B.   It is the world's only liberal arts college for the deaf.
     C.   It currently serves 2000 undergraduate deaf students.
     D.   It was signed into law by President McKinley.
     E.   It sponsors the National Technical Institute for the Deaf.

4.   Public Law 94-142 is which Congressional Act?

     A.   Education for All Handicapped Children Act
     B.   The National Technical Institute for the Deaf Act
     C.   The Bureau for Education of the Handicapped Act
     D.   The Model Secondary School for the Deaf Act
     E.   The National Interpreter Training Act

5. The Education for All Handicapped Children Act provides for all children between what ages?

   A. 6-18
   B. 3-19
   C. 4-18
   D. 3-21
   E. 0-21

6. Which of the following countries outstrips the United States in its efforts in early detection of deafness?

   A. Sweden
   B. Norway
   C. Russia
   D. Yugoslavia
   E. England

7. The National Center for Continuing Education for the Deaf is an integral part of which of the following?

   A. The National Technical Institute for the Deaf
   B. The National Center on Employment of the Deaf
   C. The National Center on Deafness in California
   D. George Washington University
   E. Gallaudet College

8. The author of the chapter offers which of the following arguments?

   A. That all teachers of the deaf need also to be certified audiologists.
   B. That all teachers of the deaf at the pre-school, elementary, and secondary levels also be qualified to teach hearing students.
   C. That all teachers of the deaf have two masters degrees.
   D. That all teachers of the deaf be certified by the American Speech-Language-Hearing Association.
   E. That all teachers of the deaf be able to teach at all levels.

9. The average age of the deaf students who enter the National Technical Institute for the Deaf is which of the following?

   A. 17 years
   B. 17.5 years
   C. 18 years
   D. 19 years
   E. 19.5 years

10. Which of the following aspects of modern day technology will be the least useful to the usual deaf person?

   A. Captioned television
   B. Interpreter television
   C. The Opticon
   D. Visual feedback devices
   E. Tactile feedback devices

11. Who are the authors of <u>The Deaf Population of the United States</u> which is based on the National Census of the Deaf Population done in 1971?


12. According to the National Census, what percent of today's deaf population have completed high school?


13. Who founded the American School for the Deaf in Hartford, Connecticu


14. Where is the Model Secondary School for the Deaf?


15. What federal legislation is leading to a proliferation of postsecondary educational programs for the deaf?

# Chapter 48

# ASPECTS OF CONTEMPORARY HEARING AIDS

*James R. Curran*

I. Introduction

    A. History of hearing aids is best summarized as "an evolutionary process of every greater miniaturization and refinement."

        1. In 1937, hearing aids weighed about 25 pounds.

        2. In 1974, hearing aids weighed less than 2 ounces.

    B. Hearing aids have nearly reached limit in size reduction.

    C. Current design attention is centered on improved performance of hearing aids.

II. Types of Hearing Aids

    A. Classed by the place where worn:

        1. Behind-the-ear.

        2. In-the-ear (increasing in sales).

        3. Eyeglass (decreasing in sales).

        4. On-the-body.

    B. Behind-the-Ear Hearing Aids:

        1. Most popular type of aid.

        2. May be high-gain, high-output, have extended frequency bandwidth; minimal problems with internal acoustic or mechanical feedback.

        3. Offers clinician greatest latitude in response and fitting modifications.

C.   In-the-Ear Aids:

   1.   "Custom instrument" in which components are assembled in a molded acrylic shell made from patient's ear impression.

   2.   "Modular instrument" in which components are pre-assembled in a small, standard case.

   3.   Early models had little gain or power – in time these limitations have been overcome.

D.   Eyeglass Aids:

   1.   Between 1959–1962, most popular type of hearing aid.

   2.   Same components as behind-the-ear aids.

   3.   Very appropriate for CROS and BiCROS fittings.

   4.   Cosmetically appealing to some patients; somewhat easier to use for persons with limitation in mobility of fingers.

E.   Body Hearing Aids:

   1.   Also called "conventional" or "pocket" aids.

   2.   Often offer greatest amount of overall power for use with severe-to-profound hearing losses.

   3.   Larger controls and switches easier for some patients to use.

   4.   Popular for children's fittings.

   5.   In general, current trend is away from body aids to behind-the-ear aids because:

      a. improved performance with microphone at ear level;

      b. minimizes resistance to use of aid because of cosmetic reasons;

      c. facilitates binaural fittings.

III.   Components of Hearing Aids

A.   Transducers (microphones and receivers):

   1.   Improved, wider bandwidth; ability to withstand shock; decreasing size.

   2.   Directional microphones.

3. Techniques for modifying receiver performance.

B. Microphones:

1. Magnetic microphone rarely used today.

2. Ceramic microphone (introduced in 1968) has excellent low frequency response; small mass – but extremely sensitive to externally generated vibrations.

3. Electret condenser microphone (1970) has low vibration sensitivity with flat, broad frequency response – has reduced susceptibility to shock, stress and damage.

4. Directional microphone:

   a. omnidirectional – equal sensitivity to sound from $360^{\circ}$ incidence;

   b. directional microphone is less sensitive to sounds which emanate from the sides and rear ($180^{\circ}$);

   c. ultracardioid response pattern is an important variation of the standard cardioid directional microphone:

      (1) has more signal rejection from the rear hemisphere and sides.

C. Receivers:

1. Internal receivers are used inside the hearing aid case.

2. External receivers are remote from the hearing aid but attached by a cord.

3. The more sensitive the receiver, the narrower its frequency bandwidth.

D. Amplifier Assemblies:

1. Amplifiers operate from one or two batteries.

2. Function is to "amplify" the small signal produced by the microphone one million times or more and transmit this power to the receiver.

3. Classified as Class A, Class B (or push-pull) AGC (or compression), diode or soft peak clipping (or curvilinear compression), or hard peak clipping.

E. Volume Control:

1. Controls the amplifier signal level.

433

IV. Hearing Aid Performance

A. Hearing aid performance is measured in accordance with ASA Standard - 1976.

B. Interpretation of Performance Data:

1. Performance is measured in a standard hard-walled 2.0 cc cavity.

2. Measurements obtained according to ASA Standard - 1976 are better viewed as a method for ensuring baseline performance and product uniformity - not necessarily for selecting and fitting aids.

C. Gain and Output Relationships:

1. Full-on gain is measured with a 60 dB input, volume control full-on.

2. Volume control should be viewed as the controller of <u>gain</u>.

3. Input level plus gain equals output level.

4. The hearing aid cannot amplify beyond SSPL90, regardless of how high the input level becomes.

5. Adjusting the SSPL90 to a level below the patient's uncomfortable level is one of the most critically important considerations in fitting a hearing aid.

D. Distortion in Hearing Aids:

1. The exact correlation, if one exists, between intelligibility, quality and distortion in hearing aids is very difficult to analyze.

2. Types of distortion available in aids includes:

a. harmonic distortion;

b. intermodulation distortion;

c. phase distortion;

d. frequency distortion;

e. transient distortion;

f. distortion from circuit noise.

3. Harmonic distortion is usually the only distortion measurement reported for hearing aids.

4.   The presence of low harmonic distortion values in an aid is no guarantee that the patient will experience success when fitted with that aid.

E.   Factors which alter the speech signal:

1.   Spectrum of the speech signal may undergo considerable transformation:

a. effects of earmold;

b. position of hearing aid microphone;

c. direction from which the speech signal comes;

d. amplifying characteristics of the hearing aid.

F.   Real Ear Performance:

1.   KEMAR - realistic mannikin uses a Zwislocki coupler to provide in situ hearing aid performance measures.

2.   More appropriate means of estimating real ear performance.

3.   Shows effects of ear canal volume on output level from hearing aid - as volume becomes smaller, SPL increases proportionately.

a. reduce volume by half, the expected increase in SPL is 6 dB.

G.   The Role of the Earmold:

1.   The response characteristics of any hearing aid can be substantially altered by earmold modifications.

2.   Also must consider the interior diameter of the tubing, changes in type and size of vent, and differences in earmold depth of insertion into the ear canal.

V.   The Contribution of CROS

A.   CROS is acronym for Contralateral Routing of Signals:

1.   Instrument's amplifier and receiver are worn on one ear, while the microphone is placed on the opposite ear.

2.   Original attempt was to overcome head shadow effect in unilaterally impaired subjects.

3.   Best candidates have some high-frequency hearing loss in the good ear.

4.   Often fitted to patients with bilateral, high frequency impairment.

5. CROS family includes BiCROS, Hi-Bi-CROS, Mini-CROS, Focal-CROS, Hi-CROS, Uni-CROS, IROS (Ipsilateral Routing of Signals.

B. As earmold vent size increases greater than .030 inch diameter, systematic changes can be observed in the hearing aid response characteristics.

1. Generally, the larger the vent, the greater the amount of low-frequency roll-off one can expect.

2. The larger the vent, the higher in frequency the vent related resonance occurs.

3. "Open mold" allows an appreciable amount of the speech signal to be heard through the vent.

4. The earmold is an important factor in clinical hearing aid selection procedures.

VI. Hearing Aid Candidacy

A. Medical clearance should be obtained for all hearing aid candidates.

B. Any hearing-impaired individual willing to try amplification should be afforded the opportunity.

C. Conventional Comparative Hearing Aid Evaluation:

1. Compares two to four hearing aids on patient with speech discrimination materials, in quiet and background noise, with aided and unaided performances.

D. Master hearing aid evaluation uses an instrument (rather than real aids) which incorporates selections of different gains, output and response characteristics.

E. Counseling Evaluation - educational in nature, leaving the actual selection of the instrument to the dispenser.

F. Real Ear (Functional) Evaluation:

1. Uses non-speech stimuli to generate data by which to specify hearing aid performance parameters.

G. Formula Methods:

1. Uses formula based on pure tone thresholds to specify frequency response, gain and SSPL 90 of the hearing aid.

H. Acoustic Impedance Measurement Method:

1. Uses acoustic reflex thresholds to specify frequency response, gain or SSPL 90 hearing aid characteristics.

I.  Problems in Hearing Aid Selection:

   1.  Time consuming techniques.

   2.  Subject fatigue.

   3.  Objective vs. subjective measurements.

   4.  The development of a reliable and valid hearing aid
       selection procedure is the single most important need
       in rehabilitative audiology today.

**REVIEW QUESTIONS**

1.  The most commonly used microphone in hearing aids today is the:

   A.  Magnetic microphone
   B.  Balanced armature microphone
   C.  Piezoelectric microphone
   D.  Electret condenser microphone
   E.  Ceramic microphone

2.  The prime determinants of the shape of the frequency response of a
    hearing aid include:

   A.  The internal receiver and associated tubing.
   B.  The amplifier and receiver responses.
   C.  The amplifier and microphone curves.
   D.  The electret condenser microphone and receiver responses.
   E.  The microphone, amplifier and receiver responses.

3.  Directional microphones are characterized by:

   A.  Distinct improvement in localization.
   B.  Reduced sensitivity to signals from the rear hemisphere.
   C.  An acoustic filter in the microphone openings.
   D.  Reduced sensitivity for all angles of incidence.
   E.  Uniform sensitivity for all angles of incidence.

4. The Reference Test Position is:

    A. Employed when determining the SSPL90.
    B. The setting of the volume control at a three frequency average level which is 17 dB less than HF-average SSPL90, with 60 dB input.
    C. Employed when measuring full on gain.
    D. The setting of the volume control at a three frequency average level which is 17 dB less than the HF-average SSPL90, with 70 dB input.
    E. Employed when measuring HF-average full on gain.

5. When the 2.0 cc coupler is used for hearing aid performance measurements (ASA Standard 1976):

    A. Its impedance resembles that of the average normal human ear.
    B. The results obtained give a good indication of the appropriateness of the instrument for a given subject.
    C. The results take into account the position of the volume control, the type of earmold used, and the position of the microphone when the aid is being worn.
    D. Pinna, head and body baffle effects, and resonant characteristics of the ear canal are present.
    E. The results are best viewed as a method of ensuring product uniformity and baseline performance.

6. The setting of SSPL90 level (maximum power output) in a hearing aid is of primary importance because:

    A. Input plus gain equals output.
    B. The volume control is the controller of gain.
    C. If the SSPL90 exceeds ULC(TD), the amplified signal may cause discomfort to the subject.
    D. The hearing aid cannot amplify beyond SSPL90.
    E. The hearing aid is exposed to very soft and extremely loud signals.

7. Indicate which of the following test conditions does not influence the scores obtained when measuring harmonic distortion:

    A. The settng of 10% as the criterion of acceptability for a hearing aid.
    B. The presence of noise either in the equipment, the aid, or the test space.
    C. Which fundamental frequency is selected for measurement.
    D. The level of the input signal.
    E. The frequency response shape of the hearing aid.

8. Which of the following factors is not a modifying influence on the shape of the amplified speech signal at the tympanic membrane:

    A. The effects of the earmold and associated tubing.
    B. The direction from which the signal comes.

C. The response characteristics of the hearing aid.
D. The long term speech spectrum.
E. The position of the hearing aid microphone.

9. CROS (Contralateral Routing of Signals) hearing aids:

A. Do best when fitted to persons having unilateral hearing loss.
B. Utilize an occluded earmold coupling.
C. Amplify low frequencies at the expense of high frequencies.
D. Deliver the sound to the poorer ear.
E. Are successfully used for subjects with bilateral, high frequency impairment.

10. An important principle in earmold venting is:

A. Parallel vents produce a rolloff in the frequencies above the vent related resonance.
B. Diagonal vents produce a rolloff in the frequencies above the vent related resonance.
C. The vent related resonance is not related to tightness of the earmold.
D. The vent related resonance decreases as the earmold is made more tight.
E. Diagonal vents produce no rolloff in the frequencies above the vent related resonance.

11. Match the following terms:

| | |
|---|---|
| ___ 1. Functional hearing aid evaluation | A. Electret condenser |
| ___ 2. HFA–FOG | B. Affects low frequency rolloff |
| ___ 3. Reference Test Position | C. Non-speech stimuli in sound field |
| ___ 4. Slit leak | |
| ___ 5. Earmold alterations | D. ASA Standard – 1976 |
| ___ 6. Low mass diaphragm | E. Directional microphone |
| ___ 7. KEMAR | F. 70 dB input signal |
| ___ 8. Harmonic distortion measurement, ASA Standard – 1976 | G. Rapid growth in popularity recently |
| ___ 9. In the ear aids | H. Frequency response |
| ___ 10. Acoustic delay "filter" | I. Causes changes in response of aid |
| | J. In situ measurements |

# ANSWERS

## CHAPTER 1
### NEUROANATOMIC BASES OF HEARING AND SPEECH

1. C
2. C
3. B
4. A
5. E
6. C
7. D

8. A
9. D
10. A
11. E
12. C
13. A
14. B
15. E

16. 1-1    A.   cerebral hemisphere
              B.   corpus callosum
              C.   cerebellum
              D.   diencephalon
              E.   midbrain
              F.   pons
              G.   medulla

       1-2    A.   soma
              B.   nucleus
              C.   dendrites
              D.   axon hillock
              E.   axon
              F.   nodes of Ranvier
              G.   myelin sheath
              H.   end feet

## CHAPTER 2
### BASIC NEUROPHYSIOLOGICAL MECHANISMS UNDERLYING ORAL COMMUNICATION

1. A. – 1
    B. – 2
    C. – 2
    D. – 2
    E. – 1

2. A.   dendritic zone
    B.   dendrites
    C.   soma
    D.   axon
    E.   hillock

3. Conduction velocity
    A.   fiber diameter
    B.   nerve temperature
    C.   presence or absence of myelin

4. A. refractory period
   B. absolute refractory period
   C. partial refractory period

5. A. electrical
   B. chemical

6. A. convergence – a single neuron is controlled by multiple, converging inputs.

   B. divergence – one neuron may innervate varying numbers of muscle fibers or multiple neuron tracts.

7. $\frac{3}{4}$ A.
   $\frac{4}{2}$ B.
   $\frac{2}{1}$ C.
   $1$ D.

8. A. striated (somatic)
   B. unstriated (smooth, visceral)
   C. cardiac

9. A. 1          E. 1
   B. 2          F. 1
   C. 2          G. 2
   D. 1          H. 1

10. Theory that a nerve fiber will transmit only one modality of sensation regardless of how the nerve is stimulated.

## CHAPTER 3
## NEUROPHYSIOLOGICAL PROCESSES OF SPEECH MOVEMENT CONTROL

1. A. electrophysiological or mechanical stimulation of various parts of the nervous system and recording evoked potentials.
   B. Observation of motor behaviors following the introduction of lesions to the animal nervous system.

2. A. The appropriate muscles must be selected.
   B. Each participating muscle must be activated or inactivated in proper temporal relation to the others.
   C. The appropriate amount of excitation or inhibition must be exerted on each muscle.

3. The phenomenon of motor equivalence.

4. perturbations

5. A. experience
   B. degree of motor skill
   C. intentions of the subject

6. closed-loop feedback system

7. A. True
   B. True
   C. True

8. Due to the concept of learned motor compensatory patterns.

## CHAPTER 4
### ANATOMY & PHYSIOLOGY OF THE ORGANS OF THE PERIPHERAL SPEECH MECHANISM

1. (1) – C        (5) – H
   (2) – A        (6) – F
   (3) – C        (7) – E
   (4) – G        (8) – B

2. D

3. E

4. C

5. – develop intrathoracic and intraabdominal pressure.
   – protection of the lower respiratory tract.
   – inlet through which air passes into and out of lower respiratory tract
   – tussive or expectorative function as exhibited in the cough reflex when a foreign substance passes through the glottis.

6. B

7. E

8. C

9. D

10. B

11. A

12. C

13. Extrinsic tongue muscles move the entire tongue within the oral cavity and outside it. They have little effect on altering the shape of the tongue dorsum. The intrinsic muscles alter the shape of the tongue dorsum such as narrowing and flattening the blade, lifting and lowering the tip.

14. E

15. D

## CHAPTER 5
## ANATOMY & PHYSIOLOGY OF THE HEARING MECHANISM

| | | | | |
|---|---|---|---|---|
| 1. | D | | 8. | C |
| 2. | C | | 9. | E |
| 3. | A | | 10. | B |
| 4. | D | | 11. | C |
| 5. | E | | 12. | C |
| 6. | A | | 13. | B |
| 7. | B | | 14. | B |
| | | | 15. | A |

16. A. middle ear transformer
    B. shearing motion of the inner ear

17. A. mechanical resistance (friction) – not frequency dependent
    B. mechanical compliance (stiffness) – low frequency influence
    C. mechanical mass (inertia) – high frequency influence

18. (a) A. inner ear           (b) A. outer ear
        B. middle ear              B. middle ear
        C. outer ear               C. inner ear

19. Contraction of the stapedius muscle causes the footplate to be moved laterally (out of the oval window) moving the long process of the incus in a lateralward direction, pulling the head of the malleus medialward and forcing the manubrium of the malleus lateralward. This causes the tympanic membrane to move in a lateral direction.

20. A. utricle
    B. saccule
    C. superior semi-circular canal
    D. posterior semi-circular canal
    E. horizontal semi-circular canal

21. A. incus
    B. tympanic membrane
    C. tensor tympani muscle
    D. internal auditory meatus
    E. mucus layer

22. When the stapes is pressed into the oval window, the round window membrane moves outward. Since the inner ear fluids are basically incompressible, the round window release permits movement of the stapes in the oval window. Of course, when the motion is reversed (stapes moving laterally), the round window membrane is pulled into the cochlear space.

## CHAPTER 6
## NEUROPHYSIOLOGY OF HEARING

| | | | |
|---|---|---|---|
| 1. | D | 8. | C |
| 2. | E | 9. | A |
| 3. | A | 10. | A |
| 4. | B | 11. | A |
| 5. | C | 12. | E |
| 6. | B | 13. | D |
| 7. | E | 14. | B |
| | | 15. | B |

## CHAPTER 7
## ACOUSTICS OF SPEECH

1.  A.  a source of energy
    B.  a vibrator
    C.  a transmitting medium

2.  vibration
    periodic or aperiodic

3.  mass
    elasticity
    inertia
    damping factor

4.  compression (or condensation)
    expansion (or rarefaction)

5.  A.  4
    B.  3
    C.  2
    D.  7
    E.  5
    F.  6
    G.  1

6.  A.  elasticity
    B.  density
    C.  temperature

7.  Fourier analysis

8.  A.  amplitude
    B.  wavelength
    C.  phase
    D.  period

9.  A.  free
    B.  forced
    C.  maintained

10. resonance

11. standing waves

12. formants
    $F_o$
    $F_1$

13. A.  children
    B.  women
    C.  men

14. the vibration of the vocal folds for voicing and the noise produced
    at the place of articulation.

15. 1,129 feet (340 meters) per second.

## CHAPTER 8
## AERODYNAMICS OF SPEECH

1.  A.  the specialized aerodynamics of speech are superimposed on a
        highly regulated respiratory system;
    B.  requirements of the body to maintain a proper chemical
        environment provide gross restraints on the availability of
        the respiratory system for speech purposes;
    C.  only a limited time interval is available for speech before
        respiratory requirements prevail.

2.  D

3.  a difference in pressure between the two areas

4.  A.  energy required to overcome elastic recoil
    B.  the magnitude of airway resistance
    C.  surface tension of the alveoli

5.  A.  25%, 1.2 to 1.5 liters of air
    B.  10% to 15%, 0.5 liter of air

6.  4 to 5 liters of air

7.  B

8.  increased

9.  <u>velopharyngeal</u> orifice, <u>nasal</u> <u>consonant</u> sound, diminished <u>nasal</u> <u>emission</u>

10. A.  3
    B.  1
    C.  2
    D.  4

# CHAPTER 9
## SPEECH PRODUCTION

| | | | | |
|---|---|---|---|---|
| 1. | A | | 8. | A |
| 2. | C | | 9. | E |
| 3. | A | | 10. | A |
| 4. | E | | 11. | A |
| 5. | A | | 12. | D |
| 6. | D | | 13. | A |
| 7. | B | | 14. | B |
| | | | 15. | E |

# CHAPTER 10
## SPEECH PERCEPTION:  AN OVERVIEW OF CURRENT ISSUES

1.  A.  auditory
    B.  phonetic
    C.  phonological
    D.  lexical, syntactic and semantic

2.  A.  perception of the <u>boundaries</u> between categories;
    B.  attempts to define the set   acoustic cues that underlie the perception of similarities (<u>constancy</u>).

3.  A.  Psychophysical
    B.  Cochlear-modeling
    C.  Neurophysiologic

4.  A.  one in which the subject <u>labels</u> each of the stimuli from an acoustic continuum that is designed to manipulate, in small steps, an acoustic cue which differentiates two consonants.
    B.  one in which the subject attempts to discriminate pairs of stimuli taken from the continuum.

5.  A.  stimulus uncertainty
    B.  memory factors

6.  True

7.  A.  the prevoiced stop
    B.  the voiceless-unaspirated stop
    C.  the voiceless-aspirated stop

8.  The Timing Hypothesis

9.  A.  Voice-Onset Time
    B.  Just-Noticeable Difference
    C.  Reaction Time
    D.  Difference Limen

## CHAPTER 11
### NEUROPSYCHOLOGICAL MODELS OF LANGUAGE

| | | | | |
|---|---|---|---|---|
| 1. | B | | 8. | C |
| 2. | D | | 9. | C |
| 3. | A | | 10. | D |
| 4. | E | | 11. | A |
| 5. | C | | 12. | E |
| 6. | B | | 13. | B |
| 7. | D | | 14. | A |

15.  (a)  5
     (b)  1
     (c)  3
     (d)  4
     (e)  2

## CHAPTER 12
### MODELS OF AUDITORY LINGUISTIC PROCESSING

| | | | | |
|---|---|---|---|---|
| 1. | D | | 9. | A |
| 2. | A | | 10. | B |
| 3. | B | | 11. | C |
| 4. | B | | 12. | C |
| 5. | E | | 13. | B |
| 6. | D | | 14. | E |
| 7. | D | | 15. | Discussion question |
| 8. | D | | 16. | Discussion question |

CHAPTER 13
## ISSUES IN CHILD LANGUAGE ACQUISITION

1. A. syntax
   B. semantics
   C. pragmatics

2. A. 8 months
   B. 10 months
   C. 12 months
   D. 20 months

3. 70%

4. The holophrase position asserts that children's one-word utterances stand for whole sentences.

5. pivot grammar is when a child produces two-word combinations by using one of a few words that occur with high frequency, in fixed position (the pivot class of words) in combination with a large number of other words that occur infrequently and also occur alone.

6. exaggerated intonation;
   higher $F_0$;
   pauses only at utterance boundaries;
   shorter, simpler, more fluent;
   less diverse and more concrete vocabulary;
   higher rates of self-repetition;
   higher rates of questioning;
   lower rates of commenting;
   topics about immediate here-and-now;
   topics about child's activities;
   use same prevalent semantic relations found in children's speech.

7. A. the mother's desire to make herself understood;
   B. the mother's desire to express affection.

8. A. 1
   B. 2
   C. 3

9. A. 4
   B. 3
   C. 1
   D. 6
   E. 5
   F. 2

10. A. 4 word
    B. 8 word

# CHAPTER 14
## TOWARD AN UNDERSTANDING OF COMMUNICATIVE DISORDERS

1. A. 4
   B. 2
   C. 1
   D. 5
   E. 6
   F. 3
   G. 2
   H. 7

2. A. Medical model
   B. Symptomatic treatment
   C. Process analysis

3. A. language
   B. speech
   C. motor speech planning

# CHAPTER 15
## THE DIAGNOSTIC PROCESS

1. B.
2. B
3. D
4. A
5. E
6. D
7. C

8. B
9. E
10. D
11. A
12. Discussion Question
13. Discussion Question
14. Discussion Question
15. Discussion Question

# CHAPTER 16
## MANAGEMENT OF SPEECH & LANGUAGE DISORDERS

1. C
2. D
3. A
4. B
5. E
6. E
7. B

8. A
9. B
10. D
11. Discussion Question
12. Discussion Question
13. Discussion Question
14. Discussion Question
15. Discussion Question

CHAPTER 17
PHONATION:  ASSESSMENT

1.  A.  True
    B.  True
    C.  False
    D.  True
    E.  False

2.  A.  1% to 9%
    B.  3% to 5%
    C.  5% to 10%

3.  (1) anxiety-related stress, (2) environmental pollutants,
    (3) excessive talking, (4) talking above background noise,
    (5) misuse of voice

4.  (1) description of the patient's voice and other existing speech
    problems, (2) history of the voice disorder, (3) description
    of the speech and voice mechanism, (4) audiometric report - if
    appropriate, (5) determination of need for referral, (6) summary
    of findings, (7) tentative diagnosis, (8) written recommendations

5.  A.  respiratory evaluation
    B.  peripheral oral
    C.  phonatory awareness
    D.  resonance
    E.  loudness

6.  "In general, as subglottic pressure increases, speaking
    fundamental frequency increases."

    "...as subglottic pressure pulse is reduced in amplitude there is
    a concomitant   lack   of vocal fold closure."

    High air flow rates have generally been associated with   lack
    of complete vocal fold closure.

7.  A.  3
    B.  1
    C.  2

8.  vocal folds  7
    tongue  6
    mouth  3
    oropharynx  4
    malocclusion  5
    lips  2
    face  1

9. A. frequency and pitch
   B. vocal intensity and loudness
   C. voice quality

10. A. motivation
    B. determination

# CHAPTER 18
## PHONATION: REMEDIATION

1. E

2. A. develop a clear voice
   B. develop an efficient voice
   C. a voice that does not contain dysphonia
   D. a voice which is not abusive to laryngeal structures

3. A. the patient's motivation
   B. the need for voice communication
   C. medical prognosis

4. A. False
   B. False
   C. True
   D. True
   E. True

5. A. improve vocal hygiene
   B. reduce or eliminate vocal abuse
   C. develop released phonation
   D. increase stability of respiratory and phonatory systems
   E. reduce situational stresses
   F. establish appropriate pitch and intonation
   G. improve patient's ability to monitor vocal output

6. Usually, as loudness increases, the mouth opens wider and there are more wrinkles along the forehead.

7. relaxation

8. A. 6
   B. 4
   C. 5
   D. 1
   E. 3
   F. 2
   G. 7

9. E

10. C

# CHAPTER 19
## ASSESSMENT OF RESONANCE DISORDERS

1. C
2. D
3. B
4. D
5. A
6. E
7. B

8. C
9. D
10. E
11. D
12. D
13. A
14. B
15. C


# CHAPTER 20
## RESONANCE DISORDERS IN STRUCTURAL DEFECTS

1. A
2. B
3. E
4. C
5. C
6. B
7. E

8. A
9. D
10. A
11. Discussion Question
12. Discussion Question
13. Discussion Question
14. Discussion Question
15. Discussion Question


# CHAPTER 21
## REMEDIATION OF IMPAIRED RESONANCE AMONG PATIENTS
## WITH NEUROPATHOLOGIES OF SPEECH

1. E.
2. A
3. A
4. B
5. C

6. B
7. A
8. D
9. E
10. D
11. B

12. Dysarthria is an impairment of the motor functions of speech resulting from lesions of the central or peripheral nervous system. The effects on speech are due to abnormalities of muscular strength, range of motion, speed, accuracy, and/or tonicity. There may be problems in respiration, phonation, resonation, articulation, and/or prosody.

13. Dysarthria results from damage to the subcortical motor nerve tracts (white matter) or in the peripheral motor pathways. Apraxia occurs from lesions in the cortex (gray matter) of the inferior frontal convolution in the dominant hemisphere (left).

4. To bring velopharyngeal muscle activity to conscious awareness. To bring it under voluntary control. To develop greater muscle strength, tone, range of movement, flexibility, and efficiency of movement.

5. The eustachian tube opens through contraction of the tensor veli palatini muscle. In patients with palatal paralysis, there is damage to the vagus nerve (cranial nerve X). Misurya states that all palatal muscles, except the tensor, are innervated by the vagus. The tensor is innervated by the trigeminal (cranial nerve V). Thus, the tensor is spared and remains active in palatal paralysis.

CHAPTER 22
ARTICULATION ASSESSMENT

1. B                                        6. B
2. C                                        7. E
3. E                                        8. D
4. D                                        9. E
5. E                                       10. D

1. A. 4
   B. 1
   C. 2
   D. 3

2. 1. 2, 3, 6
   2. 1, 4, 5

3. To identify those in need of an articulation evaluation.

4. Because the patterns represent a cultural norm for a group of people, and thus cannot be considered deviant, delayed or sub-standard.

5. 1. Is an articulation disorder present?
   2. What type of intervention program is warranted?

CHAPTER 23
ARTICULATION DISORDERS OF UNKNOWN ETIOLOGY &
THEIR REMEDIATION

1. C                                        8. E
2. A                                        9. D
3. D                                       10. B
4. A                                       11. A
5. B                                       12. D
6. C                                       13. A
7. E                                       14. C
                                           15. B

453

# CHAPTER 24

ARTICULATION DISORDERS IN OROFACIAL ANOMALIES

| | | | |
|---|---|---|---|
| 1. | A | 6. | D |
| 2. | C | 7. | D |
| 3. | B | 8. | C |
| 4. | B | 9. | D |
| 5. | E | 10. | B |

CHAPTER 25
ARTICULATION & HEARING IMPAIRMENT

| | | | |
|---|---|---|---|
| 1. | C | 6. | E |
| 2. | E | 7. | C |
| 3. | B | 8. | A |
| 4. | A | 9. | D |
| 5. | D | 10. | B |

CHAPTER 26
PROSODY IN PERCEPTION, PRODUCTION & PATHOLOGIES

1.  (a) auditory analysis
    (b) phonological analysis
    (c) syntactic analysis
    (d) semantic analysis

2.  fundamental frequency
    intensity
    temporal spacing of acoustic events

3.  pitch and loudness

4.  25 to 50

5.  (a) semantic factors
    (b) syntactic factors
    (c) stress
    (d) word and utterance length
    (e) phonetic factors

6.  intonation

7.  b, c, and d

8.  length and form

9.  T, F, and F

| 10. | ataxic dysarthria | D |
|---|---|---|
| | speech apraxia | B |
| | Parkinson Syndrome | F, E |
| | manic states | A |
| | right hemisphere lesion | F |
| | aphasia | A |
| | cerebellar ataxia | B |
| | drunk speech | C |

## CHAPTER 27
## STUTTERING

1.  A.  4
    B.  3
    C.  5
    D.  2
    E.  1

2.  A, C, E

3.  normal, stuttering

4.  blocking

5.  distraction hypothesis

6.  a.  underlying
    b.  environmental
    c.  precipitating
    d.  vocal tract

7.  F, T, T

8.  4

9.  generalize, habituate and maintain

10. a.  lower levels of laryngeal muscle activity
    b.  slower rates of vocal fold abduction and adduction
    c.  loose rather than tight vocal fold closure

11. chorea,
    Parkinsonism,
    Gilles de la Tourette's disease,
    aphasia,
    apraxia,
    presenile dementia,
    head injury, ataxia and hypokinetic dysarthria,
    spastic dysphonia

# CHAPTER 28
## THE NATURE OF APHASIA IN ADULTS

1. D

2. D

3. A. Broca
   B. Wernicke

4. (a) nonfluent
   (b) good
   (c) abnormal
   (d) abnormal

5. (a) fluent, paraphasic
   (b) abnormal
   (c) abnormal
   (d) abnormal

6. (a) fluent, paraphasic
   (b) good
   (c) abnormal
   (d) usually good

7. abnormal, abnormal, abnormal

8. verbal, nonverbal

9. A. poor
   B. poor
   C. good
   D. good
   E. good

10. D

11. normal

12. A. epileptogenic
    B. migraine-induced
    C. structural cerebral lesions

13. A. Holland
    B. Eisenson
    C. Schnell
    D. Porch

# CHAPTER 29
## THE ELEPHANT IS SOFT & MUSHY:  PROBLEMS IN ASSESSING CHILDREN'S LANGUAGE

1. E

2. aphasia
   hearing impairment
   mental retardation
   autism
   emotional disturbance

3. social deprivation,
   troubled family,
   lack of environmental stimulation,
   disadvantaged,
   maternal overprotection,
   single-parent family,
   poverty family,
   neglect,
   lack of semantic contingency in the mother's talk

4. the basic structures or units a child is thinking in as he or she understands and produces language

5. (1) deciding what to analyze
   (2) determining appropriate units that represent the child's knowledge of language
   (3) considering the role of context
   (4) developing an integrated understanding of the child

## CHAPTER 30
## LANGUAGE DELAY

| | | | | | |
|---|---|---|---|---|---|
| 1. | B | 6. | C | 11. | A |
| 2. | E | 7. | B | 12. | A |
| 3. | C | 8. | E | 13. | C |
| 4. | D | 9. | B | 14. | D |
| 5. | A | 10. | D | 15. | E |

## CHAPTER 31
## THE LANGUAGE DISORDERED CHILD

| | | | | |
|---|---|---|---|---|
| 1. | C | 6. | E | |
| 2. | D | 7. | D | |
| 3. | B | 8. | E | |
| 4. | A | 9. | A | |
| 5. | C | 10. | C | |
| | | 11. | A, B, C | |

## CHAPTER 32
## SOCIOLINGUISTICS & COMMUNICATION DISORDERS

1. speech community is any human aggregate whose members regularly and frequently interact by means of a shared set of verbal symbols and who possess shared knowledge of the rules for the production and interpretation of speech used by members of that group.

2. linguistic competence is the intuitive knowledge that a speaker/listener possesses of the grammatical rules of the language.

3. linguistic repertoire is the range of linguistic codes existing in a speech community or spoken by an individual member.

4. conversational postulates are the "rules" for interaction and communicative competence.

5. vernacular or colloquial language is a more casual, informal, intimate variety of language that is not used in writing or in school.

6. language markers are used in speech by each individual in a group in more or less the same way in any context.

7. code switching is the ability to move from one language code to another as a function of situation or audience.

8. dyadic interactions involve a speaker/hearer, an addressor/addressee, a sender/receiver, and sometimes a third participant such as an audience observing the interaction.

9. age-grading is the difference in speech relative to the age of the speaker and the listener.

10. pidgin language is very informal, consisting of many single word utterances with many gestures.

11. D

12. A. geographical features
    B. trade routes
    C. cultural and ethnic backgrounds
    D. religion
    E. politics

## CHAPTER 33
### LANGUAGE PROCESSING & READING DEFICIENCIES:  ASSESSMENT & REMEDIATION OF CHILDREN WITH SPECIAL LEARNING PROBLEMS

1. False

2. True

3. True

4. Level 1:  Surface level of comprehension; momentary storage in verbatim form.
   Level 2:  Sentence analysis; understanding relations among elements in individual sentences.
   Level 3:  Integrative analysis and synthesis of sentences with appropriate extra-sentence context.

5. A.  "The Assessment of Children's Language Comprehension"
   B.  "The Northwestern Syntax Screening Test"
   C.  "The Test for Auditory Comprehension of Language"

6. A.  "Developmental Test of Language Comprehension"
   B.  "Test of Linguistic Concepts"
   C.  "Detroit Tests of Learning Aptitude"

7. A.  "Durrell Analysis of Reading Difficulty Test"
   B.  "Gates-MacGintie Test"

8. A.  Have the child tell how many words are in a sentence.
   B.  Have the child segment words into syllables.
   C.  Have the child segment syllables into sounds.

## CHAPTER 34
## PROBLEMS OF MATHEMATICS IN CHILDREN WITH
## LANGUAGE DISORDERS

1. A. hearing evaluation
   B. vision evaluation
   C. mental abilities
   D. perceptual difficulties
   E. perceptual-motor difficulties
   F. analysis of educational background

2. A. language
   B. memory
   C. logical reasoning
   D. visual-spatial abilities

3. A. verbal comprehension
   B. auditory memory span
   C. sequencing
   D. word retrieval
   E. syntax
   F. oral formation

4. A. meaning
   B. rule acquisition
   C. reading
   D. attention
   E. organization
   F. nonverbal visual skills

5. may have difficulty with reading comprehension, with written language, and with some aspects of numerical reasoning.

6. nonverbal experience and awareness.

## CHAPTER 35
## COMMUNICATION & LANGUAGE INSTRUCTION FOR SEVERELY
## HANDICAPPED CHILDREN & YOUTH

1. A          6. C          11. B
2. C          7. A          12. E
3. B          8. D          13. A
4. B          9. E          14. D
5. E          10. C         15. E

## CHAPTER 36
## AN OVERVIEW OF AUGMENTATIVE COMMUNICATION

1. A. aided              2. 35%, 65%
   B. unaided

3.  crying
    grunting
    laughing
    pleasure sounds

4.  dysarthria
    apraxia
    aphasia
    glossectomy
    structural anomalies/laryngectomy
    autism
    deafness

5.  apraxia of speech

6.  aphasia

7.  glossectomy

8.  dysarthria

9.  communication board

10. Blissymbolics
    Rebus
    Non-speech Language Program

11. 1.5 million

## CHAPTER 37
## HEARING DISORDERS: AUDIOLOGIC MANIFESTATIONS

| | | | | | |
|---|---|---|---|---|---|
| 1. | C | 6. | B | 11. | A |
| 2. | B | 7. | A | 12. | A, B |
| 3. | E | 8. | D | 13. | D |
| 4. | B | 9. | C | 14. | E |
| 5. | E | 10. | D | 15. | B |

## CHAPTER 38
## BASIC HEARING MEASUREMENT

1.  C, D, E

2.  1933 - Sivian and White
    1938 - U.S. Public Health Survey
    1951 - A.S.A.
    1964 - I.S.O.
    1969 - ANSI

3.  The number of decibels by which the intensity of a sound exceeds the threshold of a particular ear.

4.  A.  Normal Hearing
    B.  Mild Hearing Loss
    C.  Moderate Hearing Loss
    D.  Moderately Severe Hearing Loss
    E.  Severe Hearing Loss
    F.  Profound Hearing Loss

5.  Threshold is defined clinically as the minimum effective sound pressure that a listener can detect 50% of the time.

6.  lower frequencies, 20-25 dB

7. low, high, friction

8. C

9. calibration, test environment, patient instructions, age, intelligence and/or motivation of patient, position of earphones, etc.

10. A. bone-conduction threshold
    B. air-bone gap, 0 dB

11. B and D

12. E

13. E

14. A. normal
    B. slight difficulty
    C. moderate difficulty
    D. poor
    E. very poor

15. 1. Normal
    2. Conductive
    3. Sensorineural
    4. Sensorineural
    5. Retrocochlea

## CHAPTER 39
## DIAGNOSTIC AUDIOLOGY

| | | |
|---|---|---|
| 1. D | 6. D | 11. A |
| 2. B | 7. D | 12. B |
| 3. C | 8. B | 13. E |
| 4. B | 9. C | 14. B |
| 5. A | 10. E | 15. D |

## CHAPTER 40
## IMPEDANCE AUDIOMETRY

| | | | |
|---|---|---|---|
| 1. C | 6. B | 11. A. 1 | 12. C |
| 2. C | 7. D | B. 4 | |
| 3. D | 8. C | C. 3 | 13. E |
| 4. A | 9. D | D. 4 | |
| 5. D | 10. E | E. 2 | 14. E |

6. A. tympanometry
   B. static compliance
   C. acoustic reflexes

7. C

## CHAPTER 41
## EARLY IDENTIFICATION OF HEARING LOSS

1. B

2. B

3. C

4. 1 in 750 births

5.  A.  family history of hereditary hearing loss
    B.  maternal rubella or other intrauterine infection
    C.  anomalies at birth of ear, nose or throat
    D.  birth weight less than 1500 grams
    E.  high serum bilirubin concentration

6.  D                             9.  C, E

7.  D                             10.  B

8.  C


## CHAPTER 42
## HEARING SCREENING

1.  A.  F                         2.  C
    B.  T
    C.  F                         3.  B
    D.  T
    E.  T                         4.  D
    F.  T
                                  5.  A

6.  C

7.  Eskimo, American Indians, Down's Syndrome, Cleft Palate, mentally
    impaired, psychotic children, developmentally disturbed, known
    S/N hearing loss

8.  impedance measurement and pure tone air conduction threshold

9.  D                             10.  B


## CHAPTER 43
## CENTRAL AUDITORY TESTS

1.  D                             6.  B

2.  C                             7.  B

3.  E                             8.  A, C, D

4.  1.  C                         9.  E
    2.  A
    3.  D                         10.  C
    4.  B
    5.  E                         11.  B

5.  E                             12.  D

13. A. Auditory perception is fundamental to language acquisition.
    B. Auditory perceptual deficits cause disorders of language, reading and learning.
    C. Auditory perceptual skills can be broken down into specific deficits that are amenable to training.
    D. Remediation follows a hierarchy of skills.

14. A. Auditory perceptual disorders are related to disorders of language, reading and learning but no cause and effect relationship exists.
    B. Perceptual and conceptual function are reciprocal skills rather than sequential.
    C. Perceptual deficits are secondary to verbal mediation difficulties.

15. While some poor readers have problems in auditory perception, some poor readers have adequate auditory perceptual abilities and some good readers have poor auditory perception.

## CHAPTER 44
### MEDICAL & SURGICAL TREATMENT OF HEARING LOSS

| | | | | | |
|---|---|---|---|---|---|
| 1. | C | 6. | C | 11. | A |
| 2. | B | 7. | D | 12. | B |
| 3. | C | 8. | D | 13. | C |
| 4. | A | 9. | C | 14. | C |
| 5. | B | 10. | D | 15. | C |
| | | | | 16. | C |

## CHAPTER 45
### EDUCATION OF HEARING IMPAIRED LEARNERS

| | | | | | |
|---|---|---|---|---|---|
| 1. | B | 5. | B | 11. | C |
| 2. | D | 6. | A | 12. | Gallaudet College, Washington, D.C. |
| 3. | (1) B | 7. | D | 13. | Discussion Question |
| | (2) A | 8. | E | 14. | Discussion Question |
| | (3) C | 9. | D | 15. | A |
| 4. | C | 10. | A | | |

## CHAPTER 46
### AURAL REHABILITATION IN ADULTS

| | | | | |
|---|---|---|---|---|
| 1. | B, E | 9. | 1. | B |
| 2. | A, B, C, D, E | | 2. | A |
| 3. | A | | 3. | D, E |
| 4. | A, B | 10. | D | |
| 5. | E | 11. | Discussion Question | |
| 6. | D | 12. | Discussion Question | |
| 7. | A, C, D | 13. | Discussion Question | |
| 8. | D | 14. | Discussion Question | |
| | | 15. | Discussion Question | |

463

## CHAPTER 47
## THE DEAF

| | | | | |
|---|---|---|---|---|
| 1. | D | 6. | A | |
| 2. | C | 7. | E | |
| 3. | B | 8. | B | |
| 4. | A | 9. | E | |
| 5. | D | 10. | C | |

11.   Jerome D. Schein and Marcus T. Delk

12.   34.7%

13.   Thomas Hopkins Gallaudet

14.   At Gallaudet College

15.   The 1973 Amendments to the Vocational Rehabilitation Act (or Section 504).

## CHAPTER 48
## ASPECTS OF CONTEMPORARY HEARING AIDS

| | | | | |
|---|---|---|---|---|
| 1. | D | 6. | C | |
| 2. | E | 7. | A | |
| 3. | B | 8. | D | |
| 4. | B | 9. | E | |
| 5. | E | 10. | B | |

| 11. | (1) C | (6) A |
|---|---|---|
| | (2) D | (7) J |
| | (3) H | (8) F |
| | (4) B | (9) G |
| | (5) I | (10) E |